James Atkins

The Tradesmen's Tokens of the Eighteenth Century

James Atkins

The Tradesmen's Tokens of the Eighteenth Century

ISBN/EAN: 9783744662277

Printed in Europe, USA, Canada, Australia, Japan

Cover: Foto ©ninafisch / pixelio.de

More available books at **www.hansebooks.com**

THE

TRADESMEN'S TOKENS

OF THE

EIGHTEENTH CENTURY.

BY

JAMES ATKINS

(Author of " Coins and Tokens of the British Colonies, &c.").

LONDON:

W. S. LINCOLN & SON, 69, NEW OXFORD STREET.

1892.

LONDON:
G. NORMAN AND SON, PRINTERS, HART STREET,
COVENT GARDEN.

INTRODUCTION.

———→¦←———

NO apology will be needed, in presenting to the Token collecting public, this work, which aims at supplying a want, long felt, for a thoroughly exhaustive and descriptive Catalogue of the Tradesmen's Tokens issued towards the close of the 18th Century.

Conder's "Arrangement," which is considered (and most deservedly so) as the standard work on this subject, has now had nearly a century of existence, and although far from perfect, is certainly a wonderful production, when we remember the time at which it was produced; before the age of Railways and the Penny Post, and all the other appliances which draw one part of the country so near to another. To successfully compile any list of Coins or Tokens it is necessary that much correspondence should take place with collectors scattered about in various places, and many visits paid to see their collections; and this must have been particularly difficult when Conder wrote.

Another excellent and valuable work on this subject is Sharp's Catalogue of Sir G. Chetwynd's Tokens, but being only a description of those pieces, it omits as a matter of course all mention of any not in that collection, and not only so, but being privately printed, and a small number of copies only issued, it is now exceedingly difficult to obtain, and commands when for sale, a very high price.

There is also a book of plates by C. Pye, of Birmingham, which illustrates (and so describes) a very considerable number of specimens, and if it illustrated the entire series, would be most invaluable, but in many cases only one of a type is shown; and then again there is "The Virtuoso's Companion," by Denton and Prattent, which gives a much larger number of illustrations, but *arranged* in such a peculiar manner as to be most difficult of reference.

Under these circumstances it has been thought desirable to

bring out a work, containing a complete description, not only of those Tokens already described in the before-mentioned books, but also of many others which have since become known, as well as to give a fuller description of the large series of Tokens, such as the Anglesea, Edinburgh, Liverpool, &c., which were by the authors mentioned only partially described, and to whom many of the varieties were in all probability quite unknown.

An initial difficulty in dealing with this subject has been, to decide on some plan by which the very large number of mixed dies (or *Mules* as they are generally called) might be dealt with. Doubtless a large majority of these so-called "varieties" were made to increase the sale to collectors, but on the other hand some of them at least were issued for trade purposes, and a few are even included in Pye's plates, *e.g.* Sleaford pl. 44, No. 8, which is a Lancaster obverse with a Manchester reverse and pl. 51, No. 8, where an obverse is used which has already done duty as a reverse for Emsworth and Norwich. The arrangement decided on, and which has been carried out with one or two trifling exceptions, was to place those pieces which are made up of two obverse or reverse dies, in the first county alphabetically, to which those dies belong, and when a *mule* is composed of an obverse die of one county, and a reverse of another, then it has been placed in that county to which the obverse die belongs, or to that which gave the most definite localization. In each case a reference is given to all the other places where such obverse or reverse may be found.

Whatever opinion may be held as to the desirability or otherwise of the original issue of these mixed dies, there can be no doubt as to their interest to the present day Collector, as the design and workmanship is of course equal to the genuine issues, and in many, if not most cases, they exceed them in rarity. This same remark will apply to many of the private Tokens, and those pieces made for sale, and imitations of Tokens by Westwood and others.

And here it will be advisable to make some reference to the subject of counterfeits. Of these it goes without saying, that there are a very considerable number, some of which by their

inferior workmanship, and very light weight, at once proclaim
their identity: whilst others are so excellent in execution,
as well as equal in weight to those which they are intended
to imitate, that they can scarcely be detected. In fact there
are some, generally supposed to be counterfeits, upon which
to decide positively, would require a very bold judge indeed.

Another dilemma to be met was the placing of those pieces
with incorrect edges. In many cases, artists' proofs were
doubtless struck upon already existing Tokens, the edge
inscription of which would not agree with that upon the face,
this, of course, was a matter of no moment; but then on the
other hand large numbers of Tokens were issued with edges
which were either purposely vague, such as " Current Every
Where," or what is worse, directly opposed to the legend on
their face. Under these circumstances it has been decided to
disregard the edges altogether, and to place the Tokens
according to the obverse or reverse legend, putting the correct
edge (when known) first, and the other edges to supplementary
numbers, giving also a table of the various edges at the end of
the book.

But perhaps the greatest difficulty was to decide what to
include, and what exclude, of the heterogeneous mass of
Medalets, &c., grouped by Conder under the head of " Coins
Not Local." That many small medals, not intended to pass as
Tokens, did, from the scarcity of small change, find their
way into circulation cannot be doubted ; and at the same time,
many Tokens came to be treated as Medals from their intrinsic
value and beauty, as well as from their scarcity. This being
the case, it has been thought better to err on the side of inclusion
rather than exclusion, and the result is that very few of the
pieces mentioned by Conder are left out of this work. Those
pieces struck as patterns for the Regal coinage are of course
omitted, likewise a few undoubted medals, as are also the
Colonial Coins mentioned by him. But a large number of light
coppers, struck in imitation of the Regal Currency, have been
taken from the " Not Local " section, and several others from
the Counties, and many especially from North Wales, and these
are placed in a section by themselves, together with others of

the same kind which have come to hand, where they will form the most complete list of this species that has yet been compiled.

It only remains, in conclusion, to add that although the title of this work is the "Tradesmen's Tokens of the 18th Century," yet some few have been added of the 19th, but whenever this has been done, the close connection and resemblance, as well as the short interval of time dividing these latter from the others, has been considered not only to justify such a course, but also to render it desirable. (*See* Pidcock, London, &c.)

It will be advisable also to add that no illustrations of the Tokens are given, so as not to unnecessarily increase the cost of the work, the more so that any desirous of possessing such illustrations can obtain many of them in the plates of "Pye" and "The Virtuoso's Companion," references to which will be found, as well as to "Conder," appended to the description; the first of the two numbers referring to the page or plate, and the second to the numbers upon it.

My thanks are due to the collectors (and their name is legion) scattered about all over the country, for their cheerful and valuable assistance rendered at all times during the progress of the work; also to R. S. Poole, Esq., and his assistants at the British Museum for their courteous aid in comparing my MS. notes, with the specimens in the National Collection; but most of all have I been helped by constant access to the unrivalled stock of Messrs. Lincoln & Son, Numismatists, who are also the publishers of this book. In this collection (in all probability the largest in the world), containing as it does upwards of 70,000 specimens, I found many varieties of die never before described or known, and even some proofs of dies, unfinished, and finished, which are doubtless unique. And not only so, but I have been enabled by comparing this stock with the notes on rarity by Pye and Sharp, to furnish the most reliable aid to collectors, in ascertaining the comparative rarity of the various pieces, that has ever yet been given.

JAMES ATKINS.

ENGLISH TOKENS

ISSUED IN THE FOLLOWING COUNTIES :—

BEDFORDSHIRE	.	3	LINCOLNSHIRE .	. 9
BERKSHIRE	.	1	MIDDLESEX	. 823
BUCKINGHAMSHIRE	. .	27	MONMOUTHSHIRE	. 3
CAMBRIDGESHIRE	.	36	NORFOLK	. . 55
CHESHIRE	. .	62	NORTHAMPTONSHIRE	. 1
CORNWALL	. .	4	NORTHUMBERLAND	. . 35
CUMBERLAND	. .	2	NOTTINGHAMSHIRE	. . 6
DERBYSHIRE	.	3	OXFORDSHIRE .	. 2
DEVONSHIRE	.	11	RUTLAND	. 1
DORSETSHIRE	.	13	SHROPSHIRE	. 25
DURHAM	. .	11	SOMERSETSHIRE	. 106
ESSEX	. .	43	STAFFORDSHIRE	. 25
GLOUCESTERSHIRE	. .	50	SUFFOLK	. 38
HAMPSHIRE	.	67	SURREY .	. 33
HEREFORDSHIRE	.	6	SUSSEX . .	. 38
HERTFORDSHIRE	.	5	WARWICKSHIRE	. 338
KENT	.	40	WESTMORELAND	. . 8
LANCASHIRE	. .	99	WILTSHIRE	. . 20
LEICESTERSHIRE	. .	2	WORCESTERSHIRE	. . 38

YORKSHIRE . 65

LIST OF ABBREVIATIONS.

O : or obv : = Obverse.   *E* : = Edge.

R : or rev : = Reverse.   *Ex* : = Exergue.

Virt : = Virtuoso's Companion.

Bedfordshire.

HALFPENNIES.

FLITWICK.

✓ 1. *O*: View of a church and trees. FLITWICK . CHURCH . BED-
   FORDSHIRE. *Ex*: BT. 1670 JACOBS.

   R: A cypher *P. S. Co.* and the date 1797 in a beaded
   circle. DEDICATED . TO . COLLECTORS . OF . MEDALS &
   COINS.   Conder, 15 ; 1.—Virt: 196.

   *This, with all the other tokens of the buildings series
   (see London, Bath, Birmingham, Coventry, &c.) is
   rather scarce, in fact may be considered rare.*

LEIGHTON-BUZZARD.

2. *O*: A girl sitting under a tree, making lace. LACE MANU-
   FACTORY.

   R: A lamb, with the date under 1794. PAY AT LEIGHTON
   BERKHAMSTED OR LONDON.

   E: Milled.

2a.   As last, but *E*: Plain (not in collar).
                  Conder, 85 ; 136.—Pye, 26 ; 8.—Virt: 55.

   *This also appears as a London token (Chambers') with
   inscribed edge. See Middlesex, No. 196.*

PUDDINGTON.

3. *O*: Bust to left. PUDINGTON HALFPENNY PAYE AT THE HOUSE
   OF W. WALLER.

   R: A ship sailing. KING AND CONSTITUTION. *Ex:* BRITANNIA
   1797.

   *This appears to be an artist's proof from an unfinished
   die, and is exceedingly rare.*

1

Berkshire.

HALFPENNY.

WINDSOR.

1. *O* : A stag lying under a tree.

    R : WINDSOR HALFPENNY TOKEN 1795. A crown at top, and sprigs at bottom.

    E : Plain (not in collar).   Conder, 16 ; 1.—Virt : 61

✓ 1*a*.   As last, but *E*. SKIDMORE HOLBORN LONDON.

    1*b*.   .,   *E*. SPENCE × DEALER × IN × COINS × LONDON ×

     Rare, private token.

Buckinghamshire.

HALFPENNIES.

AMERSHAM.

✓ 1. *O*: A guitar, trumpet, and music book, intertwined with flowers. AMERSHAM . TOKEN . 1797.
    R: A . SPEEDY | AND | LASTING | PEACE In four lines, within palm and laurel branches.
    E: Milled.   Conder, 17; 1.

✓ 1*a*.   As last, but *E*: Engrailed.
    Rare, private token.

AYLESBURY.

2. *O*: A cypher, *F. W.* 1797; crest, a swan, between palm and laurel branches. FRANCIS WHEELER AYLESBURY BUCKS
    R: A figure of Justice seated. AYLESBURY * HALF * PENNY *
    E: Engrailed.   Conder, 17; 3.

✓ 3. *O*: The same as last.
    R: Shield of arms, crest, a bird, between branches. MAY . THE . TRADE . OF . AYLESBURY . EVER . FLOURISH.
          Conder, 17; 4.—Pye, 4; 3.—Virt: 152.
    Very rare, 3 impressions only in silver, and 13 in copper.

✓ 4. *O*: The same as the rev. of No. 2.
    R: Shield of arms. BUCKINGHAMSHIRE . ❖ . 1796 . ❖ .
          Conder, 17; 2.—Pye, 4; 4.—Virt: 153.

5. *O*: The same as last.
    R: The same as No. 3.   Conder, 17; 5.
    The obverse of No. 2 also occurs with the following reverses :

6. *R*: Heart and hand. HONOUR &c. See Middlesex, No. 516.
    E: Milled.   Conder, 268; 38.

7. *R*: PANDORA'S BREECHES. See Middlesex, No. 522.
    E: Engrailed.   Conder, 268 ; 39.

8. *R*: A shepherd under a tree. See Middlesex, No. 524 ; and Worcestershire, No. 7.
    E: Milled.   Conder, 267; 35.

9. *R*: A true-hearted sailor. See Middlesex, No. 537.
    E: Milled.   Conder, 267 ; 37.

1 *

10. *R*: An archer standing holding a bow. ARCHERY . FOR THE
PRIZE. See Warwickshire, No. 238.

                         Conder, 267 ; 34.

11. *R*: An anchor and cable. IN COMMEMORATION OF &c. See
Not Local, No. 117.

    E: Milled.   Conder, 267 ; 36.

    The obverse of No. 4 also occurs with the following
reverses :—

12. *R*: View of a church. HENDON &c. See Middlesex, No. 155.

    E: Milled.   Conder, 267 ; 32.

13. *R*: A man with a wooden leg. MR. JOSEPH ASKINS. See
Middlesex, No. 171.

    E: Engrailed.   Conder, 266 ; 28.

14. *R*: A man hanging ; P—T &c. See Middlesex, No. 208.

    E: Milled.   Conder, 267 ; 33.

15. *R*: Laureate bust to right. LONG . LIVE . THE . KING. See
Sussex, No. 25.

    E: Milled.   Conder, 266 ; 29.

16. *R*: Bust to left. MAY THE FRENCH &c. See Not Local,
No. 117.

    E: Milled.   Conder, 267 ; 31.

17. *R*: An anchor, &c., the same as No. 11.

    E: Milled.   Conder, 267 ; 30.

    All these tokens are rare.

✓ 18. *O*: A laureate bust of William III. within a circle ; JAMES
under it. TO THE FRIENDS FOR THE ABOLITION OF
SLAVERY *

    R: A cap of liberty on a pole, radiated ; four flags across.
AYLESBURY * TOKEN * * * 1796 * * *

    E: Milled.   Conder, 17 ; 6.—Pye, 4 ; 5.—Virt: 152.

18*a*.   As last but *E*: PAYABLE AT ANGLESEY LONDON OR LIVERPOOL.

18*b*.   ,,   ,,   *E*: CELEBRATED FOR PURE AIR & SEABATHING.

✓ 18*c*.   ,,   ,,   *E*: Plain (not in collar).

    In good condition, rare.

CHESHAM.

✓ 19. *O*: A cypher *A. S.*, a crest over. CHESHAM HALFPENNY
TOKEN

    R: Shield of arms between sprigs, a ribbon under inscribed,
CAREFULLY LEARN RELIGIOUS WAYS. The date under
1795. FOR THE PUBLIC GOOD

    E: PAYABLE AT ADAM SIMPSONS × · × · ×

                  Conder, 18 ; 7.—Pye, 14 ; 1.—Virt: 21.

SLOUGH.

✔ 20. *O*: A Phœnix. SLOUGH, . BUCKS, HALFPENNY TOKEN . 1795 .
      R: Shield of arms. JOHN PECKHAM . CHEMIST & DRUGGIST .

✔ 21.   As last, but with a slight difference in the shield.
      This may be distinguished by noticing a flaw on the edge
      to the right hand side.

✔ 22. *O*: A lion rampant to left. HALFPENNY TOKEN . SLOUGH,
      BUCKS ✳ RED LION INN ✳
      R: View of the inn. *Ex*: MDCCXCIV

✔ 23. *O*: As last.
      R: Shield of arms, and ribbon with motto PRO REGE ET
      PATRIA, the date under, 1794 W. TILL . WINE & SPIRIT
      MERCHANT ✳

✔ 24. *O*: As *R*: of No. 22.
      R: As last.

✔ 25. *O*: Same as *R*: of No. 20.
      R: Same as No. 23.
      These are all rare with the exception of No. 21.

26. *O*: Lion rampant to right. RED LION INN SLOUGH BUCKS
      HALFPENNY TOKEN
      R: Same as No. 23.
      Very rare.

      Nos. 20 and 23 are struck also in gold; and Nos.
      22, 23 and 24 in silver.

FARTHING SIZE.

STOWE.

✔ 27. *O*: A tree and a building. STOWE FARTHING. Date in *Ex*:
      1796.
      R: BUILT | ANNO DOMO | 1704 in three lines with a sprig
      above and below, within a double circle, the inner
      plain, and the outer formed of leaves.
      Very rare.   Conder, 18; 8.—Virt: 159.

Cambridgeshire.

PENNIES.

CAMBRIDGE.

1. *O*: A large building. BISHOPS . HOSTELL . CAMB . A.D. 1670. *Ex*: JACOBS.
R: A globe inscribed BRITAIN between a rose and thistle. BRITISH . PENNY. Date in *Ex*: 1797.
E: I PROMISE TO PAY ON DEMAND THE BEARER ONE PENNY
Conder, 19 ; 1.

2. *O*: An ancient gateway. CHRIST . COLLEGE . GATE . CAMB. *Ex*: JACOBS.
R: and *E*: As last. Conder, 19 ; 2.—Virt: 219.

3. *O*: A public building. EMANUEL . COLLEGE . CHAPEL . CAMB. *Ex*: JACOBS.
R: and *E*: As last. Conder, 19 ; 3.—Virt: 222.

4. *O*: View of building. KINGS . COLL . CHAPEL. JACOBS under. TO THE HEADS & STUDENTS OF THE UNIVERSITY OF CAMBRIDGE.
R: A different view. WEST . FRONT . OF . THE . NEW . BUILDING . KINGS . COLL . 1796. THIS MEDAL . IS . HUMBLY . INSCRIBED . BY . THEIR . OBEDIENT . HUMBLE . SERT D. HOOD. Conder, 19 ; 4.

5. *O*: A different view of the same building. KING'S . COLLEGE . CHAPEL . CAMBRIDGE. *Ex*: JACOBS.
R: and *E*: As No. 1. Conder, 19 ; 5.

6. *O*: An ancient gateway. TRINITY . COLLEGE . GATE . CAMBRIDGE. *Ex*: JACOBS.
R: and *E*: As No. 1. Conder, 19 ; 6.

7. *O*: A man on horseback. HOBSON CAMBRIDGE CARRIER 1596 DIED 1630 AGED 86
R: A building. JAMES BURLEIGH'S TOKEN CAMBRIDGE 1799 HOBSONS CONDUIT BUILT 1614 HANCOCK
E: VALUE ONE PENNY PAYABLE AT CAMBRIDGE Pye, 15*; 1.
Very rare. 6 impressions only in silver, and 48 in copper ; a few also in tin, with plain edge.
For other Cambridge pennies, see Middlesex, No. 8, and 9.

CHESTERTON.

8. *O*: View of a church, houses, and trees. CHESTERTON . NEAR . CAMB. *Ex*: JACOBS.
R: and *E*: As No. 1. Conder, 20 ; 7.

NEWMARKET.

✔ 9. *O*: Two horses running, ridden by jockeys. PENNY TOKEN.
    Ex: NEWMARKET MDCCXCIX
    R: CRAVEN MEETING SIR. H. V. TEMPESTS HORSE HAMBLETONIAN
    RUN MR COOKSONS DIAMOND OVER THE BEACON COURSE
    IN 8 MINUTES BEING 4 M. 1 FUR. 118 YDS. & WON BY
    HALF A NECK MAR 26.
    These Pennies are all rare.

HALFPENNIES.

COUNTY.

✔ 10. *O*: A beehive and bees. INDUSTRY HAS ITS SURE REWARD.
    R: A Druid's head. CURRENT IN THE COUNTIES OF 1795
    E: CAMBRIDGE BEDFORD . AND HUNTINGTON.
                Conder, 20 ; 8.—Pye, 13 ; 7.—Virt: 107.
  10*a*. As last, but without the dot after BEDFORD
  10*b*.   ,,   ,, *E* : Plain (not in collar).
    This obverse occurs with the following reverses:—
✔ 11. *R*: A figure of Hope leaning on an anchor. SUCCESS TO
    TRADE AND COMMERCE. See Essex, No. 3.
                Conder, 228 ; 150.
✔ 12. *R*: A figure of Britannia seated. RULE BRITANNIA. *Ex*:
    1795. See Hampshire, No. 10.
    E: BERSHAM BRADLEY WILLEY SNEDSHILL.
  12*a*. As last, but *E*: PAYABLE AT THE WAREHOUSE LIVERPOOL
  12*b*.   ,,   ,, *E*: PAYABLE IN LONDON. The remainder
    engrailed.
  12*c*.   ,,   ,, *E*: Plain (not in collar).
                Conder, 228 ; 153.
✔ 13. *R*: A stork. PROMISSORY HALFPENNY. 1793. See Hamp-
    shire, No. 27.
    E: PAYABLE IN LONDON. The remainder engrailed.
✔ 13*a*. As last, but *E*: Milled.   Conder, 228 ; 152.
 14. *R*: A river deity. CLYDE . NUNQUAM ARESCERE. *Ex*: MDCCXCI.
    See Lanarkshire, No. 5.
    E: Milled.   Conder, 218 ; 74.
 15. *R*: A plough and shuttle. SUCCESS TO THE PLOUGH &
    SHUTTLE. See Norfolk, No. 19.
    E: The same as No. 12*a*.
✔ 15*a*. As last, but *E*: The same as No. 12*b*.
                Conder, 228 ; 151.
    The reverse of No. 10 occurs as an obverse with the
    following reverse:—
✔ 16. *R*: A figure of Britannia seated. RULE BRITANIA 1797.
    See Middlesex, No. 747.
    See also Lancashire, No. 91 ; and Anglesea, No. 235.

CAMBRIDGE.

17. *O*: A wheatsheaf. PEACE PLENTY & LIBERTY.

    R: DAVID HOOD | PRINT SELLER | CARVER GILDER & | PICTURE FRAME MAKER | CAMBRIDGE. In five lines.

    E: SKIDMORE HOLBORN LONDON

✔ 17a.   As last, but *E*: Plain (not in collar).

                          Conder, 20; 9.—Pye, 13; 6.

This latter is struck on both large and small flans.

This obverse occurs with the following reverses :—

18. *R*: A beggar receiving alms. I WAS HUNGRY &c. See Gloucester, No. 22.

19. *R*: TO THE ILLUSTRIOUS DUKE OF BEAUFORT &c. See Gloucester, No. 22.

✔ 20. *R*: A fat man at table eating. ENGLISH SLAVERY. See Middlesex, No. 591.   Conder, 276; 119.

✔ 21. *R*: A lean man on the ground gnawing a bone. FRENCH LIBERTY. See Middlesex, No. 605.

                          Conder, 279; 145.

✔ 22. *R*: Bishop Blaize and woolpack. See Surrey, No. 13.

                          Conder, 269; 48.

✔ 23. *R*: Bust of William III. within an oak wreath. 1688. See Not Local, No. 14.   Conder, 302; 390

24. *R*: A pair of scales. THE SALE OF CORN BY WEIGHT PROPOSED 1796. See Not Local, No. 66.

25. *R*: A pair of scales . 3½ lb.=1s. WORTH OF BREAD, &c. See Not Local, No. 67.

26. *R*: A pair of scales . 6½ lb. BREAD FOR 1s. &c. See Not Local, No. 68.

27. *R*: A crown radiated . LOYAL BRITONS LODGE. See Not Local, No. 123.   Conder, 285; 212.

See also Middlesex, No. 267, 272, and 291; Yorkshire, No. 39; Anglesea, No. 222; Cork, No. 5; and Dublin, No. 109 and 126.

The reverse of No. 17 appears as an obverse with the following reverses :—

28. *R*: Arms of Orchard. HALFPENNY 1795. See Middlesex, No. 285.   Conder, 270; 64.

29. *R*: H and a bugle horn, &c. See Dublin, No. 101.

                        Conder, 274; 99.

30. *R*: Prince of Wales' crest, &c. See Dublin, No. 116.

                        Conder, 274; 94.

31. *R*: A wheatsheaf and sickle between two doves. See Munster, No. 1.   Conder, 270; 65.

32. *R*: An anchor, &c. LIBERTY PEACE COMMERCE. See Not Local No. 123.   Conder, 270; 63.

NEWMARKET.

33. *O* : A stag lying under a tree. NEWMARKET TOKEN 1793.

R : A snail, a tree, and a bridge in the distance. A SNAIL MAY PUT HIS HORNS OUT   Conder, 20 ; 10.

Rare, in good condition.

See also Worcestershire, No. 20.

FARTHINGS.

COUNTY.

✓ 34. *O* : Beehive and bees. INDUSTRY HAS ITS SURE REWARD

R : Druid's head to right. CURRENT IN THE COUNTIES OF 1795.

E : Milled.

v 34*a*.   As last, but *E* : Plain (not in collar).

Conder, 250 ; 48.—Pye, 13 ; 8.—Virt : 122.

35. *O* : The same as last.

R : Bust to left. SR. ISAAC NEWTON. See Not Local, No. 219.

E : Milled

35*a*.   As last but *E* : Plain (not in collar).

✓ 36. *O* : The same as *R* : of No. 34.

R : Cornucopia and olive branch FARTHING 1793. See Not Local, No. 219.

Both these two latter are rare.

The obverse die of No. 10 appears to have been utilized at Birmingham for the Eighteenpence, see Warwickshire, No. 2; and the design of No. 34, but not from the same die, also occurs on a shilling, see Warwickshire, No. 4.

35*b*.

35*c*.

v 35*d*.

Cheshire.

PENNIES.
CHESTER.

✓ 1. *O*: View of an ancient fortress, a flag flying at top. CHESTER . CASTLE *Ex*: Jacobs.
R: A globe inscribed BRITAIN between a rose and thistle. BRITISH . PENNY. Date in *Ex*: 1797.
E : I PROMISE TO PAY ON DEMAND THE BEARER ONE PENNY.
Conder, 22; 1.—Virt: 208.

✓ 2. *O*: An ancient gateway, houses, and spire of a church. EAST . GATE . CHESTER. *Ex*: Jacobs.
R: and *E* : As last. Conder, 22; 2.—Virt: 208.
All the pennies of the " Globe " series are scarce.

MACCLESFIELD.

✓ 3. *O*: Bust to right. CHARLES ROE ESTABLISHED THE COPPER WORKS W 1758 D.
R: A female seated, holding mining tools. THE MACCLESFIELD PENNY 1790.
Rare. Made for sale by Westwood.

HALFPENNIES.
BEESTON.

✓ 4. *O*: Remains of a castle, a bridge, and trees. BEESTON . CASTLE
R: A cypher *S. A. C.*, and 1797 within a double circle of dots . CHESHIRE . HALFPENNY . TOKEN ·:·
E: Engrailed. Conder, 22; 3.—Virt: 183.
Rare.
4a. As last, but *E* : Plain (not in collar).

CHESTER.

✓ 5. *O*: Three castles. N S E W PROMISSORY . HALFPENNY . PAYABLE . AT ✿
R: A cypher *R. & Co.*, crest an owl . CHESTER
E: Engrailed. Conder, 22; 4.—Pye, 14; 2.

✓ 5a. As last, but *E*: Plain.

MACCLESFIELD.
1789.

6. *O*: Blank.
R: A female seated by a windlass from which a rope depends. MMACCLESFIELD (*sic*). *Ex*: 1789.
This is an artist's proof, and most probably unique.

✔ 7. *O*: A cypher *R. & Co.* crest a beehive and bees. MACCLES-
FIELD.
    R: A female as before, holding a cogwheel with 6 spokes,
there is no rope on the windlass. HALFPENNY.
    Ex: 1789.
    E : PAYABLE AT MACCLESFIELD LIVERPOOL OR CONGLETON . × .
        Conder 22 ; 5.—Pye, 36 ; 1.
    *Very rare, this reverse die failed immediately upon being
used and the following took its place.*

✔ 8. *O*: Similar to last, notice that the right-hand bee comes
under the centre of the E.
    R: Similar to last, but the cogwheel has 8 spokes.
    E: The same as last.
        Conder, 23 ; 6.—Pye, 36 ; 2.—Virt : 115.

✔ 9. Similar to last, but the right-hand bee comes between
the E and the L.

✔ 10. Similar, but the right-hand bee comes under the I.

✔ 10*bis*. Similar, but the top bee which before was between the
s and F, is now directly under the F.

11. *O*: and *E* : The same as last.
    R: Differs from preceding in the female holding the cog-
wheel so that one of the spokes comes between her
fingers, whilst before, her hand was between two of
the spokes.

✔ 11*a*. As last, but *E* : PAYABLE AT CRONEBANE OR IN DUBLIN . × .
Very rare.

1790.

✔ 12. *O*: Bust to right. CHARLES ROE ESTABLISHED THE COPPER
WORKS 1758. The front edge of coat is in a line
with the first limb of the K in "WORKS."
    R : A female seated by a windlass, holding a boring imple-
ment and a cogwheel. MACCLESFIELD HALFPENNY.
Ex : 1790. The lower handle of windlass points to
foot of the Y
    E: Same as No. 7. Conder, 23; 9.—Pye, 36; 3.—Virt: 114.

✔ 13. Similar to last, but the front edge of coat is in a line
with the second limb of the K.

✔ 14. Similar, the front edge of coat comes to second limb of
the R, and the lower handle of the windlass comes
between the foot of the Y and the period.

✔ 15. Similar, the front edge of coat is on a line with first
limb of K, windlass as last.

✔ 16. Similar to last, excepting that the front edge of coat is
in a line with second limb of K.

17. Similar to No. 15, excepting that the lower handle of
windlass is close to the period.

✔ 18. The front edge of coat in a line with second limb of R
the handle of windlass below the period.
        Conder, 23 ; 9.

19. *O*: Similar to No. 12, but on a much smaller flan.
    R: Female seated holding mining tools as before. HALF-
        PENNY. *Ex*: 1790.
    E: PAYABLE IN DUBLIN OR LONDON + . +

19*a*.   As last, but *E* : PAYABLE IN LANCASTER LONDON OR BRISTOL

✔ 19*b*.   „   „   *E*: PAYABLE IN LANCASTER LONDON OR LIVER-
        POOL

✔ 19*c*.   „   „   *E* : Plain (not in collar). Conder, 235 ; 211.

1791.

✔ 20. *O* : Similar to preceding, the front edge of coat comes to
    centre of R.
    R : As before, but dated 1791. The top bar of windlass
    points to the foot of the Y.

21.   The coat is in a line with the last limb of the R, the top
    bar of windlass points to the first limb of the second
    N, the bottom bar is just below, but does not reach
    the period.

✔ 22.   Similar, but the bottom bar of windlass projects beyond
    the period.

✔ 23.   The top bar points to second limb of the N, the bottom
    one is considerably below period.

✔ 24.   The top bar points to the foot of the Y, otherwise as
    before.

✔ 25.   The coat is in a line with the first limb of the K, the top
    bar of windlass points to first limb of the second N,
    the bottom one points to, but does not reach the
    period.

✔ 26.   Similar, but the bottom bar is just below, and projects
    beyond the period.

✔ 27.   The top bar points to the second limb of N, the bottom
    one is considerably below period.

28.   The top bar points as last, but the bottom one nearly
    touches the period.

✔ 29.   The top bar points between the N and Y, the bottom one
    considerably below period.

✔ 30.   The top bar points to foot of Y, otherwise as before.

✔ 31.   The front edge of coat comes to second limb of K, the
    rev. is like No. 25.

32.   Similar, but the rev. is like No. 26.

✔ 33.   The top bar points to the second limb of N, the bottom
    one is just below the period.

✓ 34.   The top bar points between the N and Y, the bottom is below but does not reach period.

35.   The top bar points to foot of Y, otherwise as before.

✓ 36.   The front edge of coat comes in a line with the s, the top bar of the windlass points to the second limb of the second N.

> *These are all included in Conder under No.* 10 *on page* 23. *There are many other variations too slight for description, and all the edges read the same as No.* 7.

✓ 37. *O*: Very similar to No. 12, but the coat is without buttons.
   R: Similar to preceding, the bars of windlass are at more acute angle than any others.
   E: As No. 7.

✓ 37a.   As last, but *E*: PAYABLE IN LONDON EVERYWHERE

Conder, 23 ; 11.

1792.

✓ 38. *O*: Similar to preceding, the front edge of coat comes in a line with the first limb of the K.
   R: As before, but dated 1792. The top bar of windlass points to the first limb of the N, and the other some distance below the period, the right hand points to the first C.

✓ 39.   The top bar of windlass points to second limb of N, otherwise as last.

40.   Similar to last, excepting that the hand points to the L.

41.   The top bar of windlass points to between N and Y, the right hand points to second C.

42.   Similar to last, excepting that the hand points to the first C, and no period after date on obv.
   All these have the same edge inscription as No. 7.

42a.   As last, but *E*: PAYABLE IN ANGLESEY LIVERPOOL OR CONGLETON

42b.   „ „ *E*: PAYABLE IN ANGLESEY LONDON OR LIVERPOOL . × .

42c.   „ „ *E*: PAYABLE AT MACCLESFIELD LIVERPOOL OR LONDON

43. *O*: Similar to No. 38.
   R: Top bar of windlass points to foot of Y, the hand to the first C.
   E: Same as No. 7.

43a.   As last, but *E*: PAYABLE IN LANCASTER LONDON OR BRISTOL

43b.   „ „ *E*: PAYABLE IN LONDON LIVERPOOL OR BRISTOL

44.   The front edge of coat comes in a line with the last limb of R, the top bar of windlass points to the second limb of N, the hand to the L, this is the same rev. as No. 40.

R. G.

✓ 45. *O*: A cypher *R. G.*, crest a beehive, and bees. MACCLESFIELD.
R: A female seated, holding mining tools. HALFPENNY. *Ex*: 1792.
E: BRISTOL AND LONDON Conder, 23; 7.

✓ 45*a*. As last, but *E*: PAYABLE AT LONDON OR ANGLESEY

✓ 45*b*. „ „ *E*: LONDON |||||| ANGLESEA |||||| OR |||||| BRISTOL

✓ 45*c*. „ „ *E*: LONDON BRISTOL AND LIVERPOOL

R. & C. 1793.

✓ 46. *O*: A cypher *R & C.*, crest a beehive and bees. MACCLESFIELD ♥ ♥ ♥
R: Female seated holding mining tools. HALFPENNY. *Ex*: 1793.
E: PAYABLE AT ANGLESEA LONDON OR BRISTOL
Conder, 23; 8.

46*a*. As last, but *E*: Plain.
Although from the description this obv. would appear to be the same as No. 6, there is really a very considerable difference between them, the legend of this being in much smaller letters, which required the three trefoils to make out space, and the cypher is much less ornamental.

✓ 47. *O*: Similar to No. 12, but not from the same die.
R: The same as *O*: of No. 46.
E: PAYABLE IN LANCASTER LONDON OR BRISTOL

✓ 47*a*. As last, but *E*: PAYABLE AT LONDON OR DUBLIN
Conder, 24; 14.

47*b*. „ „ *E*: PAYABLE AT LONDON .+.+.+.+.

47*c*. „ „ *E*: PAYABLE AT W. PARKERS OLD BIRMINGHAM WAREHOUSE.

47*d*. „ „ *E*: Milled.
These last three are in all probability counterfeits.

R. & Co. (without date).

✓ 48. *O*: Three castles. N S E W PROMISSORY . HALFPENNY . PAYABLE . AT ✤
R: A cypher *R. & Co.* crest, a demi-lion rampant . MACCLESFIELD. Conder, 24; 15.—Pye, 36; 4.—Virt: 115.
This obverse is the same as No. 5.

49. *O*: Bust similar to No. 36.
R: A man at table writing, a woman seated by him holding a lighted candle, a mug upon the table, a clergyman behind (intended for Dr. Priestly) putting a foolscap

with asses' ears upon the writer's head, and another
table with a larger mug upon it. TAKE THIS JOHN
NOTT WEAR IT

E : Same as No. 7.   Conder 24 ; 13.

Exceedingly rare, only 2 specimens known.

This rev. also appears with obv. Wilkinson. See
Warwickshire, No. 325.

✔ 50. *O* : As last.
   R : Figure of Vulcan seated. HALFPENNY. *Ex* : 1792.
     See Warwickshire, No. 297.
   E : PAYABLE AT G. GILBERTS NORTHIAM   Conder, 153 ; 19.

✔ 50a.   As last, but *E* : Plain (not in collar).

51. *O*: and *E* : The same as No. 49.
   R: Female seated with mining tools. HALFPENNY 1796.
     The rev. of No. 37 appears as an obv. with the
     following reverse :—

✔ 52. *R* : A plough. INDUSTRY SUPPLIETH WANT. *Ex* : 1795. See
     Middlesex, No. 750.
   E : PAYABLE IN LONDON .+.+.+.+.+.
     The rev. of No. 38 appears as an obv. with the
     following reverse :—

✔ 53. *R* : Bust to right. WILLIAM . PIT . P . M.
     Very rare.   Conder, 24 ; 18.
     The rev. of No. 43 appears as an obv. with the
     following reverses :—

✔ 54. *R* : Shield of arms, crest, an ostrich. DEUS NOBIS &c. See
     Lancashire, No. 58.
   E : PAYABLE AT LIVERPOOL OR BRISTOL   Conder, 24 ; 17.

✔ 55. *R* : Full-length figure of Bishop Blaize. ARTIS &c. See
     Yorkshire, No. 47.
   E : The same as last.   Conder, 24 ; 16.
     See also Lancashire, No. 66.

FARTHINGS.

MACCLESFIELD.

✔ 56. *O* : A cypher *R.& Co.* crest, a beehive and bees. MACCLESFIELD.
   R : A female seated holding mining tools. HALF-HALFPENNY.
       Ex : 1789.
   E : Milled.   Conder, 25 ; 20.—Virt : 213.

56a.   As last, but *E* : Engrailed.

✔ 57. *O* : Bust to right. CHARLES ROE ESTABLISHED THE COPPER-
       WORKS 1768. There are no buttons on the coat.
   R : Female seated holding mining tools. MACCLESFIELD HALF-
       PENNY. *Ex* : 1790.
   E : Engrailed.

✓ 58. *O* : Similar to last, but the coat has three buttons on it.
    R : Same as last.   Conder, 25 ; 21.—Virt : 213.
    E : Milled.

✓ 59. *O* : and *E* : Same as No. 57.
    R : Similar to last, but dated 1791.

✓ 60. *O* : and *E* : Same as No. 58.
    R : Similar to last, but the arrangement of the bars of
        windlass, and spokes of wheel, different.
                                    Conder, 25 ; 22.

✓ 61. *O* : Same as No. 57.
    R : Slightly different to any preceding and dated 1792.
    E : Milled.   Conder, 25 ; 23.

✓ 62. *O* : Same as No. 58.
    R : and *E* : Same as last.

Cornwall.

HALFPENNY.

COUNTY.

1. *O*: Blank.
   R: Shield of arms, above it, ONE AND ALL, the Cornish motto. CORNISH COPPER HALF AN OUNCE 1791.
   An artist's proof, and probably unique.

2. *O*: A Druid's head to left, within an oaken wreath. R D. under the bust.
   R: Shield of arms and coronet. Legend as before.
   Conder, 26; 1.—Pye, 15; 2.—Virt: 2.
   See also Anglesea, No. 216.

FALMOUTH.

3. *O*: A spread eagle. with a rock and pole rising from it on its breast. (The Black Rock and beacon is at the entrance to Falmouth harbour.)
   R: FALMOUTH | INDEPENDENT | VOLUNTEERS | 1797. In four lines, with an ornament over.
   E: Milled. Conder, 26; 2.—Pye, 20; 1.

PENRYN.

4. *O*: A shield of arms, supporters, crest, &c. PRO REGE ET POPULO upon a ribbon over. *Ex*: LORD DE DUNSTANVILLE COLONEL.
   R: A laureated bust upon an antique shield, surmounted by a plumed helmet, and surrounded by military trophies. PENRYN VOLUNTEERS upon a ribbon over. *Ex*: FIRST INROLLED APRIL 3. 1794.
   Struck also in silver. Conder, 26; 3.—Pye, 41; 1.

Cumberland.

HALFPENNY.

LOW HALL.

✓ 1. *O*: A man with a horse in a gin, working a coal pit.

    R: LOW HALL | COLLIERY | 1797. In three lines.

                              Conder, 230; 168.—Pye, 35; 9.

    Scarce ; only 200 impressions taken.

FARTHING.

LAKE TOKEN.

✓ 2. *O*: A tree, boats on the water, and remains of a castle on a hill. *Ex*: JAMES.

    R: Trees and railing. CUMBERLAND LAKE TOKEN. *Ex*: 1796.

                              Conder, 27; 1.—Virt: 133.

    Rare.

Derbyshire.

HALFPENNIES.

BUXTON.

✓ 1. *O*: The shield of arms, supporters, crest, and motto of the Duke of Devonshire.

R: Semicircular row of buildings. CRESCENT.

E: BUXTON TOKEN. The remainder engrailed.

Conder, 28 ; 1.—Pye, 12; 2.

Very rare, only 6 struck.

✓ 2. Similar to last, but with date 1796 added to legend on rev.

Conder, 28 ; 2.

Rare; only a few impressions.

✓ 3. *O*: Similar to No. 1, but without the helmet above the coronet.

R: and *E*: Same as last. Conder, 28 ; 3.—Pye, 12; 3.

Of this, only 200 specimens were struck.

Devonshire.

HALFPENNIES.

EXETER.

✔ 1. *O* : A three-quarter figure of Bishop Blaize holding a comb in one hand and a book in the other. SUCCESS TO THE WOOLLEN MANUFACTORY. And the date 17—92 divided by the figure.

R : Shield of arms, supporters, &c. EXETER HALFPENNY.

E : PAYABLE AT THE WAREHOUSE OF SAMUEL KINGDON . ✕ .

Very rare.   Conder, 29 ; 1.—Pye, 19 ; 5.

✔ 2.   Similar to last, but the date omitted on the *O.* and added at bottom on *R.*

Conder, 29 ; 2.—Pye, 19 ; 6.—Virt : 16.

Also struck in silver.

3.   Similar to last, but the first letter of legend on *R.* starts level with the top of the pegasus' head, and the cross of the right-hand sceptre comes by the E, whereas in the former it came to the first N, of " HALFPENNY."

E : PAYABLE AT THE WAREHOUSE OF SAMUEL KINDON . ✕ .

Very rare ; possibly unique.

The rev. of No. 2 occurs as an obv. with the following reverses :—

✔ 4. *R* : Bust to left. IOHN HOWARD F R S PHILANTHROPIST. See Hampshire, No. 34.

E : Milled.   Conder, 29 ; 3.

✔ 5. *R* : Bust to left in cocked hat. GENERAL ELLIOT. See Warwickshire, No. 166.

E : PAYABLE AT LONDON OR BRIGHTON.   Conder, 29 ; 4.

For the obverse of No. 2, see also Shropshire, No. 19.

PLYMOUTH.

✔ 6. *O* : A female spinning. SAIL CANVASS MANUFACTORY *Ex* : 1796.

R : A man in a loom weaving. PLYMOUTH above, HALFPENNY beneath.

E : PAYABLE AT SHEPHEARD DOVE HAMMETT & CO. ✕ ✕

Conder, 29 ; 5.—Pye, 41 ; 8.—Virt : 88.

6*a*.   As last. but *E* : Plain (not in collar).

✔ 7.   Similar to last, but the legend on *R.* is continuous and the loom is smaller.

E : Plain.

Rare.

✔ 8. *O* : Laureate bust to right, a small D under. GEORGIVS III REX.

R : Oval shield of arms under a draped canopy. VISITED PLYMOUTH. *Ex* : AUGUST 1789   Conder, 312 ; *5.

FARTHINGS.

EXETER.

✓ 9. *O*: Three-quarter figure of Bishop Blaize. SUCCESS TO THE
         WOOLLEN MANUFACTORY.

   R: Shield of arms, supporters, crest, &c.   EXETER HALF
         HALFPENNY . 1791

   E: Milled.   Conder, 30 ; 6.

✓ 10.   Similar to last, but dated 1792.
                              Conder, 30 ; 7.—Virt : 202.

✓ 11.   Similar to last, but the date (1792) is omitted on the *R.*
         and placed on *O.* where it is divided by the figure.
                              Conder, 30 ; 8.

Dorsetshire.

HALFPENNIES.

BLANDFORD.

✓ 1. *O*: A pair of scales above a counter, on which are tea canisters and sugar loaves. W. SANGER TEA DEALER
  R: PRO BONO PUBLICO between palm branches, an ornament above. BLANDFORD HALFPENNY 1798.
  E: Milled.   Conder, 312; *1.
1a. As last, but *E*: Plain
  Both very rare.

POOLE.

2. *O*: The Prince of Wales' crest and motto in a circle, 75 underneath in a small oval. R. ALLEN IRONMONGER POOLE 1797
  R: An anchor in an oval, formed by a cable.
  E: Engrailed.
  Very rare.   Conder, 31; 2.

✓ 3. *O*: and *E*: Same as last.
  R: POOLE | HALFPENNY | PAYABLE . IN | DORSETSHIRE | AND DEVON | 1797
  Rare.   Conder, 31; 3.

4. *O*: Same as last.
  R: A cypher *R A* and 1797 in a circle of leaves. HALF-PENNY PAYABLE IN DORSETSHIRE
  Rare.   Conder, 31; 4.

5. *O*: Same as last.
  R: A Marine Society Boy; see Middlesex, No. 532.
  E: Engrailed.
  Very rare if not unique.

✓ 6. *O*: A figure of Hope leaning upon an anchor, supporting an oval inscribed JAS | BAYLY | DRAPER | POOLE. In four lines. *Ex*: A small ornament.
  R: The Arms of Poole. PROSPERITY TO THE TOWN OF POOLE * 1795 *
  E: I PROMISE TO PAY ON DEMAND ONE HALFPENNY . + .
       Conder, 31; 1.—Pye, 42; 1.—Virt: 16.

✓ 6a. As last, but *E*: Milled.

SHERBORNE.

✓ 7. *O*: A cypher *P P & W*, crest, a beehive and bees.
  R: A spread eagle. SHERBORNE HALFPENNY . 1793
  E: PAYABLE AT THE BANK IN SHERBORNE + DORSET +
       Conder, 31; 5.—Pye, 44; 7.

8.   Similar to last, but from different reverse die, distinguishable by the size of the eagle, which has thicker
claws.

✓ 9. *O*: A building, surmounted by a small spread eagle and
motto. SHERBORNE HALFPENNY
R: PRETER | PEW & WHITTY | BANKERS | SHERBORNE | DORSET
| 1796. In six lines.
E: PAYABLE AT THE BANK IN SHERBORNE + DORSET +
Conder, 31; 6.—Virt: 237.
Very rare, only a few impressions taken.

✓ 10. *O*: A cypher *P W & P*, 1796 above. SHERBORNE TOKEN
VALUE ONE HALFPENNY
R: A spread eagle. STET FORTUNA DOMUS.
Rare.

FARTHINGS.

POOLE.

✓ 11. *O*: A figure of Hope leaning on an anchor and supporting
an oval inscribed JAS BAYLY DRAPER POOLE, in four
lines with a large dot under. *Ex*: a small
ornament.
R: The arms of Poole. PROSPERITY TO THE TOWN OF
POOLE * 1795 *
E: Milled.   Conder, 31; 7.—Pye, 41; 10.—Virt: 167.

12. *O*: Similar to last, but on the oval the small s is inverted
and the large dot omitted.
R: and *E*: Same as last.

12*a*.   As last, but *E*: Plain (not in collar).

WEYMOUTH.

13. *O*: Bust to right, c . i . under. GEORGIVS III DEI GRATIA.
R: VISITED | WEYMOUTH | JUNE 30 | 1789. In four lines, with
a small ornament above.

𝔇urham.

PENNIES.

BARNARD CASTLE.

✓ 1. *O*: An ancient ruin, and trees . BERNARDS . CASTLE . DURHAM.
Ex: JACOBS.
R: A globe inscribed BRITAIN between a rose and thistle
BRITISH . PENNY. *Ex*: 1797.
E: I PROMISE TO PAY ON DEMAND THE BEARER ONE PENNY ✕
Conder, 32; 1.

SUNDERLAND.

✓ 2. *O*: View of a bridge, part of a house and a rock, and a ship
sailing. IRON BRIDGE NEAR SUNDERLAND SPAN 236
FEET HEIGHT 100 FEET. *Ex*: OPENED AUGT. 9. 1796.
R: Two ships and a boat. PENNY TOKEN. *Ex*: SUNDER-
LAND 1797. Conder, 32; 2.—Virt: 211.

✓ 3. *O*: View of a bridge with two ships sailing under it. SUN-
DERLAND . TOKEN span . 236 . ft. Height 100 ft.
R: IRON . BRIDGE | . over . the . | RIVER . WEAR | . Built . by .
| R . BURDON . Esq. | Begun . Sep. 24. 95 | Finish'd .
Augt. | 1796. In eight lines within a wreath.
E: ON DEMAND IN LONDON LIVERPOOL OR ANGLESEY . ✕ .
Conder, 32; 3.—Virt: 174.

✓ 3a As last, but *E*: Plain (not in collar).
*These appear to have been struck over Anglesea Pennies
and show some of the former impressions.*

HALFPENNIES.

SOUTH SHIELDS.

4. *O*: A figure of Faith standing, holding a book. SOUTH
SHIELDS HALFPENNY . 1794.
R: A ship sailing. SUCCESS TO THE COAL TRADE.
E: PAYABLE AT SOUTH SHIELDS AND LONDON . ✕ ✕ .
*Very rare; these dies soon failed, and the following were
executed in consequence :—*

✓ 5. *O*: Similar to last but from a different die; the book in this
case touches the L.
R: The flag in the stern of ship is larger, and the legend
commences closer to it.
E: Same as last. Conder, 32; 4.—Pye, 44; 10.—Virt: 3.
Also struck in silver.
The rev. of No. 5 appears as an obv. with the following
reverses :—

6. *R*: A figure of Hope leaning on an anchor. SUCCESS TO
TRADE AND COMMERCE. See Essex, No. 3.
E: PAYABLE IN LONDON. The remainder engrailed.

✔ 7. *R*: MAY | PEACE | & PLENTY | ACCOMPANY | THE PRINCE | & PRINCESS | OF | WALES. See Middlesex, No. 736.

     E: Same as last.   Conder, 218; 75.

     See also Warwickshire, No. 32; and Wicklow, No. 51.

✔ 8. *O*: Shield of arms . PAYABLE . IN . DURHAM . OR . LONDON.

     R: An anchor and cable . SOUTH . SHIELDS . HALFPENNY 1796.

     E: Engrailed.   Conder, 32; 5.

STOCKTON.

9. *O*: Helmed bust of St. Bevois . PROMISSORY HALFPENNY.

     R: A large ship sailing . PRO BONO PUBLICO.   *Ex*: 1794.

     E: PAYABLE AT KINGTONS STOCKTON.   Pye, 45; 7.

     Exceedingly rare.

     A similar design appears on Hampshire, Nos. 21-23.

SUNDERLAND.

✔ 10. *O*: View of a bridge . WEARMOUTH BRIDGE . ERECTED × A.D. 1796 . SPAN . 236 F. Height 100 F.

     R: IRON | BRIDGE . | R. BURDON | × Efqr. — | INVENTr. In five lines, within a circle of leaves.

     E: Plain (not in collar).   Conder, 32; 6.—Virt: 166.

10*a*.   As last, but *E*: PAYABLE IN LANCASTER LONDON OR BRISTOL.

10*b*.   „   „ *E*: CURRENT EVERY WHERE.

     Rare, especially with inscribed edge.

✔ 11. *O*: The same as last.

     R: Arms of Orchard, &c. See Middlesex, No. 288.

                            Conder, 301; 389.

             Rare.

Essex.

SHILLING.

EPPING.

✓ 1. *O*: A stag and a tree.
    R: A star and garter 1ˢ VALUE ONE SHILLING. EPPING FOREST 1796.
    E: SPENCE × DEALER × IN × COINS × LONDON ×
1a.   As last, but *E*: Milled.
✓ 1b.   „   „   *E*: Plain (not in collar).
                     Conder, 34; 6.—Virt: 83.
    The figures 9 and 6 in date are inverted.

PENNY.

WANSTEAD.

✓ 2. *O*: View of a gentleman's seat, Jacobs under . WANSTEAD . HOUSE . ON . EPPING . FOREST.
    R: A globe inscribed BRITAIN between a rose and thistle. BRITISH . PENNY. Date in *Ex*: 1797.
    E: I PROMISE TO PAY ON DEMAND THE BEARER ONE PENNY ×
                     Conder, 33; 1.—Virt: 199.

HALFPENNIES.

BRAINTREE.

✓ 3. *O*: View of a building. BRAINTREE & BOCKING HALFPENCE.
    Ex: MDCCXCIV.
    R: Figure of Hope. SUCCESS TO TRADE AND COMMERCE. The period touches the anchor.
    E: PAYABLE AT W GOLDSMITHS BRAINTREE ESSEX . × × .
              Conder, 33; 2.—Pye, 9; 8.—Virt: 178.
                  Rare.

✓ 4.   Similar to last, but with a new reverse die, in which the period does not touch anchor.
4a.   As last, but *E*: Plain (not in collar).
    Also struck in silver.
    This rev. appears as an obv. with the following reverse:—

✓ 5. *R*: A crown, sceptre, &c. as No. 6.
    E: PAYABLE IN LONDON. The remainder engrailed.
                     Conder, 214; 36.
5a.   As last, but *E*: Plain (not in collar).
    See also Cambridgeshire, No. 11; and Durham, No. 6.

CHELMSFORD.

✓ 6. *O*: A public building. SHIRE HALL on a label underneath.
    R: A crown, sceptre, and palm branch radiated. KING AND CONSTITUTION 1794.
    E: PAYABLE AT CLACHER & CO'S CHELMSFORD ESSEX.
              Conder, 33; 3.—Pye, 13; 11.—Virt: 21.
6a.   As last, but *E*: RICHARD BACON COCKY LANE.
✓ 6b.   „   „   *E*: PAYABLE IN HULL AND IN LONDON . × ×

6c.   As last, but *E*: PAYABLE IN LONDON BRISTOL & LAN-
CASTER . × ×

6d.   As last, but *E*: Plain (not in collar).
The rev. of No. 6 appears as an obv. with the following
reverses :—

✓ 7. *R*: A figure of Hope standing. PROSPERITY TO OLD ENGLAND.
See Norfolk, No. 24.
E: Milled.   Conder, 214; 35.

✓ 8. *R*: A head in profile. EARL HOWE & THE GLORIOUS FIRST
OF JUNE. See Hampshire, No. 9.
E: PAYABLE IN HULL AND IN LONDON.

✓ 8a.   As last, but *E*: CURRENT EVERY WHERE.

✓ 8b.   „   „   *E*: Milled.

8c.   „   „   *E*: Plain (not in collar).
     Conder, 225; 130.

9. *R*: A dove flying with an olive branch, and a cornucopia.
PEACE AND PLENTY. See Hampshire, No. 7.
E: RICHARD BACON COCKEY LANE.

9a.   As last, but *E*: CURRENT EVERY WHERE.

9b.   „   „   *E*: Plain (not in collar).
     Conder, 233; 195.

See also Middlesex, No. 280.

COLCHESTER.

10. *O*: A view of Colchester Castle. *Ex*: 1794. The castle
does not extend to the edge of the coin, and a
flaw runs down the centre of the die.
R: A loom. SUCCESS TO THE BAY TRADE.
E: PAYABLE AT CHARLES HEATHS BAY MAKER COLCHESTER . ×.
     Rare.

✓ 11. *O*: A slightly different view of the Castle carried out to the
edge, from a new die.
R: and *E*: Same as last.
     Conder, 33; 4.—Pye, 15; 1.—Virt: 3.

11a.   As last, but *E*: RICHARD BACON COCKEY LANE.

11b.   „   „   *E*: WILLEY SNEDSHILL BERSHAM BRADLEY.

11c.   „   „   *E*: Plain (not in collar).

DUNMOW.

✓ 12. *O*: Shield of arms. MAY . DUNMOW . PROSPER . 1798.
R: A flitch of bacon. PAYABLE . AT . DUNMOW . ESSEX.
E: Milled.   Conder, 34; 5.—Virt: 17.

✓ 12a.   As last, but *E*: SKIDMORE HOLBORN LONDON.

12b.   „   „   *E*: Plain (not in collar).
This obv. occurs with the following reverses :—

✓ 13. *R*: Hendon Church. See Middlesex, No. 155.
     Conder, 281; 165.

14. *R*: A register stove. (Skidmore.) See Middlesex, No. 361.
    E: SKIDMORE HOLBORN LONDON.

14*a*.   As last, but *E*: Milled.

15. *R*: Two men working in a forge. (Skidmore.) See Middlesex, No. 361.
    E: Milled.

16. *R*: Ruins of St. Paul's Church, Covent Garden. See Middlesex, No. 399.
    E: SKIDMORE HOLBORN LONDON.

17. *R*: The Tree of Liberty. (Spence.) See Middlesex, No. 622.   Conder, 299 ; 368.
    E: Milled.

18. *R*: View of a street, &c. See Yorkshire, No. 11.
    E: The same as No. 16.

19. *R*: Two busts. LOUIS XVI ET M. ANTOINETTE &c. See Not Local, No. 91.
    E: Milled.   Conder, 275 ; 115.

20. *R*: As last, but with the date 17–95 at sides.
    E : SKIDMORE HOLBORN LONDON.

✓ 21. *R*: Bust of Earl Howe, &c. See Not Local, No. 117.
    E : Milled.
    The rev. of No. 12 appears as an obv. with the following reverses :—

✓ 22. *R* : Bust of David Garrick, Esq. See Middlesex, No. 155.
    E : Milled.   Conder, 275 ; 113.

22*a*   As last, but *E* : Plain (not in collar).

✓ 23. *R* : The same as No. 14.   Conder, 295 ; 319

23. *R* : and *E* : The same as No. 14.

23*a*.   As last, but *E* : Milled.

24. *R* : The same as No. 15.

25. *R* : A guillotine, &c. See Middlesex, No. 375.
    E : The same as No. 16.

✓ 26. *R* : The same as No. 16.
    E : SKIDMORE HOLBORN LONDON.

26*a*.   As last, but *E* : Milled.

27. *R* : A cat. See Middlesex, No. 574.
    E : Milled.

28. *R* : A cypher *W G M* &c. See Wiltshire, No. 12.
                    Conder, 275 ; 112.

✓ 29. *R* : A cypher *I O M* &c. See Yorkshire, No. 10.
    E : SKIDMORE HOLBORN LONDON.

30. *R* : An anchor and cable. IN COMMEMORATION &c. See Not Local, No. 117.
    E : Milled.

✓ 31. *R* : MUR'D BY THE FACTIOUS &c. See Not Local, No. 91.
    E : Milled.   Conder, 275 ; 114.
        All these pieces are scarce.

HORNCHURCH.

32. *O*: Crowned bust, with sceptre. EDWARD IV. GRANTED THE CHARTER A.D. 1465.

 R: A castle within a shield upon which is inscribed LIBERTY OF HAVERING ATTE BOWER. A crown above. HORNCHURCH ROMFORD AND HAVERING.

Conder, 34; 7.—Pye, 23; 3.—Virt: 56.

33. Similar to last, excepting that the 1 in the date has a square top.

MALDON.

34. *O*: Shield of arms, crest a dove with olive branch in its mouth. SUCCESS TO THE BOROUGH OF MALDON *

 R: The arms and crest of the Watchmakers Co. supported by Time, and a Roman soldier.

 E: PAYABLE AT W. DRAPERS WATCHMAKER MALDON ESSEX . × × .

Conder, 34; 8.—Pye, 36; 7.—Virt: 43.

Only a small quantity of these were issued.

WARLEY.

35. *O*: Bust to right. GEORGE PRINCE OF WALES.

 R: The prince's crest and motto. HALFPENNY 1794.

 E: WARLEY CAMP HALFPENNY . × . × . × .

Conder, 34; 9.—Pye, 9; 10.

35*a*. As last, but *E*: WARLEY CAMP HALFPENNY MDCCXCIV. × . × . ×

Conder, 34; 10.

36. *O*: Similar to preceding, excepting that the line of forehead comes to the letter N, whereas in the former it came to the letter E; the end of legend is closer also to the bust.

 R: and *E*: as No. 35*a*.

37. *O*: Same as last.

 R: A period at end of legend, otherwise as last.

 E: Same as No. 35.

37*a*. As last, but *E*: same as No. 35*a*.

A similar design to the preceding will be found at Sussex, Nos. 3-6; and Not Local, Nos. 159-165.

WOODFORD.

38. *O*: A wheatsheaf and sickle between doves, 1796 within a circle of leaves.

 R: A pair of compasses, wheel, saw, and axe. TOKEN ESSEX 1796 within a circle. W. BROOKS CARPENTER WOODFORD . .

 E: Plain (not in collar). Conder, 35; 11.—Virt: 151.

38*a*. As last, but *E*: PAYABLE AT HIS OFFICE NEWPORT.

They are both rare, the one with inscribed edge especially so.

This rev. appears as an obv. with the following reverses :—

 ✓ 39. *R*: The Prince of Wales' crest, &c.   See Herts, No. 2.
                                          Conder, 264 ; 8.

 ✓ 40. *R* : A man weaving in a loom.   NOTHING WITHOUT INDUSTRY
        1795.   See Dublin, No. 13.   Conder, 302 ; 400.

FARTHINGS.

LEIGH.

 ✓ 41. *O* : View of a church.   I HEMMIN LEIGH.
       R : DEALER IN ALL KIND OF HARDWARE 1796.
         Rare.   Conder, 35 ; 13.—Virt : 144.

WOODFORD.

   42. *O* : Struck from the centre of obv. die of No. 38.
       R : Struck from the centre of rev. die of No. 38.
                      Conder, 35 ; 12.—Virt : 155.

 ✓ 43. *O* : Struck from the centre of rev. die of No. 38.
       R : The Prince of Wales' crest, &c., from the centre of Hert-
          fordshire, No. 2.

      This is in effect the same as the halfpenny No. 39.

Gloucestershire.

PENNIES.

GLOUCESTER.

ᐱ 1. *O*: View of a cathedral. GLOCESTER CATHEDRAL. *Ex*: FIRST
   BUILT 1061.
   R: Arms and ducal coronet, at the sides CITY TOKEN
   P. KEMPSON FECIT   THE ARMS OF GLOCESTER. 17 97.
   Conder, 37; 1.—Virt: 233.

2. *O*: Same as last.
   R: Arms and ducal coronet. THE ARMS OF GLOUCESTER.
   Under the shield *Ottley*.

✓ 3. *O*: An ancient building and church. ST. MARY DE CRYPT
   CHURCH. *Ex*: AND SCHOOL.
   R: Same as No. 1.   Conder, 37; 2.

4. *O*: Same as last.
   R: Same as No. 2.

ᐱ 5. *O*: View of a church. ST. MARY DE LODE. *Ex*: Palm and
   laurel branches crossed.
   R: Same as No. 1.   Conder, 37; 3.

✓ 6. *O*: Similar to No. 5, but with two buttresses and a spout
   added at the east end of church.
   R: Same as No. 1.   Conder, 313; *3.

7. *O*: Same as last.
   R: Same as No. 2.

✓ 8. *O*: View of a church. ST. MICHAEL'S CHURCH. *Ex*: Two
   palm branches crossed.
   R: Same as No. 1.   Conder, 37; 4.

9. *O*: Same as last.
   R: The same as No. 2.

✓ 10. *O*: View of a church and houses. ST. NICHOLAS CHURCH.
    R: Same as No. 1.   Conder, 37; 5.

11. *O*: Same as last.
    R: Same as No. 2.

✓ 12. *O*: A large building. THE NEW COUNTY GAOL. *Ex*: A pair
    of fetters.
    R: Same as No. 1.   Conder, 37; 6.

13. *O*: Same as last.
    R: Same as No. 2.

✓ 14. *O*: A large building. ST. BARTHOLOMEW'S HOSPITAL . REBUILT .
    1789.
    R: Same as No. 1.   Conder, 37; 7.

✓ 15. *O*: An ancient cross. THE HIGH CROSS. TAKEN DOWN IN 1751.
    R: Same as No. 1.   Conder, 313; *1.

16. *O*: Same as last.
    R: Same as No. 2.

✓ 17. *O*: View of a church. ST. JOHN'S CHURCH.
    R: Same as No. 1.

✔ 18. *O* : Same as last.
　　　 R : Same as No. 2.
✔ 19. *O* : An ancient building. WHITE FRIARS. *Ex* : Palm and laurel
　　　　　 branches crossed.
　　　 R : Same as No. 1.　　　　　●　　　Conder, 313 ; *7.
　 20. *O* : Same as last.
　　　 R : Same as No. 2.
　　　　　 That portion of this series with "Ottley" on the
　　　　　 reverse is struck in copper and white metal.
✔ 21. *O* : View of a cathedral. JACOBS under it. ST. PETER .
　　　　　 GLOUCESTER . B.T. 1204.
　　　 R : A cypher *T G* between palm branches. BRITISH . PENNY.
　　　　　 1797.
　　　 E : I PROMISE TO PAY ON DEMAND THE BEARER ONE PENNY ✕
　　　　　　　　　　　　　　　　　　　　Conder, 38 ; 8.
　　　 *All these pieces are scarce, those of Ottley's being the
　　　 most so.*
　　　　　 Nos. 1, 3, 8, 10, 12, 14, 15, 17, and 19, are also struck
　　　　　 in silver.

HALFPENNIES.

BADMINGTON.

✔ 22. *O* : A beggar receiving alms. I WAS HUNGRY AND YE GAVE
　　　　　 ME MEAT.
　　　 R : TO THE ILLUSTRIOUS DUKE OF BEAUFORT THE FRIEND OF
　　　　　 MANKIND & HIS WORTHY TENANTS WHO REDUCED THE
　　　　　 PRICE OF THEIR WHEAT TO 9*s* PR. BUSHEL A.D. 1795.
　　　　　 In ten lines between sprigs of laurel and oak.
　　　 E : BADMINGTON TOKEN . ✕.✕.✕.✕.✕.✕.✕.✕.
　　　　　　　　　 Conder, 38 ; 9.—Pye, 5 ; 1.—Virt: 70.
　 22a.　 As last, but *E* : Plain.
　　　　　 *The following tokens, although not identified by the
　　　　　 inscription on the edge, were issued at the same time as
　　　　　 No. 22, and like it are illustrative of the measures then
　　　　　 adopted to reduce the price of corn during a scarcity.*
　　　　　 The obv. of No. 22 occurs with the following :—

✔ 23. *R* : Laureated bust to right. HE FEELS HIS PEOPLE'S WANTS
　　　　　 & RELIEVES THEM ✻ ✻.　See Not Local, No. 63.
　　　　　　　　　　　　　　　　Conder, 284 ; 200.
✔ 24. *R* : A ship. CORN IMPORTED BY GOVERNMENT, 1796 ✻ ✻ ✻.
　　　　　 See Not Local, No. 63.　　　　Conder, 294 ; 311.
✔ 25. *R* : A plough and harrow. A under. SUCCESS TO THE
　　　　　 CULTIVATION OF WASTE LANDS. See Not Local, No. 64.
　　　　　　　　　　　　　　　　Conder, 290 ; 265.
✔ 26. *R* : A wheatsheaf, A under. RELIEF AGAINST MONOPOLY.
　　　　　 See Not Local, No. 65.　　　　Conder, 302 ; 394.
✔ 27. *R* : A pair of scales. THE SALE OF CORN BY WEIGHT PROPOSED,
　　　　　 1796. See Not Local, No. 66.　　Conder, 294 ; 306.

✔ 28. *R*: A pair of scales 3½ lb. 1s. WORTH OF BREAD, 1795-96.
GOOD LORD, DELIVER US *. See Not Local, No. 67.
Conder, 293; 298.

✔ 29. *R*: A pair of scales 6½ lb. BREAD FOR 1s. APRIL 1796 * GOD
BE PRAISED *. See Not Local, No. 68.
Conder, 294; 303.

The rev. of No. 22 appears as an obv. with the following
reverses :—

✔ 30. *R*: Laureated bust to right. Same as No. 23.
Conder. 293; 196.

✔ 31. *R*: A ship. Same as No. 24. Conder, 294; 312.

✔ 32. *R*: A plough and harrow. As No. 25. Conder, 290; 266.

✔ 33. *R*: A wheatsheaf. Same as No. 26. Conder, 302; 395.

✔ 34. *R*: A pair of scales. As No. 27. Conder, 294; 307.

✔ 35. *R*: A pair of scales. As No. 28. Conder, 293; 299.

✔ 36. *R*: A pair of scales. As No. 29. Conder, 294; 304.

*See also Cambridgeshire, Nos. 18 and 19, and Wilt-
shire, Nos. 7 and 8.*

BRIMSCOMBE PORT.

37. *O*: A barge sailing. with striped sails. THAMES AND SEVERN
CANAL. *Ex*: MDCCXCV .— × —.
R: A view of an entrance into a tunnel.
E: PAYABLE AT BRIMSCOMBE PORT ×
Conder, 38; 11.—Pye, 10; 2.
Very rare, as the obverse die failed almost immediately.

38. Similar to last, excepting that the sails are plain.

✔ 39. Similar to No. 38, but the small ornament under the
date has not got the two dots — × —
The arrangements of the foreground of reverse is also
different.

40. *O*: Similar to last, but with a flaw on the right-hand edge
of both sails.
R: Similar to last, but a line cuts the brickwork level with
the bottom of arch.
E: Of all. As No. 37.
Conder, 38; 10.—Pye, 10; 3—Virt: 24.
Scarce. Also struck in silver.

GLOUCESTER.

41. *O*: A distant view of the city of Gloucester. SUCCESS TO
THE TRADE & COMMERCE. *Ex*: OF GLOCESTER 1797.
R: A ship sailing. GLOCESTER & BERKLEY CANAL. *Ex*: ACT
OBTAINED 1793.
E: PAYABLE AT GLOCESTER. Conder, 38; 13.—Pye, 21; 7.

✔ 41a. As last, but *E*: PAYABLE AT I.IORDANS DRAPER GOSPORT

✔ 41b. „   „   *E*: Milled.

41c. „   „   *E*: Plain (not in collar).
Very rare.

3

✓ 42.   Similar to preceding, but a new reverse die in which
          the middle E is placed in BERKELEY.

                              Conder, 38 ; 12.—.Virt : 195.

          Also struck in silver.

42a.   As last, but *E* : Plain (not in collar).

NEWENT.

✓ 43. *O* : A shield bearing a griffin's head, leaning against an
          apple-tree.   INDUSTRY LEADS TO HONOUR.

   R : SEVERAL THOUSANDS YOUNG HEALTHY & FINE CRAB APPLE &
          PEAR STOCKS RAISED FROM THE KERNEL TO BE SOLD BY
          J. MORSE NEWENT GLOCESTERSHIRE. 1796. In a con-
          tinuous spiral line.

   E : PAYABLE AT NEWENT.   The remainder engrailed.

                              Conder, 39 ; 14.—Pye, 38 ; 3.—Virt : 83.

✓ 44.   Similar to last, but THOUSAND instead of " Thousands."

44a.   As last, but *E* : Plain (not in collar).

FARTHINGS.

CHELTENHAM.

 45. *O* : Laureated bust to right, DAVIES under it.   GEORGIVS III
          DEI GRATIA.

   R : Shield crowned, the date 1788 under it.   CHELTENHAM .
          JULY . 12.

 46. *O* : Similar to last, but with W. A. & CO. under the bust.

   R : Shield as before, but the date follows the legend.

          These two are larger size than those that follow.

✓ 47. *O* : Bust as before, with C . I . under it.

   R : Similar to last.

 48. *O* : Bust as before, with I . D . under it.

   R : The same as last.

 49. *O* : Bust as before, with I . D . under it.

   R : Similar to No. 45.

          *All these have scolloped edges, and are included under
          Conder, p.* 39 ; *No.* 15.

 50. *O* : Bust as before, R . W . under it.   Legend as before, the
          whole within a beaded circle.

   R : The order and motto of the Garter.   CHELTENHAM . .
          1788 . .

          This piece is round and of rather small farthing size.

Hampshire.

SHILLING.

BASINGSTOKE.

✔ 1. *O* : A barge sailing. BASINGSTOKE CANAL. *Ex* : 1789.
   R : A spade and pickaxe, in a wheelbarrow. JOHN PINKERTON.
   Ex : VALUE ONE SHILLING.
   E : Engrailed.   Conder, 40; 3.—Pye, 5; 4.—Virt: 24.
   This piece was circulated amongst the workmen employed in cutting the canal.

PENNIES.

GOSPORT.

✔ 2.. *O* : The British standard and a drum between four flags,
       which are inscribed " PEACE "—" SPAIN "—" FRANCE "
       —" HOLLAND." The tops of the last three broken off.
       BRITAIN TRIUMPHANT.
   R : T. WOOD SALESMAN GOSPORT VALUE ONE PENNY, in a circle.
       GOSPORT PENNY TOKEN 1798.
   E : I PROMISE TO PAY ON DEMAND THE BEARER ONE PENNY ×
                                       Conder, 40; 1.
                     Rare.

✔ 3. *O* : and *E* : The same as last.
   R : A large raft. FRENCH FOLLY IN BUILDING RAFTS. *Ex* :
       A.D. 1798.   Conder, 201; 10.

NETLEY.

✔ 4. *O* : View of an ancient ruin and trees. NETLEY ABBY HANTS.
   R : A cypher *T. G.* between palm branches. BRITISH PENNY
       1797.
   E : The same as No. 2.
                                       Conder, 40; 2.
                     Rare.

HALFPENNIES.

EMSWORTH.

✔ 5. *O* : A ship sailing, at the bottom sprigs of leaves. EMSWORTH.
   R : A female seated, one arm resting upon a globe, the other
       upon an anchor, a lion crouching at her feet, with a
       crown upon its head. HALFPENNY. *Ex* : 1793.
   E : PAYABLE AT THE WAREHOUSE OF IOHN STRIDE × × × ×
                     Conder, 40; 4.—Pye, 19; 1.—Virt: 52.

✔ 6.   Similar to last, but dated 1794.   Conder, 41; 5.
       The rev. of No. 5 appears as an obv. with the following
       reverse:—
                                                  3 *

✔ 7. *R* : A dove flying, and a cornucopia. PEACE AND PLENTY.
       E : CURRENT EVERY WHERE ―◆― ―◆― ―◆―
                          Conder, 233 ; 193.—Pye, 51 ; 12.
7*a*.   As last, but *E* : EAMES HOLLAND & ANDREWS PETERSFIELD.
7*b*.   ,,   ,, *E* : PAYABLE IN LONDON BRISTOL & LANCASTER
7*c*.   ,,   ,, *E* : Plain (not in collar).
         The rev. of No. 6 appears as an obv. with the same
         reverse as follows :—
8. *R* : The same as No. 7.
   E : EMSWORTH HALFPENNY PAYABLE BY IOHN STRIDE.
                          Conder, 233 ; 194.—Virt : 53.
8*a*.   As last, but *E* : The same as No. 7*a*.
✔ 8*b*.   ,,   ,, *E* : PAYABLE IN HULL AND IN LONDON ―×―
8*c*.   ,,   ,, *E* : The same as No. 7.
8*d*.   ,,   ,, *E* : Plain (not in collar).
         See also Essex, No. 9; Norfolk, Nos. 22, 23, and 28;
         and Lancashire, No. 93.

✔ 9. *O* : Bust to left in cocked hat. EARL HOWE & THE GLORIOUS
            FIRST OF JUNE.
       R : Britannia seated. RULE BRITANNIA. *Ex* : 1794.
       E : EMSWORTH HALFPENNY PAYABLE BY IOHN STRIDE ×
                          Conder, 41 ; 6.—Pye, 19 ; 2.
✔ 9*a*.   As last, but *E* : PAYABLE AT LONDON LIVERPOOL OR BRISTOL.
9*b*.   ,,   ,, *E* : Plain (not in collar).
✔ 10.   Similar to last, but dated 1795.   Conder, 41 ; 7.
✔ 11. *O* : A larger bust, and a quatrefoil after legend, otherwise
            as before.
       R : and *E* : The same as last. Conder, 41 ; 8.—Pye, 19 ; 3.
11*a*.   As last, but *E* : PORTSMOUTH HALFPENNY PAYABLE AT
         THO'S. SHARP'S.
11*b*.   As last, but *E* : PAYABLE IN LONDON. The remainder
         engrailed.
12. *O* : A very similar bust. ADMIRAL EARL HOWE 1797.
    R : Britannia seated. ✱ ✱ RULE BRITANNIA ✱ ✱ *Ex* : 1797.
    E : PAYABLE BY IOHN STRIDE. The remainder engrailed.
         *For this obv. see also Lincolnshire, No. 7 ; and for the rev.
         Middlesex, No. 751.*
         The obv. of No. 9 occurs with the following reverses :—
✔ 13. *R* : A large ship sailing. PRO BONO PUBLICO. See No. 22.
       E : CURRENT EVERY WHERE.   Conder, 226 ; 134.
✔ 14. *R* : A ship sailing. HALFPENNY. See No. 45.
       E : The same as last.   Conder, 226 ; 133.
15. *R* : A ship sailing. VAL . T BRITTISH TARS.
    E : PAYABLE AT LONDON OR BRIGHTON . . . .
15*a*.   As last but *E* : Plain (not in collar). Conder, 225 ; 128.

✔ 16. *R* : A MAP OF FRANCE. See Not Local, No. 98.
  E : The same as No. 13.   Conder, 225 ; 131.

✔ 17. *R* : MAY GREAT BRITAIN EVER &c. See Not Local, No. 98.
  E : The same as last.

17*a*.   As last, but *E* : Milled.   Conder, 226 ; 132.
  The rev. of No. 10 appears as an obv. with the following
  reverse :—

✔ 18. *R* : THE WAY TO PREVENT KNAVES GETTING A TRICK. See Not
  Local, No. 129.
  See also Nos. 29 and 36 ; and Anglesea, No. 231 ; Cambridgeshire, No. 12; Essex, No. 8; Lanarkshire, Nos. 6
  and 9 ; Lancashire, Nos. 67 and 73 ; Norfolk, Nos. 20
  and 50 ; Sussex, No. 16 ; Warwickshire, No. 33 ;
  Yorkshire, No. 61 ; and Wicklow, No. 62.

  The obv. of No. 11 occurs with the following reverses :—

19. *R* : The same as No. 12.
  E : PAYABLE IN LONDON. The remainder engrailed.

20. *R* : A female standing. LIBERTY & COMMERCE. (*This is the
  rev. of a New York token.*)
  E : The same as last.
  Very rare, if not unique.

GOSPORT.

✔ 21. *O* : Helmed bust of Sir Bevois. PROMISSORY HALFPENNY.
  R : A large ship sailing. PRO BONO PUBLICO. *Ex* : 1794.
  The mainmast to left of O.
  E : PAYABLE AT I. IORDANS DRAPER GOSPORT × × ×
  *Very rare. This reverse die soon failed, and another was
  produced in its place as follows :—*

✔ 22. *O* : and *E* : The same as last.
  R : Similar to last, but the top of mainmast comes to centre
  of O.   Conder, 41 ; 9.—Pye, 21 ; 8.—Virt : 94.

22*a*.   As last, but *E* : Plain (not in collar).

✔ 23. *O* : Similar to preceding, but not the same die.
  R : Similar to last, but the mainmast comes between the O
  and the P.
  E : The same as No. 21.   Conder, 41 ; 10.

23*a*.   As last, but *E* : PAYABLE AT S. SALMON I. COURTNEY &
  E. FROSTS ×

23*b*.   As last, but *E* : PAYABLE IN LONDON EVERYWHERE.

23*c*.   „   „   *E* : Plain (not in collar).
  *The reverse of No. 22 is also used for a Hull token, York-
  shire, No. 24. See also Kent, No. 10 ; Norfolk, No. 37 ;
  Warwickshire, No. 38 ; and Lanarkshire, No. 8.*

  *And a very similar design appears on the Stockton token,
  Durham, No. 9.*

✔ 24. *O* : A figure of Hope standing. PAYABLE AT BENN. & IONN.
JONES GOSPORT OR SHEERNESS.
    R : A ship sailing. THE GUARD & GLORY OF GT. BRITAIN.
Ex : 1796.
    E : Milled.   Conder, 41 ; 11.—Pye, 21 ; 9.—Virt : 207.

LYNDHURST.

✔ 25. *O* : Laureated bust to right. GEORGIVS III REX.
    R : VISITED LYNDHURST LYMINGTON SOUTHAMPTON WEYMOUTH &c.
1789   Conder, 42 ; 13.

NEWPORT (ISLE OF WIGHT).

✔ 26. *O* : Bust to left. ROBERT BIRD WILKINS.
    R : An antique ship, within a beaded circle. ISLE OF WIGHT
HALFPENNY 1792.
    E : PAYABLE AT HIS OFFICE NEWPORT . . . . . ✕ . . . . .
     Conder, 41 ; 12.—Pye, 24 ; 9.—Virt : 68.

PETERSFIELD.

✔ 27. *O* : A man on horseback. PETERSFIELD.
    R : A stork, standing upon a piece of ground, the bottom
margin of which is irregular, and deeply indented,
especially on the left-hand side. PROMISSORY HALF-
PENNY . 1793.
    E : EAMES HOLLAND & ANDREWS PETERSFIELD — ✕ —

✔ 27a.   As last, but *E* : Milled.
    *In consequence of a failure in the dies of this piece others
had to be executed as follows :—*

✔ 28. *O* : The gender of the horse is distinguishable, which it is
not in the former.
    R : The under margin of the ground is in a curve parallel
with the edge of the coin.
    E : Same as No. 27.

✔ 28a.   As last, but *E* : Engrailed.
     Conder, 42 ; 14.—Pye, 41 ; 7.—Virt : 69.

✔ 28b.   ,,   ,,   *E* : Plain (not in collar).
    This obverse also occurs with the following reverses :—

✔ 29. *R* : Britannia seated. Same as No. 10.
    E : PAYABLE IN LONDON. The remainder engrailed.
     Conder, 42 ; 15.

    29a.   As last, but *E* : PAYABLE ON DEMAND. The remainder
engrailed.

✔ 29b.   As last, but *E* : Plain (not in collar).

✔ 30. *R* : Military and musical trophy. BLOFIELD CAVALRY . FIFTH-
TROOP. See Norfolk, No. 7.
    E : Engrailed.   Conder, 42 ; 16.

The reverse of No. 28, appears as an obverse with the following reverse :—

✓ 31 *R* : Female standing holding a pole with cap of liberty, &c. See No. 20.

     E : PAYABLE AT THE WAREHOUSE LIVERPOOL × × ×

                            Conder, 230 ; 167.

See also Cambridgeshire, No. 13; and Lancashire, No. 81.

PORTSMOUTH.

✓ 32. *O* : Bust to left. IOHN HOWARD . F.R.S. PHILANTHROPIST. The front edge of coat is on a line with the second limb of the N of " IOHN."

     R : A sun and moon over a castle, being the arms of the borough. PORTSMOUTH AND CHICHESTER HALF PENNY *Ex* : 1794.

     E : PAYABLE AT SHARPS PORTSMOUTH AND CHALDECOTTS CHICHESTER.   Conder, 42 ; 18.—Virt : 89.

     Very rare, as the obv. die failed when a few impressions only had been taken.

✓ 33. *O* : Similar to last, excepting that the edge of coat comes midway between the H and N, and the shape of the frill, and tie of the wig also differs.

     R : and *E* : The same as last.

33*a*.   As last, but *E* : Milled over, PAYABLE AT ANGLESEY LIVERPOOL OR CONGLETON.

33*b*.   As last, but *E* : PAYABLE AT ANGLESEY LONDON OR LIVERPOOL.

     This obv. die also failed, giving way to the following :—

34.   Very similar to last, but without a period after " HOWARD."

     A very similar token, but with the rev. legend reading " CHICHESTER AND PORTSMOUTH," will be found under Sussex, No. 18.

The obv. of No. 32 occurs with the following reverse:—

✓ 35. *R* : A female standing, &c., as No. 20.

     E : PAYABLE IN LONDON. The remainder engrailed.

     Very rare.

The obv. of No. 34 occurs with the following reverse:—

36. *R* : The same as No. 10.

     E : The same as last.

36*a*.   As last, but *E* : PAYABLE AT THE WAREHOUSE LIVERPOOL.

36*b*.   „   „   *E* : CURRENT EVERY WHERE.

36*c*.   „   „   *E* : Milled.   Conder, 224 ; 123.

See also Devonshire, No. 4; Sussex, No. 17; Yorkshire, No. 62; and Lanarkshire, No. 7.

✔ 37. *O*: An anchor and cable between sprigs of laurel. PROMISSORY HALFPENNY.

   R: Shield of arms, crest, a demi lion, holding a crescent in its paw. PAYABLE AT PORTSMOUTH 1797.

   E: BY G. ROBINSON S. MOONEY AND I. CARTER . X X.

                 Conder, 42; 19.—Pye, 42; 4.—Virt: 218.

37*a*.   As last, but *E*: PAYABLE AT ANGLESEY LONDON OR LIVERPOOL . X.

This obv. occurs with the following reverse :—

38. *R*: Bust to left. STANHOPE NOBLE WITHOUT NOBILITY. See Not Local, No. 147.

   E: YORK BUILT A.M. 1223 . CATHEDRAL REBUILT . A.D. 1075.

✔ 39. *O*: Neptune standing in his chariot is crowning with laurel a naval officer seated upon a rock.

   R: SR. JOHN JERVIS | WITH 15 SAIL | PERSUED & DEFEATED | THE SPANISH FLEET OF | 27 SAIL OF THE LINE | FEBRUARY 14th | 1797.

This inscription is in seven lines, the figure 1 being in each instance curved.

   E: PORTSMOUTH HALFPENNY PAYABLE AT THOS SHARPS . X.

               Conder, 43; 21.

Rare. Most probably in consequence of the error in spelling, this reverse die was soon laid aside, as but few specimens exist, and the following was executed in its place.

40. *O*: and *E*: Same as last.

   R: Inscription as before, the word "PURSUED" being now spelt correctly, but as if still *pursued* by fate, the engraver of the die turned the figure 4 the wrong way.

Struck also in silver.

Very rare. In all probability there were fewer of these struck than of the former, and that another die very shortly took its place as follows :—

✔ 41. *O*: and *E*: Same as last.

   R: Inscription as before, but now being quite correct, and the figures 1 straight.

The obverse die now began to show signs of failure below the feet of the figures, and was superseded by a new one, a very close copy of the old.

42. *O*: Similar to No. 39, but differs in several slight particulars, the bottom edge of the officer's coat being straight, and there is more water shown at the bottom, the trident also is less spread.

   R: and *E*: As last.

          Conder, 43; 20.—Pye, 42; 6.—Virt: 209.

✔ 43. *O*: Three-quarter bust to right. VISCOUNT JERVIS & THE GLORIOUS 14 FEBY. 1797.

R : A man-of-war sailing. UNDER PROVIDENCE YE INVINCIBLE
FIFTEEN. *Ex* : A small ornament.

E : PAYABLE AT I. BRENTS PORTSMOUTH AND PORTSEA ✕ ✕ ✕
Rare, with this edge.
*On the majority of these tokens, the name of the issuer upon
the edge has been erased, causing the edge to read,*
" PAYABLE AT PORTSMOUTH AND PORTSEA."
Conder, 43 ; 22.—Pye, 42 ; 5.

PORTSEA.

✓ 44. *O* : Shield of arms, crest, a hand holding a javelin. PORT-
SEA HALFPENNY. 1794.
R : A ship sailing, at bottom sprigs of leaves.
E : AT GEORGE EDWARD SARGEANTS PORTSEA. The remainder
engrailed.

44a. As last, but *E* : Plain (not in collar). Conder, 43 ; 23.
See also Yorkshire, No. 23.

45. Similar in all respects to last, but with HALFPENNY added
above the ship on reverse.

45a. As last, but *E* : PAYABLE AT THE STORE OF + + + +
See also No. 14 ; and Norfolk, No. 27.

46. *O* : and *E* : The same as No. 44.
R : A ship sailing, below it sprigs of leaves, above PAYABLE.
The second and third leaves on the right-hand sprig
are double, the top of mainmast is to left of, and
does not touch the A.

47. Very similar to last, but the leaves on sprigs are all
single except the middle ones, and the folds of the
pennant are different.

48. Similar, but the top of mainmast touches the first limb
of the letter A.
In the obverse of all these pieces the point of the javelin
has been just above and nearly touching the second
limb of the A in " PORTSEA."

49. *O* : Similar to preceding, but the javelin points to first
limb of A, which it does not touch.
R : Similar to No. 46, but without any lantern at stern of
ship.

✓ 50. *O* : Similar, but the javelin is above the A, and some little
distance from it.
R : The same as No. 46.
The edges of all are the same as No. 44, and all are
included under Conder, 43 ; 24.—Pye, 42 ; 2.
The rev. of No. 48 appears as an obv. with the following
reverse :—

51. *R* : Britannia seated, &c. ; as No. 12.

v 52. *O*: St. George and the Dragon. PROMISSORY-HALFPENNY. *Ex:* 1796.

  R: A man-of-war sailing, a large fish swimming under it. (Evidently intended for a *salmon* in allusion to the name of one of the proprietors of the token.)

  E: PAYABLE AT S, SALMONS I COURTNEY & E FROST PORTSEA ×
      Conder, 43; 25.—Pye, 42; 3.—Virt: 176.

52*a*. As last, but *E*: PAYABLE AT S SALMON I COURTNEY & E FROSTS ×

52*b*. As last, but *E*: Plain (not in collar).

v 53. *O*: Similar to last, but without spines on the neck of the dragon.

  R: Similar, but no stern lamp to ship, the fish and waves also different.

  E: The same as No. 52.

53*a*. As last, but *E*: PAYABLE AT SHARPS PORTSMOUTH AND CHALDECOTTS CHICHESTER.

53*b*. As last, but *E*: PAYABLE AT ANGLESEY LONDON OR LIVERPOOL . × .

53*c*. As last, but *E*: Plain (not in collar).

SOUTHAMPTON.

v 54. *O*: A helmed bust to left, SR. BEVOIS in small letters under. SOUTHAMPTON HALFPENNY.

  R: Shield of arms, 1790 above it. BREWERY AND BLOCK MANUFACTORY UNITED COMPANY.

  E: PAYABLE AT THE OFFICE OF W. TAYLOR R. V. MOODY AND CO. . × .   Conder, 43; 26.—Pye, 45; 1.

  Very rare, only a few proofs taken.

v 55. A very close copy of the last (by Westwood), may be distinguished by the branch of hops in the shield having but two blossoms, whereas on the former there were seven. Conder, 44; 27.—Virt: 94.

v 56. A rather poor copy of No. 54 (by Jacobs); this may be distinguished from the two preceding by its having no blossoms on the hop stem. Conder, 44; 28.

56*a*. As last, but *E*: PAYABLE AT H. BROWNBILLS SILVERSMITH.

56*b*. As last, but *E*: Engrailed.

v 57. *O*: Sir Bevois in a rather different helmet. SOUTHAMPTON HALFPENY (*sic*).

  R: Shield of arms, 1791 above it. SUCCESS TO THE BREWERY AND BLOCK MANUFACTORY.

  E: The same as No. 54.   Conder, 313; *28.

  These latter are all rare, although not so rare as No. 54.

✔ 58. *O:* A helmed bust to right. DUMAREST F. in small letters under it. SR. BEVOIS SOUTHAMPTON.

    R: Shield of arms of the borough (a rose and crown), the date 1791 above. PROMISSORY HALFPENNY.

    E: PAYABLE AT THE OFFICE OF W. TAYLOR R. V. MOODY & CO.

                    Conder, 44; 29.—Pye, 45; 2.—Virt: 94.

    Also struck in silver.

    There are several very slight variations in the dies used for the obv. of this piece.

✔ 59. *O:* A poor copy of the preceding, the helmet without any plume.

    R: A figure of Justice, &c. *Ex:* DEA PECUNIA. See Warwickshire, No. 162.   Conder, 44; 30.

✔ 60. *O:* A poorer piece even than the last, the helmet appears only as a skull cap.

    R: A female holding mining tools. HALFPENNY. *Ex:* 1796.

                              Conder, 44; 31.

    This appears as rev. also at Cheshire, No. 51.

✔ 61. *O:* Bust similar to last, but without skull cap, and with the hair filletted.

    R: The same as last.   Conder, 44; 32.

    These three last appear with the North Wales harp, Rule Britannia, &c. in the Imitations of Regal Halfpence, which see.

WEST COWES (ISLE OF WIGHT).

62. *O:* A draped bust of Fox, upon a large halfpenny flan.

    R: Blank.

    E: PAYABLE AT THE WAREHOUSE OF THO'S WORSWICK & SONS . × .

    This was most probably a trial of the button puncheon from which the obverse of the following token was struck. Unique.

✔ 63. *O:* The bust as before, the date 1798 under . WEST COWES HALFPENNY.

    R: Arms of the town (a chevron between three dolphins) filling the entire field.

    E: PAYABLE AT THOS. AYRTON & CO. . × . × .   Pye, 47; 10.

FARTHINGS.

PORTSEA.

✔ 64. *O:* Shield of arms, crest a hand holding a javelin. HALF HALFPENNY 1791.

    R: A ship sailing, at bottom sprigs of leaves. PAYABLE.

    E: Milled.   Conder, 44; 33.

SOUTHAMPTON.

✔ 65. *O*: A helmed bust to left. ST. BEVOIS under it. SOUTH-
         AMPTON HALF HALFPENNY.
      R: Shield of arms, the date 1790 over it. BREWERY AND
         BLOCK MANUFACTORY UNITED COMPANY.
      E: Milled.   Conder, 44; 34.

✔ 66. *O*: Bust to left, W. CRAGG under it. GEORGIVS III DEI GRATIA.
      R: Shield of arms, between laurel branches . VISITED SOUTH-
         AMPTON . JUNE . 26 . 1789.
      E: Milled.

  67. *O*: Same as last.
      R: A monogram cypher *H. S.*, a barrel above it.   Legend
         same as last.

         The two latter pieces are in brass and of large farthing size.

Herefordshire.

PENNIES.

HEREFORD.

✓ 1. *O*: A bull breaking his chains. JUNE 3D. 1796. *Ex*: J
MILTON F.
R: An apple-tree and a plough within an oaken wreath;
there is an exergue line.   Conder, 45 ; 1.
Very rare. Also struck in silver.

✓ 2. *O*: Same as last.
R: Similar to last, but without the exergue line, the handles
of the plough also are longer.
Conder, 45 ; 2.—Pye, 22 ; 9.
Rare.

3. *O*: A more powerful animal than before. HEREFORDSHIRE.
Ex: JUNE 3 1796.
R: Same as No. 1.   Pye, 22 ; 10.
✓ 4. *O*: Same as last.
R: Same as No. 2.   Conder, 45 ; 3.

HALFPENNIES.

HEREFORD.

✓ 5. *O*: An apple-tree. SUCCESS TO THE CIDER TRADE. HEREFORD
HALFPENNY C : HONIATTS. BIRMM. WAREHOUSE.
R: Figure of Justice standing with sword and scales. FOR
CHANGE NOT FRAUD. *Ex*: 1794.
E: Milled. This on both large and small flan.
Conder, 45 ; 4.—Pye, 22 ; 8.—Virt : 35.

5*a*.   As last, but *E*: PAYABLE IN ANGLESEY LONDON OR LIVER-
POOL . X .

5*b*.   As last, but *E*: Plain (rounded).
*The reverse of this piece, which appears to be a common
one, is also found upon the Bungay and Kendal tokens :
see Suffolk, No. 20 ; and Westmoreland, No. 5.*

✓ 6. *O*: Bust to left. T. GORTON HEREFORD. 1794 (the 4 inverted).
R: An apple-tree and a cask. CYDER . MERCHT.
Conder, 45 ; 5.
Very rare.
*There is a striking resemblance between the bust on this
piece and that on Wiltshire, No. 12, which see.*

Hertfordshire.

PENNY.

SAWBRIDGEWORTH.

1. *O* : Full face bust in very high relief. ROBERT . ORCHARD . SAWBRIDGEWORTH . HERTS . .

   R : A book lying at the foot of a tree, a church in the distance. ✳ SAWBRIDGEWORTH ✳ PENNY ✳ TOKEN ✳

   Ex : ✳ ✳ PAYABLE ✳ ✳ FEBY. XI ✳ 1801 ✳

   This is exceedingly rare, as the die failed almost immediately.

HALFPENNIES.

ST. ALBANS.

✓ 2. *O* : The Prince of Wales' crest, and motto between sprigs. PAYABLE AT ST. ALBANS HERTS ❖ 1796 ❖

   R : A crown, 1796 over it, within a radiation, and a circle of lions, at bottom sprigs of leaves.

   Conder, 46 ; 1.—Virt : 151.

   Scarce.

   See also Essex, No. 39.

SAWBRIDGEWORTH.

✓ 3. *O* : A church with arms above, JACOBS under. ROBT. ORCHARD SAWBRIDGEWORTH HERTS.

   R : A shepherd under a tree. *Ex* : 1790.

   E : COVENTRY TOKEN.

3a. As last, but *E* : Milled.

   Rare.

   This reverse, which is common to several, also appears at Middlesex, No. 524, &c., and Worcester, No. 21.

   For other tokens of Robert Orchard see Middlesex, Nos. 74 and 285-299.

STORTFORD.

✓ 4. *O* : Shield of arms, crest, and motto. SIR GEORGE JACKSON BAR : SOLE PROPRIETOR.

   R : View of a river, with barges, &c. STORT NAVIGATION SOURCE OF TRADE . 1795 .

   E : PAYABLE AT BISHOPS STORTFORD .

4a. As last, but *E* : Plain.

   Conder, 46 ; 2.—Pye, 9 ; 5.—Virt : 166.

FARTHING.

ST. ALBANS.

✔ 5. *O*: The Prince of Wales' crest, and motto.

    R: A crown with the date 1796 above it, within a radiation. This is made from the dies of the halfpenny, No. 2.

    See also Essex, No. 43.

Kent.

PENNY.

GRAVESEND.

v 1. *O*: A Gravesend boat sailing. GRAVESEND TOKEN.
   R: A crown and naval coronet between sprigs of laurel.
   NAVAL ∴ PENNY. 17 ∴ 97.

Conder, 50; 19.—Virt: 183.

This piece, which is of small halfpenny size, is very rare.

HALFPENCE.

APPLEDORE.

✓ 2. *O*: A man carrying a sack to a windmill, and part of a
      house, in a beaded circle. THE UNION OF APPLEDORE
      KENT. 1794.
   R: A lion and lamb lying together in standing corn. PEACE
      INNOCENCE AND PLENTY.
   E: PAYABLE AT W. PECKHAM'S APPLEDORE . × . × . × .

Conder, 48; 1.—Pye, 4; 2.—Virt: 10.

✓ 2a.   As last, but *E*: PAYABLE BY W. FRIGGLES GOUDHURST

BENENDEN.

✓ 3. *O*: A wheatsheaf. PEACE AND PLENTY.
   R: Shield of arms. BENENDEN HALFPENNY. 1794.
   E: PAYABLE BY THOMAS REEVES BENENDEN + + +

Conder, 48; 2.—Pye, 7; 2.—Virt: 2.

*Only a small number of these pieces were circulated, the
remainder being destroyed; there were originally 4 cwt.
They are now rare.*

3a.   As last, but *E*: PAYABLE BY F. HEATH BATH.

BROOKLAND.

✓ 4. *O*: The Kentish horse in a beaded oval. KENT HALFPENNY
      PAYABLE AT .
   R: A cypher *I K*, over it a fleece. GROCER AND DRAPER. 1794.
   E: PAYABLE BY THOMAS KING'S BROOKLAND + . + . + . +

Conder, 48; 3.—Pye, 25; 4.—Virt: 9.

This piece also is scarce.

We now arrive at a point where, for the first time, we break
through our rule of giving a number to tokens only which have
something different on obverse or reverse, but in this county,
in three or more instances, the same token was struck with a
different edge for two persons in the same town (see also Goudhurst).

CANTERBURY.

✔ 5. *O*: A side view of Canterbury Cathedral. UNITY PEACE AND
   CONCORD: GOODWILL TO ALL MEN ❖ *Ex*: CANTERBURY
   TOKEN in two lines.

   R: Shield of arms of the city of Canterbury, and a mural
   crown. PROTECTION TO OUR KING AND COUNTRY LAWS
   AND TRADE +1795+

   E: PAYABLE AT JOHN MATHEWS'S + + + +
   Conder, 48; 4.—Pye, 13; 9.—Virt: 66.

   5*a*. As last, but *E*: PAYABLE IN LANCASTER LONDON OR BRISTOL
   This is an artist's proof and probably unique.

✔ 6. *O*: and *R*: same as No. 5.
   E: PAYABLE AT JAMES ROBERTSONS + + + +
   Conder, 48; 5.

✔ 7. *O*: A similar view. CANTERBURY TOKEN. *Ex*: a cypher *E. P.*

   R: Same arms and crown as before. OUR KING AND COUNTRY
   LAWS AND TRADE. 1795. A Maltese cross before and
   after date.

   E: PAYABLE AT CANTERBURY + + + +
   Conder, 49; 6.—Pye, 6.—Virt: 66.

✔ 8. *O*: Similar to last but from different dies, the cypher is
   larger, and there is no period at end of legend.

   R: and *E*: Same as last.

   9. *O*: and *E*: Same as last.

   R: Similar to No. 7, but with a dot on each side of date in
   place of Maltese cross, and a dot in the legend after
   " COUNTRY."
   Conder, 49; 7.

   These pieces are rare, especially the two latter.

   10. *O*: As *R*: of No. 5.

   R: An armoured bust of Sir Bevois. PROMISSORY HALF-
   PENNY. See Hampshire, No. 21. Conder, 234; 204.

DEAL.

✔ 11. *O*: A man of war sailing. THE GUARD & GLORY OF G' BRITAIN.

   R: Shield of arms of the Cinque Ports, between branches
   of oak. DEAL HALFPENNY TOKEN. 1794 above the
   shield.

   E: PAYABLE AT RICHARD LONG'S LIBRARY . × .
   Conder, 49; 8.—Pye, 16; 1.—Virt: 46.

   11*a*. As last, but *E*: MASONIC TOKEN I SCETCHLEY·FECIT.

   11*b*.   „   „ *E*: Plain (not in collar).

   A similar design but from different die to this obverse
   occurs on Hampshire, No. 24.

   4

DEPTFORD.

✓ 12. *O*: The Kentish men meeting William the Conqueror. KENTISH LIBERTY PRESERVED BY VIRTUE & COURAGE. *Ex*: 1067.

R: The stern of the "ROYAL GEORGE," under it KENT HALF-PENNY 1795 T H D   PROSPERITY TO THE WOODEN WALLS OF OLD ENGLAND

E: PAYABLE AT THO'S HAYCRAFTS DEPTFORD.

Conder, 49; 9.—Pye, 16; 2.

✓ 12a.   As last, but *E*: PAYABLE AT DEPTFORD CHATHAM AND DOVER. A flaw is observable on the *O*: of this piece.

Conder, 49; 10.—Virt: 48.

13. *O*: The same as last, but without the flaw.

R: The water-line does not extend beyond the ship, and the centre lamp does not touch E in "WOODEN."

E: The same as last.

✓ 14. *O*: Similar to last, but with a small cross instead of a dot at end of legend.

R: Similar, but from different die, chiefly noticeable in the date and the word "WOODEN."

E: The same as last.

Both these varieties are very rare.

DIMCHURCH.

✓ 15. *O*: A cypher *W.P.* crest, a lamb. ROMNEY MARSH HALFPENNY.

R: Figure of Justice standing.   FOR THE HONOR AND USE OF TRADE.

E: PAYABLE AT W. PARRIS DIMCHURCH . × . × . × .

Conder, 49; 11.—Pye, 43; 4.—Virt: 2.

15a.   As last, but *E*: Plain.

DOVER.

✓ 16. *O*: Bust to right.   THE. R. HON. W. PITT . LORD WARDEN CINQUE PORTS :

R: The arms of Dover. 1795 over the shield.   CINQUE PORTS TOKEN PAYABLE AT DOVER :

E: AT HORN'S LIBRARY.   The remainder engrailed.

Conder, 49; 12.—Pye, 14; 6.

16a.   As last, but *E*: PAYABLE IN LANCASTER LONDON OR BRISTOL.

16b.   „   „   *E*: PAYABLE AT LONDON OR DUBLIN.

17. *O*: Bust full face. R. HON.W.PITT. LORD WARDEN CINQUE PORTS :

R: Same as last.

E: Same as No. 16a.   Conder, 50; 13.—Virt: 46.

Very rare.

✓ 18. *O*: and *E*: Same as last.

R: A ship sailing.   THE WOODEN WALLS OF OLD ENGLAND ∴

18a. As last, but *E*: PAYABLE IN LONDON. The remainder
engrailed. Conder, 234; 206.—Pye, 14; 5.
Both rare.

✓ 19. *O*: Dover Castle and a distant view of ships at sea. *Ex*:
DOVER TOKEN.
R: Military trophy within a laurel wreath. DEDICATED.TO.
COLLECTORS.OF.PROVINCIAL.COINS.1795.
E: PAYABLE IN LONDON. The remainder engrailed.
Conder, 50; 14.—Virt: 74.
This also is rare.

FAVERSHAM.

✓ 20. *O*: An ancient sloop. PAYABLE AT FEVERSHAM.
R: Shield of arms of the Cinque Ports. CINQUE PORT HALF-
PENNY. 17 94.
E: PAYABLE AT IOHN CROWS COPPER SMITH × . ×
Conder, 50; 15.—Pye, 20; 2.—Virt: 47.
This reverse is used again for the Hythe token, No. 27.

FOLKESTONE.

✓ 21. *O*: Ships lying at a quay. MAY.COMMERCE.FLOURISH.
R: PAYABLE.AT.FOLKSTONE.KENT. VALUE ONE.HALFPENNY. 1796.
In two circles with date in centre.
E: Milled over inscription. Conder, 50; 16.—Virt: 193.
Rare.

GODINGTON.

✓ 22. *O*: A monogram TOKE (the name of the proprietor).
GODINTON. HOP-TOKEN. 1767. The two T's of the
legend come by the corners of the T of the monogram.
R: A basket heaping full of hops. NO PAINS NO GAINS.
There is no band round the basket.

23. *O*: Similar to last, but without a dot after TOKEN. The
first N of GODINTON and the P of HOP come by the
corners of large T.
R: Similar to last, but no dot after legend; and there is a
band round the basket, which is only level full.

24. *O*: There is no dot after GODINTON nor hyphen after HOP,
but there is a dot after TOKEN.
The T of GODINTON and the P of HOP come by the
corners of large T.
R: Similar to last, but not from the same die.
These three are struck in brass.

25. *O*: The monogram as before. GODINGTON HOP TOKEN. 1767.
R: A basket full of hops. NO PAINS NO GAINS.
*This is inserted on the authority of Sharp, and placed in
error by him at Herefordshire, No. 1. All these pieces
are very rare.*

4 *

GOUDHURST.

26. *O*: The Kentish horse. KENT HALFPENNY TOKEN. *Ex*: 1794.
    R: Shield of arms of the City of Canterbury. FOR GENERAL
        CONVENIENCE.
    E: PAYABLE BY W. FRIGGLES GOUDHURST + + + + +
        *The name on the edge of this piece being spelt wrong it
        was suppressed, and when any are met with an attempt
        has usually been made to erase the name.*
✓ 26a.   As last, but *E*: PAYABLE BY W. FUGGLES GOUDHURST
         . × . × . × . ×   Conder, 50; 18.
✓ 27. *O*: and *R*: Same as last.
    E: PAYABLE BY W. MYNS GOUDHURST + + + +
                             Conder, 50; 17.—Pye, 25; 3.
        *These pieces are met with countermarked; No. 26a with
        an F, and No. 27 with an M.*

HAWKHURST.

✓ 28. *O*: A cypher, *C. H.*, crest a wheatsheaf. HAWKHURST HALF-
        PENNY PAYABLE AT
    R: The Kentish horse in a shield. JUSTICE & CONFIDENCE
        THE BASIS OF TRADE.
    E: CHARLES HIDER'S. The remainder milled.
                    Conder, 51; 20.—Pye, 22; 5.—Virt: 48.

HYTHE.

✓ 29. *O*: An ancient sloop. PAYABLE AT HYTH.
    R: Shield of arms of Cinque ports. CINQUE PORT HALFPENNY.
        1794.
    E: AT RICHARD SHIPDEN'S . × . × . × . × . ×
                    Conder, 51; 21.—Pye, 14; 7.—Virt: 47.
29a.   As last, but *E*: Plain (not in collar).
        This reverse is the same as No. 20; *the obverse also is
        similar.*

LAMBERHURST.

30. *O*: A man picking hops, within a circle of dots. MAY HOPS
        FOR EVER FLOURISH.
    R: Shield of arms, between sprigs of leaves. SUSSEX HALF-
        PENNY TOKEN. 1794.
    E: PAYABLE BY T. FOSTER LAMBERHURST + + + +
30a.   As last, but *E*: PAYABLE AT RICHARD MAPLESDEN'S
        WINCHELSEA. × . × .
31. *O*: Similar to last, but varies in several particulars, and
        may be distinguished by noticing that the corner of
        the hop bin comes to the letter R in FLOURISH,
        whilst in the former it came to the letter U.
    R: and *E*: The same as last.
        Both these pieces are very rare, as the obverse die of
        each appears to have failed after very few impres-
        sions had been taken, giving way to the following :—

✔ 32. *O*: Similar to preceding, but the formation of the hop
plants differ, and the legend is closer; the hop bin
comes near the letter s in FLOURISH.

   R: and *E*: The same as last.

                     Conder, 51 ; 22.—Pye, 45 ; 10.—Virt : 36.

✔ 33. *O*: Shield of arms of the city of Chichester. FOR CHANGE
NOT FRAUD. Upon a label at bottom SUSSEX.

   R: Shield of arms of Canterbury. KENT HALFPENNY
TOKEN. 1794.

   E: PAYABLE BY I. GIBB'S LAMBERHURST + + +

                     Conder, 51 ; 23.—Pye, 25 ; 5.—Virt : 36.

33*a*.   As last, but *E* : PAYABLE BY + I + GIBB'S SUSSEX.

33*b*.   ,,   ,,   *E* : PAYABLE IN LANCASTER LONDON OR BRISTOL.
The latter edge is rarely met with.

MAIDSTONE.

✔ 34. *O*: Shield of arms, and supporters of the borough of Maidstone. 1794 above. MAIDSTONE HALFPENNY.

   R: A figure of Justice standing. THE SPRING OF FREEDOM
ENGLANDS BLESSING. *Ex*: KENT.

   E: PAYABLE BY HENRY CHILVERS + +

                     Conder, 51 ; 24.—Pye, 36 ; 5.—Virt : 48.

✔ 35. *O*: Shield of arms and supporters as before. MAIDSTONE
above, HALFPENNY under.

   R: View of a paper mill. PAYABLE BY J. SMYTH AT PADSOLE
PAPERMILL 1795.

   E: Milled.   Conder, 51 ; 25.—Pye, 36 ; 6.—Virt : 48.

ROMNEY.

✔ 36. *O*: A small antique sloop, between sprigs of laurel. THE
SUCCESS.

   R: Shield of arms of the town of Romney. ROMNEY HALF-
PENNY TOKEN 1794.

   E: PAYABLE AT IOHN SAWYER'S ROMNEY . × .

                     Conder, 52 ; 26.—Pye, 43 ; 3.—Virt : 2.

SANDWICH.

✔ 37. *O*: An ancient sloop. SANDWICH HALFPENNY TOKEN FOR

   R: Shield of arms of the Cinque Ports. MANUFACTURERS
TRADE AND COMMERCE.

   E: PAYABLE AT THOMAS BUNDOCKS × . × . × . ×

                     Conder, 52 ; 27.—Pye, 44 ; 3.—Virt: 47.

37*a*.   As last, but *E* : PAYABLE AT LANCASTER LONDON OR BRISTOL.

37*b*.   ,,   ,,   *E* : BRIGHTON CAMP HALFPENNY.

SHEERNESS.

*For a token issued jointly for Sheerness and Gosport see
Hampshire, No. 24.*

STAPLEHURST.

v 38. *O*: The Kentish horse. FOR CHANGE NOT FRAUD *Ex*: 1794.
     R: A cypher *I. S.*, crest a stag's head. STAPLEHURST HALF-
        PENNY 1794.
     E: PAYABLE BY I: SIMMONS STAPLEHURST ❖ ❖ ❖ ❖ ❖ ❖ ❖
                  Conder, 52; 28.—Pye, 45; 6.—Virt: 16.

STONE.

v 39. *O*: A thistle between sprigs. HALFPENNY.
     R: A cypher *M. S.* within a circle. M . SNOW . HOP . FACTOR .
        STONE . 1797.
     E: COVENTRY TOKEN and a wavy line.   Conder, 314; *28.
     Very rare.

TENTERDEN.

v 40. *O*: A horse and dray, and part of a brewhouse. *Ex*: TO
        CHEER OUR HEARTS.
     R: Shield of arms of the Brewers' Company. TENTERDEN
        HALFPENNY 1796.
     E: PAYABLE AT I & T CLOAKES BREW HOUSE . ✕ ✕ .
            Conder, 52; 29.—Pye, 46; 7.—Virt: 179.
   40*a*.   As last, but *E*: BIRMINGHAM REDRUTH & SWANSEA.

Lancashire.

PENNIES.

HALSALL.

✔ 1. *O*: Shield of arms, supporters, and crest. NEC PLACIDER CONTENT QUIETE EST upon a ribbon under.
 R: HALSALL D
 E: Engrailed.   Conder, 55 ; 1.—Virt : 187.
                      Rare.

LANCASTER.

✔ 2. *O*: View of a castle and tree. LANCASTER CASTLE.
 R: View of a bridge. LANCASTER BRIDGE *Ex* : A . SEWARD .
      1794.   Conder, 55 ; 2.
      Scarce, in both copper and brass.

MANCHESTER.

3. *O*: The Grocer's arms, supporters, &c. MANCHESTER PROMIS-SORY HALFPENNY 1793.
 R: East India Co.'s Tea Mark. PAYABLE AT INO. FIELDINGS GROCER & TEA DEALER.   Conder, 55 ; 3.
    Very rare.
    This is struck from the dies of the halfpenny, No. 77, upon a penny blank.

HALFPENNIES.

LANCASTER.

1791.

✔ 4. *O*: A crowned bust to left, a pentagonal star under. IOHN OF GAUNT DUKE OF LANCASTER.
 R: Shield of arms of the borough of Lancaster. LANCASTER HALFPENNY 1791.
 E: PAYABLE AT THE WAREHOUSE OF THOS. WORSWICK & SONS . X .

5. *O*: Differs from preceding, the centre point of crown comes to the letter U of DUKE whilst in the former it came between the D and the U.
 R: Differs from preceding, the centre line of shield comes to the centre of the C, but before, between C and A.

6. *O*: Centre point of crown comes between the U and the K.
 R: Same as No. 4.

7. *O*: Same as last.
 R: Same as No. 5.

✓ 8.　*O* : The centre point of crown comes to the K.

　　　R : Same as No. 4.　　　　　　　　　　　Pye, 26 ; 2.

　　　The edges of all these are the same as No. 4, and all are
　　　included under Conder, p. 55, No. 4.

1792.

9.　*O* : As before.　The centre of crown points to the D, the
　　　front point reaches to the U of " GAUNT."

　　　R : As No. 4, but dated 1792.

10.　*O* : As before.　The centre of crown points to the D, the
　　　front point comes to the N.　　　　　　　Virt : 12.

✓ 11.　*O* : The centre is between the D and the U, the front point
　　　comes to the U.

✓ 12.　*O* : Centre as last, front point comes to the N.

13.　*O* : The centre of crown points to K, the front points to T.

　　　The reverse and edge of all these are the same, and are
　　　included under Conder, p. 55, No. 5.

✓ 14.　*O* : The front point of crown curls over more than any of
　　　the others, reaching to the N, whilst the centre points
　　　to the K.　There is a flaw in the die which gives an
　　　impression of a *nose-ring*.

　　　R : Date much more spread, and a period after legend.

　　　E : PAYABLE IN LONDON BRISTOL AND LANCASTER — × —

　　　　　　　　　　　　　　　　　　　　　Conder, 55 ; 6.

✓ 14a.　　As last, but *E* : CAMBRIDGE BEDFORD AND HUNTINGDON

　　　　　　　　　　　　　　　　　　　　　Conder, 56 ; 7.

✓ 14b.　　　　"　　　"　　*E* : PAYABLE AT CLOUGHER OR IN DUBLIN

✿ 14c.　　　　"　　　"　　*E* : PAYABLE IN HULL AND IN LONDON.

✔ 14d.　　　　"　　　"　　*E* : CURRENT　EVERY　WHERE.

14e.　　　　"　　　"　　*E* : Milled.

14f.　　　　"　　　"　　*E* : Plain (not in collar).

15.　*O* : A very poor imitation of No. 13.

　　　R : Similar to No. 4, but the centre line of shield comes
　　　between the A and S of " LANCASTER."

　　　E : Same as No. 14b.　　　　　　　　Conder, 55 ; 8.

15a.　　As last, but *E* : Plain (not in collar).

16.　*O* : Similar to No. 13, but with a hexagonal star under the
　　　bust.

　　　R : Very nearly like No. 14.

　　　E : Same as No. 14.

17.　*O* : Similar to No. 12, but without any star under bust.

　　　R : Same as No. 9.

　　　E : PAYABLE IN LANCASTER LONDON OR BRISTOL.

　　　　　　　　　　　　　　　　　　　　　Conder, 56 ; 9.

✓ 17a.　　As last, but *E* : Plain (rounded).

　　　A flaw runs from the top left-hand side of shield to the
　　　edge.

17a - ℛ.O. ℛ...... .. ..t . ... flaw .
*　　ℰ . .. last .*

1794.

✓ 18. *O* : Similar to No. 13, but with a hexagonal star under bust, the centre of crown comes between U and K.

     R : As before, but dated 1794, and a period after legend.

     E : Same as No. 17.   Conder, 56 ; 11.

18*a*.   As last, but *E* : PAYABLE AT W. GYE'S PRINTER BATH ×.×

18*b*.   „   „   *E* : PAYABLE AT W. PARKER'S OLD BIRMINGHAM WAREHOUSE.

18*c*.   As last, but *E* : PAYABLE IN CHANDOS STREET CONVENT GARDEN + +

18*d*.   As last, but *E* : PAYABLE IN SUFFOLK-STREET HAY-MARKET .×. .×.

18*e*.   As last, but *E* : Plain (not in collar).

✓ 19. *O* : Similar to No. 12, but without a star under the bust, the centre of crown comes between D and U.

     R : and *E* : Same as No. 18.   Conder, 56 ; 10.

✓ 20. *O* : Similar to last, but the bust is smaller, the centre of crown comes to left of D.

     R : Similar, but there is a large space dividing " LANCASTER " and " HALFPENNY," and the date is badly formed.

     E : AN ASYLUM FOR THE OPRESS'D OF ALL NATIONS.

✓ 20*a* *E* : Plain (not in collar).   Conder, 56 ; 12.

21.   Similar to last, but the centre of crown comes to right of the D.

22. *O* : Similar to No. 18, but the star is not quite so large, and there is a period after legend.

     R : Shield of arms as before. HALFPENNY. 17 94. Two small ornaments between legend and date.

     E : Same as No. 18.   Conder, 56 ; 13.—Virt : 12.

22*a*.   As last, but *E* : PAYABLE AT S. & T. ASHLEY.

                                     Conder, 223 ; 109.

✓ 22*b*.   „   „   *E* : PAYABLE AT THE TEMPLE OF THE MUSES In these pieces the centre point of shield comes just midway between the 7 and 9 of date.

✓ 23. *O* : Similar, but without period after legend, the centre of crown comes to last limb of K.

     R : Similar to last, but the centre of shield comes nearer the 9 than the 7.

     E : Same as No. 17.

23*a*.   As last, but *E* : PAYABLE AT LONDON OR DUBLIN ×.×.×.

23*b*.   „   „   *E* : CURRENT EVERY WHERE.

24. *O* : and *E* : Same as No. 23.

     R : There is a period after " HALFPENNY," and the two halves of the date are a little farther apart.

24*a*.   As last, but *E* : PAYABLE AT LONDON .+.+.+.+.+.+.

24b.   As last, but *E*: Milled.

✔ 25. *O*: and *E*: Same as No. 18.
   R: There is no period after "HALFPENNY," and the two
      halves of the date are much wider apart.

   There are several minor variations in both *O*: and *R*:
   of these tokens, Nos. 4 to 25, but the differences are
   too minute to specify.

   The obverse of No. 12 also occurs with the following
   reverses:—

✔ 26. *R*: Arms, crest an ostrich, &c. DEUS NOBIS HÆC OTIA FECIT.
      1793. See No. 58.
   E: PAYABLE AT LIVERPOOL OR BRISTOL.   Conder, 59; 37.

✔ 27. *R*: Bishop Blaize and lamb. ARTIS NOSTRÆ CONDITORE. See
      Yorkshire, No. 47.
   E: Same as last.   Conder, 222; 107.

   The obverse of No. 14 occurs with the following
   reverses:—

✔ 28. *R*: A river god, &c. NUN QUAM ARESCERE. *Ex*: MDCCXCI.
      See Lanarkshire, No. 3.
   E: PAYABLE IN LONDON. The remainder engrailed.
                                Conder, 222; 106.

✔ 29. *R*: Figure of Britannia standing. SUCCESS TO THE COMMERCE
      OF BRITAIN. See Lincolnshire, No. 5.
                                Conder, 222; 105.

   The reverse of No. 24 appears as an obverse with the
   following reverse:—

✔ 30. *R*: Bust to right. GEORGE PRINCE OF WALES. See Not Local,
      No. 158.
   E: PAYABLE IN LANCASTER LONDON OR LIVERPOOL.

30a.   As last, but *E*: PAYABLE AT BANBURY OXFORD OR READING +
                                Conder, 240; 253.
   *See also No. 61, and Lincolnshire, No. 3; Middlesex, No.
   245; Warwickshire, No. 193; Yorkshire, Nos. 49, 50
   and 52; Dublin, No. 74; and Wicklow, Nos. 53 and 57.*

31. *O*: Bust to left. DANIEL ECCLESTON LANCASTER. In raised
      letters.
   R: A ship, plough, and shuttle. THE LANCASHIRE HALF-
      PENNY 1794, above upon a label. *Ex*: AGRICULT.
      MANUFACT. & COMMERCE.
   E: Milled.   *Possibly unique. (See Sharp, p.* 54; *No.* 7.)

✔ 32. *O*: Similar, but the legend is incuse, and there is PONTHON
      on the bust.
   R: Similar, but the legend is not on a label, but incuse
      upon a broad rim.
   E: PAYABLE.IN.LANCASTER.LIVERPOOL.&.MANCHESTER.
                        Conder, 56; 15.—Pye, 26; 1.—Virt: 46.

✓ 33. *O* : A hand holding a scroll inscribed " OUR CAUSE IS JUST "
UNANIMITY IS THE STRENGTH OF SOCIETY ❖

R : Fifteen stars radiated. E PLURIBUS UNUM.

E : PAYABLE IN LANCASTER LONDON OR BRISTOL.

Conder, 57; 16.—Virt: 104.

33*a*. As last, but *E* : AN ASYLUM FOR THE OPPRESS'D OF ALL
NATIONS.

33*b*. As last, but *E* : Milled.

✓ 33*c*.   „   „   *E* : Plain (not in collar).

LIVERPOOL.

1791. (Straight 1's in date.)

34. *O* : A ship sailing, at bottom sprigs of leaves. LIVERPOOL
HALFPENNY.

R : The arms, and crest, of Liverpool, between bulrushes;
there are no heads to the rushes. DEUS NOBIS HÆC
OTIA FECIT 1791.

E : PAYABLE AT THE WAREHOUSE OF THOMAS CLARKE . ✕ ✕ .

Pye, 27; 3.

*Very rare. This reverse die failed immediately, giving
place to the following :—*

✓ 35 *O* : The same as last. The mainmast of the ship just touches
the last letter of " LIVERPOOL."

R : Similar, but with two heads added to the rushes on
either side.   Conder, 57; 19.—Pye, 27; 4.

*The position of the mainmast is wrong in both Pye's illus-
trations.*

36. *O* : Similar, but the bowsprit of ship is closer to the foot
of the Y, and the mainmast is just clear of the letter
L, which before it touched.

R : The upper and lower of the four flags on right-hand
side point to the E and T, which in the previous ones
pointed to the F and I.

37. *O* : The mainmast comes to centre of foot of the L, the bowsprit in the bend of the Y.

R : Nearly as last.

✓ 38. *O* : The mast comes to the end of foot of the L, the bowsprit
to top of the Y.

R : Same as last.

39. *O* : The mast comes between L and H and nearly to the edge
of the coin.

R : The bulrushes come higher than any previous, the left-
hand one reaching the B, and the right hand one the I.

40. *O* : Top of mast touches foot of H.

R : Slightly differing from any preceding.

41. *O*: Very similar to No. 34, but there is a period at end of legend.

    R: Same as No. 36.

42. *O*: The top of mast comes between and *just below* the L and H, the end of the left-hand sprig touches the beginning of legend. There is a flaw in "HALFPENNY."

    R: There is a period at end of legend, and the left-hand bulrush touches the I.

43.   There is a period at end of legend on both *O*: and *R*:

44.   Differs in several particulars from the preceding, but may best be identified by the period on *O*: being above the line nearly in the bend of the Y.

     These are all included in Conder under No. 19 on page 57.

(Curved 1's in date.)

✓ 45. *O*: Similar, top of mast nearly touches the L, bowsprit touches foot of the Y.

    R: Similar to preceding, but the 1's in date are curved.

✓ 46.   Top of mast comes midway between the L and H.

46a.   As last, but *E*: PAYABLE AT THE WAREHOUSE LIVERPOOL

✓ 47.   Top of mast nearly touches the left-hand side of the H.

✓ 48.   Top of mast comes to the middle of the foot of the first limb of H.

     These are included in Conder under No. 20 on page 57, and all from No. 34 onwards have the same inscription on edge.

✓ 49. *O*: A good imitation of preceding, the mast touches end of letter L, bowsprit foot of Y.

    R: Similar to No. 36.

    E: PAYABLE IN ANGLESEY LONDON OR LIVERPOOL.

49a.   As last, but *E*: PAYABLE AT LANCASTER LONDON OR BRISTOL.

✓49b.   „   „   *E*: PAYABLE AT LONDON OR ANGLESEY.

49c.   „   „   *E*: LONDON ANGLESEA OR BRISTOL.

49d.   „   „   *E*: LONDON BRISTOL AND LIVERPOOL.

49e.   „   „   *E*: LONDON LIVERPOOL OR BRISTOL.

49f.   „   „   *E*: AT NUNEATON HINKLEY OR BEDWORTH.

49g.   „   „   *E*: NUNEATON BEDWORTH AND HINKLEY.

49h.   „   „   *E*: Milled to right.

49i.   „   „   *E*: Milled to left.

50. *O*: and *R*: A very poor imitation of the preceding.

    E: PAYABLE AT ANGLESEA LONDON OR LIVERPOOL.

                                   Conder, 57; 21.

1792.

51. *O*: Similar to preceding ones, but with no stern lamp.
    R: As before, but dated 1792.
    E: PAYABLE AT THE WAREHOUSE OF THOMAS CLACKE . × × .

52.   Similar to No. 46, but dated 1792. Bowsprit touches
         foot of Y.   Pye, 27; 5.

✓ **53.** *O*: Tip of bowsprit some little distance below the Y.
    R: The position of reeds and legend slightly different from
       last.

54.   Similar to preceding, but with period after legends on
         both *O*: and *R*:
         Nos. 52-54 are included in Conder under No. 22 on page 57.

✓ **55.** *O*: and *R*: A poor copy of No. 52, but without stern lantern.
    E: PAYABLE AT BIRMINGHAM LONDON OR BRISTOL.

55a.   As last, but *E*: PAYABLE ✳ AT ✳ CRONEBANE ✳ OR ✳ IN ✳
         LONDON ✳

55b.   As last, but *E*: PAYABLE IN LANCASTER LONDON OR BRISTOL.
                               Conder, 57; 23.

55c.   „   „   *E*: PAYABLE IN SUFFOLK BATH OR MANCHESTER.

56.   A rather better copy of No. 52; this has a stern lantern
         and a small dot under it looks like a pendant.
    E: PAYABLE IN HULL AND IN LONDON.

✓ **56a.**   As last, but *E*: CURRENT EVERYWHERE.
                               Conder, 58; 24.

1793.

✓ **57.** *O*: and *R*: Similar to last, but dated 1793. There is no
         pendant to stern lantern.
    E: PAYABLE AT ANGLESEA LONDON OR BRISTOL.
                               Conder, 58; 25.

57a.   As last, but *E*: LONDON ||||| ANGLESEA ||||| OR ||||| BRISTOL.

58. *O*: Similar, but with oak branches under ship.
    R: As before, but with a period at end of legend.
    E: PAYABLE IN ANGLESEY LONDON OR LIVERPOOL.
                               Conder, 58; 26.

✓ **58a.**   As last, but *E*: PAYABLE IN LONDON LIVERPOOL OR BRISTOL.

58b.   „   „   *E*: Milled.   Pye, 27; 6.

58c.   „   „   *E*: Plain (not in collar).

59. *O*: and *R*: A poor copy of preceding.
    E: PAYABLE AT LONDON & LIVERPOOL.   Conder, 58; 27.

1794.

✓ **60.** *O*: and *R*: Similar to preceding, but dated 1794.
    E: Same as No. 58.   Conder, 58; 28.

60a.   As last, but *E*: AT instead of IN.

60b.   „   „   *E*: PAYABLE BY IOHN PILMER CHURCH LANE.

60c.   As last, but *E* : PAYABLE IN HULL AND IN LONDON.

60d.   „   · „   *E* : PAYABLE AT LONDON LIVERPOOL OR BRISTOL.

60e.   „   „   *E* : PAYABLE AT LONDON CORK OR BELFAST.

60f.   „   „   *E* : PAYABLE AT DUBLIN CORK OR BELFAST.

60g.   „   „   *E* : Plain (not in collar).

There are a number of variations of Nos. 34-60 too minute to specify.

The obv. of No. 56 occurs with the following reverse :—

✓ 61. *R* : Crowned bust to left. IOHN OF GAUNT DUKE OF LAN-
CASTER. See No. 14 *ante*.
     E : CURRENT EVERY WHERE.   Conder, 58 ; 30.

61a.   As last, but *E* : Plain (not in collar).

The obv. of No. 58 occurs with the following reverses :—

62. *R* : Bust to left in cocked hat. The date 1795 and HALF-
PENNY under the bust. EARL HOWE & THE FIRST OF
JUNE, 1794. See Not Local, No. 112.
     E : PAYABLE AT SHARP'S PORTSMOUTH AND CHALDECOTT'S
        CHICHESTER.   Conder, 59 ; 34.

✓ 63. *R* : Bishop Blaze and lamb. ARTIS NOSTRÆ CONDITORE. See
Yorkshire, No. 47.
     E : PAYABLE IN ANGLESEY LONDON OR LIVERPOOL.
                                   Conder, 59 ; 36.

✓ 64. *R* : Bust to left. WASHINGTON PRESIDENT 1791. See Not
Local, No. 172.5
     E : Same as last.   Conder, 59 ; 35.

The obv. of No. 60 occurs with the following reverses :—

✓ 65. *R* : Female seated holding fasces. METAL & COPPER COMPANY
HALFPENNY. *Ex* : 1795. See Warwickshire, No. 78.
     E : Same as last.   Conder, 58 ; 31.

66. *R* : Bust of "CHARLES ROE, &c." See Cheshire, No. 38.
     E : PAYABLE IN ANGLESEY LONDON OR LIVERPOOL . × .

✓ 67. *R* : Bust of " EARL HOWE, &c." See Hampshire, No. 9.
     E : BIRMINGHAM REDRUTH & SWANSEA.   Conder, 59 ; 33.

67a.   As last, but *E* : AN ASYLUM FOR THE OPPRESS'D OF ALL
NATIONS.

✓ 67b.   As last, but *E* : PAYABLE AT DUBLIN CORK OR BELFAST.

67c.   „   „   *E* : PAYABLE AT LONDON CORK OR BELFAST.

67d.   „   „   *E* : The same as No. 62.

67e.   „   „   *E* : Plain (not in collar). .

68. *R* : Bust to right. GEORGE PRINCE OF WALES. See Not Local,
No. 158.
     E : The same as No. 63.   Conder, 59 ; 32.

68a.   As last, but *E* : PAYABLE IN LONDON OR BRIGHTON.

68b.   „   „   *E* : Plain (not in collar).

69. *R*: Bust to left. STANHOPE NOBLE WITHOUT NOBILITY. See Not Local, No. 147.

   E: PAYABLE AT ADAM SIMPSON'S ROMNEY.

70. *R*: A bishop's head with crozier, &c.   See Wicklow, No. 1.

   E: BIRMINGHAM REDRUTH & SWANSEA.

71. *O*: An imitation of N̄o. 47.

   R: Britannia seated. BRUNSWICK HALFPENNY. See Middle-sex, No. 241.

   E: The same as No. 63.   Conder, 58; 29.

71a.   As last, but *E*: PAYABLE IN LONDON. The remainder engrailed.

71b.   As last, but *E*: COVENTRY TOKEN. The remainder engrailed.

✓ 71c.   As last, but *E*: PAYABLE BY IOHN PILMER CHURCH LANE × ×

   The rev. of No. 58 appears as an obv. with the following reverses :—

✓ 72.   *R*: Bishop Blaize and lamb, the same as No. 63.

   E: PAYABLE AT LIVERPOOL OR BRISTOL.   Conder, 314; *37.

73.   *R*: Female seated holding fasces, the same as No. 65.

   E: PAYABLE IN LONDON. The remainder engrailed.

   The rev. of No. 60 appears as an obv. with the following reverses :—

74.   *R*: Britannia seated. RULE BRITANNIA. 1794. See Hamp-shire, No. 9.   Conder, 214; 32.

   See also No. 26; and Cheshire, No. 52; and Middlesex, No. 256.

✓ 75.   *O*: Bust to left. IOHN HOWARD F.R.S PHILANTHROPIST. See Hampshire, No. 34.

   R: Similar to last, but dated 1795. See Hampshire, No. 10.

   E: PAYABLE AT THE WAREHOUSE LIVERPOOL × × ×

MANCHESTER.

✓ 76.   *O*: Front view of India House. EAST INDIA HOUSE.

   R: The Grocers' arms, supporters, &c. HALFPENNY . 1792

   E: PAYABLE AT I. FIELDINGL ✝ MANCHESTER ○

                 Conder, 59; 38.—Pye, 36; 8.

✓ 76a.   As last, but *E*: LONDON BRISTOL AND LIVERPOOL.

76b.   „   „   *E*: Plain (not in collar).

   This token is also used, with a different edge, for Hudders-field. See also Warwickshire, No. 190.

✓ 77.   *O*: The Grocers' arms, supporters, &c. MANCHESTER PROMIS-SORY HALFPENNY 1793.

   R: East India Co.'s bale mark. PAYABLE AT INO. FIELDINGS GROCER & TEA DEALER ·

✓ 78. *O*: Similar to last, but with several minor distinctions, chief amongst which is the fact that whereas on the former the two centre figures only of the date come under the middle ribbon, in this case the entire date comes there.

  R: May be distinguished from the last by the tail of the & curling *downwards*.

✓ 79. *O*: Differs from last in the tufts at end of Griffins' tails being *solid* which before were made of two distinct lines, the shape of the Camel's rein is different, as is also the end of ribbon which approaches date.

  R: As last. Conder, 59 ; 39.—Pye, 36 ; 9.—Virt : 110.
  There are other slight varieties in these pieces, all scarce.

✓ 80. *O*: A porter carrying a pack. MANCHESTER HALFPENNY. *Ex* : 1793.

  R: Shield of arms, SIC DONEC on a ribbon under. SUCCESS TO NAVIGATION.

  E: Same as No. 75.
       Conder, 59 ; 40.—Pye, 36 ; 10.—Virt : 95.

✓ 80*a*. As last, but *E* : PAYABLE AT BIRMINGHAM LONDON OR BRISTOL.

80*b*. As last, but *E* : PAYABLE IN DUBLIN OR LONDON.

✓ 80*c*. „ „ *E* : PAYABLE IN LANCASTER LONDON OR BRISTOL.

80*d*. „ „ *E* : LONDON ||||| ANGLESEA ||||| OR ||||| BRISTOL.

✓ 80*e*. „ „ *E* : Engrailed.

✓ 80*f*. „ „ *E* : Plain (not in collar). This latter occurs on both large and small flans.

  This obv. occurs with the following reverses :—

81. *R*: A stork. PROMISSORY HALFPENNY 1793. See Hampshire, No. 31.   Conder, 60 ; 41.

82. *R*: A stork on a cornucopia. HALFPENNY PAYABLE AT See Warwickshire, No. 48.

  E: Engrailed.   Conder, 60 ; 42.
  See also Lincolnshire, No. 3, and Westmoreland, No. 8.

✓ 83. *O*: A head, front-face. FREDERICK DUKE OF YORK.

  R: The Bricklayers' arms and crest. HALFPENNY PAYABLE AT J. RAYNER & CO. MANCHESTER 1793.

  E: ANGLESEY LONDON OR LIVERPOOL.
       Conder, 60 ; 43.—Pye, 37 ; 1.—Virt : 81.

83*a*. As last, but *E* : BIRMINGHAM REDRUTH & SWANSEA.

83*b*. „ „ *E* : Plain (not in collar).

ROCHDALE.

✓ 84. *O*: A fleece. ROCHDALE 1791.

  R: A man weaving in a loom. HALFPENNY.

  E: PAYABLE AT THE WAREHOUSE OF IOHN KERSHAW . × .
       Conder, 60 ; 44.—Pye, 43 ; 1.—Virt : 23.

84*a*.　　As last, but *E*: Plain (not in collar).

✓ 85. *O*: and *R*: A very close copy of the preceding.
　　E: PAYABLE IN ANGLESEY LONDON OR LIVERPOOL . × .
　　Rare.

✓ 86.　　Similar to No. 84, but dated 1792.　　Conder, 60; 45.
　　This is an imitation by Westwood, and rare.　Also struck in silver.

✓ 87. *O*: Arms and crest of the Clothworkers' Company. ROCH-
　　DALE HALFPENNY. 1792.　The left-hand point of the
　　shield comes to the lower part of the letter L of
　　"ROCHDALE." There is a flaw, like a comma, between
　　the end of legend and the period.
　　R: A man weaving in a loom.
　　E: Same as No. 84.

87*a*.　　Same as last, but *E*: Plain (not in collar).

88.　　Similar to last, but the shield comes to top of letter L.

89.　　Similar to last, but the shield nearly touches the letter E.

✓ 90.　　As last, but with only three treadles to loom on *R*.
　　*The edges of all are the same as No. 84, and Nos. 87-90
　　are included in Conder under No. 46 on page 60—Pye,
　　43; 2—Virt: 23.　No. 89 is also struck in silver.*

The obverse of No. 88 occurs with the following
reverses :—

✓ 91. *R*: Beehive and bees. INDUSTRY HAS ITS SURE REWARD.　See
　　Cambridgeshire, No. 10.
　　E: PAYABLE IN LONDON.　The remainder engrailed.
　　　　　　　　　　　　　　Conder, 60; 48.

91*a*.　　As last, but *E*: Plain (not in collar).

✓ 92. *R*: A mounted dragoon. PRO REGE ET PATRIA.　*Ex*: QUEENS
　　BAYS.　See Norfolk, No. 47.
　　E: Same as No. 91.　　　　　　Conder, 60; 47.

92*a*.　　As last, but *E*: Plain (not in collar).

The reverse of No. 90 also appears as an obverse with
the following :—

✓ 93. *R*: Dove and olive branch. PEACE AND PLENTY.　See Hamp-
　　shire, No. 7.
　　E: PAYABLE IN HULL AND IN LONDON — × × —

FARTHINGS.

LANCASTER.

✓ 94. *O*: Crowned bust to left. IOHN OF GAUNT DUKE OF LANCASTER.
　　R: Shield of arms. LANCASTER HALF HALFPENNY 1791.
　　E: Milled.　　　　　　　　　Conder, 61; 49.

✓ 95　　Similar to last, but dated 1792.　　Conder, 61; 50.
　　　　　　　　　　　　　　　　　　　　5

LIVERPOOL.

✓ 96. *O*: A ship sailing, at bottom sprigs of leaves. LIVERPOOL HALF HALFPENNY.
    R: Shield of arms between bulrushes, crest an ostrich. DEUS NOBIS HÆC OTIA FECIT 1791.
    E: Milled.   Conder, 61 ; 51.—Virt : 212.
✓ 97.   Similar to last, but dated 1792.   Conder, 61 ; 52.

ROCHDALE.

✓ 98. *O*: A fleece. ROCHDALE 1791.
    R: A man weaving in a loom. HALF HALFPENNY.
    E: Milled.   Conder, 61 ; 53.
✓ 99.   Similar to last, but dated 1792.
                  Conder, 61 ; 54.—Virt : 240.

Leicestershire.

HALFPENNIES.

ELMSTHORPE.

1. *O* : View of a church in ruins.   RUINS OF ELMSTHORP CHURCH
   Ex : 1800.

   R : A wheatsheaf, with plough and harrow.   HALFPENNY
   PAYABLE BY RICHD. FOWKE.

   E : Plain in collar.

   This piece is an artist's proof struck in tin.

2. *O* : Similar to last, but with the legend corrected by adding
   the final letter E to " ELMSTHORPE."

   R : Similar to last, but with GOD SPEED THE PLOUGH added in
   Ex :   Pye, 18* ; 8.

   Very rare, only 3 impressions in silver and 18 in copper.

Lincolnshire.

HALFPENNIES.

LINCOLN.

✓ 1. *O* : A wheatsheaf. PEACE . AND . PLENTY . HALFPENNY.
   R : The arms of Lincoln. PAYABLE . AT . LINCOLN . OR . LONDON.
   1795.   Conder, 63 ; 1.—Virt: 161.

2. *O* : Same as last.
   R : The arms of London. SCALES WEIGHTS & STEELYARDS.
   See Middlesex, No. 265.

SLEAFORD.

✓ 3. *O* : Crowned bust to left. IOHN OF GAUNT DUKE OF LANCASTER.
   See Lancashire, No. 17.
   R : Arms, SIC DONEC under.   SUCCESS TO NAVIGATION.
   See Lancashire, No. 80.
   E : PAYABLE BY THOMAS BALL SLEAFORD . ✛ . ✛ . ✛ . ✛ .
                                 Conder, 63 ; 2.—Pye, 44 ; 8.

✓ 3a.   As last, but *E* : Plain (rounded).

SPALDING.

✓ 4. *O* : Figure of Britannia standing, at a distance men plough-
   ing and ships sailing. A small lion *above* Britannia.
   SUCCESS TO THE COMMERCE OF BRITAIN.
   R : A cypher *T. I.* in a shield between sprigs of flowers, ·
   crest a demi-lion.
   E : PAYABLE AT T. IENNINGS'S SPALDING & HOLBEACH — × —
                                 Conder, 63 ; 3.—Pye, 45 ; 3.
   *A flaw runs along the right-hand side of obverse, which
   necessitated the making of a new die after a few only
   of these had been struck.*

✓ 5. *O* : Similar to last, but the small lion is now *below* the figure,
   the legend commences at the bottom instead of the
   top, and there is a small sprig between lion and end
   of legend.
   R : and *E* : Same as last.   Pye, 45 ; 4.

✓ 6. *O* : and *E* : Same as last.
   R : The tail of the demi-lion is much nearer the letter H, and
   the festoon to left of shield has only four leaves
   below the rose, where before there were five.

✓ 6a.   As last, but *E* : PAYABLE AT I. IORDANS SPALDING & HOL-
   BEACH — × —   Conder, 63 ; 4.
   This is also struck in silver.

6b.   As last, but *E* : PAYABLE AT IOHN FINCHAMS SUFFOLK.
6c.   „   „   *E* : PAYABLE IN LONDON BRISTOL & LAN-
   CASTER.

6*d*.   As last, but *E* : PAYABLE AT LEEK STAFFORDSHIRE.

6*e*.   „   „   *E* : Plain (not in collar).

✔ 7. *O* : Same as No. 5.

    R : Bust to left in cocked hat. ADMIRAL EARL HOWE 1797. See Hampshire, No. 12.

    E : BUXTON TOKEN.   The remainder engrailed.

Conder, 227 ; 141.

    See also Lancashire, No. 29.

WAINFLEET.

8. *O* : View of Wainfleet Abbey.   FOUNDED BY WILLIAM WAYNE-FLETE ✱ 1459.

    R : A figure of Hope standing, a ship in the distance. WAIN-FLEET HALFPENNY. *Ex* : 1793.   The finger of the figure points to the second letter E in "WAINFLEET."

    E : BIRMINGHAM REDRUTH & SWANSEA.
An artist's proof, and possibly unique.

✔ 9. *O* : The same as last.

    R : Similar, but the figure is not so large, and its pointing finger touches the first E.

    E : PAYABLE AT THE WAREHOUSE OF D. WRIGHT & S. PALMER . ✕ .

Conder, 63 ; 5.—Pye, 47 ; 1.—Virt : 3.

9*a*.   As last, but *E* : reads WAREHOUSES.

9*b*.   „   „   *E* : PAYABLE IN HULL AND IN LONDON.

9*c*.   „   „   *E* : PAYABLE IN LONDON BRISTOL & LANCASTER.

Middlesex.

SIXPENCES.

CHRIST'S HOSPITAL.

In another's cabinet.

1. O: A monogram cypher *C C H.* The down strokes are formed of double lines; under it, the date 1800 in a curved line.
   R: SIX PENCE. (Octagonal flan.)
2. O: Similar to last, but the down strokes of the monogram are solid, and there is a period after the date, which is in a straight line.
   R: As before. (Struck upon octagonal, and also round flans.)
   In good condition rare.

THREEPENCE.

GOODMAN'S FIELDS.

3. O: A bear chained to a double ring above his back. GOODMANS . FEILDS . BREWHOUSE . 1760.
   R: THOMAS JORDAN AND CO. THREEPENCE. A double ring above similar to that on the obverse.

THREEHALFPENCE.

4. Similar, but the reverse legend reads "THREEHALFPENCE" instead of "THREEPENCE."
   Both these pieces are very rare.

PENNIES.

COUNTY.

5. O: An ancient building. WESTMINSTER HALL . BT. 1397. *Ex:* JAcobs.
   R: A portcullis and scales, between sprigs of oak and laurel. MIDDLESEX PENNY . 1797.
   E: I PROMISE TO PAY ON DEMAND THE BEARER ONE PENNY
   Conder, 68; 1.—Virt: 179.
6. O: A large building. THE BANQUETING HOUSE WHITEHALL. *Ex:* JAcobs.
   R: and *E:* The same as last.
7. O: An ancient building. THE HOUSE OF COMMONS FROM THE THAMES. *Ex:* BUILT 1552. JAcobs.
   R: and *E:* The same as last.
   This obverse occurs again at No. 99.

✓ 8. *O*: An ancient gateway. QUEENS . COLL . GATE . CAMB.   *Ex*:
JACOBS.
   R: and *E*: The same as last.   Conder, 68 ; 3.

✓ 9. *O*: A public building. TRINITY . COLL . LIBRARY . CAMB.   *Ex*:
JACOBS.
   R: and *E*: The same as last.   Conder, 68 ; 4.

✓ 10. *O*: A swan swimming.
   R: Three swords in a shield between sprigs. PAYABLE IN
   MIDDLESEX 1797.
   E: The same as last.   Conder, 68 ; 5.—Virt: 193.

✓ 11. *O*: and *E*: The same as last.
   R: An urn between scythes and sprigs of laurel, an arrow,
   skull, and hour-glass under the urn. TIME DESTROYS
   ALL THINGS. See Yorkshire, No. 1.
   All these pennies are rare, especially the two latter.

HACKNEY.

✓ 12. *O*: View of a church, and a small shield of arms. HACKNEY
   CHURCH. *Ex*: MDC.
   R: A cypher *D A R*, a knife and palm-branch under.
   HACKNEY PROMISSORY TOKEN 1795.
   E: ON DEMAND WE PROMISE TO PAY ONE PENNY.
                     Conder, 68 ; 6.—Virt: 138.

✓ 12a.   As last, but *E*: Plain (not in collar).
   This is struck from the dies of the imitation Hackney
   halfpenny, No. 153.

✓ 13. *O*: View of a church, and tombs. HACKNEY CHURCH MCCXC.
   Ex: *I Milton F.*
   R: A figure of Time, seated on a cabinet supporting a
   medallion inscribed "*David Alves Rebello.*" A
   globe, lyre, plants, &c. on the ground. MEMORIA IN
   ÆTERNA. *Ex*: 1796.
   E: Plain (in collar).   Conder, 69 ; 7.—Pye, 22 ; 2.
   Very rare, 8 impressions in silver, 28 in copper, and 1
   (unfinished) in tin.
   The obv. of No. 12 occurs with the following reverses:—

14 *R*: A cap of liberty on a pole between oak branches. PRO
   PATRIA upon a label across the pole. SHEFFIELD CON-
   STITUTIONAL SOCIETY. See Yorkshire, No. 6.
                     Conder, 263 ; 3.
   E: The same as No. 12.

✓ 14a.   As last, but *E*: Plain (not in collar).

15. *R*: A monogram cypher *P M Co.* ornamented. WE .
   PROMISE . TO . PAY . THE . BEARER . ON . DEMAND . ONE .
   PENNY. See Anglesea, No. 118.

✓ 16. *R*: A lion rampant supporting shield. REVOLUTION PENNY.
See Not Local, No. 14.   Conder, 264; 4.
The rev. of No. 12 appears as an obv. with the following
reverses:—

✓ 17. *R*: An oval shield, flags, &c. See Yorkshire, No, 6.
     Conder, 263; 2.

18. *R*: Bust of William III., &c. See Not Local, No. 14.
See also Anglesea, No. 124.

KEW.

✓ 19. *O*: A large building and trees. KEW . PALACE . MIDDX. *Ex*:
JACOBS.
     R: A globe inscribed BRITAIN between a rose and thistle.
BRITISH . PENNY. *Ex*: 1797.
     E: I PROMISE TO PAY ON DEMAND THE BEARER ONE PENNY
     Conder, 69; 8.

LONDON.

Christ's Hospital.

✓ 20. *O*: A monogram cypher *C C H*, the down strokes solid.
The date 1800 under, the top of the figure 1 is sloping.
     R: PENNY across the centre of field.   Pye, 35*; 3.

✓ 21. *O*: The same as last.
     R: PENNY in the centre with a sprig above and below.

✓ 22. *O*: Similar, but the down strokes of cypher in double lines,
the top of the 1 flat, no period after date.
     R: The same as last.

✓ 23. *O*: Similar, but the down strokes are solid, the 1 flat on
top, and no period after date.
     R: Similar to last. This piece is of finer work than any of
the others; it has a beaded rim, and is usually
struck upon a thicker flan.
     In good condition rare.

✓ 23*a*.   **Dennis'.**

✓ 24. *O*: A wheatsheaf. BAKERS HALFPENNY 1795.
     R: TO LESSEN | THE SLAVERY | OF | SUNDAY BAKING | AND PRO-
VIDE FOR | PUBLIC WANTS : | AN ACT WAS | PASSED. |
A.D. 1794.
     E: ON DEMAND WE PROMISE TO PAY ONE PENNY
     This is struck from the dies of the halfpenny, No. 214.

Gorton's.

✔ 25. *O* : A fender and fire-irons. T. GORTON . DEALER . IN . FENDERS, &C. . CLERKENWEL . LONDON.

    R : A cypher *T G* between palm-branches. BRITISH . PENNY . 1797 . in raised letters on a broad rim.

    E : I PROMISE TO PAY ON DEMAND THE BEARER ONE PENNY ×

Conder, 315; *9.

    For this reverse see also Hampshire, No. 4; Argyleshire, Nos. 1 and 2 ; and Not Local, Nos. 5 and 18.

Hall's.

✔ 26. *O* : Three quadrupeds. THE . KANGUROO THE . ARMADILLO THE . RHINOCEROS.

    R : T. HALL | CITTY ROAD | NEAR | FINSBURY SQUARE | LONDON | 1795 in six lines. THE FIRST ARTIST IN EUROPE FOR PRESERVING BIRDS BEASTS &.

    E : MANUFACTURED BY W. LUTWYCHE BIRMINGHAM . × .

Conder, 69; 10.—Virt: 140.

✔ 27. *O* : A deformed dwarf. SIR JEFFERY DUNSTAN MAYOR OF GARRAT.

    R : and *E* : The same as last. Conder, 69; 11.—Virt: 141.

✔ 27a.   As last, but *E* : ON DEMAND WE PROMISE TO PAY ONE PENNY *

27b.   „   „   *E* : Plain (not in collar).

✔ 28. *O* : A female standing. MRS. NEWSHAM THE WHITE NEGRESS.

    R : and *E* : The same as No. 26.

29. *O* : Similar to last, but with something like a necklace round the neck of the figure.

    R : TO BE HAD AT THE CURIOSITY HOUSE CITY ROAD * NEAR | FINSBURY SQUARE | LONDON | 1795.

    E : ON DEMAND WE PROMISE TO PAY ONE PENNY.

Conder, 69; 12.—Virt: 145.

29a.   As last, but *E* : Plain (not in collar).

30. *O* : The same as last.

    R : and *E* : The same as No. 26.

    The two latter are very rare.

Hardy's.

✔ 31. *O* : Full-face bust. THOS. HARDY SECRETARY TO THE LONDON CORRESPONDING SOCY. NOT GUILTY NOVR. 5. 1794.

    R : Names of jury in centre. BY THE INTEGRITY OF THE JURY WHO ARE JUDGES OF LAW AS WELL AS FACT.

Conder, 203 ; 23.

James'.

✓ 32. *O* : A lion couchant, holding a shield, inscribed, No. 6
MARTLETT COURT BOW STREET LONDON in four lines. C.
JAMES ENGRAVER.

R : A vulture. MEDALS DIES CRESTS COATS OF ARMS UNIFORMS
&c.   Conder, 70; 13.—Pye, 30; 10.
Very rare; about two dozen struck.

✓ 33. *O* : The same as last.

R : A crown between sprigs of oak, rays of sun at top.
ROYAL PENNY.

E : I PROMISE TO PAY ON DEMAND THE BEARER ONE PENNY ✕
Conder, 70; 14.

Also rare.

Kempson's.

✓ 34. *O* : View of a building. GUILD-HALL. *Ex* : LONDON .
MDCCXCVI.

R : The arms of London between palm-branches. LONDON
PROMISSORY PENNY TOKEN ✱

E : The same as last.   Conder, 70; 15.—Virt: 131.

✓ 35. *O* : A large building. *Ex* : MANSION . HOUSE . ERECTED .
MDCCLIII.

· *R* : The same as last.   Conder, 70; 16.—Virt: 132.

✓ 36. *O* : A public building. BACK FRONT OF SOMERSET HOUSE. *Ex* :
LONDON.

R : The same as last.   Conder, 70; 17.—Virt: 133.

✓ 37. *O* : A public building. BANK OF ENGLAND. *Ex* : ERECTED 1734.

R : Arms of London as before. LONDON PENNY TOKEN ✱
Conder, 70; 18.—Virt: 143.

✓ 38. *O* : A public building. ST. BARTHOLOMEW'S HOSPITAL. *Ex* :
ERECTED MDCCXXIX.

R : The same as last.   Conder, 70; 19.—Virt: 142.

✓ 39. *O* : A public building. BETHLEM HOSPITAL. *Ex* : ERECTED
MDCLXXV between sprigs of leaves.

R : The same as last.   Conder, 70; 20.—Virt: 172.

✓ 40. *O* : A large building. CARLETON HOUSE. *Ex* : AS IN 1788.
And a sprig of leaves.

R : The same as last.   Conder, 70; 21.—Virt: 144.

✓ 41. *O* : A public building. CHELSEA HOSPITAL. *Ex* : ERECTED
MDCXC.

R : The same as last.   Conder, 71; 22.—Virt: 137.

✓ 42. *O* : An ancient building. CHRIST'S CHURCH HOSPITAL.
Ex : FOUNDED 1552.

R : The same as last. NOTE.—Although the description
appears similar, this is quite distinct from Nos. 78
and 100.   Conder, 71; 23.—Virt: 142.

✓ 43. *O* : A church. ST. PAUL'S CHURCH COVENT GARDEN ERECTD 1640 DESTROYD. BY FIRE 1795.
R : The same as last.   Conder, 71 ; 24.—Virt : 135.

✓ 44. *O* : A public building. FOUNDLING HOSPITAL LAMBS CONDUIT FIELDS. *Ex* : COMPLEATED 1741.
R : The same as last.   Conder, 71 ; 25.—Virt : 135.

✓ 45. *O* : A public building. ST. GEORGE'S HOSPITAL. ERECTED. *Ex* : MDCCXXXIV.
R : The same as last.   Conder, 71 ; 26.—Virt : 136.

✓ 46. *O* : A large building. GOLDSMITH'S HALL AS REBUILT AFTER THE FIRE. *Ex* : MDCLXVI.
R : The same as last.   Conder, 71 ; 27.—Virt : 173.

✓ 47. *O* : A public building. GREENWICH HOSPITAL. *Ex* : COMPLEATD. IN THE REIGN OF KING CHARLES IIND.
R : The same as last.   Conder, 71 ; 28.—Virt : 174.

✓ 48. *O* : A public building. GUY'S HOSPITAL. *Ex* : ERECTED MDCCXXII.
R : The same as last.   Conder, 71 ; 29.—Virt : 172.

✓ 49. *O* : An ancient building. ST. JAMES'S FIRST USED AS A ROYAL PALACE. *Ex* : MDCXCVII.
R : The same as last.   Conder, 71 ; 30.—Virt : 134.

✓ 50. *O* : A large building. IRONMONGERS ALMSHOUSES. *Ex* : ERECTED MDCCXIII between sprigs of leaves.
R : The same as last.   Conder, 71 ; 31.—Virt : 173.

✓ 51. *O* : A public building. ST. LUKE'S HOSPITAL. *Ex* : INSTITUTED MDCCLI.
R : The same as last.   Conder, 72 ; 32.—Virt : 180.

✓ 52. *O* : A public building. MIDDLESEX HOSPITAL. *Ex* : ERECTED MDCCLV.
R : The same as last.   Conder, '72 ; 33.—Virt : 136.

✓ 53. *O* : A public building. MONTAGUE HOUSE ALTERD FOR THE BRITISH. *Ex* : MUSEUM 1754.
R : The same as last.   Conder, 72 ; 34.—Virt : 144.

✓ 54. *O* : A monument and houses. MONUMENT . ERECTED . 1677.
R : The same as last.   Conder, 72 ; 35.—Virt : 133.

✓ 55. *O* : A public building. ORDNANCE OFFICE OLD PALACE YARD.
R : The same as last.   Conder, 72 ; 36.—Virt : 134.

✓ 56. *O* : A public building. ROYAL EXCHANGE ERECTD. 1669.
R : The same as last.   Conder, 72 ; 37.—Virt : 132.

✓ 57. *O* : A public building. ST. THOMAS'S HOSPITAL COMPLEATD. *Ex* : MDCCVIII.
R : The same as last.   Conder, 72 ; 38.—Virt : 180.

✓ 58. *O* : A large building. TRINITY ALMS HOUSE. *Ex* : INSTITUTED MDCXCV.
R : The same as last.   Conder, 72 ; 39.—Virt : 173.

59. *O*: View of a bridge. LONDON BRIDGE THE FIRST OF STONE COMPLEATED 1209. *Ex*: THE HOUSES ON THE BRIDGE TAKEN DOWN & THE BRIDGE REPAIRD. 1758.

R: Britannia seated. *Ex*: A cypher *P K* and MDCCXCVII. On a raised circle BRITISH PENNY TOKEN.

E: I PROMISE TO PAY ON DEMAND THE BEARER ONE PENNY ×
                       Conder, 72; 40.—Virt: 211.

60. *O*: View of a bridge. WESTMINSTER BRIDGE. *Ex*: COMPLEATED NOVR. 1750.

R: and *E*: The same as last.   Conder, 73; 41.

61. *O*: The same as last.

R: A figure of Justice standing. BRITISH . PENNY . TOKEN 1797.

E: The same as last.   Conder, 73; 42.—Virt: 217.

62. *O*: View of a bridge. BLACK-FRIARS BRIDGE. *Ex*: COMPLEATED MDCCLXX.

R: and *E*: The same as last. Conder, 73; 43.—Virt: 217.

63. *O*: An ancient gateway. ALDGATE. *Ex*: ERECTED 1609 TAKEN DOWN 1766.

R: The same as last.   Conder, 73; 44.

64. *O*: An ancient gateway. ALDERSGATE AS REBUILT 1616. *Ex*: TAKEN DOWN 1766.

R: The same as last.   Conder. 73; 45.

65. *O*: An ancient gateway. BISHOPSGATE AS REBUILT 1729. *Ex*: TAKEN DOWN 1766.

R: The same as last.   Conder, 73; 46.

66. *O*: An ancient gateway. BRIDGE GATE AS REBUILT 1728. *Ex*: TAKEN DOWN 1766.

R: The same as last.   Conder, 73; 47.

67. *O*: An ancient gateway. CRIPPLEGATE AS REPAIR'D &C. MDCLXIII. *Ex*: TAKEN DOWN MDCCLXVI.

R: The same as last.   Conder, 73; 48.—Virt: 231.

68. *O*: An ancient gateway. LUDGATE AS ENLARGE'D &C. MCCCCLIIII. *Ex*: TAKEN DOWN MDCCLXVI.

R: The same as last.   Conder, 73; 49.—Virt: 231.

69. *O*: An ancient gateway. MOORGATE AS ERECTED MDCLXXIIII. *Ex*: TAKEN DOWN MDCCLXVI.

R: The same as last.   Conder, 74; 50.—Virt: 230.

70. *O*: An ancient gateway. NEWGATE AS REPAIRD MDCLXXII. *Ex*: BURNT AT THE RIOTS MDCCLXXX.

R: The same as last.   Conder, 74; 51.—Virt: 230.

Of these pennies, Nos. 54 and 55 are scarcer than the others, especially if without flaw.

Masonic.

71. *O*: The Freemasons' arms, supporters, motto, and crest.
         * PRO BONO PUBLICO *

R: A cupid and masonic emblems in a triangle. MASONIC PENNY * 1795.

E: MANUFACTURED BY W. LUTWYCHE BIRMINGHAM . × .
                    Conder, 205; 32.—Virt: 141.

Mendoza.

72. *O*: Two heads in profile.   D. MENDOZA   W. WARD
    R: Two men boxing.   *Ex*: 1791.   Conder, 205; 33.
    This penny is rare.

Milton's.

✓ 73. *O*: A figure emblematic of the Sciences, seated amidst the clouds.
    R: A figure of Time (?) leading Pegasus, a figure climbing a rock in the distance.   *Ex*: MILTON . MEDALIST | SEALS . COINS &C. | 1800.
    In consequence of a failure in reverse die, a few impressions in tin only were taken.   Very rare.

Orchard's.

✓ 74. *O*: Bust to right.   ROBERT ORCHARD Nº. 34 GREEK STREET CORNER OF CHURCH STREET SOHO LONDON * 1803.
    R: AND AT SAWBRIDGEWORTH HERTS MANUFACTURER OF CHOCOLATE & COCOA ON A NEW AND IMPROVED PRINCIPLE. GROCER & TEA DEALER WHOLESALE RETAIL & FOR EXPORTATION.
    See Herts, No. 1, for another penny of Orchard's.   This token also, strictly speaking, belongs to the 19th century.

Skidmore's.

75. *O*: View of a church.   WEST VIEW OF BOSTON CHURCH IN THE COUNTY OF LINCOLN   *Ex*: JACOBS.
    R: A cypher *P S* 1797 in a circle of flowers.   P. SKIDMORE . MEDAL . MAKER . NO. 15 COPPICE . ROW . CLERKENWELL . LONDON.
    E: I PROMISE TO PAY ON DEMAND THE BEARER ONE PENNY . × .
                                                   Conder, 76; 64.
✓ 76. *O*: A large building.   ADDINGTON . PLACE . NEAR . CROYDON . IN . SURRY .   *Ex*: JACOBS.
    R: Shield of arms.   P . SKIDMORE . MEDAL . MAKER . COPPICE . ROW . CLERKENWELL . LONDON.
    E: The same as last.   Conder, 76; 65.—Virt: 198.
✓ 77. *O*: An ancient fortress.   CARISBROOK . CASTLE . ISLE . OF . WIGHT.
    R: and *E*: The same as last.   Conder, 76; 66.
78. *O*: An ancient building.   CHRIST'S . HOSPITAL NEWGATE ST.   *Ex*: JACOBS.
    R: and *E*: The same as last.
    This obverse occurs again at No. 100.
✓ 79. *O*: An ancient fortress and trees.   COWS . CASTLE . ISLE . OF . WIGHT.
    R: and *E*: The same as last.   Conder, 76; 67.

80. *O* : Part of an ancient fortress. TOWER OF DUDLEY CASTLE 1797. See Worcestershire, No. 5.
    R : and *E* : The same as last.

✔ 81. *O* : View of a church, with trees and houses. DULWICH . COLLEGE . IN . SURRY. *Ex* : JACOBS.
    R : and *E* : The same as last. Conder, 76 ; 68.—Virt : 198.

✔ 82. *O* : A building and trees. THE . BISHOP . OF . LONDON'S . SEAT . AT . FULHAM . MIDDLESEX. *Ex* : JACOBS.
    R : and *E* : The same as last. Conder, 76 ; 69.

✔ 83. *O* : A building and trees. THE . SEAT . OF . DAVID . GARRICK . ESQR. AT . HAMPTON. *Ex* : JACOBS.
    R : and *E* : The same as last. Conder, 76 ; 70.—Virt : 194.

✔ 84. *O* : An ancient building. THE . HOUSE OF LORDS. *Ex* : JACOBS.
    R : and *E* : The same as last. Conder, 76 ; 71.—Virt : 202.

✔ 85. *O* : An ancient fortress. FORT . GEORGE . INVERNESS . SCOTLAND ✣
    R : and *E* : The same as last. Conder, 77 ; 72.—Virt : 213.

✔ 86. *O* : View of a church with trees and houses. PART . OF . ISLEWORTH . IN . MIDDLESEX. *Ex* : JACOBS.
    R : and *E* : The same as last. Conder, 77 ; 73.—Virt : 199.

✔ 87. *O* : A public building. ST. PAUL'S . SCHOOL . LONDON. *Ex* : JACOBS.
    R : and *E* : The same as last. Conder, 77 ; 74.

✔ 88. *O* : An ancient abbey and trees. RIVALX . ABBEY . YORKSHIRE. *Ex* : JACOBS.
    R : and *E* : The same as last. Conder, 77 ; 75.

✔ 89. *O* : A large building. SION-HOUSE . NEAR BRENTFORD . MIDDLESEX. *Ex* : JACOBS.
    R : and *E* : The same as last. Conder, 77 ; 76.

✔ 90. *O* : A public building. THE SMALL-POX HOSPITAL NEAR ST. PANCRASS. *Ex* : JACOBS.
    R : and *E* : The same as last. Conder, 77 ; 77.—Virt : 194.

✔ 91. *O* : A public building. THE . SOUTH . SEA . HOUSE . LONDON. *Ex* : JACOBS.
    R : and *E* : The same as last. Conder, 77 ; 78.—Virt : 204.

92. *O* : A large building. SURGEONS . HALL . OLD . BAILEY. *Ex* : JACOBS.
    R : and *E* : The same as last. Conder, 77 ; 79.

✔ 93. *O* : A large building. LORD . STORMONT'S . WANDSWORTH. *Ex* : JACOBS.
    R : and *E* : The same as last. Conder, 77 ; 80.—Virt : 200.

✔ 94. *O* : A large building and trees. WEST . CLANDON . PLACE . SURRY. *Ex* : JACOBS.
    R : and *E* : The same as last. Conder, 78 ; 81.—Virt : 200.
    All these pennies are rare, No. 76 especially so, as the obverse die broke immediately upon being used. An engraving of it appears in Conder on pl. 1 ; 3.

Young's.

✓ 95. *O :* View of St. Paul's. *Ex :* 1794.

R : A star and garter. H. YOUNG . DEALER . IN . COINS . NO. 18 . LUDGATE . ST. LONDON.

Conder, 78; 83.—Pye, 35; 3.

Struck also in silver.

96. *O :* Britannia seated, St. Paul's in the distance. CIVITAS LONDINI MDCCXCVIII. *Ex :* I Milton F.

R : MATHEW . YOUNG . GOLDSMITH . AND . JEWELLER ✣ Upon a raised rim, and in the centre, DEALER . IN | COINS & MEDALS | ANTIENT & MODERN | NO. 16 | LUDGATE . STREET | LONDON in six lines.

Owing to the mistake in the name only one impression in tin was taken of this piece when it was corrected as follows :—

✓ 97. Similar in all respects to last, excepting that the name is correctly spelt MATTHEW.

E : PROMISSORY PENNY TOKEN PAYABLE ON DEMAND. ✣ ✣

Pye, pl. 35; 4.

Rare ; only six dozen struck.

In consequence of the alteration, a failure is noticeable in the die. A failure also frequently occurs on the obv. of No. 95, which causes the absence of the date. See Virt: 137.

Miscellaneous.

98. *O :* A figure of Britannia seated. BRITANIA . THE . BRITISH . PENNY . TOKEN. .

R : A cypher *T W R*, and the date 1797 upon a label, within a circle of leaves. LONDON . MIDDLESEX . AND . SURRY . PENNY.

E : I PROMISE TO PAY ON DEMAND THE BEARER ONE PENNY ✕

Conder, 74; 52.

✓ 99. *O :* An ancient building. THE . HOUSE . OF . COMMONS . FROM . THE . THAMES . BUILT . 1552. *Ex :* Jacobs.

R : A cap of Liberty over a coronet upon a pole, between a palm-branch and a cornucopia. PEACE . LIBERTY . AND . PLENTY . 1797.

E : The same as last. Conder, 74 ; 53.—Virt: 179.

This obverse is the same as No. 7, *ante.*

✓ 100. *O :* An ancient building. CHRIST'S . HOSPITAL NEWGATE ST. *Ex :* Jacobs.

R : A globe inscribed BRITAIN between a rose and thistle. BRITISH . PENNY. *Ex :* 1797.

E : The same as last. Conder, 74; 55.—Virt: 213.

This obverse is the same as No. 78, *ante.*

✓ 101. *O :* A public building. THE . NEW . EXCISE . OFFICE . LONDON. *Ex :* Jacobs.

R : and *E :* The same as last. Conder, 74; 56.

✓ 102. *O* : A large building. GOLDSMITHS . HALL . FOSTER . LANE.
Ex : JACOBS.
R : Shield of arms. TO . THE . WORSHIPFUL . COMPY. OF .
GOLDSMITHS.
E : The same as last. Conder, 74 ; 54.
*All these pennies are difficult to obtain, especially No.
98, which in good condition is very rare.*

✓ 103. *O* : Laureate bust to right. GEORGIVS . III . DEI . GRATIA.
R : Rays of sun over the arms of London, supported by
the sword and mace. VISITED ST. PAULS. *Ex* :
23 APRIL 1789. Conder, 75 ; 58.
Also struck in silver.

104. *O* : The same as last.
R : Similar to last, but does not show the sun above the
arms.

✓ 105. *O* : Laureate bust to right between G III 1788 . GOD SAVE
THE KING.
R : The same as last. Conder, 75 ; 59.

✓ 106. *O* : Laureate bust to right. GEORGIVS . III . DEI . GRATIA.
Under the bust, MILTON.
R : Regalia lying upon a pedestal inscribed HOWE ST.
VINCENT DUNCAN. Three fleur-de-lis above the top
·word. ROYAL . THANKSGIVING . AT . ST . PAULS. *Ex* :
DEC . 19 . 1797. Conder, 75 ; 60.

107. *O* : The same as last.
R : Similar to last, but without the three fleur-de-lis.

✓ 108. *O* : Laureate bust to right between G-III . VISITED ST PAULS
DECEMBER 19 1797.
R : Arms of London radiated, supported by the sword and
mace. IN HONOR OF LORD DUNCANS VICTORY OVER THE
DUTCH FLEET OCT 11 1797. Conder, 75 ; 61.

✓ 109. *O* : Laureate bust to right. · GEORGIVS III REX ATTENDED
DIVINE SERVICE AT ST PAULS LONDON DECr. 19 1797. .
R : PROVIDENCE | THIS DAY ACKNOW | -LEDGED IN THE MA- | -NY
SIGNAL VICTO- | RIES OBTAINED | DURING THE | WAR.
Conder, 75 ; 62.
*It is difficult to regard the foregoing in any other light
than that of medalets, especially those which are
struck in white metal.*

110. *O* : A deer. FREEDOM WITH INNOCENCE.·
R : A plough. INDUSTRY PRODUCETH WEALTH.
Also struck in silver.

111. *O* : Similar to last, and with *Westwood fecit* added in *Ex* :
R : As last with initials A & S added in *Ex* :
—. *See a very similar design upon the halfpenny, No.* 749.

LONDON AND WESTMINSTER.

✔ 112. *O*: A public building. BANK OF ENGLAND NEW BUILDINGS.
Ex: BUT. 1796.

　　R: The arms of London and Westminster between palm
　　and laurel branches, the date at top 1797. LONDON
　　AND WESTMINSTER PENNY.

　　E: I PROMISE TO PAY ON DEMAND THE BEARER ONE PENNY ✕
　　　　　　　　Conder, 78; 84.—Virt: 188.

✔ 113. *O*: A public building. DRURY LANE THEATRE. *Ex*: BT.
1794.

　　R: and *E*: The same as last. Conder, 78; 85.—Virt: 188.

✔ 114. *O*: A public building. KINGS THEATRE HAYMARKET. *Ex*:
BT. 1794.

　　R: and *E*: The same as last. Conder, 78; 86.—Virt: 189.

✔ 115. *O*: A large building. TRINITY HOUSE BUILT 1795.

　　R: and *E*: The same as last. Conder, 78; 87.—Virt: 187.

✔ 116. *O*: A public building. CITY OF LONDON LYING-IN HOSPITAL BT.
1771. *Ex*: An anchor and a cross radiated.

　　R: The arms of London and Westminster with a mural
　　coronet. LONDON AND WESTMINSTER PENNY 1797.
　　Within a circle of leaves.

　　E: The same as No. 112.　　Conder, 78; 88.—Virt: 191.

✔ 117. *O*: An ancient building. LAMBETH PALACE. *Ex*: BT. 1557.
A mitre between two crosiers.

　　R: The arms as before between palm and laurel branches,
　　a cap of maintenance above. LONDON AND WEST-
　　MINSTER PENNY. 1797.

　　E: The same as No. 112.　　Conder, 79; 89.—Virt: 190.

✔ 118. *O*: A public building. SESSIONS HOUSE OLD BAILEY BT. 1774.
Ex: Sword, scales and palm radiated.

　　R: and *E*: The same as last. Conder, 79; 90.—Virt: 192.

✔ 119. *O*: A public building. TREASURY. ST. JAMES'S PARK.

　　R: and *E*: The same as last. Conder, 79; 91.—Virt; 190.

✔ 120. *O*: An ancient fortress. TOWER OF LONDON. *Ex*: BT. 1079.
R: and *E*: The same as last. Conder, 79; 92.—Virt: 189.

✔ 121. *O*: View of the Abbey. WESTMINSTER ABBEY BT. 1245.
R: and *E*: The same as last.　　　　Conder, 79; 93.

✔ 122. *O*: and *E*: The same as last.

　　R: Arms as before surrounded with drapery, crest a cap
　　of maintenance · which divides the date 17-97.
　　LONDON AND WESTMINSTER PENNY.
　　　　　　　　Conder, 79; 94.—Virt: 192.

✔ 123. *O*: A large building. ALBION MILL BUILT 1787 BEFORE THE
FIRE. S. Wyatt Archt.

　　R: Arms and mural crown. LONDON AND WESTMINSTER
　　PENNY 1797. The same as No. 116.

　　E: The same as No. 112.　　Conder, 79; 95.—Virt: 193.

　　　　　　　　　　　　　　　　6

124. *O*: A public building. HORSE AND FOOT GUARDS WHITEHALL.
   Ex: A sword and gun crossed.
   R: and *E*: The same as last. Conder, 79 ; 96.—Virt: 191.

125. *O*: A public building, under it a book radiated. ST. PAUL'S
   SCHOOL FOUNDED 1509.
   R: and *E*: The same as last. Conder, 80; 97.—Virt: 202.

126. *O*: A building and trees. BARBER'S HALL, MONKWELL
   STREET.
   R: and *E*: The same as last. Conder, 80; 98.—Virt: 214.

127. *O*: A large building. BREWERS HALL. *Ex*: FINISHED 1673.
   R: and *E*: The same as last. Conder, 80; 99.—Virt: 216.

128. *O*: A building, with arms under it. CORDWAINERS HALL
   BUILT 1790.
   R: and *E*: The same as last. Conder, 80 ; 100.—Virt: 212.

129. *O*: The inner court of a large building. DRAPERS HALL
   BUIL ʬ + D. 1672.
   R: and *E*: The same as last. Conder, 80 ; 101.—Virt: 226.

130. *O*: A large building, with arms over it. DYERS HALL BUILT
   A.D. 1770.
   R: and *E*: The same as last. Conder, 80 ; 102.—Virt: 206.

131. *O*: A large building, with arms under it. FISHMONGERS
   HALL FOUNDED 1536.
   R: and *E*: The same as last. Conder, 80; 103.—Virt: 204.

132. *O*: An ancient building, arms under it. GROCERS HALL
   FOUNDED A.D. 1411.
   R: and *E*: The same as last. Conder, 80; 104.—Virt: 203.

133. *O*: An ancient building. HABERDASHERS HALL BUILT 1671.
   R: and *E*: The same as last. Conder, 80 ; 105.—Virt: 220.

134. *O*: A large building. IRONMONGERS HALL BUILT 1748 A.D.
   R: and *E*: The same as last. Conder, 81 ; 106.—Virt: 206.

135. *O*: An ancient building. LEADENHALL BUILT A.D. 1419 TAKEN
   DOWN 1794.
   R: and *E*: The same as last. Conder, 81 ; 107.—Virt: 205.

136. *O*: An ancient building. LEATHERSELLERS HALL BUILT A.D.
   1567.
   R: and *E*: The same as last. Conder, 81 ; 108.—Virt: 228.

137. *O*: An ancient building. MERCHANT TAYLORS HALL.
   R: and *E*: The same as last. Conder, 81 ; 109.—Virt: 226.

138. *O*: A building, with a small horse above and below. SADLERS
   HALL.
   R: and *E*: The same as last. Conder, 81 ; 110.—Virt: 228.

139. *O*: A building, with arms under it. SKINNERS HALL BUILT
   A.D. 1667.
   R: and *E*: The same as last. Conder, 81 ; 111.—Virt: 205.

140. *O*: A large building. STATIONERS HALL, NEAR LUDGATE ST.
   R: and *E*: The same as last. Conder, 81 ; 112.—Virt: 223.

✓ 141. *O*: A large building. LATE SURGEONS HALL . OLD BAILEY.
    R: and *E*: The same as last. Conder, 81 ; 113.—Virt: 212.

✓ 142. *O*: A large building, with arms under it. TALLOW CHANDLER
    HALL BUILT A.D. 1671.
    R: and *E* : The same as last. Conder, 81; 114.—Virt: 223.

✓ 143. *O*: An ancient courtyard. VINTERS HALL FOUNDED 1437.
    Ex: Arms between bunches of grapes.
    R: and *E*: The same as last. Conder, 82 ; 115.—Virt: 207.

✓ 144. *O*: A large building. WAX CHANDLERS HALL. *Ex*: BUILT
    1792.
    R: and *E* : The same as last. Conder, 82; 116.—Virt: 220.

WESTMINSTER.

✓ 145. *O*: A front face bust. THE RIGHT HON. CHAS. JAS. FOX.
    R: TO THE | FREE AND | INDEPENDENT | ELECTORS | OF | WEST-
    MINSTER | 1789.   In seven lines.   Conder, 202 ; 19.

✓ 146. *O* : A different bust. GLORY BE THINE INTREPID FOX FIRM AS
    OLD ALBIENS BATTER'D ROCKS.
    R: RESISTLESS | SPEAKER | FAITHFUL GUIDE | THE COURTIERS
    | DREAD | THE PATRIOTS | PRIDE.   In seven lines.
                                    Conder, 202 ; 18.
    Both these are struck in white metal.

✓ 147. *O*: Similar to last, but the letters of outer legend larger,
    and ALBIONS correctly spelt.
    R: Similar to last, but the letters rather smaller, and a
    wreath of oak and laurel added.
    E: MANUFACTURED BY W. LUTWYCHE BIRMINGHAM. ×.×.
                                    Conder, 202; 17.—Virt: 129.
    Struck in copper, brass and white metal.

✓ 148. *O*: Similar to No. 146, but with the word ALBIONS spelt
    correctly.
    R: and *E*: The same as last.
    Exceedingly rare.

✓ 149. *O*: A naval officer standing against a cannon. ADMIRAL
    GARDNER WORTHY THE FLEET OR THE SENATE. ELECTION
    TOKEN.
    R: A fox holding a pole standing upon three blocks,
    inscribed 'CORRESPONDG SOCIETY' 'RIGHTS OF MAN'
    and 'WHIG CLUB.' On a label from the fox's mouth
    'NO MAJESTY BUT THAT OF THE PEOPLE.' The top
    stone supported by a prop inscribed 'SEDITION' held
    by a clergyman with a label from his mouth 'THIS
    IS YOUR ONLY PROP.' A crown radiated over a sword
    and sceptre upon a monument inscribed 'BILL OF
    RIGHTS' MAG. CHA. A branch of oak behind the
    monument. SOME OF THE FOXES TRICKS ON A WESTMIN-
    STER POLE 1796.   Conder, 203 ; 21.—Virt: 128.
    It has been thought that there was sufficient ground for
                                    6 *

these Tokens, or Medalets, to be removed from the Not Local section, and placed to Westminster; as they (like the Hereford pennies) were doubtless struck upon the occasion of the Parliamentary Elections there, contested by Fox and Gardner.

HALFPENNIES.

BOW.

150. *O*: Arms between branches of leaves. HALFPENNY 1797.
    R: A cypher *S M* in a circle. MOSES STONE CABINET MAKER BOW 1797.
    E: Engrailed.   Conder, 83; 118.—Virt: 196.
✓ 150*a*.   As last, but *E*: Plain (not in collar).
       Rare.

CHELSEA.

✓ 151. *O*: A sailor with a wooden leg presenting a petition to Britannia. CHELSEA. *Ex*: HALFPENNY.
    R: A figure of Hope leaning on an anchor. THE SUPPORT OF OUR ENDEAVOUR.
    E: Milled.   Conder, 83; 119.—Pye 13; 12.—Virt: 73.

151*a*.   As last, but *E*: PAYABLE IN ANGLESEY LONDON OR LIVERPOOL.

151*b*.   As last, but *E*: Plain (not in collar).

HACKNEY.

✓ 152. *O*: View of a church, shield of arms at top, J. M. on the ground. HACKNEY CHURCH. *Ex*: MDCXC.
    R: A cypher *D A R*, a knife and palm-branch crossed below, a small wreath above. HACKNEY PROMISSORY TOKEN 1795.
           Conder, 83; 120.—Pye, 22; 1.—Virt: 102.
    Very rare; 10 impressions in silver, and 24 in copper.

153. *O*: A very close imitation of the preceding, but without the "J. M." and poorer work.
    R: Not such fine work as last, the 1 in date is straight.
    E: PAYABLE AT MACCLESFIELD LIVERPOOL OR CONGLETON.

153*a*.   As last, but *E*: Plain (not in collar).
                   Conder, 83; 121.
    This is from the same dies as the penny, No. 12.

154. *O*: A paint-pot, cask, and two brushes crossed, within a circle. GEORGE . BUTLER . OILMAN . HACKNEY.
    R: A cypher *G B*. FOR THE USE OF TRADE. *See also Sussex, No. 32, for this reverse.*
    E: PAYABLE IN LONDON. The remainder engrailed.

154*a*.   As last, but *E* : Engrailed.

154*b*.   „   „   *E* : Milled.   Conder, 83 ; 122.
            Rare.

HENDON.

155. *O* : View of a church. HENDON . VALUE . ONE . HALFPENNY.
            Ex : 1794.
      R : A greyhound. I . PROMISE TO PAY ON DEMAND. *Ex* : B.
       · PRICE.   Conder, 84 ; 123.—Pye, 22 ; 6.—Virt : 24.
      This obv. occurs with the following reverses :—

156. *R* : Bust to left. DAVID GARRICK . ESQR.
                  Conder, 281 ; 164.—Pye, 22 ; 7.—Virt : 111.

157. *R* : A register stove. PAYABLE AT SKIDMORES &c. See No.
            361.
      E : SKIDMORE HOLBORN LONDON.   Conder, 280 ; 162.

157*a*.   As last, but *E* : Milled.

158. *R* : A guillotine and part of a house. HALFPENNY. See
            No. 375.
      E : The same as No. 157.   Conder, 281 ; 168.

159. *R* : Ruins of a church. DESTROY'D, BY, FIRE, SEPT. 17tb,
            1795. See No. 399.

160. *R* : Bust to right. CHURCH AND KING. See No. 400.
      E : PAYABLE IN LONDON. The remainder engrailed.
                        Conder, 281 ; 166.—Virt : 76.

160*a*.   As last, but *E* : Milled.
160*b*.   „   „   *E* : Plain (not in collar).

161. *R* : A cat. MY FREEDOM I AMONG SLAVES ENJOY. See No.
            514.
      E : Milled.

162. *R* : The heads of a lion and ass conjoined. ODD FELLOWS,
            &c. See No. 520.
      E : Engrailed.

162*a*.   As last, but *E* : Milled.   Conder, 281 ; 170.

163. *R* : A cypher *J O M.* JAMES . METCALF . BEDAL . YORKSH.
            See Yorkshire, No. 11.
      E : The same as No. 157.   Conder, 281 ; 167.

164. *R* : An anchor and cable. IN COMMEMORATION, &c. See
            Not Local, No. 117.
      E : Milled.   Conder, 281 ; 169.

165. *R* : MUR'D BY THE FACTIOUS, &c. See Not Local, No. 91.
      E : Milled.   Conder, 280 ; 163.
            See also Buckinghamshire, No. 12 ; Essex, Nos. 13
            and 21 ; and Warwickshire, Nos. 86 and 91.

HORNSEY.

✓ 166. *O*: View of a church, behind trees. HORNSEY . HALFPENNY.
      Ex: 1797.
    R: A . SPEEDY . | AND . | LASTING | PEACE . in four lines,
      between palm and laurel branches.
    E: Engrailed.   Conder, 84; 124.—Virt: 194.
166*a*.   As last, but *E* : Plain (not in collar).

LONDON.
Allen's.

✓ 167. *O*: Shield of arms, crest a goat's head; between sprigs
      and within a circle. PROMISSORY HALFPENNY. An
      ornament at top and bottom.
    R: Shield of arms, draped, crest a bird, within a circle.
      WILLIAM ALLEN LONDON, 1795.
    E: PAYABLE IN CHANDOS STREET CONVENT GARDEN.
                Conder, 84; 125.—Pye, 27; 7.—Virt: 75.
167*a*.   As last, but *E*: PAYABLE AT LONDON . + . + . + . + . + .
167*b*.   „   „ *E*: Milled.

Anderson's.

168. *O*: Shield of the arms of London (the cross not shaded).
      LONDON CITY TOKEN.
    R: A monogram cypher *PA*, 1795 above, HALFPENNY
      below.
    E: PAYABLE AT THE HOUSE OF PETER ANDERSON.
    Very rare.   Conder, 84; 127.
✓ 169. *O*: Similar to last, but the cross on the arms is shaded.
    R: Same as last.
    E: LONDON added to inscription.
               Conder, 84; 126.—Pye, 27; 8.
169*a*.   As last, but *E* : PAYABLE AT LONDON.
169*b*.   „   „ *E*: Milled.
    All these are very rare.
✓ 170. *O*: Similar to last, but with DOMINE DIRIGE NOS . added above
      the shield.
    R: Similar to preceding, but with the monogram orna-
      mental.
    E: The same as No. 169.   Conder, 84; 128.—Pye, 27; 9.
    Very rare, only 8 specimens struck.

Askins'.

171. *O*: A man with a wooden leg walking. MR. JOSEPH ASKINS.
    R: An anchor in a circle of leaves. THE CELIBRATED
      VENTRILOQUIST 1796.
    E : Milled.   •   Conder, 210; 4.
    Very rare.

✓ 172. *O* : The same as last.

   R : A cypher *I A* within a wreath. The legend the same
   as before.

   E : Engrailed.   Conder, 210 ; 5.
   Rare.

173. *O* : and *E* : The same as last.

   R : THE | CELIBRATED | VENTRILOQUIST | 1796.   In four
   lines.   Conder, 210 ; 6.

173*a*.   As last, but *E* : Milled.

173*b*.   „   „   *E* : Plain (not in collar).
   See also Buckinghamshire, No. 13.

Bayly's.

✓ 174. *O* : A crocodile and a tree. A CROCODILE TO BE SEEN ALIVE
   AT G. BAYLYS MUSEUM FOR.

   R : A rattlesnake and a tree. ALL SORTS OF NATURAL
   HISTORY 242 PICCADILLY. Under the rattlesnake the
   word . JAMES . in minute letters.
                     Conder, 84 ; 129.—Pye, 28 ; 1.—Virt : 25.

Bebbington's.

✓ 175. *O* : Laureate bust to right. LONDON & MIDDLESEX . HALF-
   PENNY.

   R : The Prince of Wales's crest in a shield, under an
   umbrella. FOR . CHANGE . NO . FRAUD . IOHN . BEBBING-
   TON.   Conder, 85 ; 131.—Pye, 35 ; 5.—Virt : 100.
   In good condition rare.

Biggar's.

176. *O* : C : BIGGAR | SPRING GARDEN | COFFEE HOUSE | AND HOTEL .
   | FOR | GENTLEMEN | AND | FAMILIES. In eight lines.

   R : BIGGAR'S | CORRECTED MSS | ARMY LIST | BY | SUBSCRIP-
   TION | COMMENCING | JANY. 1ST. | 1796. In eight lines
   within an inner circle. CONTINUED ANNUALLY SUB-
   SCRIPTION TWO SHILLS. & SIX PENCE EACH *

   E : Milled.

176*a*.   As last, but *E* : Plain (not in collar).
   *This obverse die failed after a few impressions only had
   been taken, when the following was executed in its
   place :—*

✓ 177. *O* : Similar to last, but with a hyphen in SPRING-GARDEN and
   COFFEE-HOUSE and a dash at the bottom.

   R : The same as last.
                        Conder, 85 ; 132.—Pye, 27 ; 10.

Black Friars.

178. *O*: Figure of a friar. PAYABLE IN BLACK FRIARS LONDON.
    R: The arms, supporters, crest, and motto of the City of London.
    E: Milled.

v 178*a*.   As last, but *E*: Plain (not in collar).
           Conder, 85; 130.—Pye, 28; 2.—Virt: 40.

Burchell's.

179. *O*: BASIL BURCHELL SOLE PROPRIETOR OF THE FAMOUS SUGAR-PLUMBS FOR WORMS 78 . LONG-ACRE.
    R: BASIL BURCHELL SOLE PROPRIETOR OF THE ANODYNE NECKLACE FOR CHILDREN . CUTTING TEETH.
    Rare.

180. *O*: Similar to last, but *N*. 79 for the number, and a small quatrefoil before and after "LONG ACRE." The W of "WORMS" is larger than the other letters.
    R: Differs from last in the N of "NECKLACE" touching the U of "CUTTING," and a hyphen connects "CUTTING-TEETH."

v 181. *O*: The tail of the *N* forms an o and there is no hyphen to LONG ACRE. Crosses instead of quatrefoils.
    R: The same as last.

182. *O*: Differs from the last in the figures being much larger and a dot between "LONG" and "ACRE."
    R: The same as last.

183. *O*: The tail of the *N* comes just over the o. There is a hyphen in "LONG-ACRE." W of "WORMS" is large.
    R: The same as last.

184. *O*: The tail of the *N* comes just over the o. There is no hyphen in "LONG ACRE." All the letters are the same size in "WORMS." There is a large quatrefoil before and after "LONG ACRE."
    R: Very nearly like No. 179. This is struck in tin.

185. *O*: The tail of the *N* comes partly round the o; there is no dot under it. A hyphen in "LONG-ACRE" and "*WORMS*" is in Italics. There is a small quatrefoil before and after "LONG ACRE."
    R: The same as No. 180.

186. *O*: The tail of the *N* comes over the 79 which is in very small figures; there is no dot under o. There is a hyphen in "LONG-ACRE" and a dot before and after it. W of "WORMS" is large.
    R: Very nearly like No. 179.   Pye, 28; 4.

187. *O*: The *N* is badly shaped, the o is smaller, and the figures larger than last. The 9 touches the top of the A in "ACRE."
    R: The same as No. 184.

188. *O*: The *N* comes over the figures very nearly as last, but the tail of the 7 touches the top of the A of "ACRE." There is one large dot and two small ones each side of "LONG-ACRE" and the W of "WORMS" is large. There is no dot under the O.

    R: The P of "PROPRIETOR" touches the foot of I of "BASIL." A flaw runs through "FOR CHILDREN."

189. *O*: There is a dot under the O. *WORMS* is in Italics, and a small quatrefoil before and after "LONG ACRE."

    R: The word "*PROPRIETOR*" is in Italics; there are one large and two small dots on each side "CUTTING TEETH," and the P of "*PROPRIETOR*" comes just above the foot of the I of "BASIL."

190. *O*: The words *PROPRIETOR*, *FAMOUS*, and *WORMS* are in Italics. Three dots before and after "LONG-ACRE."

    R: The same as last.   Pye, 28; 3.

191. *O*: The same as last.

    R: Very similar to last, but the upper and lower legends are closer together, and there is only one large dot on either side.

✓ 192. *O*: The word *WORMS* only in Italics. There is a scroll on each side OF THE. A small quatrefoil before and after LONG-ACRE.

    R: The same as last.

    All these have plain edges, and must be included under Conder, p. 85; No. 133.

✓ 193. *O*: The *N* and figures are larger than any previous ones, the letter s of "WORMS" is smaller than the other letters. There are three dots before and after "LONG-ACRE."

    R: The centre legend is lower than any of the others, the N of "NECKLACE" touching the last limb of the U of "CUTTING." There are three dots between the upper and lower legends.

    E: THIS IS NOT A COIN BUT A MEDAL . + . + . + . + .
               Conder, 85; 134.—Pye, 28; 5.—Virt: 111.

193*a*.   As last, but *E*: PAYABLE IN DUBLIN OR LONDON . | . | . | . |

193*b*.   ,,   ,, *E*: Milled. This is struck on a smaller flan.

Carter's.

✓ 194. *O*: A lady's slipper. CARTER 32 JERMYN STREET LONDON 1795. The toe of the slipper points just above the T in "CARTER."

    R: LADIES SHOE ✱ MANUFACTORY ✱ A floral ornament above and below.

    E: Milled.   Pye, 28; 6.

194*a*.   As last, but *E* : Plain (not in collar).
    A flaw appears on both dics of this piece, and others were executed as follows :—

v   195.   *O* : The legend is farther from date than before, otherwise a very close copy. This may be identified by notic-ing the toe of the slipper, which in this points below the T of " CARTER."
    R : Very nearly as last; the floral ornaments a little larger.
    E : As before.   Conder, 85 ; 135.—Virt : 71.

Chambers'.

v   196.   *O* : A girl sitting under a tree. LACE MANUFACTORY.
    R : A lamb. PAY AT LEIGHTON BERKHAMSTED OR LONDON.
    E : CHAMBERS . LANGSTON HALL & CO . × × × × .
                      Conder, 85 ; 136.—Pye, 26 ; 8.—Virt : 55.
    This same token, with a plain edge, appears at Bedford-shire, No. 2. Struck also in silver and brass.

Ching's.

v   197.   *O* : Bust to left. I. CHING PATENTEE FOR WORM LOZENGES THE BEST MEDICINE IN THE WORLD.   SOLD IN BOXES AT 3/6 . PACKETS 1S. AND IN SMALL PACKETS AT 6D. EACH.
    R : The Royal arms, supporters, crest, and motto. BY EVERY PRINCIPAL MEDICINE VENDER IN THE KINGDOM.
    E : Milled.   Conder, 218 ; 69.—Pye, 28 ; 7.

197*a*.   As last, but *E* : Plain (not in collar).

Christ's Hospital.

v   198.   *O* : A monogram cypher *O O H* 1800. The down strokes of the letters are solid, and the top of the 1 is sloping, there is a period after the date.
    R : HALF | PENNY In two lines in the centre of the field.

v   199.   *O* : Similar to last, but the top of the 1 is square, and there is no period.
    R : The same as last.

v   200.   *O* : The down strokes of the monogram are formed of double lines.
    R : Similar to last, but the letters are formed better.
                           Pye, 35* ; 4.
    In good condition rare.

Clark's.

v   201.   *O* : Bust to right. G. WASHINGTON . THE FRIEND TO PEACE & HUMANITY *
    R : A stove. PAYABLE BY CLARK & HARRIS 13 . WORMWOOD ST. BISHOPSGATE . LONDON 1795.
    E : PAYABLE AT LONDON LIVERPOOL OR BRISTOL.

201*a*.   As last, but *E* : Milled to right.

v   201*b*.   „   „   *E* : Milled to left.
                      Conder, 86 ; 137.—Pye, 28 ; 8.

202. *O* : The end of the legend is farther from the star, and from
　　　　the bust.
　　R : and *E* : The same as last.

Corresponding Society.

203. *O* : The fable of the bundle of sticks. LONDON CORRESPOND-
　　　　ING SOCIETY. The first letter of the legend is some
　　　　distance from the old man's robe.
　　R : A dove flying, with an olive branch. UNITED FOR A
　　　　REFORM OF PARLIAMENT. *Ex* : 1795.
　　E : Milled.

　　　　*Very rare. A flaw in the obverse die across the heads of
　　　　the young men necessitated the production of a fresh
　　　　die, when a very few pieces of this had been struck;
　　　　the new piece being as follows :—*

✔ 204. *O* : Very similar to last, but the first letter of legend
　　　　touches the old man's robe.
　　R : and *E* : The same as last.　　　　Conder, 86 ; 138.

✔ 204*a*.　　As last, but *E* : BIRMINGHAM OR IN SWANSEA.

204*b*.　　　　,,　　,,　　*E* : PAYABLE AT DUBLIN CORK OR BEL-
　　　　FAST . × × .

204*c*.　　As last, but *E* : PAYABLE AT LONDON LIVERPOOL OR BRISTOL.

204*d*.　　　　,,　　,,　　*E* : Plain (not in collar).

✔ 205. *O* : The same as last.
　　R : Bust to right. GEORGE PRINCE OF WALES. See Not
　　　　Local, No. 159.
　　E : AN ASYLUM FOR THE OPPRESS'D OF ALL NATIONS— × —
　　　　　　　　　　　　　　　　　　Conder, 86 ; 139.
205*a*.　　As last, but *E* : Plain (not in collar).
　　　　See also No. 281.

　　　　The rev. of No. 203 occurs as an obv. with the
　　　　following reverses :—

206. *R* : Two hands united. MAY SLAVERY & OPPRESSION CEASE
　　　　THROUGHOUT THE WORLD. See Not Local, No. 145.
　　E : PAYABLE IN ANGLESEY LONDON OR LIVERPOOL.

206*a*.　　As last, but *E* : PAYABLE AT LONDON OR BRIGHTON.

206*b*.　　　　,,　　,,　　*E* : PAYABLE AT LONDON CORK OR BELFAST.

206*c*.　　　　,,　　,,　　*E* : CELEBRATED FOR PURE AIR & SEA
　　　　BATHING.

✔ 206*d*.　　As last, but *E* : AN ASYLUM FOR THE OPPRESS'D OF ALL
　　　　NATIONS.
206*e*.　　As last, but *E* : Plain (not in collar).
　　　　　　　　　　　　　　　　Conder, 235 ; 207.

207. *R*: Britannia seated with spear and shield. RULE
BRITANNIA. *Ex*: 1794.   Conder, 235 ; 208.
This is a reverse common to several tokens. See
Hampshire, No. 7.
See also Wicklow, Nos. 49 and 54.

✓ 208. *O*: *A* man hanging P⌒T, a cap of liberty on a pole, a
medallion bearing an anchor, HOPE, a cross, crown, &c.
on the ground, LIBERTY . AND . NOT . SLAVERY, and a
monument inscribed PEACE 1796.
R: A cypher *L C S* in a circle of leaves. DEDICATED . TO .
THE . LONDON . CORRESPONDING . SOCIETY. And in an
inner circle MAY . THEIR . ENDEAVOURS . MEET .
REWARD.
E: Milled.   Conder, 86 ; 140.

209. *O*: The same as last.
R: An obelisk, and masonic emblems. GOD . THE . FIRST .
ARCHITECT. *Ex*: JACOBS.
E: Engrailed.   Conder, 230 ; 166.

209*a*.   As last, but *E*: Engrailed over AT GEORGE EDWARD SAR-
GEANT'S PORTSEA.
See also Buckinghamshire, No. 14.

Coventry Street.

✓ 210. *O*: A filtering stone. FOR PURIFYING WATER. *Ex*: 1795.
R: THE FILTERING STONE WARE-HOUSE * COVENTRY STREET
LONDON.
Conder, 86 ; 141.—Pye, 29 ; 4.—Virt: 21.

Davidson's.

211. *O*: A female seated, holding a sword and a shield bearing
the arms of London, a distant view of St. Paul's.
SISE LANE HALFPENNY. *Ex*: 1795.
R: A crown upon a triangle, held by two hands. BR. CON-
STITUTION radiated in the centre. KING . LORDS .
COMMONS. The cross on the crown is some distance
from IN of " KING."
E: Milled. This is struck in silver, copper and tin, only
six having been struck in copper.

✓ 212. *O*: Similar to last, but the shield is quite close to legend.
R: Similar to last, but the cross on top of crown touches
IN of " KING."
E: PAYABLE AT THE HOUSE OF T. & R. DAVIDSON.
Conder, 86 ; 142.—Pye, 28 ; 9.—Virt : 32.

The rev. of No. 211 occurs as an obv. with the
following reverse :—

213. *R*: Bust to right. GEORGE PRINCE OF WALES. See Not
Local, No. 159.
E: Milled.   Conder, 240 ; 252.

213a.   As last, but E : Plain (not in collar).
See also No. 749.

Dennis'.

✓ 214. O : A wheatsheaf. BAKERS HALFPENNY 1795.
R : TO LESSEN | THE SLAVERY OF | SUNDAY BAKING | AND PRO-
VIDE FOR | PUBLIC WANTS : | AN ACT WAS | PASSED. | A.D.
1794. In eight lines.
E : PAYABLE AT I + DENNIS LONDON . × . × .
Conder, 87 ; 143.—Pye, 5 ; 2.—Virt: 51.

214a.   As last, but E : PAYABLE IN ANGLESEY LONDON OR LIVER-
POOL.

214b.   As last, but F : PAYABLE IN DUBLIN OR LONDON.

214c.   „   „ E : PAYABLE IN LANCASTER LONDON OR BRISTOL.

214d.   „   „ E : Milled. These are on large and small
flans.

✓ 214e.   As last, but E : Plain (not in collar).
This halfpenny die is used also for the penny, No. 24.

Dodd's.

✓ 215. O : Bust to right. ✱ HANDEL ✱ INSTRUMENTS TUN'D & LENT TO
HIRE.
R : A harp in a radiated circle. DODD'S CHEAP SHOP FOR
MUSICAL INSTRUMENTS NEW STREET COVENT GARDEN.
Conder, 87 ; 144.—Pye, 29 ; 1.
Some of these are struck on much thicker flans than
others.

Eaton's.

✓ 216. O : Bust to left, with FRANGAS NON FLECTES on a ribbon
under.   D . I . EATON THREE TIMES ACQUITTED OF
SEDITION.
R : A cock crowing over pigs in a sty. PRINTER TO THE
MAJESTY OF THE PEOPLE . LONDON . 1795.
E : Milled.   Conder, 87 ; 145.—Pye, 29 ; 2.

Forster's.

✓ 217. O : A crown, and the date 1795, encircled with the notes
of " GOD SAVE THE KING."
R : The Prince of Wales's crest, within a double circle. WM.
FORSTER . VIOLIN . TENOR . & VIOLONCELLO MAKER . NO.
348 STRAND . LONDON.
E : Plain rounded.
Conder, 87 ; 146.—Pye, 29 ; 5.—Virt: 61.
Also struck in silver with a milled edge.

Foundling Fields.

218. *O* : A lamb, within a circle. FOUNDLING FIELDS. 1795.
   R : A cypher *I B* within a circle. PAYABLE ON DEMAND.
The *I* is much smaller than the *B*, and a diamond-shaped stop comes midway between the beginning and end of legend.
   E : Milled.   Conder, 87 ; 147.—Pye, 29 ; 6.

219. *O* : The same as last.
   R : The beginning and end of legend are much closer, the stop is a round dot, and the *I* and *B* are the same size.
   E : Milled.   Pye, 29 ; 7.
Both very rare; these reverse dies appear to have failed, after a very few impressions had been taken, the following taking their place :—

✓ 220. *O* : The same as last.
   R : The cypher as last, with the beginning and end of legend further apart as in No. 218, but with a round dot only, close after "DEMAND." A flaw which occurs just on the period, makes it in most cases invisible.
   E : Milled.   Conder, 87 ; 148.—Virt : 57.

Fowler's.

✓ 221. *O* : Head of Neptune with his trident. HALFPENNY.
   R : Whale fishery. PAYABLE AT I. FOWLERS LONDON. *Ex* : WHALE FISHERY 1794.
      Conder, 87 ; 149.—Pye, 29 ; 8.—Virt : 72.

Franklin Press.

222. *O* : A printing press. SIC ORITUR DOCTRINA SURGETQUE LIBERTAS . 1794.
   R : PAYABLE | AT | THE FRANKLIN | PRESS | LONDON. In five straight lines.
   E : AN ASYLUM FOR THE OPPRESS'D OF ALL NATIONS.
✓ 222*a*.   As last, but *E* : Plain (not in collar).
      Conder, 88 ; 150.—Pye, 29 ; 9.—Virt : 21.

Guest's.

✓ 223. *O* : Royal arms, supporters, and crest. GUESTS PATENT BOOTS & SHOES ✱
   R : A boot, shoe, and lady's slipper. NO. 9 . SURRY ST. BLACKFRIARS . ROAD . HALFPENNY 1797.
   E : PAYABLE AT LONDON . + . + . + . + . + .
223*a*.   As last, but *E* : PAYABLE AT LONDON BATH OR MANCHESTER.
223*b*.   „   „ *E* : PAYABLE IN DUBLIN OR LONDON.
223*c*.   „   „ *E* : PAYABLE IN DUBLIN OR AT BALLY-MURTAGH . + . + .

223*d.*   As last, but *E* : PAYABLE IN LANCASTER LONDON OR
          BRISTOL.
ᵛ 223*e.*   As last, but *E* : Milled.
                    Conder, 88 ; 151.—Pye, 29 ; 10.—Virt : 67.

Hall's.

ᵛ 224.   *O* : Three quadrupeds. " THE KANGUROO " " THE ARMADILLO "
          " THE RHINOCEROS ".
     R : T. HALL | CITTY ROAD | NEAR | FINSBURY SQUARE | LONDON
          | 1795. In six lines in the centre. THE FIRST ARTIST
          IN EUROPE FOR PRESERVING BIRDS BEASTS & :
                    Conder, 88 ; 152.—Pye, 30 ; 3.—Virt : 27.
ᵛ 225. *O* : The same as last.
     R : TO BE HAD AT THE CURIOSITY HOUSE CITY ROAD + NEAR
          | FINSBURY SQUARE | LONDON | 1795.
                                        Conder, 88 ; 153.
ᵛ 226. *O* : A deformed dwarf. SIR JEFFERY DUNSTAN MAYOR OF
          GARRAT.
     R : The same as last.
     E : Milled.
ᵛ 226*a.*   As last, but *E* : Plain (not in collar).
                    Conder, 88 ; 154.—Pye, 30 ; 1.—Virt : 27.
ᵛ 227. *O* : The same as last.
     R : The same as No. 224.   Conder, 88 ; 155.
ᵛ 228. *O* : A woman standing. MRS. NEWSHAM THE WHITE NEGRESS.
     R : The same as No. 225.
                    Conder, 88 ; 156.—Pye, 30 ; 2.—Virt : 27.
          *These halfpenny dies have appeared before as pennies;
          see Nos. 26-29.*

228. *O* : A Toucan sitting on the branch of a tree. TO . THE .
          CURIOUS . OBSERVERS . OF . NATURAL . PHENOMENA.
     R : THE 1ST ARTIST IN EUROPE. in four lines in the centre.
          T . HALL . PRESERVER . OF . BIRDS . BEASTS . OR . REPTILES.
          CITTY . ROAD . NEAR . FINSBURY . SQUARE. in a double
          circle.
     E : PAYABLE AT LONDON . + . + . + . +
          Extremely rare. The obv. die shows a flaw through S . OBS
          *and only a very few were struck when the die failed,
          and the following was produced in its place :—*

230. *O* : Similar to last, but the Toucan is larger and there is
          no flaw.
     R : and *E* : The same as last.
230*a.*   As last, but *E* : PAYABLE IN DUBLIN OR LONDON × ×
230*b.*   „   „   *E* : PAYABLE IN LANCASTER LONDON OR
          BRISTOL.
ᵛ 230*c.*   As last, but *E* : Milled.
                    Conder, 88 ; 157.—Pye, 30 ; 4.—Virt : 28.
          This obv. occurs also with one of Pidcock's ; see No. 311.

Hancock's.

✔ 231. *O*: A shop front and a small umbrella.   I . HANCOCK . 19 .
LEATHER . LANE . HOLBORN . LONDON.

    R: A cypher *I H* and 1796 in a circle of leaves.   UMBRELLA .
MAKER . & . DEALER . IN . PROVINCIAL . COINS.

         Conder, 89 ; 159.—Pye, 30 ; 6.—Virt : 176.

    Rare ; only a few impressions taken when the obv. die broke.

✔ 232. *O*: A large umbrella.   Legend as before.

    R: Same as last.

         Conder, 89 ; 158.—Pye, 30 ; 5.—Virt : 85.

    Scarce.

✔ 233. *O*: Three umbrellas in a shield, dividing the date 17-98.
IOHN HANCOCK UMBRELLA MAKER . NO. 19 LEATHER LANE.
HOLBORN LONDON.

    R: A naked boy holding a coin tray.   DEALER IN COINS AND
MEDALS.   *Ex* : HALFPENNY.

    E : Milled.   Pye, 30 ; 7.

    Very rare.

Hatfield's.

✔ 234. *O*: A naked leg within a circle. I . HATFIELD GOLDEN-LEGG +
SNOW-HILL + LONDON.

    R: BOOT & SHOE MANUFACTORY SHOPKEEPERS SUPPLIED ON
REASONABLE TERMS 1795. In seven lines, with a small
ornament above.

         Conder, 89 ; 160.—Pye, 30 ; 8.—Virt : 41.

Heslop's.

235. *O*: A man and a monkey in antic postures.   CAN YOU DO SO.

    R: R. HESLOP NO. 86 CHISWELL STREET FINSBURY SQUARE .
THE FIRST | SHOP IN LONDON FOR | NATURAL CURIOSITY'S
| PAINTINGS, COINS | COLOURS FOR | ATISTS &c.

    E : Engrailed.

235*a*.   As last, but *E* : Milled.

✔ 235*b*.   ,,   ,,   *E* : Plain (not in collar).

         Conder, 89 ; 161.—Pye, 30 ; 9.—Virt : 25.

Some of these latter are struck on very large flans.

Ibberson's.

✔ 236. *O*: St. George killing the dragon, crest, a boar.   HOLBORN
LONDON.   *Ex*: C . IBBERSON.

    R: MAIL & POST COACHES TO ALL PARTS OF ENGLAND. In
four lines within a laurel wreath.

    E : PAYABLE AT THE GEORGE & BLUE BOAR LONDON.

         Conder, 89 ; 164.—Pye, 31 ; 1.

*Very rare ; a few specimens only struck in silver and cop-
per ; a recent imitation has also been struck. An artist's
proof in tin of the obv. die is in the National collection, without any boar ; and there is also a singular
piece there which appears to have been struck from this
obv. die and having rev.* NO. — | SIX | PENCE | 1800.

v 237. *O*: Similar to last, but the boar is larger, and with PONTHON
in minute letters on the *Ex*: line.
R: and *E*: The same as No. 236.
Conder, 89 ; 163.—Pye, 31 ; 2.—Virt: 14.
Also struck in silver.

238. *O*: The same as No. 236.
R: A cypher *R W* on a shield, hanging on a tree, &c. See
Wexford, No. 1.

James'.

v 239. *O*: A lion couchant, holding a shield inscribed NO. 6
MARTLETT COURT BOW STREET LONDON. Under this is
C JAMES, and when the flan is large enough to show it,
ENGRAVER under it, being from the same dies as the
penny No. 32.
R: A tiger. ROYAL MALE TIGER ❖ 1796 ❖   See Pidcock's
No. 304.
E: SPENCE ✕ DEALER ✕ IN ✕ COINS ✕ LONDON ✕
Conder, 89 ; 162.
239*a*.   As last, but *E*: Plain (not in collar).

Kelly's.

v 240. *O*: A postilion holding a harnessed horse. KELLY'S LIGHT
HARNESS &c. *Ex*: SOLD CHEAP AT THEIR | MANUFACTORY
| STRAND | LONDON. In four lines, the last one curved.
R: A saddle, spur, and umbrella, two bits, and two whips.
KELLY'S PATENT SADDLERY &c. SOLD CHEAP.
E: PAYABLE AT LONDON . ✛ . ✛ . ✛ . ✛ . ✛ .
Conder, 90 ; 165.—Pye, 31 ; 3.—Virt: 42.
240*a*.   As last, but *E*: PAYABLE AT LONDON BATH OR MANCHESTER.
240*b*.   „   „   *E*: PAYABLE IN ANGLESEY LONDON OR LIVER-
POOL.
v 240*c*.   As last, but *E*: PAYABLE IN DUBLIN OR LONDON . ✕ .
240*d*.   „   „   *E*: PAYABLE BY HENRY OLIVERS.
240*e*.   „   „   *E*: Milled. Some of these are struck in
white metal.
240*f*.   As last, but *E*: Plain (not in collar).

Kilvington's.

v 241. *O*: Laureate bust to left. PAYABLE AT J. KILVINGTONS.
The point of laurel comes under the J.
R: Figure of Britannia seated holding a spear. BRUNSWICK
HALFPENNY. *Ex*: 1795.
E: Engrailed.   Conder, 217 ; 63.—Pye, 11 ; 1.
241*a*.   As last, but *E*: RICHARD BACON COCKEY LANE.
241*b*.   „   „   *E*: Plain (not in collar).

7

✓ 242. *O*: Similar to last, but the tip of the laurel points to the T
of " AT."

     R: and *E*: The same as No. 241.   Conder, 217; 64.

243. *O*: Very similar bust to preceding. BRUNSWICK HALFPENNY
1795.

     R: Britannia seated holding a spear. RULE BRITANNIA.

     E: PAYABLE IN DUBLIN OR LONDON . × . × .

243*a*.   As last, but *E*: Plain (not in collar).

                                   Conder, 217; 65.

244. *O*: The same as last.

     R: A man of war sailing. THE GUARD & GLORY OF BRITAIN.
See Not Local, No. 112.

     E: Engrailed.

244*a*.   As last, but *E*: Plain (not in collar).

                                   Conder, 217; 66.

✓ 245. *O*: The same as last.

     R: Shield of Arms of Lancaster. HALFPENNY 1794. See
Lancashire, No. 18.

     E: PAYABLE AT G. GILBERTS NORTHIAM . × × × ×.

                                   Conder, 153; 20.

245*a*.   As last, but *E*: Plain (not in collar).

246. *O*: The same as *R*: of No. 241, but dated 1796.

     R: Bust to left. SHAKESPEAR.   Conder, 217; 67.
See also Lancashire, No. 71.

Lackington's.

✓ 247. *O*: A three-quarter bust to left. J. LACKINGTON. 1794

     R: A figure of Fame, blowing a trumpet. HALFPENNY OF
J. LACKINGTON & CO. CHEAPEST BOOKSELLERS IN
THE WORLD. Notice that the Y of " HALFPENNY "
comes between the O's, and the initial J just over the
first E of " BOOKSELLERS."

     E: Milled.   Conder, 90; 166.

247*a*.   As last, but *E*: AN ASYLUM FOR THE OPPRESS'D OF ALL
NATIONS.

247*b*.   As last, but *E*: BIRMINGHAM OR IN SWANSEA.

247*c*.   ,,   ,,   *E*: PAYABLE AT LONDON LIVERPOOL OR BRISTOL.

✓ 248. *O*: The same as last.

     R: Similar to last, but the J is over the first L of " BOOK-
SELLERS."

     E: PAYABLE AT LACKINGTON & CO.S FINSBURY SQUARE +
LONDON +   Conder, 90; 167.—Pye, 31; 4.

248*a*.   As last, but *E*: PAYABLE IN ANGLESEY LONDON OR LIVER-
POOL . ×.

✓ 249. *O*: Similar to preceding, but with a quatrefoil after legend. The 1 of date is just under and nearly touches the bottom button of coat.

    R: Fame as before. HALFPENNY OF LACKINGTON . ALLEN & CO.✱ The inner legend as before, but with a dot at the end instead of an annulet, and a line dividing it from the outer.

    E: PAYABLE AT THE TEMPLE OF THE MUSES ✱ / ✱ / ✱ /
                          Conder, 90 ; 168.—Pye, 31 ; 6.

249*a*.   As last, but *E*: PAYABLE IN LANCASTER LONDON OR BRISTOL.

249*b*.   ,,   ,,   *E*: HALFPENNY PAYABLE AT THE BLACK HORSE TOWER HILL.

✓ 250. *O*: Similar to last, but the 1 of date is some little distance to the right of the button.

    R: and *E*: the same as No. 249.   Virt: 42.

251. *O*: and *E*: The same as last.

    R: Similar to last, but position of the outer and inner legends vary, which may be detected by noticing that in this piece the period after "LACKINGTON" is over the N of "IN," whilst before it was over the T of "THE." There are other differences, but this will be sufficient to distinguish by.

✓ 252. *O*: Profile bust to right. J. LACKINGTON. A small cross below bust.

    R: The same as last.

    E: PAYABLE AT LONDON OR DUBLIN . × . ×.   Pye, 31 ; 5.
    Rare.

✓ 253. *O*: Similar to last, but with FINSBURY SQUARE 1795 in place of cross under the bust.

    R: The same as last.

    E: The same as No. 249.   Conder, 90 ; 169.—Virt: 42.

253*a*.   As last, but *E*: Milled.

✓ 254. *O*: The same as last.

    R: A smaller figure of Fame. The same legend as No. 249, but without the dividing line.

    E: Milled to right.

✓ 254*a*.   As last, but *E*: Milled to left.
                 Conder 90 ; 170.—Pye, 31 ; 7.

254*b*.   ,,   ,,   *E*: Plain (not in collar).

The obv. of No. 247 occurs with the following reverse :—

255. *R*: Figure of Vulcan at work. HALFPENNY. *Ex*: 1793. See Warwickshire, No. 303.

    E: AN ASYLUM FOR THE OPPRESS'D OF ALL NATIONS.
                        Conder, 229 ; 165.

The rev. of No. 247 appears as an obv. with the following reverse :—

                                  7 ✱

256. *R*: Arms of Liverpool between reeds. DEUS NOBIS HÆC
OTIA FECIT 1794. See Lancashire, No. 60.
Conder, 90; 171.
See also Shropshire, No. 22; and Dublin, No. 7.

For London and Middlesex, &c., see Miscellaneous at end.

Lyceum.

257. *O*: Mercury standing on a galloping horse. THE . FIRST
EQUESTN. . PERFORMANCE . IN . EUROPE. *Ex*: LYCEUM
STRAND LONDON.
R: A man balancing himself upon his head on the point of
a sword, the hilt of which rests upon a table.
SINGING DANCING TUMBLING SLACK WIRE &c. *Ex*:
EVERY EVENING.
E: PAYABLE AT LONDON OR MANCHESTER.
Condor, 92; 182.—Pye, 29; 3.—Virt: 51.

v 257*a*.   As last, but *E*: PAYABLE AT LONDON BATH OR MAN-
CHESTER +

257*b*.   As last, but *E*: PAYABLE IN DUBLIN OR LONDON . + . + .

257*c*.   „   „   *E*: PAYABLE IN LANCASTER LONDON OR
BRISTOL × ×

257*d*.   As last, but *E*: PAYABLE AT W. PARKERS OLD BIRMING-
HAM WAREHOUSE.

257*e*.   As last, but *E*: PAYABLE BY HENRY OLIVERS.

257*f*.   „   „   *E*: Milled.

Mail Coach.

v 258. *O*: A mail coach travelling. MAIL COACH HALFPENNY
PAYABLE IN LONDON *Ex*: TO TRADE EXPEDITION &
TO PROPERTY PROTECTION.
R: TO | J. PALMER. ES. | THIS IS INSCRIBED | AS A TOKEN OF |
GRATITUDE | FOR BENEFITS RECD. | FROM THE ESTAB-
LISHMENT | OF MAIL COACHES. In eight lines with a
cypher *J F* under, the whole within branches of
palm.   Conder, 92; 183.—Pye, 31; 8.—Virt: 72.

v 259. *O*: Similar to last, but with a period after "PROPERTY,"
and the upper legend nearer the horses' heads.
R: Similar to last, but with 1797 in place of the cypher.
Rare.

v 260. *O*: A mail coach as before. HALFPENNY PAYA-BLE IN
LONDON *Ex*: TO TRADE EXPEDIN. & TO PROPERTY
PROTECTION.
R: A cypher *A F H* between palm branches. TO J.
PALMER ESQ. THIS IS INSCRIBED
Condor, 92 : 184.—Pye, 31 ; 9.—Virt : 72.

Masonic.

261. *O*: The Freemasons' arms, supporters, crest, and motto.
PRINCE OF WALES ELECTED G.M + 24 Nov 1790.
The bodies of the supporters are ribbed.

    R: A cupid and Masonic emblems within a triangle.
WISDOM STRENGTH & BEAUTY. The rays are formed
of lines of dots, and do not descend below the left
arm of the cupid. SIT LUX ET LUX FUIT.

    E: HALFPENNY PAYABLE AT THE BLACK HORSE TOWER
HILL . × .

261*a*.   As last, but *E*: MASONIC TOKEN I. SCETCHLEY FECIT
1794 . + . + . + .

v 261*b*.   As last, but *E*: PAYABLE IN LANCASTER LONDON OR
BRISTOL.

261*c*.   As last, but *E*: PAYABLE AT LONDON . + . + . + . +

261*d*.   „   „   *E*: PAYABLE AT LONDON OR DUBLIN.

v 262. *O*: The same as last.

    R: Similar to last, but the rays are composed of alternate
lines and dots, which descend below the arm and
robe of the cupid, and there is no period after
" FUIT."

    E: HALFPENNY PAYABLE AT THE BLACK HORSE TOWER
HILL . × .

v 262*a*.   As last, but *E*: MASONIC TOKEN I SCETCHLEY FECIT
1794 . + . + . + .

262*b*.   As last, but *E*: PAYABLE IN LANCASTER LONDON OR
BRISTOL.

262*c*.   As last, but *E*: PAYABLE AT LONDON . + . + . + . + .

262*d*.   „   „   *E*: MASONIC HALFPENNY TOKEN MDCCXCIV.

263. *O*: The same as last.

    R: The rays, which are all composed of lines, descend to
the ground, and there is a period after BEAUTY and
after FUIT.

    E: MASONIC HALFPENNY TOKEN MDCCXCIV . × . ×

v 263*a*.   As last, but *E*: MASONIC TOKEN BROTHER SCETCHLEY BIR-
MINGHAM FACIT.

263*b*.   As last, but *E*: PAYABLE AT LONDON . + . + . + . +

✔ 264. *O*: Similar to preceding, but the bodies of the supporters
are not ribbed, and there is a comma after NOV.

    R: and *E*: The same as No. 261.

v 264*a*.   As last, but *E*: MASONIC TOKEN I SCETCHLEY FECIT
1794 . + . + . + .

v 264*b*.   As last, but *E*: MASONIC HALFPENNY TOKEN MDCCXCIV. × . × .

264c.   As last, but *E*: MASONIC TOKEN J. SKETCHLEY R.A. & P.G.S. BIRMINGHAM FECIT ✳

264d.   As last, but *E*: HALFPENNY PAYABLE AT DUBLIN CORK OR DERRY.

264e.   As last, but *E*: PAYABLE IN LANCASTER LONDON OR BRISTOL.

264f.   As last, but *E*: PAYABLE AT RICHARD LONG'S LIBRARY . ✕ .

264g.   „   „   *E*: PAYABLE AT W. PARKERS OLD BIRMINGHAM WAREHOUSE.

264h.   As last, but *E*: Plain (not in collar).
         These are found in Conder at p. 111, No. 343 ; p. 230, No. 172 ; p. 231, Nos. 173-5, and in Pye at pl. 37, No. 2.

Meymott's.

265. *O*: Britannia seated holding a pair of scales and a spear. MEYMOTT + & + SON + LONDON. *Ex*: + 1795 +
      The point of the spear touches the o of "SON."

      R: The arms of London. SCALES + WEIGHTS + & + STEEL-YARDS +

      E: CORNER OF WORMWOOD STREET BISHOPSGATE ✕ In raised letters.   Conder, 92 ; 185.—Pye, 32 ; 1.

265a.   As last, but *E*: Plain (not in collar).
         Struck in silver, copper, and tin ; and one in gold.
         Very rare, the obverse die failed when but very few impressions had been taken, which necessitated the making of a fresh one, as follows :—

✔ 266. *O*. Similar to last, but there are no crosses in the legend, and the spear reaches the edge of the coin between "SON" and "LONDON." There is a dot before and after the date.

      R: and *E*: The same as No. 265. ·
         Also struck in silver.
                     Conder, 92 ; 186.—Pye, 32 ; 2.—Virt : 52.

266a.   As last, but *E*: Plain (not in collar).
         This latter is struck in white metal.

         The obv. of No. 266 appears with the following reverses :—

267. *R*: A wheatsheaf. PEACE PLENTY AND LIBERTY. See Cambridgeshire, No. 17.   Conder, 286 ; 219.

268. *R*: The arms of Orchard. See No. 285.

269. *R*: A cypher *J E & Co*. HALFPENNY PAYABLE IN CORK OR DUBLIN. See Cork, No. 1.

✔ 270. *R*: A wheatsheaf and doves. PEACE AND PLENTY HALF-PENNY. See Munster, No. 2.   Conder, 286 ; 218.

271. *R*: An anchor and cap of Liberty radiated. LIBERTY *
PEACE * COMMERCE.   See Not Local, No. 123.

Conder, 286 ; 220.

The rev. also occurs as an obv. with the following
reverses :—

272. *R*: A wheatsheaf.   The same as No. 267.

Conder 302; 392.

v 273. *R*: The arms of London crowned. FEAR GOD AND HONOUR
THE KING 1795.   See No. 729.   Conder 265 ; 19.

274. *R*: Anchor, &c. The same as No. 271.   Conder 264; 9.
See also Nos. 592 and 606; Lincolnshire, No. 2 ;
Dublin, No. 118; and Munster, No. 12.

Moore's.

v 275. *O*: A girl sitting under a tree making lace. LACE MANU-
FACTORY. 1795 within a double circle.
R: A scroll inscribed MUSLINS IRISH CLOTH HOSE &c. within
a circle. MOORE.NO.116 GREAT PORTLAND STREET *
E: Milled.   Conder, 92; 187.—Pye, 32 ; 3.—Virt: 55.

Neeton's.

v 276. *O*: A Saracen's head. EDWARD * NEETON * ST. MARY LE
BONE *
R: A puncheon. WINE * RUM * AND * BRANDY * VAULTS *
1795 *   Conder, 93 ; 188.—Pye, 32 ; 4.—Virt: 72.
Some of these are on much larger flans than others.

Newgate.

277. *O*: Front view of a prison. NEWGATE. *Ex*: MDCCXCIV.
R: PAYABLE | AT | THE RESIDENCE | OF MESSRS SYMONDS |
WINTERBOTHAM | RIDGWAY | & | HOLT. In eight lines.
E: Milled.

v 278. *O*: and *E*: The same as last.
R: Differs from the last in the tail of the " & " hanging
down, and the letters of abbreviation in "MESSRS." are
smaller.
Both these are scarce.

v 279. *O*: Similar to preceding, but the gratings over the side
doors have cross bars as well as upright ones, and
there is no period after date.
R: Similar to last, but the tail of the " & " turns up.
E: As before. Conder, 93 ; 189.—Pye, 32 ; 5.—Virt: 41.
Also struck in silver.

279a.   As last, but *E*: PAYABLE IN HULL AND IN LONDON.
This obv. occurs with the following reverses :—

v 280. *R*: A crown, sceptre, and palm branch radiated. KING
          AND CONSTITUTION 1794. See Essex, No. 6.
     E: CURRENT EVERYWHERE.   Conder, 93; 190.
   280*a*.   As last, but *E*: Plain (not in collar).
   281. *R*: Old man and sons. LONDON CORRESPONDING SOCIETY.
          See No. 204.
   282. *O*: A different view with a square tower in the centre.
          NEWGATE. *Ex*: 1795 between sprigs.
     R: Similar to No. 279 but not from the same die.
     E: CURRENT EVERY WHERE.
   282*a*.   As last, but *E*: PAYABLE AT THE WAREHOUSES OF D.
          WRIGHT & S. PALMER . × .
v 282*b*.   As last, but *E*: Milled.
v 282*c*.   Conder, 93; 191.—Pye, 32; 6.—Virt: 41.
          This obv. occurs with the following reverse:—
v 283. *R*: Three men hanging. NOTED ADVOCATES FOR THE RIGHTS
          OF MAN 1796. See Not Local, No. 129.
                              Conder, 93; 192.
          See also Wicklow, No. 38.

Oppenheim's.

v 284. *O*: A view of St. Paul's Cathedral. *Ex*: 1797.
     R: A man weaving in a loom. SUCCESS TO THE MANUFAC-
          TURERS OF GLASGOW.
     E: PAYABLE AT M & H OPPENHEIMS TOY WAREHOUSE LONDON.
     Very rare.

Orchard's.

v 285. *O*: Draped bust to left. JACOBS under it. ROBERT ORCHARD.
     R: Orchard's arms on a shield. HALFPENNY 1795.
                              Conder, 232; 183.—Virt: 49.
v 286. *O*: Bust to right. JAMES under it.   * ROBERT ORCHARD *
     R: The arms of London in an ornamental border, &c.
          See No. 341.   Conder, 232; 184.—Virt: 164.
   287. *O*: The same as last.
     R: A beehive with sprigs under it. SMITHFIELD TOKEN
          1797.   Conder, 107; 309.
          This is most probably unique.
v 288. *O*: Draped bust to right. JAMES under it.   * ROBERT
          ORCHARD * LONDON TOKEN 1797.
     R: Orchard's arms on a shield between two branches.
          An o is above the shield.   Conder, 107: 310.
v 289. *O*: View of a church. JACOBS under, and arms above it.
          ISLINGTON . OLD . CHURCH . ROBERT . ORCHARD.
     R: A large cypher *R O*. HALFPENNY 1798.
     E: COVENTRY TOKEN.

289*a*. As last, but *E* : Plain.

290. *O* : The same as No. 285.
  R : The same as the obverse of No. 286.
  Conder, 289 ; 257.
  The obverse of No. 285 occurs with the following reverses :—

291. *R* : A wheatsheaf. PEACE PLENTY & LIBERTY. See Cambridgeshire, No. 17. Conder, 288 ; 250.

292. *R* : An anchor in a shield, &c. See No. 341.
  E : PAYABLE IN ANGLESEY LONDON OR LIVERPOOL.

292*a*. As last, but *E* : CURRENT EVERYWHERE.

292*b*.   „   „   *E* : Plain (not in collar).
  Conder, 285 ; 210.

293. *R* : A cypher *J E & Co.* HALFPENNY PAYABLE IN CORK OR DUBLIN. See Cork, No. 1. Conder, 289 ; 253.

294. *R* : A wheatsheaf and sickle between two doves. See Munster, No. 1. Conder, 288 ; 248.

295. *R* : Anchor and cap of Liberty radiated. LIBERTY.PEACE. COMMERCE. See Not Local, No. 123.
  Conder, 288 ; 248.
  The obverse of No. 286 occurs with the following reverse :—

296. *R* : Figure of Fame flying. See Cork, No. 1.
  Conder, 289 ; 254.
  The reverse of No. 285 appears as an obverse with the following reverses : —

297. *R* : Bust of William III. in a wreath of oak. 1688. From the die of Not Local Penny, No. 14.
  Conder, 215 ; 38.

298. *R* : A cypher *H. S. Co.* between laurel branches. See Dublin, No. 116. Conder, 265 ; 20.

299. *R* : Hope holding a quadrant. FOR THE GOOD OF TRADE. See Dublin, No. 18. Conder, 282 ; 174.
  Another halfpenny of Orchard's is described at Hertfordshire, No. 3.
  See also No. 268, *ante;* Cambridgeshire, No. 28 ; Durham, No. 11 ; Northumberland, No. 27 ; Cork, No. 6 ; Dublin, Nos. 21, 104, 110, and 119 ; and Munster, Nos. 5 and 6.

St. Paul's. (*See* Miscellaneous.)

Pidcock's.

300. *O* : A lion couchant, holding a shield inscribed EXETER CHANGE LONDON in three lines, C. JAMES. F. under the lion. PIDCOCKS EXIBITION.
  R : An eagle, BIRDS . AND BEAST. .
  Conder, 93 ; 194.—Pye, 32 ; 7.—Virt : 26.

✔ 301. *O*: Similar to last, but the word EXHIBITION correctly spelt.
    R: An eagle with a radiation above, and BIRDS.AND.BEASTS.
    1795. below.
    E: PAYABLE IN DUBLIN OR LONDON + . +
              Conder, 93; 195.—Pye, 32; 8.—Virt: 26.

301*a*.   As last, but *E*: Milled.

✔ 301*b*.   „   „ *E*: Plain (not in collar).
    The remainder of Pidcock's tokens will now be given
    in the following list, commencing with the more
    important animals, and bringing in every known
    variety, and conjunction of obv. or rev.

Elephant.

O: An elephant. JAMES under it. PIDCOCKS * * * EXHI-
BITION *
This obv. occurs with the following reverses:—

302. *R*: A rhinoceros looking to the right. EXETER * CHANGE
* STRAND * LONDON *
E: SPENCE × DEALER × IN × COINS × LONDON ×

302*a*.   As last, but *E*: Milled.
          Conder, 291; 277.—Pye, 32; 7.—Virt: 26.

✔ 302*b*.   As last, but *E*: Plain (not in collar).

✔ 303. *R*: A rhinoceros looking to the left. PIDCOCK EXETER
CHANGE LONDON.

304. *R*: A tiger. JAMES under it. ROYAL MALE TIGER ÷ 1796 ÷
See No. 239, *ante.*
E: The same as No. 302.   Conder, 276; 116.

305. *R*: A nylghau looking to the right. JAMES under it.
* PIDCOCKS * EXHIBITION.   Conder, 265; 16.

306. *R*: An antelope looking to the left. ÷ PIDCOCK'S ÷ EXHI-
BITION ÷ ALIVE. *Ex*: 1795.
E: Milled.   Conder, 265; 14.

306*a*.   As last, but *E*: Plain (not in collar).

307. *R*: A zebra. PIDCOCK'S * GRAND . MENAGERIE . EXETER .
CHANGE . LONDON *

308. *R*: A two-headed cow. EXETER CHANGE * STRAND LONDON * .
E: Milled.   Conder, 94; 196.—Pye, 32; 9.—Virt: 26.

✔ 308*a*.   As last, but *E*: Plain (not in collar).
    Struck also in tin.

✔ 309. *R*: A kangaroo. THIS . KANGAROO'S . BIRTH . SEP. 10 . 1800.

310. *R*: A monkey. THE WAN-DEROW . 1801 PIDCOCKS * GRAND .
MENAGERIE . EXETER . CHANGE . LONDON *

✔ 311. *R*: A toucan. TO . THE . CURIOUS . OBSERVERS &c. See
No. 230, *ante.*

Lion (and dog).

O: A lion with a dog upon its back. LION AND DOG. 1801.
This obv. occurs with the following reverses:—

312. *R*: A rhinoceros to left.. As No. 303.
313. *R*: A zebra. As No. 307.
314. *R*: A two-headed cow. As No. 308.
315. *R*: A kangaroo. As No. 309.
316. *R*: The wanderow. As No. 310.

Lion (lying down).

O: A lion lying down, fondling a dog. PIDCOCK'S * GRAND .
MENAGERIE . EXETER . CHANGE . LONDON * .
This obv. occurs with the following reverses :—

317. *R*: A two-headed cow. As No. 308.
318. *R*: A kangaroo. As No. 309.
319. *R*: A cockatoo. ORANGE CRESTED COCKATOO 1801.
320. *R*: A crane. THE AFRICAN CROWN CRANE * PIDCOCK'S EXHI-
BITION * .

Rhinoceros (to right).

O: A rhinoceros looking to the right. As No. 302.
This obv. occurs with the following reverses :—

321. *R*: A tiger. As No. 304.
E: SPENCE × DEALER × IN × COINS × LONDON × .
.... ·Conder, 291 ; 276.

322. *R*: An antelope looking to the left. As No. 306.
E: Milled.   Conder 94; 197.—Virt: 69.

322a.   As last, but *E*: Plain (not in collar).

323. *R*: A kangaroo. As No. 309.

Rhinoceros (to left).

O: A rhinoceros looking to the left. As No. 303.
This obv. occurs with the following reverse :—

324. *R*: A two-headed cow. As No. 308.

Tiger.

O: A tiger. As No. 304.
This obv. occurs with the following reverses :—

325. *R*: A two-headed cow. As last.
E: SPENCE × DEALER × IN × COINS × LONDON ×

325a.   As last, but *E*: Milled.

326. *R*: An ostrich, JAMES under it. ❖ EXETER CHANGE STRAND
LONDON ❖
E: SPENCE × DEALER × IN × COINS × LONDON ×
Conder, 94; 199.

326*bis R* : Eagle, &c. As No. 301.
    E : Same as last.

Nylghau.

O : A nylghau looking to the right,   As No. 305.
    This obv. occurs with the following reverses :—
327. *R* : A two-headed cow. As No. 308.   Conder, 265 ; 15.
✓ 328. *R* : An ostrich. As No. 326.
        Conder, 94 ; 198.—Pye, 33 ; 1.—Virt : 69.
329. *R* : Bust to right. LOUIS REX. Conder, 265, 17.—Pye, 33 ; 2.

Antelope.

O : An antelope looking to the left. As No. 306.
    This obv. occurs with the following reverse:—
330. *R* : An ostrich. As No. 326.
    E : Milled.   Conder, 265 ; 13.—Virt : 27.
✓ 330*a*.   As last, but *E* : Plain (not in collar).
        Some of these are on very small flans, with a rounded
        edge.

Zebra.

O : A zebra. As No. 307.
    This obv. occurs with the following reverses :—
331. *R* : A two-headed cow. As No. 308.
✓ 332. *R* : A cockatoo. As No. 319.
✓ 333. *R* : A crane. As No. 320.

Two-headed Cow.

O : A two-headed cow. As No. 308.
    This obv. occurs with the following reverses :—
✓ 334. *R* : A kangaroo. As No. 309.
✓ 335. *R* : The wanderow. As No. 310.
✓ 336. *R* : A toucan. As No. 311.   Conder, 272 ; 76.
✓ 337. *R* : The Prince of Wales' arms, crest, &c. LONDON &
    MIDDLESEX HALFPENNY. See No. 740.
        Conder, 272 ; 75.

Kangaroo.

O : The kangaroo. As No. 309.
    This obv. occurs with the following reverse :—
✓ 338. *R* : A cockatoo. As No. 319.

Wanderow.

O : The wanderow. As No. 310.
    This obv. occurs with the following reverses :—
✓ 339. *R* : A cockatoo. As No. 319.

✔ 340. *R* : A crane. As No. 320.

> *Some of these pieces were struck in the 19th century,
> but the connection between them is so close as to make
> it desirable to include them all.*

Prattent's.

✔ 341. *O* : An anchor in a shield, between sprigs of laurel, crest
a cap of Liberty radiated. LONDON COMMERCIAL
TOKEN 1796.

R : The arms of London, in an ornamental circle, upon a
sword and mace crossed.

Conder, 94 ; 200.—Virt : 167.

This obv. occurs with the following reverses :—

342. *R* : A man smoking. SR. GEORGE COOK &c. See Surrey,
No. 15.   Conder, 285 ; 208.

343. *R* : Fame flying, &c. See Cork, No. 1.

E : ANGLESEA LONDON OR LIVERPOOL.

343*a*.   As last, but *E* : PAYABLE AT JAMES ROBERTSONS.

343*b*.   „   „   *E* : Plain (not in collar). Conder, 285 ; 207.

344. *R* : Crowned bust. BRYEN BOIROIMBE &c. See Munster,
No. 1.

E : PAYABLE AT N. BOLINBROKES HABERDASHER NORWICH.

344*a*.   As last, but *E* : Plain (not in collar). Conder, 284 ; 206.

✔ 345. *R* : A crown radiated. LOYAL * BRITONS * LODGE * See
Not Local, No. 123.   Conder, 285 ; 209.

See also Nos. 286, 292 ; Surrey, No. 17 ; and Dublin,
No. 22.

Presbury's.

✔ 346. *O* : Robed and crowned bust. QUEEN ELIZABETH. See
Sussex, No. 14.

R : PAYABLE BY C. PRESBURY & CO. JEWELLERY & HARDWARE
MANUFACTORY LONDON.

E : PAYABLE IN LONDON $+ . + . + . \times$.

Conder, 94 ; 201.—Pye, 33 ; 7.

> *Very rare in good condition ; the obv. being merely the
> worn-out die of the Chichester token.   There were
> about three dozen struck.*

Ratley's.

347 *O* : A man holding a picture, which another is looking at.
P. RATLEY DUKES COURT ST. MARTINS . DEALER IN
DRAWGS. PICTRS. & CURIOSOTIES.

R : Shells lying on the sea shore, a rocky cliff, and a ship
on the sea. SHELLS . ORES & MINERALS . BOT. SOLD .
OR EXCHANGED . 1795. The top of the cliff comes
between the "OR" and "EXCHANGED."

> *Exceedingly rare ; the rev. die failed almost immediately.*

v 348. *O*: The same as last.
  R: Similar to last, but the top of the cliff comes between SOLD and OR.
  Rare. Only about six dozen struck. Also struck in silver.
  Conder, 94; 202.—Pye, 33; 8.—Virt: 22.

349. *O*: A bust, and a shield of arms, in two small circles. RATLEY DEALER IN COINS DUKES COURT ST. MARTINS LANE. The whole within a circle. A GREAT VARIETY OF PROVINCIAL COINS TRADESMENS TOKENS 1801.
  R: Blank.
  Very rare.

Richardson's.

v 350. *O*: A figure of Fortune standing between two lottery wheels. NOTHING VENTURE NOTHING HAVE. *Ex*: 1795.
  R: AT THE OFFICES OF | RICHARDSON GOODLUCK & CO | NO | 12807 | THE LAST PRIZE OF | £30000 | SHARED | WAS SOLD IN SIXTEENTHS. Displayed in eight lines. The A in top line comes over the HA of the second, and the F at end of top line comes over the K.

351. *O*: The same as last.
  R: Similar, but the letters of second line are smaller, the A of top line comes over the H of the second and the F comes over the C.

v 352. *O*: Similar to preceding, but the letters of legend are smaller, and the figures of date larger.
  R: The same as last.
  Conder, 94; 203.—Pye, 33; 9.—Virt: 40.

v 353. *O*: A bluecoat boy preparing to draw from a lottery wheel. NOTHING VENTURE NOTHING HAVE. *Ex*: A cornucopia of money dividing the date 17—95.
  R: RICHARDSON GOODLUCK & CO | SOLD | NO | 12807 | THE LAST PRIZE OF | £30000 | SHARED | IN | SIXTEENTHS. Displayed in nine lines, the top and bottom ones being curved.
  Conder, 95; 204.—Pye, 33; 10.—Virt: 40

There is a slight variation in the reverse die of this piece.

Nos. 350 and 353 are struck also in silver.

Rupert Street.

v 354. *O*: Arms, supporters, crest, and motto, of the Curriers' Company. HALFPENNY.
  R: A plough. GOD SPEED THE PLOUGH on a label above it. PAYABLE IN RUPERT STREET ST. JAMES'S below.
  E: Plain (not in collar).
  Conder, 95; 205.—Pye, 33; 6.—Virt: 17.

354a. As last, but *E*: BIRMINGHAM REDRUTH & SWANSEA.
  In good condition scarce.

Salter's.

⌄ 355. *O*: Hatmakers at work. SALTER'S . 47 CHARING . CROSS
LONDON.

   R: A shop-front within a circle. CHEAPEST HAT-WAREHOUSE
IN THE WORLD. *

           Conder, 95; 206.—Pye, 34; 1.—Virt: 32.

Schooling's.

⌄ 356. *O*: A figure of Justice standing between weights of various
kinds. SCHOOLING & SON SCALE MAKERS. *Ex*:
NO. 44 BISHOPSGATE WITHIN LONDON.

   R: A tea kettle standing on a stove. FURNISHING IRON-
MONGERS & SMITHS AT THEIR MANUFACTORY. *Ex*:
CRISPIN STREET SPITALFIELDS 1795.

           Conder, 95; 207.—Pye, 34; 2.—Virt: 74.

Shackleton's.

357. *O*: The royal arms, crest, and supporters. FRANCIS
SHACKLETON LODON ❖

   R: A candle mould. FINE MOULD AND STORE CANDLES ❖
1794.

   E: PAYABLE IN SUFFOLK-STREET HAY-MARKET . × . . × .
              Conder, 95; 209.—Pye, 34; 3.

✓ 357*a*.   As last, but *E*: PAYABLE IN LANCASTER LONDON OR
BRISTOL.

357*b*.   As last, but *E*: Plain (not in collar).

   *Very rare. Only about twelve impressions struck, when, in
consequence of the error in spelling "LONDON," the
obverse die was rejected and the following executed
in its place:—*

⌄ 358. *O*: Similar to last, but LONDON correctly spelt. The
unicorn's tail comes to L of "LONDON."

   R: and *E*: The same as No. 357.
   Scarce.

359. *O*: Similar to last, but the tail of unicorn comes to the O
of "LONDON."

   R: and *E*: The same as last.

           Conder, 95; 208.—Pye, 34; 4.—Virt: 32.

359*a*.   As last, but *E*: PAYABLE IN DUBLIN OR LONDON . + . + .

359*b*.   „   „ *E*: Plain (not in collar).

Sims'.

⌄ 360. *O*: Bust of Garrick to right. C. JAMES . F. under it. WE .
NE'ER . SHALL . LOOK . UPON . HIS . LIKE . AGAIN.

   R: Tragic and comic masks, a thistle and crown above,
sprigs below. SIMS . RUSSELL . COURT.

   E: Milled. These are struck on large flans.

⌄ 360*a*.   As last, but *E*: Plain (not in collar).

           Conder, 96; 210.—Pye, 34; 5.—Virt: 40.

Skidmore's.

v 361. *O*: A register stove. NO. 123 HIGH HOLBORN LONDON within
a circle. PAYABLE AT SKIDMORES FURNISHING REPOSI-
TORY *
R : Two men at a forge. MANUFACTORY . & . IRON FOUNDRY.
CLERKENWELL * *Ex* : 1795.
E : Milled.   Conder, 96 ; 211—Pye, 34 ; 6—Virt : 17.
Struck also in silver.
This obv. occurs with the following reverses :—

362. *R* : Various ornaments. ORNAMENT MAKER.

363. *R* : A star. STAR Halfpenny 1791.

364. *R* : An anchor and cable. M. PINTOSH HORSHAM 1791. See
Sussex, No. 25.
E : SKIDMORE HOLBORN LONDON.   Conder, 295 ; 320.

365. *R* : Bust to left of WILLIAM HALLAN. See Warwickshire,
No. 84.
E : The same as last.   Conder, 280 ; 160.

366. *R* : Bust in cocked hat of GENERAL ELLIOT. See Warwickshire, No. 167.
E : Milled.

367. *R* : Bust to left. PAYABLE AT SALISBURY. See Wiltshire,
No. 12.
E : The same as No. 364.   Conder, 295 ; 318.

368. *R* : A woolpack. PAYABLE AT T. SANTER KIDDERMINSTER. See
Worcestershire, No. 22.
E : The same as No. 364.

v 369. *R* : Arms, &c. See Worcestershire, No. 22.

v 370. *R* : View of a street, &c. See Yorkshire, No. 11.
E : The same as No. 364.

371. *R* : A cypher, *I O M*, &c. See Yorkshire, No. 11.

372. *R* : Two busts. LOUIS XVI ET M. ANTIONETTE, &c. See Not
Local, No. 91.
E : Milled.   Conder, 278 ; 142.

373. *R* : Similar to last, but with the date 17—95 at the sides.
See Not Local, No. 95.
E : The same as No. 364.

373*a*. As last, but *E* : Milled.

374. *R* : Bust in cocked hat. MAY THE FRENCH &c. See Not
Local, No. 117.
E : The same as No. 364.   Conder, 282 ; 184.
The rev. of No. 361 appears as an obv. with the fol-
lowing reverses :—

375. *R* : A guillotine, and part of a house. HALFPENNY.
E : The same as No. 364.   Conder, 96 ; 212.

376. *R* : Ornament, &c., as No. 362.   Conder, 96 ; 213.

377. *R* : A star, as No. 363.   Conder, 96 ; 214.

378. *R*: Bust to left of DAVID GARRICK ESQ. See No. 155.
   E: Milled over SKIDMORE HOLBORN LONDON.

379. *R*: Heart in hand, &c. See No. 516.
   E: Milled.   Conder, 277 ; 129.

380. *R*: Laureate bust. LONG . LIVE . THE . KING. See Sussex, No. 25.
   E: SKIDMORE HOLBORN LONDON.

381. *R*: A cypher, *G. B.* FOR . THE . USE . OF . TRADE. See Sussex, No. 33.

382. *R*: Bust in cocked hat of GENERAL ELLIOT. See Warwickshire, No. 167.
   E: Engrailed.   Conder, 277 ; 128.

382*a*. As last, but *E*: Milled.

383. *R*: A woolpack, &c. As No. 368.
   E: Milled.   Conder, 283 ; 193.

384. *R*: A cypher, *W. G. M.* &c. See Wiltshire, No. 12.
   E: Milled.   Conder, 277 ; 130.

385. *R*: Arms, &c. As No. 369.
   E: Milled.   Conder, 277 ; 177.

386. *R*: A cypher, *I O M.* As No. 371.
   E: The same as No. 364.

387. *R*: Two busts, with date at sides. See Not Local, No. 95.

388. *R*: MUR'D BY THE FACTIOUS, &c. See Not Local, No. 91.
   E: Milled.

389. *R*: An anchor and cable. IN COMMEMORATION OF &c. See Not Local, No. 117.
   See also Nos. 401, 404, and 405 ; and Essex, Nos. 14, 15, 23, and 24.

   The rev. of No. 363 (a star) appears as an obv. with the following reverses :—

390. *R*: A cypher *W. G. M.* &c. As No. 384.
   E: Milled.

391. *R*: MUR'D BY THE FACTIOUS, &c. As No. 388.
   E: The same as last.

392. *R*: Anchor and cable. As No. 389.
   E: The same as last.

   The rev. of No. 375 (a guillotine) appears as an obv. with the following reverse :—

393. *R*: Two busts with the date at the sides as No. 387.
   See also Nos. 158, 573, 668, 708, and 719 ; Essex, No. 25 ; and Worcestershire, No. 26.

394. *O*: A figure of Minerva, TRUTH FOR MY HELM & JUSTICE FOR MY SHIELD.
   R: A cap of liberty radiated upon a pole. LIBERTAS 1796.
   E: SKIDMORE HOLBORN LONDON.   Conder, 96, 215.

This obv. occurs with the following reverses :—

395. *R*: A cypher *P. S. Co.* 1797 &c.   See No. 420.
Conder, 300 ; 371.

396. *R*: Three fleur-de-lis. 1790.
E: SPENCE × DEALER × IN × COINS × LONDON.
Conder, 300 ; 372.
See also Nos. 533, 677, 678, 684, and 713; Sussex, No. 34; and Warwickshire, No. 169.

397. *O*: Arms between branches. DEALER IN COINS MEDALS &c. within a circle. SKIDMORE . 123 HIGH . HOLBORN . LONDON.
R: An open book. HOLY BIBLE &c. See Nos. 435 and 436.
Conder, 265 ; 18.

398. *O*: The same as last.
R: A free-born Englishman. See No. 542.
Conder also gives at page 96, No. 217, this obv. with the rev. DUKE OF YORK, *but I have not seen the piece, nor have I heard of anyone else who has done so.*
The Church of St. Paul, Covent Garden, is so different to the remainder of Skidmore's churches, that it has been thought advisable to place it here, together with its various combinations.

✔ 399. *O*: View of a church, JAMES under. ST. PAULS COVENT GARDEN LONDON.
R: View of the same in ruins. DESTROY'D, BY, FIRE, SEPR. 17th . 1795.
E: SKIDMORE HOLBORN LONDON.

✔ 399*a*.   As last, but *E*: Milled. Conder, 100; 244.—Virt: 31.
399*b*.   „   „   *E*: Plain (not in collar).

This obv. occurs with the following reverses :—
✔ 400. *R*: Laureate bust to right. CHURCH AND KING.
E: Milled.   Conder, 100 ; 245.

✔ 401. *R*: A register stove, &c. as No. 361.
E: The same as No. 399.

402. *R*: Laureate bust to right. LONG . LIVE . THE . KING. See Sussex, No. 25.
E: The same as last.

403. *R*: A cypher. *I O M* &c. See Yorkshire, No. 11.
E: The same as last.   Conder, 268 ; 44.

The rev. of No. 399 appears as an obv. with the following reverses :—

404. *R*: Register stove, &c. as No. 361.

405. *R*: Two men at a forge, &c. as No. 361.
E: SKIDMORE HOLBORN LONDON.
405*a*.   As last, but *E*: Milled.

✔ 406. *R*: Bust to right. LONG . LIVE . THE . KING. As No. 402.
E: As No. 405.

407. *R* : Arms, &c. See Worcestershire, No. 22.
    E : As last.

408. *R* : A street, and spire of a church. See Yorkshire, No. 11.
    E : As last.   Conder, 268; 41.

409. *R* : Two busts, with the date at sides. See Not Local,
    No. 95.
    E : As last.

410. *R* : Bust in cocked hat. MAY THE FRENCH &c. See Not
    Local, No. 117.
    See also No. 159 ; *Essex, Nos.* 16 *and* 26 ; *Northumber-*
    land, No. 18 ; *Sussex, No.* 29 ; *Warwickshire, No.* 88 ;
    and Wiltshire, No. 13.

✓ 411. *O* : A man skating. HYDE PARK.
    R : A cypher *G. S.* HALFPENNY 1797.
    E : Milled.   Conder, 96 ; 216.—Virt : 168.

✓ 412. *O* : and *E* : The same as last.
    R : A cypher *G. B.* FOR THE USE OF TRADE. See Sussex,
    No. 33.   Conder, 283 ; 186.
    Many of these varieties of Skidmore's are rare, and some
    are exceedingly so.

Skidmore's Churches and Gates.

✓ 413. *O* : View of a church and houses. ST. MARY ABCHURCH LANE.
    Ex : JAcobs.
    R : A cypher *P. S. Co.* in a circle. DEDICATED TO COL-
    LECTORS OF MEDALS & COINS.   Conder, 97 ; 218.

✓ 414. *O* : View of a church.
    R : BUILT ANNO DOMO 1676 within a circle. ST. MARYS .
    ALDERMAN BURY.
    E : Milled.   Conder, 97 ; 219.—Virt : 44.

✓ 415. *O* : View of a church. ST. ANN'S ALDERSGATE. *Ex* : BT.
    1680.
    R : Cypher. As No. 413.   Conder, 97 ; 220.

✓ 416. *O* : View of a church. ST. BOTOLPH . ALDERSGATE . BUILT .
    1734. *Ex* : JAcobs.
    R : Cypher. As last.   Conder, 97 ; 221.—Virt : 180.

✓ 417. *O* : View of a church and houses. ST. BARTHOLOMEW THE
    GREAT . BT. 1628. *Ex* : JAcobs.
    R : Cypher. As last.   Conder, 97 ; 222.—Virt : 175.

✓ 418. *O* : View of a church. ST. BARTHOLOMEW . THE . LESS. *Ex* :
    JAcobs.
    R : Cypher. As last.   Conder, 97 ; 223.

✓ 419. *O* : View of a church. ST. MICHAEL . BASING-HALL ST. B. T.
    1679.
    R : Cypher. As last.   Conder, 97 ; 224.

420. *O*: View of a church. ST. MATHEWS'S . BETHNAL . GREEN . BT. 1740. *Ex*: JACOBS.
R: Cypher as before, with the date 1797 under. The legend as before. Conder, 83; 117.

421. *O*: View of a church. ST. MARY-AT-HILL BILLINGSGATE. *Ex*: JACOBS.
R: Cypher. As No. 413. Conder, 97; 225.

422. *O*: View of a church. ST. BOTOLPH . BISHOPSGATE . BUIT. 1727. *Ex*: JACOBS.
R: Cypher. As last. Conder, 98; 226.

423. *O*: View of a church. ST. ETHELBURGE . BISHOPSGATE . ST. A.D. 1701.
R: Cypher and date. As No. 420. Conder, 98; 227.

424. *O*: View of a church. GREAT ST. HELEN'S BISHOPSGATE ST. BT. 1669. *Ex*: JACOBS.
R: Cypher and date. As last. Conder, 98; 228.—Virt: 200.

425. *O*: View of a church. ST. ANN'S . BLACK-FRYARS. *Ex*: JACOBS.
R: Cypher and date. As last. Conder, 98; 229.

426. *O*: View of a church. ST. GEORGE'S BLOOMSBURY. BT. 1731.
R: Cypher. As No. 413. Conder, 112; 350.
Very rare.

427. *O*: View of a church and houses. ST. BOTOLPH . BOTOLPH LANE. *Ex*: JACOBS.
R: Cypher. As last. Conder, 98; 230.

428. *O*: View of a church. ST. MARY . BOW . LANE. *Ex*: JACOBS.
R: Cypher and date. As No. 420. Conder, 98; 231.

429. *O*: View of a church. ST. MILDRED'S . BREAD . ST. . BT. 1683. *Ex*: JACOBS.
R: Cypher and date. As last. Conder, 98; 232.

430. *O*: View of a church. ST. SWITHIN . CANNON . ST. *Ex*: JACOBS.
R: Cypher. As No. 413. Conder, 98; 233.—Virt: 233.

431. *O*: View of a church. ST. LAWRENCE . CATEATON . ST. B.T. *Ex*: 1677.
R: Cypher. As last. Conder, 99; 234.

432. *O*: View of a church. ST: MARY-LE-BOW CHEAPSIDE. 1673. *Ex*: JACOBS.
R: Cypher and date. As No. 420. Conder, 99; 235.

433. *O*: View of a church and houses. ST. JAMES'S CLERKENWELL BT. 1626. *Ex*: JACOBS.
R: Cypher and date. As last. Conder, 99; 236.

434. *O*: A different view. ST. JAMES . CLERKENWELL.
R: BUILT ANNO . DOMO 1792 in a circle between sprigs of leaves.
E: SKIDMORE HOLBORN LONDON. Conder, 99; 237.—Virt: 58.

' 434*a*.   As last, but *E* : Plain (in collar).

✓ 435. *O* : The same as last.
  R : Arms between small branches.   SKIDMORE . 123 . HIGH-
    HOLBORN . LONDON . DEALER IN COINS MEDALS &c.   See
    No. 397, *ante*.
  E : The same as No. 434.   Conder, 99 ; 238.—Virt : 58.
435*a*.   As last, but *E* : Plain (in collar).

✓ 436. *O* : The same as last.   See No. 397, *ante*.
  R : An open book inscribed HOLY BIBLE EXI CHAP. I radiated,
    RELIGION above, branches below.
  E : The same as No. 434.   Conder, 99 ; 239.—Virt : 58.

436*bis*. *O* : and *E* : The same as No. 434.
  R : Knife and fork.   USELESS.

✓ 437. *O* : View of a church.   ST. CATHERINE . COLEMAN . STREET .
    BT. 1714.   *Ex* : JACOBS.
  R : Cypher and date.   As No. 420.
                        Conder, 101 ; 250.—Virt : 199.
  This should have been Fenchurch Street.

✓ 438. *O* : View of a church and houses.   ST. STEPHENS . COLEMAN .
    ST. BT. 1670.   *Ex* : JACOBS.
  R : Cypher.   As No. 413.   Conder, 99 ; 240.—Virt : 96.

✓ 439. *O* : View of a church.   ST. MICHAEL . COLLEGE . HILL.   *Ex* :
    JACOBS.
  R : Cypher.   As last.   Conder, 100 ; 241.—Virt : 232.

✓ 440. *O* : View of a church.   ST. MICHAEL'S CORNHILL BT. 1670.
    Ex : JACOBS.
  R : Cypher and date.   As No. 420.
                        Conder, 100 ; 242.—Virt : 210.

✓ 441. *O* : View of a church.   ST. PETER'S CORNHILL BT. 1670.
    Ex : JACOBS.
  R : Cypher and date.   As last.   Conder, 100 ; 243.
  For St. Paul's, Covent Garden, see No. 399, &c., ante.

✓ 442. *O* : View of a church.   ST. GILES'S CRIPPLEGATE 1547.
  R : Cypher.   As No. 413.   Conder, 100 ; 246.

443. *O* : View of a church.   ALHALLOWS CRUTCH'D FRYERS.
    Ex : JACOBS.
  R : Cypher and date.   As No. 420.   Conder, 100 ; 247.

✓ 444. *O* : View of a church.   ST. JAMES'S . DUKES-PLACE . B . T .
    1622.
  R : Cypher.   As No. 413.   Conder, 100 ; 248.

445. *O* : View of a church.   ST. CLEMENTS EAST CHEAP.   *Ex* :
    JACOBS.
  R : Cypher.   As last.   Conder, 101 ; 249.

✓ 446. *O* : View of a church.   ST. MARY . MAGDALEN . OLD . FISH . ST.
    1685.   *Ex* : JACOBS.
  R : Cypher and date.   As No. 420.   Conder, 101 ; 251.

✓ 447. *O*: View of a church. ST. NICHOLAS . OLD . FISH-STREET.
   Ex: JACOBS.
  R: Cypher. As No. 413.   Conder, 101 ; 252.

  448. *O*: View of a church and houses. ST. BRIDE . FLEET ST. . B . T .
   1731.
  R: Cypher. As last.
  E: COVENTRY TOKEN.

448*a*.   As last, but *E*: Plain (in collar).   Conder, 101 ; 253.

✓ 449. *O*: View of a church. ST. DUNSTAN'S FLEET ST.   *Ex*: B . T .
   1701.
  R: Cypher. As last.   Conder, 101 ; 254.

✓ 450. *O*: View of a church. ST. MATHEW'S FRIDAY STREET BUILT
   1670. *Ex*: JACOBS.
  R: Cypher. As last.   Condor, 101 ; 255.—Virt: 175.

✓ 451. *O*: View of a' church. ST. JAMES'S GARLICK . HITH. *Ex*:
   B . T . 1683.
  R: Cypher. As last.   Conder, 101 ; 256.

✓ 452. *O*: View of a church. ST. GILES'S . IN . THE . FIELDS . B . T .
   1733.
  R: Cypher. As last.   Conder, 102 ; 257.

✓ 453. *O*: View of a church. ST. BENNET . GRACECHURCH ST. A.D.
   1685. *Ex*: JACOBS.
  R: Cypher and date. As No. 420.   Conder, 102 ; 258.

  454. *O*: View of a church. ST. GEORGE'S HANOVER SQUARE. *Ex*:
   BUILT 1724 JACOBS.
  R: A dove flying with an olive branch, in a wreath.
   DEDICATED . TO . COLLECTORS . OF . MEDALS . & COINS.
   There are no berries in the wreath, excepting at the
   tips, where there are spikes of them.
         Conder, 102 ; 259.—Virt: 74.

   Also struck in white metal.

✓ 455. *O*: The same as last.
  R: Similar, but there are berries in the wreath, which
   terminates with leaves; the outside leaves next to the
   tie are double.   Conder, 102 ; 260.

   These are both rare, the former especially so.

✓ 456. *O*: The same as last.
  R: The wreath similar to last, but the outside bottom
   leaves are single. There are no dots in legends.
         Conder, 102 ; 261.

   The rev. of No. 456 occurs as an obv. with the
   following reverse:—

✓ 457. *R*: A cypher *G B* FOR THE USE OF TRADE. See Sussex,
   No. 33.

   See also Warwickshire, No. 237.

458. *O* : View of a church and part of a house. JACOBS on the
left-hand side.
  R : ST. ANDREW'S . HOLBORN (No. 2).   Three circles, and in
the centre, BUILT . ANNO DOMO 1704 . in three lines,
with a small ornament top and bottom.
  E : SKIDMORE HOLBORN LONDON.
                          Conder, 102 ; 262.—Virt : 58.

459. *O* : View of a church. ST. ANDREW . LEADENHALL ST.   *Ex* :
Jacobs.
  R : Cypher and date.   As No. 420.   Conder, 102 ; 263.

460. *O* : View of a church.   ALLHALLOWS . LOMBARD . STREET
BUILT 1672.
  R : Cypher and date.   As last.   Conder, 102 ; 264.

461. *O* : View of a church and part of a house.   ST. EDMOND .
THE . KING . LOMBARD ST.   *Ex* : Jacobs.
  R : Cypher.   As No. 413.   Conder, 103 ; 265.—Virt : 232.

462. *O* : View of a church. ST. MARY . WOOLNORTH . LOMBARD . ST.
Ex : Jacobs.
  R : Cypher.   As last.   Conder, 103 ; 266.—Virt. 233.

463. *O* : View of a church.   ST. MAGNUS LONDON . BRIDGE 1676.
  R : Cypher.   As last.   Conder, 103 ; 267.

464. *O* : View of a church. ST. ALPHAGE LONDON-WALL . A . D .
1701.   *Ex* : Jacobs.
  R : Cypher and date.   As No. 420.   Conder, 103 ; 268.

465. *O* : View of a church and houses.   ST. MARGARETS . LOTH-
BURY . BT. 1690.   *Ex* : Jacobs.
  R : Cypher.   As No. 413.   Conder, 103 ; 269.

466. *O* : View of a church. ST. MARY'S . LOVE . LANE. *Ex*: B . T .
1781.
  R : Cypher.   As last.   Conder, 103 ; 270.

467. *O* : View of a church and houses.   ST. MARTIN'S LUDGATE.
Ex : BUILT 1672 Jacobs.
  R : Cypher.   As last.   Conder, 103 ; 271.—Virt : 83.

468. *O* : Similar to last, but not showing the houses at sides.
  R : Cypher.   As last.   Conder, 103 ; 272.—Virt : 83.

469. *O* : View of a church. ST. TRINITY . MINORIES. *Ex* : Jacobs.
  R : Cypher.   As last.   Conder, 103 ; 273.

470. *O* : View of a church and a pump.   ST. OLIVES . OLD-JEWRY.
B . T.   *Ex* : 1710.
  R : Cypher.   As last.   Conder, 104 ; 274.

471. *O* : View of a church. ST. LUKE'S . OLD ST. BUILT . 1732.
Ex : Jacobs.
  R : An open book.   As No. 436.
  E : SKIDMORE HOLBORN LONDON.

471*a*.   As last, but *E* : Plain (in collar).
                          Conder, 104 ; 275.—Virt : 61.

v 472. *O*: View of a church. PADDINGTON . NEW-CHURCH. *Ex*:
       A.D. 1791.
       R: Cypher and date. As No. 420.   Conder, 113; 353.

v 473. *O*: View of a church. ST. BENNET'S . PAUL'S . WHARF . built .
       1670. *Ex*: JACOBS.
       R: Cypher and date. As last.   Conder, 104; 276.

v 474. *O*: A similar view. ST. BENNET PAUL'S-WHARF. *Ex*: A.D.
       1691.
       R: Cypher and date. As last.   Conder, 104; 277.

v 475. *O*: View of a church. ST. MILDRED'S . IN . THE . POULTRY .
       BT. 1671. *Ex*: JACOBS..
       R: Cypher and date. As last.   Conder, 104; 278.

v 476. *O*: View of a church. ST. MICHAEL . QUEENHITHE . B . T .
       1676.
       R: Cypher. As No. 413.

v 477. *O*: View of a church. ST. GEORGE'S . QUEEN . SQUARE BT.
       1706. *Ex*: JACOBS.
       R: Cypher. As No. 420. Conder, 104; 280.—Virt: 223.

v 478. *O*: View of a church. ST. PAULS . SHADWEL.. *Ex*: JACOBS.
       R: Cypher. As No. 413.   Conder, 104; 281.

v 479. *O*: View of a church. ST. SEPULCHER . SNOW-HILL. *Ex*:
       JACOBS.
       R: Cypher and date. As No. 420.   Conder, 104; 282.

v 480. *O*: View of a church. SHOREDITCH CHURCH . B. T. 1791.
       R: Cypher. As No. 413.
       E: COVENTRY TOKEN.

   480a.   As last, but *E*: Plain (in collar).   Conder, 105; 283.

v 481. *O*: View of a church. ST. ANN'S SOHO. *Ex*: B . T . 1686.
       R: Cypher. As last.   Conder, 105; 284.

v 482. *O*: View of a church. SPITALFIELDS CHURCH . B . T . 1727.
       R: Cypher. As last.
       E: COVENTRY TOKEN.

   482a.   As last, but *E*: Plain (in collar).   Conder, 105; 285.

   483. *O*: View of a church. STEPNEY CHURCH . A . D . 1612.
       R: Cypher. As last.
       E: The same as No. 482.

v 483a.   As last, but *E*: Plain (in collar).   Conder, 113; 354.

v 484. *O*: View of a church. STOKE . NEWINGTON . CHURCH . *Ex*:
       JACOBS.
       R: Cypher. As last.   Conder, 113; 355.—Virt: 232.

v 485. *O*: View of a church. ST. CLEMENT'S . STRAND . *Ex*:
       JACOBS.
       R: Cypher. As last.   Conder, 105; 286.

✓ 486. *O*: View of a church and part of a house. ALHALLOWS . THAMES ST. *Ex*: BT. 1683. JACOBS.
   R: Cypher. As last.   Conder, 105; 287.—Virt: 96.

✓ 487. *O*: View of a church. ST. MARTIN. OUTWICH THREADNEEDLE ST. BT. 1540. *Ex*: JACOBS.
   R: Cypher. As last.   Conder, 105; 288.—Virt: 171.

✓ 488. *O*: An ancient edifice and houses. THE . CHAPEL . IN . THE . TOWER . BUILT . 1371. *Ex*: JACOBS.
   R: Cypher and date. As No. 420.
                   Conder, 105; 289.—Virt: 211.

✓ 489. *O*: View of a church. ST. MARGARET PATTENS . LITTLE . TOWER . ST. *Ex*: JACOBS.
   R: Cypher. As No. 413.   Conder, 105; 290.

✓ 490. *O*: View of a church, and part of a house. ST. STEPHEN'S : WALBROOK . BT. *Ex*: -1676- JACOBS.
   R: Cypher. As last.   Conder, 105; 291.—Virt: 90.

491. *O*: View of a church. ST. JOHN'S WAPPING. *Ex*: JACOBS.
   R: Cypher. As last.   Conder, 106; 292.

✓ 492. *O*: View of a church. ST. JAMES'S WESTMINSTER . BT. *Ex*: 1684. JACOBS.
   R: Cypher and date. As No. 420.
                   Conder, 112; 351.—Virt: 200.

✓ 493. *O*: View of a church. ST. MARY'S . WHITECHAPEL . *Ex*: JACOBS.
   R: Cypher. As No. 413. Conder, 106; 293.—Virt: 233.

✓ 494. *O*: View of a church. WILLSDON CHURCH . MIDDX. A . D . 1217.
   R: Cypher. As last.   Conder, 113; 356.

✓ 495. *O*: View of a church. ST. ALBANS . WOOD ST. B . T . 1685.
   R: Cypher. As last.
   E: COVENTRY TOKEN.

495a.   As last, but *E*: Plain (in collar). Conder, 106; 294.

✓ 496. *O*: View of a church and houses. ST. MICHAEL WOOD . ST. BUILT . 1671. *Ex*: JACOBS.
   R: Cypher and date. As No. 420.
                   Conder, 106; 295.—Virt: 211.

Other views of churches by Skidmore will be found at Bedfordshire, No. 1; and Surrey, Nos. 6, 7, and 20-25.

✓ 497. *O*: An ancient gateway. ALDGATE 1796. *Ex*: JACOBS.
   R: Cypher. As No. 413. Conder, 106; 296.—Virt: 96.

✓ 498. *O*: An ancient gateway. ALDERSGATE . BUILT 1670. *Ex*: JACOBS.
   R: Cypher and date. As No. 420. Conder, 106; 297.

v 499. *O*: The same gateway. ALDERSGATE. *Ex*: BT. 1670. JACOBS.
    R: Cypher and date. As last.
                    Conder, 106 ; 298.—Virt: 198.

v 500. *O*: An ancient gateway. BISHOPSGATE . BT. 1733. *Ex*: JACOBS.
    R: Cypher. As No. 413. Conder, 106 ; 299.—Virt : 170.

v 501. *O*: An ancient gateway. BRIDGE-GATE . BT. 1728. In the gateway. JACOBS.
    R: Cypher. As last.   Conder, 106 ; 300.—Virt : 170.

v 502. *O*: An ancient gateway. CRIPPLEGATE. *Ex*: 1796. JACOBS.
    R: Cypher. As last.   Conder, 107 ; 302.—Virt: 169.

v 503. *O*: An ancient gateway. SAINT JOHN'S-GATE. *Ex*: JACOBS.
    R: Cypher and date. As No. 420.   Conder, 106 ; 301.

504. *O*: An ancient gateway. LUDGATE BT. 1586. *Ex*: JACOBS. (The legend is above the gate.)
    R: Cypher. As No. 413. Conder, 107 ; 304.—Virt: 171.

505. *O*: The same gateway. LUDGATE . BUILT . 1586. *Ex*: JACOBS.
    R: Cypher. As last.   Conder, 107 ; 303.

v 506. *O*: The same gateway. LUDGATE BT. 1586. *Ex*: JACOBS. (The legend is at the sides of the gate.)
    R: Cypher. As last.   Conder, 107 ; 304.

v 507. *O*: An ancient gateway. MOORGATE. *Ex*: 1796. JACOBS.
    R: Cypher. As last.   Conder, 107 ; 306.—Virt: 102.

v 508. *O*: An ancient gateway with a ventilator at top. NEWGATE . BT. 1670. On the ground JACOBS.
    R: Cypher. As last.   Conder, 107 ; 307.—Virt: 169.

v 509. *O*: An ancient gateway and houses. TEMPLE BAR 1796. *Ex*: JACOBS.
    R: Cypher. As last.   Conder, 107 ; 308.—Virt: 96.

v 510. *O*: An ancient gateway. WHITEHALL GATE BT. 1532. *Ex*: JACOBS.
    R: Cypher. As last.   Conder, 113; 352.—Virt: 177.

Spence's.

v 511. *O*: Bust to left. JAMES under it. . T. SPENCE ❖ 7 MONTHS IMPRISON'D FOR HIGH TREASON ❖
    R: THOS. SPENCE | Sir THOS. MORE | THOS. PAINE | NOTED ADVOCATES FOR THE RIGHTS OF MAN *
                  Conder, 296 ; 326.
    For this rev. see also Nos. 549, 559, 623, 634, 639, 653, 685, and 695; and Northumberland, Nos. 5 and 19. This obverse occurs with the following reverses :—

v 512. *R*: Britannia seated, a cap of liberty falling from her
      spear. ROUSE BRITANNIA.
                    Conder, 296; 330.—Virt: 112.

v 513. *R*: A caduceus between a crown and cap of liberty. WE
      WERE BORN FREE AND WILL NEVER DIE SLAVES.
      E: SPENCE × DEALER × IN × COINS × LONDON ×
                    Conder, 297; 336.

514. *R*: A cat. MY FREEDOM I AMONG SLAVES ENJOY.
      E: The same as last.   Conder, 297; 337.

515. *R*: Three citizens armed. WHO KNOW THEIR RIGHTS AND
      KNOWING DARE MAINTAIN. *Ex*: 1795.
      E: As last, but stars instead of crosses.
                    Conder, 296; 331.

515*a*.   As last, but *E*: Engrailed.
515*b*.   „   „   *E*: Milled.
515*c*.   „   „   *E*: Plain (not in collar).

516. *R*: A heart in a hand, JAMES under, within a wreath of
      laurel. HONOUR.
      E: The same as No. 513.

516*a*.   As last, but *E*: Milled.
v 516*b*.   „   „   *E*: Plain (not in collar).
                    Conder, 296; 328.

517. *R*: A Highlander. THE GALLANT GARB OF SCOTLAND·ː· See
      Lothian, No. 13.
      E: The same as No. 513.   Conder, 296; 335.

v 518. *R*: An Indian. IF RENTS I ONCE CONSENT TO PAY MY LIBERTY
      IS PAST AWAY.
      E: The same as last.   Conder, 110; 331.

519. *R*: A lion dismayed at a cock crowing. LET TYRANTS TREMBLE
      AT THE CROW OF LIBERTY. *Ex*: 1795.
      E: The same as last.   Conder, 296; 332.

519*a*.   As last, but *E*: The same as No. 515.
519*b*.   „   „   *E*: Engrailed.
519*c*.   „   „   *E*: Plain (not in collar).

520. *R*: The head of a man and an ass conjoined. ODD * FEL-
      LOWS * A MILLION HOGG . A GUINEA PIG * 1795.
      E: The same as No. 513.

520*a*.   As last, but *E*: The same as No. 515.
520*b*.   „   „   *E*: Milled.
520*c*.   „   „   *E*: Plain (not in collar).
                    Conder, 296; 329.

521. *R*: Cain killing Abel. THE BEGINING OF OPPRESSION. (The
      N's are retrograde.)
      E: The same as No. 513.   Conder, 296; 333.

522. *R:* A pair of breeches on fire, a serpent with a man's head under. PANDORAS . BREECHES.
   E: Milled.

✔ 523. *R:* Three men dancing and one eating at a table, under a tree. AFTER THE REVOLUTION.
   E: The same as No. 513   Conder, 296; 334.

524. *R:* A shepherd lying under a tree. *Ex:* 1790. See Worcestershire, No. 7.
   E: The same as last.   Conder, 296; 327.

524*a.*   As last; but *E:* Milled.

✔ 524*b.*   „   „   *E:* Plain (not in collar).

525. *R:* A soldier shaking hands with two citizens. WE ALSO ARE THE PEOPLE. *Ex:* 1796.
   E: The same as No. 513.   Conder, 297; 338.—Virt: 225.

525*a.*   As last, but *E:* Plain (not in collar).

526. *R:* Soldiers besieging a city. See Sussex, No. 7.
          Conder, 296; 325.

✔ 527. *R:* Two boys at a turnstile. LITTLE TURNSTILE HALFPENNY. 1796.   Conder, 297; 339.

528. *R:* T. SPENCE | BOOKSELLER | DEALER IN | PRINTS & COINS | N 8 | LITTLE | TURNSTILE HOLBORN | LONDON.
          Conder, 296; 324.
   This rev. becomes an obverse with the following reverses:—

529. *R:* Bust to right. JAMES under it. RT. HE. C. J. FOX.
          Conder, 277; 131.

530. *R:* Bust to left in broad-brimmed hat. LD. GEO. GORDON DIED IN NEWGATE NOV. 1 . 1793.   Conder, 279; 151.

531. *R:* An Indian. As No. 518.

✔ 532. *R:* A sailor boy. MARINE SOCIETY BOY.
   E: The same as No. 513.   Conder, 109; 322.

532*a.*   As last, but *E:* Plain (not in collar).

533. *R:* A figure of Minerva standing. TRUTH FOR MY HELM & JUSTICE FOR MY SHIELD. See *ante,* No. 393.

534. *R:* A Spaniard. ❖ THE HABIT OF A SPANIARD ❖
   E: The same as No. 513.

✔ 534*a,*   As last, but *E:* Plain (not in collar).
          Conder, 110; 330.

535. *R:* Bust to right. JAMES under it. JOHN THELWALL.
          Conder, 297; 340.

536. *R:* Bust to right. JACOBS . F. under it. HORNE TOOKE ESQ.
          Conder, 298; 348.

✔ 537. *R:* A Turk. THE HABIT OF A TURK.   Conder, 110; 335.

538. *R*: A collegian. A . WESTMINSTER . SCHOLAR.
    E: The same as No. 513.   Conder, 111; 338.
538*a*.   As last, but *E*: Plain (not in collar).
539. *R*: T | SPENCE | BOOKSELLER | DEALER ⸪ IN | PRINTS | . & . |
    COINS | displayed in seven lines with a radiation above,
    LITTLE TURNSTILE NO. 8 HOLBORN LONDON.

    This rev. becomes an obverse with the following
    reverses :—

540. *R*: A Christ's Hospital scholar. ⸪ A BLUE COAT BOY ⸪
    E: The same as No. 513.   Conder, 108; 312.
540*a*.   As last, but *E*: Plain (not in collar).
541. *R*: A youth with a stick in his hand. * A BRIDEWELL BOY *
    E: The same as No. 513.   Conder, 108; 313.
542. *R*: A man fettered, and a padlock on his mouth. A FREE-
    BORN '. ENGLISHMAN 1796.   Conder, 108; 317.
543. *R*: A Highlander. As No. 517.   Conder, 109; 238.
544. *R*: An Indian. As No. 518.
545. *R*: After the Revolution. As No. 523. Conder, 293; 273.
546. *R*: A sailor. A TRUE HEARTED SAILOR. *Ex*: JAMES.
    E: The same as No. 513.   Conder, 293; 294.
547. *R*: A snail, &c. A SNAIL MAY PUT ITS HORNS OUT. See
    Worcester, No. 20.
    E: The same as No. 513.   Conder, 295; 321.
547*a*.   As last, but *E*: Plain (not in collar).
548. *R*: A turnstile. As No. 527.   Conder, 300; 375.
    See also Anglesea, No. 226.

Ass.

O: An ass bearing two pairs of paniers, labelled " RENTS "
    and " TAXES." I WAS AN ASS TO BEAR THE FIRST PAIR ⸪
    This obv. occurs with the following reverses:—

549. *R*: THOS. SPENCE, &c. As No. 511.
    E: The same as No. 513.   Conder, 107; 311.
549*a*.   As last, but *E*: SKIDMORE HOLBORN LONDON.
550. *R*: Britannia. As No. 512.
    E: The same as No. 513.   Conder, 266; 22.
551. *R*: Free-born Englishman. As No. 542.
    Conder, 266; 25.—Virt: 225.
552. *R*: Indian. As No. 518.
    E: The same as No. 513.   Conder, 266; 26.—Virt: 224.
553. *R*: Lion dismayed. As No. 519.
    E: The same as last.   Conder, 266; 24.
554. *R*: Odd Fellows. As No. 520.
    E: Milled.
554*a*.   As last, but *E*: Plain (not in collar).

555. *R*: After the Revolution. As No. 523.   Conder, 266; 23.
556. *R*: Turnstile. As No. 527.   Conder, 266; 27.

Blue Coat Boy.

✓ 557. *O*: Figure of a scholar. As No. 540.
     R: Figure of a collegian. As No. 538. Conder, 301; 387.

Bridewell Bay.

558. *O*: Figure of a youth. As No. 541.
     R: Bust to left. ✳ D. MENDOZA ✳   Conder, 269; 49,

     Britannia (Rouse). See Nos. 512, 550, 561, 578, 594,
       607, 604, 654, 660, 694 ; Northumberland, No. 6 ;
       and Worcester, No. 9.

British Liberty.

   O: A sailor seizing a landsman. ✳ BRITISH ✳ LIBERTY ✳
     DISPLAYED ✳ *Ex*: 1795.

   This obv. occurs with the following reverses :—
559. *R*: THOS. SPENCE &c.   As No. 511.
     E: PAYABLE IN LONDON.   The remainder engrailed.
                       Conder, 269; 50.
560. *R*: Two men boxing. FASHIONABLE AMUSEMENTS.
     R: The same as No. 513.   Conder, 270; 61.
560*a*.   As last, but *E*: Milled.
✓ 561. *R*: Britannia. As No. 512.
     E.R: The same as No. 559.   Conder, 108; 314.
562. *R*: Caduceus. As No. 513.
     E: The same as No. 513.   Conder, 270; 60.
563. *R*: Citizens armed. As No. 515.
     E: The same as No. 513.
     E: SKIDMORE HOLBORN LONDON.
563*a*.   As last, but *E*: The same as No. 513.
563*b*.   „   „   *E*: Plain (not in collar). Conder, 269; 55.
564. *R*: Free-born Englishman. As No. 542.
     E: The same as No. 513.   Conder, 270; 58.
564*a*.   As last, but *E*: Milled.
565. *R*: Heart and hand. As No 516.
     E: The same as No. 559.   Conder, 269; 52.
566. *R*: Indian. As No. 518.
     E: The same as No. 513.   Conder, 270; 59.
567. *R*: Lion dismayed. As No. 519.   Conder, 269; 53.
568. *R*: Odd Fellows. As No. 520.
     E: The same as No. 559.   Conder, 269; 54.
569. *R*: The beginning of Oppression. As No. 521.
     E: The same as No. 513.   Conder, 270; 56.

570. *R*: After the Revolution. As No. 523. Conder, 270; 57.
571. *R*: Shepherd. As No. 524.
      E: The same as No. 559.   Conder, 269; 51.
572. *R*: Turnstile. As No. 527.   Conder, 270; 62.
573. *R*: A guillotine and part of a house. See No. 375, *ante*.

> *Cat.* See Nos. 514, 585, 625, and 662; Essex, No. 27;
> Northumberland, No. 7; Worcestershire, No. 11; and
> Not Local, No. 119.
> *Citizens armed.* See Nos. 515, 563, 596, 626, 642,
> 655, 663, 686, and 698; Northumberland, No. 8;
> and Worcestershire, No. 12.

Coining Press.

O: A " COINING PRESS." INSCRIBED TO THE COLLECTORS OF
MEDALS * 1796.

This obv. occurs with the following reverses :—
574. *R*: Two men boxing. As No. 560.
      E: The same as No. 513.   Conder, 271; 72.
574*a*.   As last, but *E*: Plain (not in collar).
575. *R*: A harp crowned, between thistles. ENGLAND . IRELAND .
      SCOTLAND.
      E: The same as No. 513.   Conder, 271; 73.
576. *R*: Highlander. As No. 517.
      E: The same as last.   Conder, 271; 71.—Virt: 74.
v 577. *R*: Turnstile. As No. 527.   Conder, 108; 315.

Deserted Village.

O: A village in ruins. ONE ONLY MASTER GRASPS THE WHOLE
DOMAIN.

This obv. occurs with the following reverses :—
v 578. *R*: Britannia, &c. As No. 512.   Conder, 301; 383.
579. *R*: Highlander. As No. 517.
      E: The same as No. 513.   Conder, 301; 386.
579*a*.   As last, but *E*: Milled.
580. *R*: Indian. As No. 518.
      E: The same as last.   Conder, 301; 385.
v 581. *R*: Lion dismayed. As. No. 519.
      E: The same as last.   Conder, 111; 337.
581*a*.   As last, but *E*: Plain (not in collar).
582. *R*: The beginning of Oppression. As No. 521.
      E: The same as No. 513.   Conder, 301; 384.
583. *R*: Shepherd. As No. 524.   Conder, 301; 382.

Dog.

O: A dog. MUCH GRATITUDE BRINGS SERVITUDE.
This obv. occurs with the following reverses :—
584. *R*: A caduceus. As No. 513.
      E: The same as No. 513.   Conder, 272; 81.

v 585. *R* : A cat. As No. 514.
  E : The same as last.   Conder, 108 ; 316.
 586. *R* : Free-born Englishman. As No. 542. Conder, 272 ; 79.
 587. *R* : Highlander. As No. 517.
  E : The same as No. 513.   Conder, 272 ; 80.
 587*bis*. *R* : The beginning of Oppression. As No. 521.
  E : The same as last.   Conder, 272 ; 77.
 588. *R* : After the Revolution. As No. 523.
  E : The same as last.   Conder, 272 ; 78,
 588*a*. As last, but *E* : Milled.
 589. *R* : Turnstile. As No. 527.   Conder, 272 ; 82.

Englishman (Freeborn.)

 O : A man fettered, &c. As No. 542.
  This obv. occurs with the following reverse :—
 590. *R* : Three citizens armed. As No. 515.
  E : Milled.
  See also Nos. 398, 551, 564, 586, 619, and 676.

English Slavery.

 O : A fat man, sitting at a table eating. ENGLISH SLAVERY.
  This obv. occurs with the following reverses :—
 591. *R* : A lean man on the ground, gnawing a bone. FRENCH
  LIBERTY.   Conder, 221 ; 92.
 592. *R* : Arms of London. SCALES WEIGHTS & STEELYARDS. See
  No. 265, *ante*.   Conder, 276 ; 120.
 593. *R* : An anchor, and cap of liberty. LIBERTY . PEACE .
  COMMERCE. See Not Local, No. 123.
        Conder, 276 ; 117.
  *See also Nos. 605 and 734; Cambridgeshire, No. 20;
  and Munster, No. 14.*

Fox.

 O : Bust of Fox. As No. 529.
  This obv. occurs with the following reverses :—
 ·594. *R* : Britannia. As No. 512.
  E : The same as No. 513. Conder, 278 ; 135.
 594*a*. As last, but *E* : Plain (not in collar).
v 595. *R* : Caduceus. As No. 513.
  E : The same as No. 513. Conder, 108 ; 319.—Virt : 60.
 595*a*. As last, but *E* : Milled.
 596. *R* : Citizens armed. As No. 515.
  E : The same as No. 513. Conder, 278 ; 136.
 596*a*. As last, but *E* : Milled.
 596*b*. „ „ *E* : Engrailed.

✔ 597. *R* : Indian. As No. 518.
    E : The same as No. 513.   Conder, 278 ; 138.
✔ 598. *R* : Lion dismayed. As No. 519.
    E : The same as last.   Conder, 277 ; 133.
  599. *R* : Odd Fellows. As No. 520.
    E : The same as last.   Conder, 277 ; 134.
  600. *R* : The beginning of Oppression. As No. 521.
    E : The same as last.   Conder, 278 ; 137.
  601. *R* : Shepherd. As No. 524.
    E : The same as last.   Conder, 277 ; 132.
  601*a*. As last, but *E* : Engrailed.
  601*b*.   „   „   *E* : Plain (not in collar).
✔ 602. *R* : Soldier and two citizens. As No. 525.
    E : The same as last.   Conder, 108 ; 318.
✔ 603. *R* : Turnstile. As No. 527.   Conder, 278 ; 139.
  604. *R* : A tree with two shields leaning against it. A.FRIEND.
    TO.PEACE.AND.LIBERTY. *Ex* : Jacobs.
    E : Engrailed.   Conder, 221 ; 97.
  604*a*. As last, but *E* : Milled.
  604*b*.   „   „   *E* : Plain (not in collar).
    See Somersetshire, No. 39 ; and Not Local, Nos. 88
    and 89.

French Liberty.

    O : A lean man gnawing a bone, &c. As No. 591.
    This obv. occurs with the following reverses :—
  605. *R* : The arms of London, &c. As No. 592.
                                       Conder, 279 ; 146.
  606. *R* : An anchor, &c. As No. 593.   Conder, 279 ; 149.
    See also Nos. 591 and 735 ; Cambridgeshire, No. 21 ;
    Northumberland, No. 26 ; Surrey, No. 17 ; and
    Munster, No. 15.

Gordon.

    O : Bust of Ld. Geo. Gordon. As No. 530.
    This obv. occurs with the following reverses :—
  607. *R* : Britannia. As No. 512.
    E : The same as No. 513.   Conder, 279 ; 153.
  608. *R* : Caduceus. As No. 513.
    E : The same as last.   Conder, 280 ; 155.
  609. *R* : Heart and hand. As No. 516.
    E : The same as last.   Conder, 279 ; 152.
  610. *R* : The beginning of Oppression. As No. 521.
    E : The same as last.   Conder, 279 ; 154.
  611. *R* : After the Revolution. As No. 523.   Conder, 280 ; 156.
✔ 612. *R* : View of a public building. SESSIONS-HOUSE OLD BAILY.
    E : The same as No. 513.   Conder, 109 ; 321.

612*a*.   As last, but *E*: Plain (not in collar).

613. *R*: Turnstile. As No. 527.   Conder, 280; 157.

∨ 614. *O*: Bust to left, without any legend.
    R: LORD | GEORGE | GORDON | 1780.
    E: The same as No. 513.   Conder, 109; 320.—Virt: 60.

> *Heart and hand.* See Nos. 379, 516, 565, 609, 627,
> 628, 643, 649, 656, 687, 699, 711; also Bucking-
> hamshire, No. 6; Northumberland, Nos. 9 and 20;
> and Worcestershire, No. 13.
> *Highlander.* See Nos. 517, 543, 576, 579, 587, 629,
> 700 and 718; Northumberland, Nos. 10 and 21; and
> Worcestershire, No. 14.
> *Indian.* See Nos. 518, 531, 544, 552, 566, 580, 597,
> 635, 644, 657, and 701.
> *Lion dismayed.* See Nos. 519, 552, 566, 580, 630,
> 658, 664, and 702; Northumberland, No. 11; and
> Worcestershire, No. 15.

Marine Society Boy.

O: A sailor boy. As No. 532.
This obv. occurs with the following reverses:—

615. *R*: A true-hearted sailor. As No. 537.
    E: The same as No. 513.   Conder, 285; 215.

615*a*.   As last, but *E*: Plain (not in collar).

616. *R*: Turnstile. As No. 527.   Conder, 285; 216.

Mendoza.

O: A bust of D. Mendoza. As No. 558.
This obv. occurs with the following reverses:—

∨ 617. *R*: Two men boxing. As No. 560.
    E: The same as No. 513.   Conder, 109; 323.—Virt: 75.

618. *R*: Shepherd. As No. 524.   Conder, 285; 217.

Odd Fellows.

O: Head of man and ass conjoined. As No. 520.
This obv. occurs with the following reverses:—

619. *R*: Free-born Englishman. As No. 542.

620. *R*: Two men dancing round a fire. THE END OF OPPRESSION.
    E: The same as No. 513.

621. *R*: The heads of Pitt and Fox conjoined. ODD . FELLOWS.
    QUIS RIDES.
    E: The same as last.   Conder, 232; 182.

621*a*.   As last, but *E*: The same as No. 515.

621*b*.   ,,   ,,   *E*: Plain.

622. *R*: Four men dancing round a pole, surmounted by a head
    radiated. TREE OF LIBERTY.
    E: Milled.

622a.   As last, but *E*: Plain (not in collar). Conder, 299; 360.

    See also Nos. 568, 599, 659, *and* 688; *Northumberland,
    No.* 12; *and Worcestershire, No.* 16.

Odd Fellows (Quis Rides).

O: The same as *R*: of No. 621.
    This obv. occurs with the following reverses :—

✔ 623. *R*: THOS. SPENCE, &c. As No. 511.   Conder, 287; 230.

623*bis*. *R*: Britannia. As No. 512.
    E: The same as No. 513.   Conder, 288; 242.

624. *R*: Caduceus. As No. 513.
    E: The same as last.   Conder, 287; 236.

625. *R*: Cat. As No. 514.
    E: The same as last.   Conder, 287; 237.

626. *R*: Citizens armed. As No. 515.
    E: PAYABLE IN LONDON. Remainder engrailed.

626a.   As last, but *E*: Milled.   Conder, 287; 233.

626b.   ,,   ,, *E*: Plain (not in collar).

627. *R*: Heart in hand. As No. 516.
    E: The same as No. 513.

627a.   As last, but *E*: Milled.   Conder, 231; 181.

✔ 627b.   ,,   ,, *E*: Plain (not in collar). This latter is
    sometimes found on very small flans.

628.   Similar to last, but with the addition of a neat border
    of dots on both sides.   Conder, 231; 180.

629. *R*: Highlander. As No. 517.
    E: The same as No. 513.   Conder, 287; 235.

630. *R*: Lion dismayed. As No. 519.
    E: The same as No. 515.

630a.   As last, but *E*: As No. 626.

630b.   ,,   ,, *E*: Plain (not in collar). Conder, 287; 232.

631. *R*: Shepherd. As No. 524.
    E: The same as No. 626.   Conder, 287; 231.

631a.   As last, but *E*: Plain (not in collar).

632. *R*: Soldiers besieging a city. As No. 526.
                                Conder, 286; 229.

633. *R*: Turnstile. As No. 527.   Conder, 287; 238.

Oppression (Beginning of).

O: Cain killing Abel. As No. 521.
    This obv. occurs with the following reverses :—

634. *R*: THOS. SPENCE, &c. As No. 511.

9 *

635. *R*: Indian. As No. 518.
ᵥ 636. *R*: End of Oppression. As No. 620.
　　E: The same as No. 513.   Conder, 109; 324.
ᵥ 637. *R*: Odd Fellows (Quis Rides). As No. 621.
　　E: The same as last.   Conder, 287; 234.
637*a*.   As last, but *E*: Milled.
638. *R*: Shepherd. As No. 524.
　　E: The same as last.

Oppression (End of).

O: Two men dancing. As No. 620.
　　This obv. occurs with the following reverses :—
639. *R*: THOS. SPENCE, &c. As No. 511.
　　E: The same as 513.   Conder, 287; 239.—Virt: 224.
640. *R*: Britannia. As No. 512.
　　E: The same as last.   Conder, 288; 242.
641. *R*: Caduceus. As No. 513.
　　E: The same as last.   Conder, 288; 246.
642. *R*: Citizens armed. As No. 515.
　　E: The same as last.   Conder, 288; 243.
642*a*.   As last, but *E*: SKIDMORE HOLBORN LONDON.
643. *R*: Heart and hand. As No. 516.
　　E: The same as No. 513.   Conder, 288; 241.
643*a*.   As last, but *E*: The same as No. 642*a*.
644. *R*: Indian. As No. 518.
　　E: The same as No. 513.   Conder, 288; 245.
645. *R*: After the Revolution. As No. 523.
　　E: The same as last.   Conder, 288; 244.
645*a*.   As last, but *E*: Plain.   Conder, 291; 275.
646. *R*: Shepherd. As No. 524.
　　E: The same as No. 513.   Conder, 288; 240.
646*a*.   As last, but *E*: SKIDMORE HOLBORN LONDON.
646*b*.   „   „   *E*: The same as No. 626.
647. *R*: Turnstile. As No. 527.
　　E: The same as No. 626.
647*a*.   As last, but *E*: The same as No. 513.
647*b*.   „   „   *E*: Plain (not in collar).
        Conder, 288; 247.

Pandora's Breeches.

O: A pair of breeches on fire. As No. 522.
　　This obv. occurs with the following reverses :—
648. *R*: A crown and anchor, between two hearts. WHEN THIS
        YOU SEE REMEMBER ME.
　E: PAYABLE IN ANGLESEY LONDON OR LIVERPOOL.
648*a*.   As last, but *E*: Plain (not in collar). Conder, 289; 256.

649. *R*: Heart and hand. As No. 516.

650. *R*: Bust of Mendoza. As No. 558.   Conder, 289 ; 258.

✓ 651. *R*: A man hanging on a gibbet with a church in the distance. END OF PAIN. See Not Local, No. 131.

Conder, 232 ; 185.

This piece has a border of hands pointing, surrounding it on both sides.

652. *R*: Similar to last, but without the border, and without the angular support to gibbet.   Conder, 232 ; 186.

See also Anglesea, No. 227 ; *Buckinghamshire, No.* 7 ; *Northumberland, No.* 13 ; *and Warwickshire, Nos.* 244 *and* 247.

Pig.

O: A pig trampling upon emblems of royalty, &c. Pigs meat Published by T. Spence London.

This obv. occurs with the following reverses :—

653. *R*: THOS. SPENCE, &c. As No. 511.

E: The same as No. 513.   Conder, 109 ; 325.

653*a*.   As last, but *E*: Milled.

✓ 653*b*.   „   „   *E*: Plain (not in collar).

654. *R*: Britannia. As No. 512.

E: Milled.

654*a*.   As last, but *E*: Plain (not in collar).

Conder, 290 ; 264.

655. *R*: Citizens armed. As No. 515.

656. *R*: Heart and hand. As No. 516.   Conder, 290 ; 262.

657. *R*: Indian. As No. 518.

658. *R*: Lion dismayed. As No. 519.

E: The same as No. 513.

659. *R*: Odd Fellows. As No. 520.

E: The same as last.   Conder, 290 ; 263.

659*a*.   As last, but *E*: Milled.

659*b*.   „   „   *E*: Plain (not in collar).

660. *R*: Shepherd. As No. 524.   Conder, 290 ; 261.

Revolution (Before).

O: A man sitting in prison gnawing a bone. BEFORE THE REVOLUTION. *Ex*: 1795.

This obv. occurs with the following reverses :—

661. *R*: Britannia. As No. 512.   Conder, 291 ; 271.

✓ 662. *R*: Cat. As No. 514.

E: The same as No. 513. Conder, 109 ; 327.—Virt: 239.

663. *R*: Citizens armed. As No. 515.
    E: The same as No. 626.   Conder, 290 ; 269.
664. *R*: Lion dismayed. As No. 519.
    E: The same as last.   Conder, 290 ; 268.
664*a*.   As last, but *E*: Plain (not in collar).
665. *R*: Odd Fellows. As No. 520.
    E: The same as No. 513.
✓ 665*a*.   As last, but *E*: Plain (not in collar). Conder, 291 ; 270.
666. *R*: Shepherd. As No. 524.
    E: The same as No. 626.   Conder, 290 ; 267.
✓ 667. *R*: After the Revolution. As No. 523.
    E: The same as No. 513.   Conder, 109 ; 326.
667*a*.   As last, but *E*: Plain (not in collar).
668. *R*: A guillotine and part of a house. See *ante*, No. 375.
    E: Milled.
668*a*.   As last, but *E*: Plain (not in collar). Conder, 291 ; 272.

Revolution (After).

669. *O*: Three men dancing round a tree, &c. As No. 523.
    R: A stag under a tree. See Essex, No. 1.
                            Conder, 291 ; 274.
      See also Nos. 523, 545, 555, 570, 588, 611, 645, 667,
        679, 690, *and* 705 ; *Northumberland, No.* 14 ; *and*
        Worcestershire, No. 17.

Sailor (True-hearted).

    O: A sailor. As No. 546.
    This obv. occurs with the following reverses :—
✓ 670. *R*: Crown and anchor between hearts. As No. 648.
    E: The same as No. 513.   Conder, 110; 329.—Virt: 67.
671. *R*: Anchor and cable. IN COMMEMORATION, &c. See Not
        Local, No. 117.
    E: Milled.   Conder, 293 ; 295.
    See also Buckinghamshire, No. 9.

Sessions House.—See Nos. 612, 680, and 691.

Shepherd.

    O: A shepherd under a tree. As No. 524.
    This obv. occurs with the following reverses :—
672. *R*: Soldier and two citizens. As No. 525.
✓ 673. *R*: Stag and tree. As No. 669.   Conder, 294 ; 310.
    See also Northumberland, Nos. 15 *and* 22.

Snail.

674. *O*: A snail putting out its horns. As No. 547.
    R: Stag and tree. As last.   Conder, 295 ; 322.

Spaniard.

675. *O*: A figure of a Spaniard. As No. 534.
    R: Turnstile. As No. 527.   Conder, 295 ; 323.

Thelwall.

    O: Bust of Thelwall. As No. 535.
    This obv. occurs with the following reverses :—
676. *R*: Free-born Englishman. As No. 546.
    E: The same as No. 513.   Conder, 297 ; 343.
676*a*.   As last, but *E* : PAYABLE AT YORK × × × × × ×
677. *R*: Cap of Liberty. As No. 393 of Skidmore's.
    E : SKIDMORE HOLBORN LONDON.
                  Conder, 297 ; 344.—Virt : 60.
677*a*.   As last, but *E* : Plain (not in collar).
v 678. *R* : Minerva. As No. 533.
    E : The same as No. 513.   Conder, 110 ; 332.—Virt : 60.
678*a*.   As last, but *E* : Plain (not in collar).
    Also struck in white metal.
679. *R*: After the Revolution. As No. 523. Conder, 297 ; 345.
680. *R*: Sessions House. As No. 612.   Conder, 297 ; 341.
681. *R*: A snail. As No. 547.   Conder, 297 ; 346.
682. *R*: A tiger. As No. 239 of James'.
    E : The same as No. 513.   Conder, 297 ; 342.
683. *R*: Turnstile. As No. 527.   Conder, 298 ; 347.
684. *R*: Three fleurs-de-lis. As No. 396 of Skidmore's.
                  Conder, 238 ; 235.

Tooke.

    O: Bust of Tooke. As No. 536.
    This obv. occurs with the following reverses :—
685. *R*: THOS. SPENCE, &c. As No. 511.
v 686. *R*: Citizens armed. As No. 515.
    E : The same as No. 513.   Conder, 298 ; 352.
v 687. *R* : Heart and hand. As No. 516.
    E : The same as No. 513.   Conder, 110 ; 333.
687*a*.   As last, but *E* : PAYABLE IN LONDON. The remainder
      engrailed.
v 688. *R*: Odd Fellows. As No. 520.
    E: The same as No. 513.   Conder, 298 ; 351.
688*a*.   As last, but *E* : Milled.
689. *R*: Pandora's breeches. As No. 522. Conder, 298 ; 354.
690. *R*: After the Revolution. As No. 523. Conder, 298 ; 353.

√ 691. *R* : Sessions House. As No. 612.   Conder, 78 ; 82.
      Some of these are <u>on very large flans</u>. Also struck in white metal.

692. *R* : Turnstile. As No. 527.   Conder, 298 ; 355.

693. *R* : Bust to right. CHURCH AND KING. See *ante*, No. 400.
    E : Milled.   Conder, 298 ; 349.

694. *R* : Bust to right. LONG LIVE THE KING. See Sussex, No. 25.
    E : The same as last.   Conder, 298 ; 350.

Tree of Liberty.

O : Four men dancing. As No. 622.
    This obv. occurs with the following reverses :—

695. *R* : THOS. SPENCE, &c. As No. 511.   Conder, 298 ; 356.

696. *R* : Britannia. As No. 512.
    E : The same as No. 513.

696*a*.   As last, but *E* : Milled.

√ 696*b*.   ,,   ,,   *E* : Plain (not in collar).Conder, 299 ; 361.

697. *R* : Caduceus. As No. 513.
    E : The same as No. 513.   Conder, 299 ; 366.

√ 698. *R* : Citizens armed. As No. 515.
    E : The same as last.   Conder, 110 ; 334.

698*a*.   As last, but *E* : Plain (not in collar).

699. *R* : Heart and hand. As No. 516.
    E : The same as No. 515.

699*a*.   As last, but *E* : Milled.

699*b*.   ,,   ,,   *E* : Plain (not in collar).
                      Conder, 299 ; 358.

700. *R* : Highlander. As No. 517.
    E : The same as No. 513.   Conder, 299 ; 365.

701. *R* : Indian. As No. 518.   Conder, 299 ; 364.

702. *R* : Lion dismayed. As No. 519.
    E : The same as No. 513.   Conder, 299 ; 359.

702*a*.   As last, but *E* : Plain (not in collar).

√ 703. *R* : Odd Fellows. As No. 520.   Conder, 299 ; 360.
    E : Milled.

703*a*.   As last, but *E* : Plain (not in collar).
                      Conder, 299 ; 360.

704. *R* : The beginning of Oppression. As No. 521.
    E : The same as No. 513.   Conder, 299 ; 362.

705. *R* : After the Revolution. As No. 523. Conder, 299 ; 363.

706. *R* : Shepherd. As No. 524.
    E : The same as No. 515.

706*a*.   As last, but *E* : Plain (not in collar). Conder, 298 ; 357.

707. *R* : Turnstile. As No. 527.   Conder, 299 ; 369.

708. *R* : Guillotine. As No. 668.   Conder, 299 ; 367.
    See also Essex, No. 17.

Turk.

709. *O* : The figure of a Turk. As No. 537.
   R : Turnstile. As No. 527.   Conder, 300 ; 374.

Turnstile.

O : A turnstile. As *R* : of last.
   This obv. occurs with the following reverses :—
710. *R* : Crown and anchor. As No. 648.   Conder, 300 ; 377.
711. *R* : Heart and hand. As No. 516.
712. *R* : Bust of Mendoza. As No. 558.   Conder, 300 ; 378.
713. *R* : Figure of Minerva. As No. 533.   Conder, 300 ; 373.
714. *R* : A man hanging on a gibbet and a church in the
         distance. END OF PAIN. See Not Local, No. 131.
                                    Conder, 289 ; 255.
715. *R* : Stag under a tree. As No. 669.   Conder, 300 ; 376.
716. *R* : Westminster scholar. As No. 541. Conder, 301 ; 388.
         See also Anglesea, No. 228 ; Northumberland, Nos. 16
         and 23 ; Warwickshire, Nos. 245 and 247 ; and
         Worcestershire, No. 19.

United Token.

O : Laureate bust to right, a star radiated above. UNITED
   TOKEN.
   This obv. occurs with the following reverses :—
717. *R* : A crowned harp. As No. 575.
   E : The same as No. 513.   Conder, 110 ; 336.—Virt: 76.
717*a*.   As last but *E* : Plain (not in collar).
718. *R* : Highlander. As No. 517.
   E : The same as No. 513.   Conder, 301 ; 381.
719. *R* : A guillotine. As on No. 375 of Skidmore's.

Westminster Scholar. See Nos. 541, 557, and 716.

   The arrangement of the very numerous varieties of
   Spence's tokens has been, with the exception of
   those bearing his bust, or address, strictly alphabetical, taking the leading word or idea as a guide.
   A considerable number of other varieties will be
   found in the different counties to which reference
   has been made. It will be noticed that obverses are
   sometimes treated as reverses, and *vice versa*, but
   this was a difficulty impossible to avoid.

Spittle's.

720. *O* : View of St. Paul's. LONDON AND BRIGHTON HALFPENNY.
   R : Shield of Arms (of Brighton?) between laurel branches.
      PAYABLE AT THE WAREHOUSE OF J. SPITTLE LONDON OR
      OF J. KIRBY OR R. LASHMAR BRIGHTON 1795.
                                    Conder, 111 ; 340.

v 721. *O*: Similar to last, but with ST. PAULS added in *Ex*:
        and the initials I.P. in small letters.
      R: The same as last.   Conder, 111; 339.

Stinton's.

v 722. *O*: A grasshopper. FINE TEAS OF THE ROUGH FLAVOUR.
      R: WM. STINTON . ST. JAMES'S STREET . LONDON + PATENT
        COCAO WAREHOUSE 1795.
      E: ITALIAN FRENCH & PORTUGAL FRUIT WAREHOUSE .+.
                      Conder, 111; 341.—Pye, 34; 9.—Virt: 42.

✓ 722a.   As last, but *E*: PAYABLE IN DUBLIN OR LONDON.

   722b.   „   „   *E*: Plain (not in collar).

Summers'.

   723. *O*: The head of a wild man, full face. A WILD MANS HEAD
        FROM THE LAND OF JESSO TO BE SEEN AT ·:·
      R: A cypher *R . S* . DEALER IN CURIOSITIES &c. in a scallop
        shell. SUMMERS'S MUSEUM No. 24 OLD CAVENDISH
        STREET OXFORD STREET . PAINTINGS BOUGHT SOLD AND
        EXCHANGED . 1797. In two circles. Notice that the
        A of " AND " comes below the D of " CAVENDISH " and
        the first part of the *S* in cypher does not cross the
        top of the *R*.
        *Very rare; this obverse die failed after a few impressions
        only had been taken.*

v 724. *O*: The same as last.
      R: Similar, but the cypher is larger; the first stroke of the
        S crosses the top of *R*, and nearly touches the C of
        " CURIOSITIES." The A of " AND " comes under the
        IS of " CAVENDISH." Conder, 111; 342.—Pye, 35; 1.
        Rare.

Swainson's.

   725. *O*: Bust to left. ISAAC SUAINSON.
      R: A female dropping herbs into a still. HYGEIA PRE-
        PARING VELNOS' VEGETABLE SYRUP ✱
                      Conder, 238; 234.—Pye, 34; 10.
        *Very rare; 12 impressions in silver and copper only taken,
        in consequence of a mistake in spelling the name.*
        See also Ayrshire, No. 4.

        For Tower Hill, see " Masonic," *Nos. 261-264.*

Whitfield's.

   726. *O*: A bust to left.
      R: A hand from the clouds holding a balance, LONDON
        between the scales. PAYABLE AT JOHN WHITFIELDS.
                      Conder, 112; 346.

▾ 727. *O*: Bust similar to last. ✱ ✱ ✱ LONG ✱ LIVE ✱ THE ✱ KING ✱
　　　R: Similar to last, but nothing between the scales.
　　　　　　　　　　　　　Conder, 112; 345.—Virt: 28.
　　　Both these pieces are rare.

▾ 728. *O*: Similar to last.
　　　R: A large cypher *I M & Co.*, the date 1795 under.
　　　　　　　　　　　　　Conder, 213; 27.

Williams'.

▾ 729. *O*: The Prince of Wales' crest upon a portcullis. w.
　　　WILLIAMS LONDON, under. RENDER TO CÆSAR THE
　　　THINGS THAT ARE CÆSAR'S. Notice that the second
　　　bar of portcullis from the right hand comes between
　　　the letters A and M of " WILLIAMS."
　　　R: A crown on the arms of London. FEAR GOD AND HONOUR
　　　THE KING 1795.

▾ 730. *O*: Similar to last, but the second bar of portcullis comes
　　　directly above the A.
　　　R: Similar to last, but not the same die.
　　　　　　　　Conder, 112; 348.—Pye, 35; 2.—Virt: 63.
　　　There are at least three different dies used for this re-
　　　verse, the difference being in the shape and position of
　　　the crown, but very slight, and impossible to describe.
　　　The obv. of No. 729 occurs with the following reverses:

731. *R*: A wheatsheaf. PEACE PLENTY & LIBERTY. See Cam-
　　　bridgeshire, No. 17.　　　　　Conder, 302; 393.

732. *R*: An anchor, and cap of Liberty radiated. LIBERTY ✱
　　　PEACE ✱ COMMERCE. See Not Local, No. 123.
　　　　　　　　　　　　　Conder, 264; 10.
　　　The rev. of No. 729 appears as an obv. with the fol-
　　　lowing reverses:—

733. *R*: Bishop Blaze and woolpack. See Surrey, No. 13.
　　　　　　　　　　　　　Conder, 269; 46.

734. *R*: A fat man at table, eating. See No. 591.
　　　　　　　　　　　　　Conder, 276; 120.

735. *R*: A man on the ground gnawing a bone. See No. 591.
　　　　　　　　　　　　　Conder, 279; 146.
　　　See also No. 273, *ante*; and Anglesea, No. 222.

Miscellaneous.

London, Essex, and Norfolk.

✓ 736. *O*: PAYABLE | LONDON ESSEX | AND | NORFOLK. In four
　　　straight lines across the field.
　　　R: MAY | PEACE | & PLENTY | ACCOMPANY | THE PRINCE | &
　　　PRINCESS | OF | WALES. In eight lines.
　　　　　　　　Conder, 91; 178.—Pye, 35; 6.—Virt: 79.
　　　There are two different dies used for this piece, in one
　　　of which the letters are sharper and better formed
　　　than the other, though not quite so large.
　　　For this reverse, see also Durham, No. 7.

London, Leeds and Birmingham.

✔ 737. *O*: Crest, a ram. PAYABLE AT LONDON LEEDS AND BIRMING-
HAM ✳
     R: A ship, with sprigs of leaves under. FOR THE HONOR
AND USE OF TRADE ✳
     E: Plain (not in collar).

737*a*.   As last, but *E*: PAYABLE IN DUBLIN OR AT BALLY
MURTAGH +
     This reverse also occurs on a Dublin token, No. 5.

738. *O*: The same as last.
     R: Crest, a leopard's head, crowned, VI ET VIRTUTE on a
label under. FOR THE HONOR AND USE OF TRADE +
     Both these pieces are scarce, and in good condition rare.

St. Paul's.

✔ 739. *O*: Bust to right. GEORGIVS III REX.
     R: The arms of London, with the sword and mace crossed
behind, an eye radiated above. VISITED ST. PAULS.
     Ex: 23 APRIL 1789.   Conder, 93; 193.

London and Middlesex.

✔ 740. *O*: Bust of Shakespeare to left. LONDON & MIDDLESEX.
     R: A female seated holding a cornucopia, part of a ship in
the distance. HALFPENNY. *Ex*: 1792.
     E: Upright milling.

740*a*.   As last, but *E*: Oblique milling.
               Conder, 90; 172.—Pye, 35; 8.—Virt: 119.

740*b*.   As last, but *E*: Plain (not in collar).

✔ 741. *O*: The royal arms, &c. with the Prince of Wales' motto
under. LONDON AND MIDDLESEX. HALFPENNY.
     R: Three-quarter bust to right. GEO. PRINCE OF WALES.
The Prince of Wales' crest below the bust.
     E: BRIGHTON CAMP HALFPENNY MDCCXCIV . ✕.✕
               Conder, 91; 173.—Pye, 35; 7.

✔ 741*a*.   As last, but *E*: PAYABLE IN LANCASTER LONDON OR
BRISTOL.

741*b*.   As last, but *E*: PAYABLE AT THE TEMPLE OF THE MUSES

742. *O*: The same as last.
     R: Similar to last, but with HALFPENNY under the bust
instead of the crest.
     E: The same as No. 741*a*.

✔ 742*a*.   As last, but *E*: PAYABLE AT LONDON OR DUBLIN ° ✕ ° ✕ °
               Conder, 91; 174.

✔ 743. *O*: The same as last.
     R: Profile bust to right. GEORGE PRINCE OF WALES. The
line of forehead comes to E of " PRINCE."
     E: The same as No. 741*a*. Conder, 91; 175.—Virt: 78.

744. *O*: and *E*: The same as last.

R: Similar to last, but the line of forehead comes between the N and C of " PRINCE."

745. *O*: Similar to preceding, but without period before or after " HALFPENNY."

R: Similar to last, but without a period at end of legend.

E: PAYABLE AT THE WAREHOUSE OF THOMAS CLACKE.

This piece is very rare.

The obv. of No. 741 occurs with the following reverses :—

✔ 746. *R*: Crowned bust to left. IOHN OF GAUNT DUKE OF LAN- CASTER ✳ See Lancashire, No. 18.

E: The same as No. 741*a*.   Conder, 91 ; 177.

747. *R*: The Freemason's arms, &c. See *ante*, No. 261.

E: The same as last.

748. *R*: The Prince of Wales' crest, &c., 1795 under. INDUSTRY IS THE PARENT OF SUCCESS. See Norfolk, No. 6.

E: The same as last.

✔ 749. *R*: A triangle supported by two hands. KING LORDS COMMONS. See *ante*, No. 211.

E: Milled.   Conder, 91 ; 176.

See also *ante*, No. 337.

Stag.

✔ 750. *O*: A stag. FREEDOM WITH INNOCENCE.

R: A plough. INDUSTRY ✳ SUPPLIETH WANT. *Ex*: 1796.

E: PAYABLE IN LONDON. The remainder engrailed.
Conder, 91 ; 179.—Pye, 35✳ ; 8.—Virt: 89.

750*a*. As last, but *E*: The remainder dots and crosses.

750*b*.   „   „   *E*: Milled.
For this reverse see Cheshire, No. 52, and Not Local, No. 103.

See also a very similar design upon the penny, *ante*, No. 110.

✔ 751. *O*: The same as last.

R: Figure of Britannia seated holding a spear and a palm branch. ✳ ✳ RULE BRITANNIA ✳ ✳ *Ex*: 1797.

E: The same as No. 750. Conder, 91 ; 180.—Pye, 35✳ ; 7.

751*a*. As last, but *E*: The remainder dots and crosses.

751*b*.   „   „   *E*: Plain (not in collar).
For this reverse see also Cambridgeshire, No. 16; Hampshire, Nos. 12 and 19; Staffordshire, No. 16; and Not Local, No. 102.

Westminster.

✔ 752. *O* : Bust to left.   IOHN HOWARD . F . R . S .
   R : An ornamental cypher *H H*, WESTMINSTER HALFPENNY
      1792.
   E : PAYABLE AT THE IRON WAREHOUSE NO. 3 EGBASTON STRT.
      BIRM.   Conder, 112 ; 349.—Pye, 48 ; 1.—Virt : 90.
   This obverse with a very similar reverse appears as a
   Birmingham halfpenny. See Warwickshire, No. 92.

FARTHINGS.

LONDON.

Denton's.

✔ 753. *O* : DENTON DEALER IN COINS HOSPITAL GATE SMITHFIELD.
   R : Two busts facing. WE THREE BLOCKHEADS BE 1795.
                           Conder, 114 ; 360.
   This obv. occurs with the following reverses :—
✔ 754. *R* : A crown, within a radiation. Struck from the die of
      the halfpenny, Hertfordshire, No. 2.
                           Conder, 114 ; 361.—Virt : 131.
✔ 755. *R* : A cart unloading into a ship, lying at a quay. Struck
      from the die of the halfpenny, Northumberland,
      No. 25.   Conder, 114 : 362.—Virt : 131.
✔ 756. *R* : A deformed dwarf. SIR JEFFERY DUNSTAN. See Surrey,
      No. 29.   Conder, 114 ; 363.—Virt : 130.
   The rev. of No. 753 appears as an obv. with the following reverses :—
✔ 757. *R* : The same as No. 756. Conder, 303 ; 404.—Virt : 132.
✔ 758. *R* : Prince of Wales' crest, &c. Struck from the die of the
      halfpenny, Hertfordshire, No. 2.
                           Conder, 303 ; 402.—Virt : 156.
   See also Dublin, No. 182.

Harrison's.

✔ 759. *O* : . Harrison . Hair ❖ Dresser ❖ No. 64 . Long ❖ Lane
      West Smithfield.
   R : Two busts facing, similar to No. 753. . Bleeding &
      Tooth Drawing 1797.
                           Conder, 114 ; 364.—Virt : 166.

Orchard's.

✔ 760. *O* : Bust to left with a hat on, JACOBS under it. ROBERT
      ORCHARD . 1796.
   R : A large cypher *R O*.   Conder, 251 ; 65.
   See also Anglesea, No. 261 ; and Dublin, No. 185.

761. *O* : ROBERT ORCHARD | GROCER | & | TEA DEALER | NO. 34 GREEK ST. | SOHO | LONDON | WHOLESALE & RETAIL 1803.

> *R* : A Turk standing amongst bales, &c. FARTHING MAKER OF CHOCOLATE & COCOA ON A NEW PRINCIPLE. (Inverted N's.)

762. *O* : The same as last.

> *R* : A building. ROBERT . ORCHARD . TEA . WAREHOUSE . CORNER OF CHURCH ST . AND . AT SAWBRIDGEWORTH HARTS.

763. *O* : Bust to right. ROBERT ORCHARD GROCER & TEA DEALER NO. 34 GREEK ST. CORNER CHURCH ST. SOHO LONDON 1804.

> *R* : Similar to last, but HERTS instead of HARTS.

> It will be perceived that we have again entered upon the Nineteenth Century, but the close connection of these pieces makes it undesirable to separate them. The same remark will apply to some of Pidcock's, next following.

Pidcock's.

764. *O* : An elephant, JAMES under it. * PIDCOCK'S * * EXHIBITION.

> *R* : A lion fondling a dog.   EXETER CHANGE LONDON PIDCOCK.

765. *O* : The same as last.

> *R* : A two-headed cow.   EXETER * CHANGE * * STRAND LONDON.   The cow's horns divide the two stars.

> *E* : Milled.   Conder, 115 ; 366.—Pye, 33 ; 4.—Virt : 143. Some of these are on much thicker flans than others.

766. *O* : Similar to last, but different die.   The artist's name does not appear.

> *R* : Similar to last, but the horns of cow come into the word " CHANGE."

> *E* : Plain (not in collar).

767. *O* : The same as No. 764.

> *R* : A cockatoo standing on a branch of a tree.   EXETER CHANGE STRAND LONDON.

> *E* : Milled.

767*a*.   As last, but *E* : Plain (not in collar).
>   Conder, 114 ; 365.—Pye, 33 ; 3.—Virt : 143.

768. *O* : The same as last.

> *R* : A pelican.   PIDCOCK . EXETER CHANGE LONDON.

769. *O* : A lion.   As No. 764.

> *R* : A beaver.   THE BEAVER 1801.

770. *O* : The same as last.

> *R* : A monkey.   THE WANDEROW 1801.

771. *O* : A beaver.   As No. 769.

> *R* : A cockatoo.   As No. 767.

✔ 772. *O* : The same as last.
     R : A pelican. As No. 768.
✔ 773. *O* : The wanderow. As No. 770.
     R : The same as last.

Skidmore's.

✔ 774. *O* : A register stove. NO. 123 HIGH HOLBORN LONDON.
     R : Two men working in a foundry. *Ex* : 1795.
                              Conder, 115 ; 367.
     This is struck from the halfpenny dies of No. 361, *ante*.
✔ 775. *O* : Shield of arms between sprigs. DEALER IN COINS
          MEDALS. From the halfpenny die of No. 397, *ante*.
     R : A man hanging from a gallows. END OF PAIN. See
          Not Local, No. 232.
     E : Milled.   Conder, 252 ; 71.
     See also Anglesea, Nos. 260 and 262.

Spence's.

✔ 776. *O* : Bust to left, JACOBS under. T. SPENCE . A . STATE
          PRISONER IN 1794.
     R : Britannia seated, a cap of Liberty falling. ROUSE
          BRITANNIA.   Conder, 253 ; 77.—Virt : 160.
     This obv. occurs with the following reverses :—
✔ 777. *R* : A man riding on a bull with an ass's head. AM I NOT
          THINE ASS.   Conder, 305 ; 419.
  778. *R* : A man and ass's heads conjoined. ODD FELLOWS. A
          MILLION HOG. A GUINEA PIG.   Conder, 305 ; 427.
✔ 779. *R* : A padlock. MUM 1796.   Conder, 306 ; 432.
✔ 780. *R* : A pig trampling on a crown, crozier, &c. PIGS MEAT
          PUBLISHED BY T. SPENCE LONDON.
                              Conder, 306 ; 435.—Virt : 160.
✔ 781. *R* : A slave kneeling. AM I NOT A MAN AND A BROTHER.
          Ex : JAMES.   Conder, 307 ; 444.

Adam and Eve.

✔ 782. *O* : Adam and Eve in the garden of Eden. MAN OVER MAN
          HE MADE NOT LORD. *Ex* : C. JAMES . F.
     R : A pig. As No. 780.   Conder, 115 ; 369.
✔ 783. *O* : Similar to last, but with lines in place of artist's name
          in *Ex*.
     R : A bull with ass's head. As No. 777. Conder, 304 ; 416.
     This obv. appears with the following reverses :—
✔ 784. *R* : Britannia seated. As No. 776.   Conder, 304 ; 411.
✔ 785. *R* : Odd Fellows. As No. 778.   Conder, 305 ; 426.
  786. *R* : A padlock. As No 779.   Conder, 306 ; 431.
✔ 787. *R* : A pig. As No. 780.   Conder, 115 ; 369.
✔ 788. *R* : A slave. As No. 781.   Conder, 307 ; 442.

Bull.

O : A bull with ass's head, &c. As No. 777.
This obv. occurs with the following reverses :—

ᴠ 789. *R* : THOS. SPENCE | SIR THOS. MORE | THOS. PAINE | 1795. In the centre in four lines. ADVOCATES FOR THE RIGHTS OF MAN. Conder, 246 ; 18.

790. *R* : The faces of a man and a demon joined. EVEN FELLOWS Conder, 304 ; 418.

791. *R* : A man on all fours. IF THE LAW REQUIRES IT WE WILL WALK THUS. Conder, 247 ; 19.
See also Northumberland, Nos. 29 and 33.

Britannia.

O : Figure of Britannia. As No. 776.
This obv. occurs with the following reverses :—

792. *R* : THOS. SPENCE, &c. As No. 789. Conder, 304 ; 410.
793. *R* : Even Fellows. As No. 790. Conder, 304 ; 413.—Virt : 128.
794. *R* : Man on all fours. As No. 791. Conder, 304 ; 415.—Virt : 129.
795. *R* : An anchor and cable. PROMISSORY NAVAL FARTHING. See not Local, No. 204. Conder, 304 ; 414.
See also Northumberland, No. 30.

Cat.

O : A cat. IN . SOCIETY . LIVE . FREE . LIKE . ME . 1795. Under the cat JAMES.

This obv. occurs with the following reverses :—

796. *R* : THOS. SPENCE, &c. As No. 789.

797. *R* : A hand holding an open book, inscribed PIGS MEAT ✳ ✳ IF LORDS ALL MANKIND ARE ✳ THEN THEY YE RENTS SHOUD SHARE. Conder, 247 ; 21.—Virt : 129.

Even Fellows.

798. O : Faces of man and demon. As No. 790.
R : A man hanging on a gibbet against which a ladder is resting. END OF PƆT. See Not Local, No. 237.
E : Milled. Conder, 306 ; 439.

Odd Fellows.

O : Heads of man and ass. As No. 778.
This obv. occurs with the following reverses :—

799. *R* : THOS. SPENCE, &c. As No. 789. Conder, 305 ; 425.

800. *R* : Three men hanging on a gibbet. THE THREE THOMAS'S 1796.
E : Milled. Conder, 307 ; 447.

801. *R* : Even Fellows. As No. 790. Conder, 248 ; 30.

802. *R* : Man on all fours. As No. 791.
See also Northumberland, No. 31.

Padlock.

O : A padlock. As No. 779.

This obv. occurs with the following reverses :—

v 803. R : THOS. SPENCE, &c. As No. 789.   Conder, 306 ; 430.

v 804. R : Even Fellows. As No. 790.
                                 Conder, 248 ; 29.—Virt : 171.

805. R : Man on all fours. As No. 791.

Pandora's Breeches.

O : A pair of breeches on fire, a snake with a man's head under. PANDORAS BREECHES.

This obv. occurs with the following reverses :—

806. R : Man on all fours. As No. 791.   Conder, 304 ; 409.

v 807. R : The three Thomases. As No. 800.
       E : Milled.   Conder, 307 ; 448.

v 808. R : A man hanging. END OF PAIN. See Not Local, No. 232.
                                 Conder, 251 ; 66.—Virt : 149.

Pig.

O : A pig trampling on emblems of royalty, &c. As No. 780.

This obv. occurs with the following reverses :—

v 809. R : THOS. SPENCE, &c. As No. 789.   Conder, 115 ; 368.

v 810. R : Even Fellows. As No. 790.   Conder, 306 ; 434.

See also Northumberland, No. 32.

Slave.

O : A slave kneeling. As No. 781.

This obv. occurs with the following reverses :—

v 811. R : THOS. SPENCE, &c. As No. 789.   Conder, 307 ; 441.

v 812. R : Even Fellows. As No. 790.   Conder, 307 ; 445.

v 813. R : Man on all fours. As No. 791.   Conder, 253 ; 76.

See also Northumberland, No. 34.

Three Thomases.

O : Three men hanging. As No. 800.

This obv. occurs with the following reverses :—

v 814. R : THOS. SPENCE, &c. As No. 789.
       E : Milled.   Conder, 307 ; 446.

815. R : An open book inscribed "JANY. 21, 1793." THE . WRONGS . OF . MAN. See Not Local, No. 234.
                                 Conder 307 ; 449.

v 816. R : MAY THE 3 KNAVES OF JACOBIN CLUBS NEVER GET A TRICK.
                                 Conder, 253 ; 78.—Virt : 154.

Miscellaneous.

v 817. *O*: Profile bust to right. LONDON & MIDDLESEX FARTHING.
     R: Prince of Wales' crest in a shield. PRO BONO PUBLICO
     1793 above, and two sprigs under.
                             Conder, 114 ; 357.—Virt : 142.
     This reverse appears also at North Wales, No. 14.

v 818. *O*: Two busts. GEORGE AND CAROLINA.
     R: A stork standing upon a cornucopia. PAYABLE IN
     LONDON * 1795.   Conder, 114 ; 358.—Virt : 164.
     This obv. appears also with the following reverses :—

✓ 819. *R*: A pig, with the Prince of Wales' crest on its head,
     trampling upon "HONOUR," cards, dice, &c., strewn
     on the ground, LONG LIVE THE KING.
                              Conder, 253 ; 81.

820. *R*: Similar to last, but the legend reads—FREEDOM TO THE
     SLAVE.

821. *R*: PEACE in the centre, a beehive above, and sprigs of
     laurel below.

v 822. *O*: Laureate bust to left. IULIOUS CEASER . 1795.
     R: PAYABLE | IN LONDON | LIVERPOOL | OR BATH. In four
     lines.   Conder, 114; 359.

823. *O*: A stag. FREEDOM . WITH . INNOCENCE ∴
     R: A plough. INDUSTRY . PRODUCETH . WEALTH.
     See a similar design on the halfpenny, No. 750.

10 *

Monmouthshire.

HALFPENNIES.

ABERGAVENNY.

1. *O* : A cask. JAMES POWELL IMPORTER . 1795.
   R : J. POWELL WINE & BRANDY MERCHANT . ABERGAVENNY.   A small ornament at top, and a bunch of grapes under the word " MERCHANT."
   E : PAYABLE AT MONMOUTH AND ABERGAVENNY . ✕ .
   Conder, 116 ; 1.—Pye, 4 ; 1.—Virt : 22.

1a.   As last, but *E* : LONDON LIVERPOOL OR MONTROSE . ✕ .
1b.   „   „   *E* : Milled.
1c.   „   „   *E* : Plain (not in collar).

MONMOUTH.

2. *O* : and *E* : Same as No. 1.
   R : J. POWELL | WINE & BRANDY | MERCHANT | MONMOUTH.   In four lines, with a bunch of grapes top and bottom.
   Conder, 116 ; 3.

   Very rare ; the reverse die failed when only a few impressions had been taken, giving way to the one following.

3.   Similar to last, but with a vine sprig at bottom instead of a bunch of grapes.
   Conder, 116 ; 2.—Pye, 37 ; 3.—Virt : 100.

3a.   As last, but *E* : Plain (not in collar).

Norfolk.

THREEPENCE.

WROXHAM.

✔ 1. *O* : A spade and pickaxe across a wheelbarrow. MARLE . PIT
TOKEN in two lines under. TO . PAY . WORKMEN . AND .
PROMOTE . AGRICULTURE ❖

R : 3 PENCE PAYABLE AT WROXHAM   D. COLLYER . PROPRIETOR
. 1797.   Conder, 117 ; 3.—Pye, 49 ; 5.—Virt : 229.

PENNIES.

LYNN.

✔ 2. *O* : A plough and harrow. A . COOK . CORN . FACTOR . NORFOLK.
R : A cypher *A C* within a circle.   LYNN . PENNY . TOKEN . 1798.
E : I PROMISE TO PAY ON DEMAND THE BEARER ONE PENNY.
Conder, 117 ; 1.
Rare.

NORWICH.

✔ 3. *O* : View of an ancient fortress and bridge. NORWICH . CASTLE.
Ex : JAcobs.
R : A globe inscribed BRITAIN between a rose and thistle.
BRITISH . PENNY. *Ex* : 1797.
E : Same as last.   Conder, 117 ; 2.—Virt : 209.

✔ 4. *O* : A soldier carrying arms in front of a range of tents,
Norwich Castle and Cathedral in the distance.
NORWICH . LOYAL . MILITARY . ASSOCIATION . 1797.
R : The arms of Norwich and military ensigns. PATRIÆ . ET .
DECUS . ET . TVTAMEN ❖
Also struck in silver.

YARMOUTH.

5. *O* : A female seated holding a scroll inscribed, BOULTER'S
EXHIBITION OF NATURAL AND ARTIFICIAL CURIOSITIES.
Various curiosities lying on the ground. *Ex* :
YARMOUTH.
R : Three figures (representing Asia, Africa, and America)
presenting curiosities to Britannia, who is recording
them in a book. UNDIQUAQUE COLLIGITUR. *Ex* : 1796.
E : Same as No. 2   Conder, 117 ; 4.
Very rare.
This is struck from the dies of the halfpenny, No. 54.

HALFPENNIES.

AYLSHAM.

6. *O* : The Grocers' arms, supporters, &c. PROSPERITY TO THE
TOWN OF AYLSHAM.
R : The Prince of Wales' crest and motto. INDUSTRY IS THE
PARENT OF SUCCESS HALFPENNY 1795.
E : PAYABLE AT S & T ASHLEY . + . + . + . +
Conder, 118 ; 5.—Pye, 4 ; 6—Virt : 110.
Rarely found with this edge.

꒦ 6*a*.   As last, but *E* : S & T ASHLEY.   The remainder crosses
and dots.

6*b*.   As last, but *E* : PAYABLE AT I + H BOORMAN O × O × O.

6*c*.   „   „   *E* : PAYABLE AT THE TEMPLE OF THE MUSES.
For this reverse see also Middlesex, No. 748, and Not
Local, Nos. 158 and 160.

BLOFIELD.

꒦ 7. *O* : A group of weapons and musical instruments. BLOFIELD
CAVALRY.   On a label FIFTH TROOP.
R : A mounted dragoon. LOYAL NORFOLK YEOMANRY. *Ex* :
MDCCXCVI.
E : FEAR GOD AND HONOUR THE KING . × × .
Conder, 118 ; 6.—Pye, 9 ; 6.—Virt : 73.

7*a*.   As last, but *E* : Milled.

7*b*.   „   „   *E* : Plain.
Scarce ; there were only 12 *lbs. struck.   Also struck in
silver.*

This obv. occurs with the following reverses :—

꒦ 8. *R* : A dragoon mounted. PRO REGE ET PATRIA. *Ex* : QUEENS
BAYS.   See No. 47.   Conder, 118 ; 9.

꒦ 9. *R* : Bust to left. DR. SAML. IOHNSON. See Staffordshire,
No. 15.
E : BUXTON TOKEN . × .   The remainder engrailed.
Conder, 118 ; 11.

꒦ 10. *R* : Front face of Queen Elizabeth, &c. See Sussex, No. 14.
E : Engrailed.   Conder, 118 ; 7.—Virt : 181.

꒦ 11. *R* : A female standing. LIBERTY & COMMERCE. *Ex* : 1795.
The rev. of a New York Token.
E : Same as last.   Conder, 118 ; 8.

꒦ 12. *R* : An armoured bust to right. FOR GENERAL CONVENIENCE.
See Not Local, No. 101.
E : Same as No. 9.   Conder, 118 ; 10.—Virt : 184.
See also Hampshire, No. 30.

NORWICH.

✓ 13. *O*: View of a castle and bridge with shrubs, &c. NORWICH
CASTLE. The period touches the shrubs on the bridge.
R: A fleece. GOOD TIMES WILL COME . MDCCXCIV.
E: RICHARD BACON COCKEY LANE.

13*a*. As last, but *E*: PAYABLE AT DALLYS CHICHESTER -:- -:- -:-

13*b*. „ „ *E*: PAYABLE AT CHARLES HEATHS BAY MAKER
COLCHESTER . ✕ .

13*c*. As last, but *E*: CURRENT EVERY WHERE

13*d*. „ „ *E*: Milled.

13*e*. „ „ *E*: Plain (not in collar).

14. *O*: Similar to last, but the period is midway between end of
legend and the shrubs on the bridge.
R: and *E*: Same as No. 13.
Also struck in silver.

14*a*. As last, but *E*: PAYABLE AT THE WAREHOUSE OF THOMAS
CLARKE.

14*b*. As last, but *E*: PAYABLE AT SOUTH SHIELDS AND LONDON . ✕

14*c*. „ „ *E*: CURRENT EVERY WHERE

14*d*. „ „ *E*: Plain (not in collar).
Conder, 119; 12.—Pye, 40; 2.—Virt: 37.

✓ 15. *O*: The arms of Norwich. MAY NORWICH FLOURISH. PRO
BONO PUBLICO.
R: Shield of arms of the county. NORFOLK AND NORWICH
HALFPENNY . 1792.
E: PAYABLE AT N. BOLINGBROKES HABERDASHER &c. NOR-
WICH . ✕ .

✓ 16. *O*: Similar to last, but with a small annulet instead of period
after " FLOURISH."
R: Similar, but the ends of batons come in different position
with legend.
E: The same as last.

16*a*. As last, but *E*: Plain (not in collar).

✓ 17. *O*: Similar to preceding, but without period or annulet at
end of legend.
R: and *E*: Same as No. 16.

17*a*. As last, but *E*: Plain (not in collar).
Conder, 119; 13.—Pye, 38; 8.—Virt: 38.

✓ 18. *O*: The same as last.
R: A plough and shuttle. SUCCESS TO THE PLOUGH AND
SHUTTLE. Conder, 119; 14.
See also Cambridgeshire, No. 15; and Suffolk, No. 30.

19. *O*: Same as the rev. of last.
R: Bust to left in cocked hat. EARL HOWE, &c. See
Hampshire, No. 9. Conder, 226; 136.

✓ 20. *O*: A key suspended from an iron archway. PAYABLE AT BULLEN AND MARTINS. *Ex*: MARKET PLACE NORWICH.

R: Same as No. 18. Conder, 119; 15.—Pye, 39; 3.—Virt: 37. *Also struck in silver.*

20*a*. As last, but *E*: PAYABLE AT IOHN FINCHAMS SUFFOLK.

✓ 21. *O*: A straight stocking and a glove, and a knife and fork crossed. R ✕ CAMPIN ✕ HABERDASHER. *Ex*: ✕ GOAT ✕ LANE ✕ NORWICH.

R: A female seated between an anchor and a globe, a crowned lion lying at her feet. HALFPENNY. *Ex*: 1793. *This is the same as Hampshire, No. 4.*

E: CURRENT EVERY WHERE
Conder, 119; 16.—Pye, 39; 10.—Virt: 39.

21*a*. As last, but *E*: BIRMINGHAM LIVERPOOL OR LONDON.

21*b*.   „   „   *E*: Plain (not in collar).

✓ 22. *O*: A bent stocking and a glove, and a knife and fork crossed in an opposite direction, the legend as before.

R: Similar to last but dated 1794. *This is the same as Hampshire, No. 5.*

E: Same as No. 21.
Conder, 119; 17.—Pye, 39; 3.—Virt: 39.

22*a*. As last, but *E*: PAYABLE AT T. IENNING'S SPALDING & HOLBEACH — ✕ —

22*b*. As last, but *E*: PAYABLE AT THE WAREHOUSE OF IOHN STRIDE ✕ ✕ ✕

✓ 22*c*. As last, but *E*: Plain (not in collar).

✓ 23. *O*: A muff and tippet. PAYABLE AT J. CLARKE'S MARKET PLACE NORWICH.

R: An umbrella, stocking, hat, and glove. No. 2 GENTLEMAN'S WALK 17—94.

E: Plain rounded; these are struck on large and small flans.
Conder, 119; 18.—Pye, 40; 1.—Virt: 38.

23*a*. As last, but *E*: PAYABLE ✕ AT ✕ CRONEBANE ✕ ✕ OR ✻ IN ✻ DUBLIN ✕ O ✕

23*b*. As last, but *E*: PAYABLE IN LANCASTER LONDON OR BRISTOL.

23*c*.   „   „   *E*: Milled.

✓ 24. *O*: A bottle. MORE TRADE AND FEWER TAXES.

R: A figure of Hope standing. PROSPERITY TO OLD ENGLAND.

E: RICHARD DINMORE & SON NORWICH. ✕ ✕ ✕ ✕ .
Conder, 119; 19.—Pye, 40; 3.—Virt: 38.

✓ 24*a*. As last, but *E*: Plain (not in collar).

✓ 25. *O*: and *E*: Same as No. 24.

R: Similar to last, but from a different die, which may be distinguished by the figure in this one pointing to the letter Y, and in the former to the T of "PROSPERITY."

25*a*.   As last, but *E*: PAYABLE IN LONDON BRISTOL & LAN-
CASTER — × —

25*b*.   As last, but *E*: Plain (not in collar).
Also struck in silver.

The rev. of No. 25 appears as an obv. with the following
reverses :—

✓ 26. *R*: A ship sailing. HALFPENNY.   See Hampshire, No. 45.
E: CURRENT EVERY WHERE   Conder, 214 ; 34.

26*a*.   As last, but *E*: Plain (not in collar).

✔ 27. *R*: A dove flying, and a cornucopia. PEACE AND PLENTY.
See Hampshire, No. 7.
E: Same as last.

27*a*.   As last, but *E*: BERSHAM BRADLEY WILLEY SNEDSHILL.

27*b*.   „   „   *E*: PAYABLE AT THE SHOP OF DUNHAM &
YALLOP GOLDSMITHS.

27*c*.   As last, but *E*: EMSWORTH HALFPENNY PAYABLE BY IOHN
STRIDE.

27*d*.   As last, but *E*: Engrailed.

27*e*.   „   „   *E*: Plain (not in collar).
Conder, 233 ; 196.—Virt: 53.

See also Essex, No. 7 ; and Yorkshire, No. 25.

28. *O*: Shield of arms of the city of Norwich, upon a sword
and mace in saltire, between palm branches. SUCCESS
TO THE CITY OF NORWICH.

R: A shop front in a circle. NORWICH HALFPENNY.   1792.

E: PAYABLE AT THE SHOP OF DUNHAM & YALLOP GOLD-SMITHS.
*Very rare ; a flaw runs diagonally across the shield, which
caused a failure of the die when a very few only had
been struck, upon which the following took its place :—*

✓ 29.   Very similar to proceding, but from a new obv. die
which differs in the shape of the palm branches, and
is without the flaw.
Conder, 120 ; 20.—Pye, 39 ; 1.—Virt: 39.

30. *O*: Similar to last, but the hilt of the sword points to the
foot of the F, whereas in the former it pointed to
the o of " OF."

R: Similar to last, but dated 1793.

E: Same as last.   Conder, 121 ; 21.—Pye, 39 ; 2.
*Very rare; Sharp says:—"Not more than three are certainly
known."*

31. *O*: Same as last.

R: An eagle with wings expanded. NORWICH HALFPENNY.
Ex: 1793.

E: Plain (rounded).
Exceedingly rare ; possibly unique.

⌄ 32. *O* : Similar to No. 28, but the shield is flat, whereas in the former it was raised, and the palm branches are tied with a ribbon, which they were not before.
R : Same as last.
E : Same as No. 28.
Conder, 120 ; 22.—Pye, 39 ; 6.—Virt : 39.

32*a*.   As last but *E* : Plain (not in collar).

⌄ 33.   Similar to last, but the shield is emblazoned *or*, and there are two small ornaments following the legend on obverse.   Conder, 120 ; 23.—Pye, 39 ; 5.

⌄ 34. *O* : A figure of Hope standing, supporting a shield inscribed, DUNHAM AND YALLOP GOLD SMITHS.
R : A shop front within a circle. NORWICH HALFPENNY. 1796.
E : Milled.   Conder, 120 ; 24.—Pye, 39 ; 4.—Virt : 95.

⌄ 35. *O* : View of the Cathedral. NORWICH CATHEDRAL. *Ex* : 1797.
R : Bust of Handel. GEORGE FREDERICK HANDEL.
E : PAYABLE BY HARDINGHAM MUSICIAN.   Conder, 120 ; 25.

35*a*.   As last, but *E* : Plain (in collar).
Rare ; only about four dozen struck. Also struck in silver.

36.   Very similar to last, but with a slightly different bust, which may be distinguished by noticing the hair, of which there is less, and it is farther from the ear.
E : Plain (in collar).   Conder, 315 ; 25.—Pye, 40 ; 4.
Very rare.
This bust of Handel also appears upon a set of Coventry Buildings, which see.
The obv. of No. 35 occurs with the following reverses :—

⌄ 37. *R* : Armoured bust to left. PROMISSORY HALFPENNY.   See Hampshire, No. 21.   Conder, 120 ; 26.
Rare.

38. *R* : Armoured bust to right. FOR GENERAL CONVENIENCE. See Not Local, No. 101.
Very rare.

⌄ 39. *O* : Shield of arms of the city of Norwich, the shield plain. The date 1 7 9 2 around.
R : A man working in a loom.
E : IOHN HARVEY OF NORWICH . × × × ×.
In this specimen the 2 of the date is in a line with the lower loop-hole of castle, and on the reverse the wheel of the loom appears to have nine spokes, none of which are quite perpendicular or horizontal.

40.   Similar to last, but there is no tuft about the middle of the lion's tail.
This may be identified by a small comma-like flaw between the base of the castle and left hand edge of the shield.

41. Similar to No. 39, but the 2 of date comes between the two loop-holes.

42. *O* : Similar to No. 39.

    R : Similar, but there are eight spokes to wheel, two of which are perpendicular and two horizontal. The loop of cord hanging from the top beams describes a regular curve.

43. *O* : Same as No. 40.

    R : Similar to last, but the loop of the cord does not describe a regular curve.

44. *O* : Same as No. 41.

    R : Same as last.

    E : Of all, the same as No. 39.

44*a*. As last, but *E* : Plain. These are all included under Conder, 120; 27.—Pye, 38; 9.

45. *O* : Similar to preceding, but with the shield emblazoned *gules*.

    R : The same as No. 42.

46. *O* : Same as last.

    R : Same as No. 43.

    Edges of both, the same as No. 39.

These are included under Conder, 120; 28.—Pye, 38; 10. Pye was evidently in error in his attribution of rarity to these pieces, as he says of No. 9, r., about 10 doz., and of No. 10, 1 ton. Now unquestionably the latter is by far the rarer of the two, and the most reasonable explanation would be to transpose the numbers.

47. *O* : A mounted dragoon. PRO REGE ET PATRIA. *Ex* : QUEENS BAYS.

    R : View of the barracks. NORWICH BARRACKS 1793 upon a label above.

    E : PAYABLE AT IOHN ROOKS NORWICH. × × × .

47*a*. As last, but *E* : Plain (not in collar).

    Also struck in silver and brass.

    In this obverse the cockade in dragoon's hat points between the E and T, whilst the point of the sword is near the second E of "REGE."   Pye, 39; 7.

48. *O* : Similar to last, but the cockade in this instance points to the foot of the T, and the point of the sword is near the E of "ET"; the legend also is in smaller letters and the tail of the horse is quite near the period at end of legend.

    R : and *E* : The same as No. 47.

48*a*. As last, but *E* : Plain (not in collar).   Pye, 39; 8.

49. *O* : Same as last.
  R : Differs in several small particulars; the building on left is farther from edge, the post on right of entrance is taller and farther from the others, but may best be identified by the lines marking the brickwork of wall being sunken, whereas in the former they were raised.
  E : Plain (not in collar).
  Rare.
  These three are included under Conder, 121 ; 29.
  The obv. of No. 47 occurs with the following reverse :—

✓ 50. *R* : A figure of Britannia seated. RULE BRITANNIA. *Ex* : 1795. See Hampshire, No. 10.
  E : PAYABLE IN LONDON. The remainder engrailed.

50*a.*   As last, but *E* : Plain (not in collar). Conder, 234; 206. See also No. 8, *ante;* Lancashire, No. 92; Somerset, No. 75; Warwickshire, No. 39; and Yorkshire, No. 73.

YARMOUTH.

51. *O* : Blank.
  R: Shield of arms of the borough of Yarmouth, between sprigs of oak. LET YARMOUTH FLOURISH.
  E : PAYABLE AT THE WAREHOUSE OF SAMUEL KINGDON – – ✗ – –
  The oak sprigs are small, barely reaching the beginning and end of legend, and there is a wide toothed border. This is doubtless the proof of a die, which failed before any use could be made of it.

✓ 52. *O* : A ship in full sail. YARMOUTH HALFPENNY. *Ex* : 1792.
  R : Similar to last, but the sprigs are larger, and overlap the legend two or three letters at either end.
  E : PAYABLE AT THE GLASS WAREHOUSE OF W. ABSOLON . ✗ .
                           Conder, 121 ; 30.
  These pieces are mostly found with a countermark (a rose formed of six dots thus :—∴) on the reverse, just above the last leaf of the oak sprig, usually on the right-hand side, and, but very rarely, on the left.

53. *O* : A female seated, holding a scroll, which is inscribed, BOULTER'S EXHIBITION *of* NATURAL AND ARTIFICIAL CURIOSITIES. *Ex* : YARMOUTH in a curved line.
  R : Three figures, representative of Asia, Africa, and America presenting various curiosities to Britannia, who is recording them in a book. *Ex* : 1796.
  E : PUBLISHED BY JOS. DANL. & JNO. BOULTER .. ✱ ..
                 Conder, 121 ; 31.—Pye, 50 ; 2.

53*a.*   As last, but *E* : PAYABLE AT LONDON LIVERPOOL OR BRISTOL.

53*b*.   As last, but *E* : Plain (in collar).
   Very rare; only a few specimens struck.

v 54. *O* : Similar to last, but *Ex* : straight.
   R : The same as last, with a legend added, UNDIQUAQUE
      COLLIGITUR. *Ex* : 1796.
   E : The same as No. 53.
   Also struck in silver.

v 54*a*.   As last, but *E* : Plain.
               Conder, 121 ; 32.—Pye, 50 ; 3.—Virt : 116.
   These latter are larger than those with inscribed edge.

FARTHING.

YARMOUTH.

55. *O* : A ship in full sail. YARMOUTH HALF HALFPENNY. *Ex* :
      1792.
   R : Shield of arms, between sprigs of oak. LET YARMOUTH
      FLOURISH.
   E : Engrailed.   Conder, 121 ; No. 33.

v 55*a*.   As last, but *E* : Milled.

Northamptonshire.

HALFPENNY.

NORTHAMPTON.

✔ 1. *O* : Bust to left.   GEORGE JOBSON . BANKER.   *Ex* : 1794.
   R : A castle and lion.   MAY NORTHAMPTON FLOURISH.
   E : PAYABLE IN LANCASTER LONDON OR BRISTOL.

   Conder, 122 ; 1.—Pye, 38 ; 5.—Virt : 75.

1*a*.   As last but *E* : Plain (not in collar).
   *This piece is struck upon a much thicker and heavier flan
   than the former one, but is not intended for a penny.*

Northumberland.

PENNIES.

ALNWICK.

✔ 1. *O*: An ancient fortress and spire of a church. ALNWICK. CASTLE . NORTHUMBD. *Ex*: Jacobs.

R: A globe inscribed BRITAIN between a rose and thistle. BRITISH . PENNY. *Ex*: 1797.

E: I PROMISE TO PAY THE BEARER ONE PENNY. Conder, 123; 1.

NEWCASTLE.

✔ 2. *O*: Justice supporting a shield on which are an anchor and a key. JUSTICE RESTING ON THE EMBLEMS OF SECURITY.

R: MATHER | IRONMONGER | DEALER IN | HARDWARE | STOVES GRATES | &c. In six lines within a circle. NEWCASTLE UPON TYNE 1797. Pye, 38; 1.

There were about 2 gross struck of these, the majority being in yellow metal. There are a few in tin.

HALFPENNIES.

NEWCASTLE.

∨ 3. *O*: A sailor. ✱ J. SPENCE ✱ SLOP-SELLER ✱ NEWCASTLE ✱ *Ex*: JAMES.

R: A man in a barge sailing. ✱ COALY ✕ TYNE ✱ *Ex*: 1795. Conder, 123; 2.—Pye, 38; 2.—Virt: 37.

Very rare, only 26 impressions struck.

∨ 4. *O*: The same as last.

R: A barge sailing. COALY . TYNE. *Ex*: 1797.

E: Milled. Conder, 123; 3.

This obv. occurs with the following reverses :—

5. *R*: THOS. SPENCE SIR THOS. MORE THOS. PAINE &c. See Middlesex, No. 511.

E: SPENCE ✕ DEALER ✕ IN ✕ COINS ✕ LONDON ✕ Conder, 292 ; 282.

6. *R*: Britannia seated. ROUSE BRITANNIA. See Middlesex, No. 512.

E: The same as last.

6*a*. As last, but *E*: PAYABLE AT THE WAREHOUSE OF ALEXR. MOLISON. Conder, 293; 291.

6*b*. As last, but *E*: Milled.

7. *R* : A cat. See Middlesex, No. 514.
    E : The same as No. 5.   Conder, 293 ; 290.

8. *R* : Three citizens armed. See Middlesex, No. 515.
    E : The same as last.   Conder, 292 ; 287.

8*a*.   As last, but *E* : Milled.

9. *R* : Heart and hand. See Middlesex, No. 516.
    E : SPENCE × DEALER × IN × COINS × LONDON ×
                                 Conder, 292 ; 284.

9*a*.   As last, but *E* : Plain (not in collar).

10. *R* : An armed Highlander. See Middlesex, No. 517, and
       Lothian, No. 13.
    E : The same as No. 9.   Conder, 292 ; 289.

11. *R* : A lion dismayed. See Middlesex, No. 519.
    E : The same as last.   Conder, 292 ; 285.

12. *R* : A man and ass's heads joined. ODD FELLOWS. See
       Middlesex, No. 520.
    E : The same as last.   Conder, 292 ; 286.

13. *R* : Breeches on fire. PANDORAS BREECHES. See Middlesex,
       No. 522.   Conder, 293 ; 292.

14. *R* : Three men dancing round a tree, &c. AFTER THE
       REVOLUTION. See Middlesex, No. 523.
    E : The same as No. 9.   Conder, 292 ; 288.

15. *R* : A shepherd lying under a tree. See Middlesex, No. 524.
    E : The same as last.   Conder, 292 ; 283.

16. *R* : A turnstile with two boys. See Middlesex, No. 527.
                                   Conder, 293 ; 293.

17. *R* : An anchor and cable. IN COMMEMORATION OF &c. See
       Not Local, No. 117.
    E : The same as No. 9.   Conder, 292 ; 281.

17*a*.   As last, but *E* : Milled.

The rev. of No. 3, appears as an obv. with the following
       reverses :—

18. *R* : Laureate bust to right. CHURCH AND KING. See Middle-
       sex, No. 400.   Conder, 271 ; 66.

19. *R* : THOS. SPENCE, &c. As No. 5.
    E : SPENCE × DEALER × IN × COINS × LONDON ×
                                     Conder, 271 ; 67.

20. *R* : Heart and hand. As No. 9.
    E : The same as last.   Conder, 271 ; 69.

21. *R* : Highlander. As No. 10.
    E : The same as last.   Conder, 271 ; 70.

22. *R* : Shepherd. As No. 15.
    E : The same as last.   Conder, 271 ; 68.

23. *R* : Two boys at a turnstile. As No. 16.
    E : The same as last.

23a.   As last, but *E*: Plain (not in collar). Conder, 300 ; 380.
    All these pieces are scarce.

24. *O*: View of a building.   *Ex*: NEWCASTLE 1800.
    R: A jockey holding a'horse.
    E: PAYABLE AT THE WAREHOUSE LONDON OR LIVERPOOL.
    Exceedingly rare, if not unique. An artist's proof.

NORTH SHIELDS.

✔ 25. *O*: A cart unloading into a ship, moored alongside a quay.
    MAY NORTH SHIELDS FLOURISH.
    R: A cypher *I P R* in monogram, 1795 under it, within a
    wreath. NORTH SHIELDS HALFPENNY.
                            Conder, 123 ; 4.—Virt : 82.
        Rare.
26. *O*: The same as last.
    R: A man on the ground gnawing a bone. FRENCH LIBERTY.
        See Middlesex, No. 591.   Conder, 279 ; 148.
✔ 27. *O*: The same as *R*: of No. 25.
    R: Bust to left. ROBERT ORCHARD. *Ex*: JACOBS. See Mid-
        dlesex, No. 285.   Conder, 289 ; 252.
    The centre of obv. die of No. 25 appears as a farthing.
    See Surrey, No. 32.

FARTHINGS.

NEWCASTLE.

✔ 28. *O*: A barge sailing. ✶ COALY ✶ TYNE ✶
    R: A sailor. NEWCASTLE FARTHING.
                            Conder, 123 ; 5.—Virt : 172.
    This obv. occurs with the following reverses :—
29. *R*: A man riding upon a bull with an ass's head.   See
        Middlesex, No. 777.
    E: Milled.
29a.   As last, but *E*: Plain.   Conder, 304 ; 417.
30. *R*: Britannia seated. ROUSE BRITANNIA. See Middlesex,
        No. 776.
    E: Milled.   Conder, 304 ; 412.
30a.   As last, but *E*: Plain.
✔ 31. *R*: Odd Fellows. See Middlesex, No. 778.
32. *R*: A pig trampling on emblems of Church and State. See
        Middlesex, No. 780.   Conder, 306 ; 433.
33. *R*: A man walking on all fours. See Middlesex, No. 791.
                            Conder, 305 ; 420.
✔ 34. *R*: A slave kneeling. See Middlesex, No. 781.
                            Conder, 307 ; 443.
    The rev. of No. 28 appears as an obv. with the follow-
    ing reverse :—
35. *R*: An anchor and cable. PROMISSORY NAVAL FARTHING. See
        Not Local, No. 204.   Conder, 123 ; 6.—Virt : 172.
                            11

Nottinghamshire.

PENNY.

NEWSTEAD.

∨ 1. *O* : The remains of an ancient abbey. NEWSTEAD ABBEY. On a raised circle, NOTTINGHAMSHIRE Jacobs.

R : A cypher *T. G.* between palm branches. BRITISH PENNY 1797, on a raised circle.

E : I PROMISE TO PAY ON DEMAND THE BEARER ONE PENNY.

Conder, 124: 1.

Very rare.

HALFPENNIES.

NOTTINGHAM.

2. *O* : DONALD & CO | STOCKING | MANUFACTURERS | WHOLESALE & | RETAIL. In five lines within an oval. PROMISSORY HALFPENNY PAYABLE AT NOTTINGM OR

R : A behive and bees within a circle. NO 29 BULL STREET BIRMINGHAM 1792.

∨ 3. *O* : Similar to last. The die has been altered from PROMISSARY to PROMISSORY.

R : Same as last, but a flaw now appears running through the word BIRMINGHAM.

4. *O* : Similar to No. 2, but the small M nearly touches the OR and the latter touches the oval.

R : As before, but the flaw is still further developed especially at the IR of BIRMINGHAM.

One instance of No. 4 has been seen in which the flaw is in the same condition as on No. 3.

Conder, 124; 2.—Pye, 7; 7.—Virt: 11.

See a very similar token at Warwickshire, No. 82.

5. *O* : As last.

R : A man working at a loom. NO 29 BULL STREET *Ex* : BIRMINGHAM 1792.   Pye, 7; 9.

6. *O* : A man working a machine. INCLINED PLANE AT KETLEY 1789. See Shropshire, No. 4.

R : Similar to last.

These two pieces are of extreme rarity (if not unique) and are in all probability trial pieces of a new die, struck upon any reverse which came to hand; the centre of No. 5, is engraved in the only specimen known.

Oxfordshire.

PENNY.

SHERBORNE.

∨ 1. *O*: View of an ancient fortress, and trees. SHERBORNE CASTLE OXFORDSHIRE. *Ex*: Jacobs.

 R: A globe inscribed BRITAIN between a rose and thistle. BRITISH PENNY. *Ex*: 1797.

 E: 1 PROMISE TO PAY ON DEMAND THE BEARER ONE PENNY.

Conder, 125; 1.

HALFPENNY.

BANBURY.

∨ 2. *O*: A three-quarter face bust. WM. RUSHER HATTER BOOKSELR. & STATIONER . BANBURY.

 R: The sun. DEUS . EST . NOBIS . SOL . ET . SCUTUM .

 E: PAYABLE AT BANBURY OXFORD OR READING.

Conder, 125; 2.—Pye, 5; 3.—Virt: 14.

These are made on large and small flans, there being a very considerable difference between the two, and of course in the amount of border showing, as all are from the same pair of dies.

 2*a*. As last, but *E*: Plain (not in collar).

Rutland.

HALFPENNY.

COUNTY.

✓ 1. *O*: COL, NOEL, | OF THE RUTLAND | FENCIBLES M.P. | FOR THE
COUNTY— | LONG LIFE ATTEND | HIM AND HIS | FAMILY.
In seven lines.

R: WHOSE | EXAMPLE IN | LIFE CONSISTS | IN BEING BRAVE |
HUMANE NOBLE | & GENEROUS.   In six lines.

Rare.

Shropshire.

PENNIES.

DUDMASTON.

✔ 1. *O*: A large building. DUDMASTON SHROPSHIRE. *Ex*: Jacobs.
R: A globe inscribed BRITAIN between a rose and thistle.
BRITISH . PENNY. *Ex*: 1797
E: I PROMISE TO PAY ON DEMAND THE BEARER ONE PENNY.
Conder, 128; 1.—Virt: 222.

LUDLOW.

✔ 2. *O*: An ancient fortress. LUDLOW CASTLE . SALOP. *Ex*: Jacobs.
R: and *E*: Same as last.   Conder, 128; 2.—Virt: 210.

HALFPENNIES.

BOSCOBEL.

✔ 3. *O*: Laureated bust to right. CHARLES THE SECOND OF ENG-
LAND 1650.
R: An oak tree. BOSCOBEL HALFPENNY.
E: PAYABLE AT CRONEBANE LODGE OR IN DUBLIN.

3*a*.   As last, but *E*: WILLEY SNEDSHILL BERSHAM BRADLEY.
Conder, 316; 2.
3*b*.   „   „   *E*: Plain.
Rare.

COALBROOK DALE.

✔ 4. *O*: View of a bridge. IRON BRIDGE AT COALBROOK DALE
1779.
R: A man working a machine. INCLINED PLANE | AT KET-
LEY | 1789. In three lines under. The 1 in date
slopes to right.
E: PAYABLE AT COALBROOK-DALE AND KETLEY.
Conder, 128; 3.—Pye, 14; 8.
Very rare; the obverse die broke when only a few impres-
sions had been taken.

5. *O*: Similar to last, but with a vessel sailing under the bridge,
and the following legend above it in three lines :—
ERECTED | ANNO. 1779 | SPAN 100 FT. HEIT. 50 FT.
The outer legend as before, but dated 1792.
R: A very ornamental pattern in seven alternate bands
of straight lines and scrolls.
E: BIRMINGHAM REDRUTH & SWANSEA.
This is an artist's proof, and in all probability unique.

6. *O*: Similar to last, but not from the same die.
   R: The same as No. 4.

7. *O*: The same as last.
   R: Similar, but the 1 of date slopes to left in the ordinary way, and there is a period after KETLEY. Pye, 14; 10.

8. *O*: Similar to last, but the legend over the bridge is ERECTED | ANNO 1779. | SPAN 100 FT. The 1's slope to the right.
   R: Similar, but the 1 of date slopes to right, and there is a period after the date as well as KETLEY.
   These three are patterns, and all exceedingly rare.

✓ 9. *O*: View of a bridge with a vessel sailing under. ERECTED | ANNO 1779. | SPAN 100 FEET. In three lines above the bridge; the whole within an inner circle; outer legend as last, the 1's slope to the right.
   R: The same as No. 4.

10. *O*: The same as last.
    R: Similar to last, but the 1 in date has a *flat* top.
    Pye, 14; 9.

11. *O*: The same as last.
    R: Similar to last, but with a period after KETLEY.

12. *O*: The same as last.
    R: Similar to last, but with a period after the date, as well as KETLEY.
    This variety is very rare.

13. *O*: Similar to No. 9, but the 1's slope to the left, the position of the ends of the bridge to the legend is also different, there is a flaw between the L and B of "COALBROOK," and another under the E of "FEET."
    R: The same as No. 11.
    Also struck in silver.

14. *O*: The same as last.
    R: The same as No. 12.

15. *O*: Very similar to No. 13, but the lamps upon the bridge have only single supports, whereas before they were supported upon triangles.
    R: The same as No. 4.
    This variety also is rare.

✓ 16. *O*: The same as last.
    R: The same as No. 10.
    The edges of all are the same as No. 4, and Nos. 9 to 16 are included under Conder, 128; 4.—Virt: 43.
    For this reverse see also Nottinghamshire, No. 6.

SHREWSBURY.

17. *O* : Shield of arms of the borough of Shrewsbury. SHREWSBURY HALFPENNY 1792.

    R : Blank.

    E : PAYABLE AT MACCLESFIELD LIVERPOOL OR CONGLETON . × .

    This is doubtless an artist's proof, which was not proceeded with in consequence of an error in date, as the 2 is partially erased.

18. *O* : Similar to last, but dated 1793.

    R : A woolpack. SALOP WOOLEEN MANUFACTORY *

    E : PAYABLE AT SHREWSBURY + +

v 19. *O* : Similar to last, but the legend beneath the shield is more divided.

    R : Similar to last, but the top right-hand corner of woolpack, which before pointed to the second limb of the N of " MANUFACTORY," now points to the U.

    E : Same as last.

v 20. *O* : and *E* : Same as last.

    R : Similar, but the right-hand top corner of woolpack now points between the ᴧ and the N of " MANUFACTORY."

                  Conder, 128; 5.—Pye, 44; 2.

    The obv. of No. 18 occurs with the following reverses :—

v 21. *R* : Bishop Blaze holding a woolcomb. SUCCESS TO THE WOOLLEN MANUFACTORY. See Devonshire, No. 2.

    E : PAYABLE IN ANGLESEY LONDON OR LIVERPOOL .×.

                       Conder, 129 ; 6.

22. *R* : Bishop Blaze holding a chalice. Legend as before. See Yorkshire, No. 48.

    E : Same as last.

    See also Anglesea, No. 224.

23. *O* : A close copy of No. 17, but dated 1794.

    R : Similar to preceding, but with a hexagonal star instead of a pentagonal one.

    E : AN ASYLUM FOR THE OPPRESS'D OF ALL NATIONS.

23*a*.   As last, but *E* : BIRMINGHAM REDRUTH & SWANSEA.

23*b*.   „   „   *E* : PAYABLE AT CRONEBANE OR IN BUBLIN.

23*c*.   „   „   *E* : PAYABLE AT LONDON CORK OR BELFAST . × × .

v 23*d*.   „   „   *E* : PAYABLE AT LONDON LIVERPOOL OR BRISTOL.

                      Conder, 129 ; 7.

23*e*.   „   „   *E* : Milled.

23*f*.   „   „   *E* : Plain (not in collar).

    This obv. occurs with the following reverse :—

v 24. *R* : Fame blowing a trumpet. HALFPENNY OF J. LACKINGTON &c. See Middlesex, No. 247.   Conder, 129 ; 8.

FARTHING.

SHREWSBURY.

25. *O* : Shield of arms.   SHREWSBURY HALF HALFPENNY 1792.
   R : A woolpack.   SALOP WOOLLEN MANUFACTORY.
   E : Milled.   Conder, 129; 9.—Virt : 218.

Somersetshire.

PENNIES.

COUNTY.

1. *O* : A sword, spear, and trumpet, crossed, a hat and pair of spurs. SOMERSET YEOMANRY CAVALRY ✳ 1796. ✳
   R : Three horsemen, one carrying a flag. THEIR TOKEN. *Ex* : P . A . ET . F.
   E : Indistinct from one inscription being struck over another.
   This is from the halfpenny dies of No. 21.

BATH.

✓ 2. *O* : View of a cathedral. ABBEY CHURCH BATH.
   R : View of a public building. GUILD-HALL BATH.
   E : Plain (in collar). Conder, 130 ; 1.
   This is struck in copper, brass, and white metal.

✓ 3. *O* : View of entrance to the BOTANIC GARDEN. A small letter A on the bricks leading to the entrance. HE SPAKE OF TREES FROM THE CEDAR TREE THAT IS IN LEBANON + *Ex* : BATH TOKEN.
   R : Shrubs growing on a wall and a large tree. EVEN UNTO THE HYSSOP THAT SPRINGETH OUT OF THE WALL + *Ex* : 1 . KINGS : CH : 4 V : 33.
   E : ON DEMAND WE PROMISE TO PAY ONE PENNY . ×
   Conder, 130 ; 2.—Virt : 12.

4. *O* : GLOVERS LONDON SHEFFIELD & BIRMINGM. WAREROOMS . BATH.
   R : Bust to left. STANHOPE NOBLE WITHOUT NOBILITY.
   E : Same as No. 1.

5. *O* : Crowned bust to right. ALFRED YE GREAT REFOUNDED BATH . A.D. 900 .
   R : A tower within a wall. AND SURROUNDED IT WITH WALLS & TOWERS .
   E : Same as No. 3.

✓ 6. *O* : A camel, and rays of sun. TEAS COFFEE SPICES & SUGARS.
   Ex : A five-pointed star.
   R : View of a building. INDIA HOUSE 1794 within a circle. M . LAMBE & SON TEA-DEALERS & GROCERS BATH
   E : As before. Conder, 130 ; 3.—Virt : 123.

7. Similar to last, excepting date, which is 1795.
   Conder, 130 ; 4.

8.   „   „   „   „   „   1796.
   Conder, 130 ; 5.

The two latter are exceedingly rare.

9. *O*: A scroll inscribed READY MONEY ONLY within a circle. WOOD & CO LINENDRAPERS &c.
　R: Perspective view of a street. BATH STREET. *Ex*: BATH.
　　　　　　　　　　　　　　　Conder, 131; 6.

10. *O*: Shield of arms of the city of Bath. THE ARMS OF THE CITY OF BATH
　R: View of a building. INDIA HOUSE above, 1794 below; the whole within a circle. M. LAMBE & SON TEA DEALERS & GROCERS BATH (The same as No. 6.)
　E: The same as No. 3.

11. Similar to last, but dated 1795.

12. 　　 „　　 „　　 „　 1796.

13. *O*: As No. 10.
　R: Arms, supporters, &c., of the city of Bath. W. GYE PRINTER & STATIONER BATH 1794
　E: The same as No. 3.

14. *O*: As No. 10.
　R: A female seated, directing a boy with a key to open the prison doors. GO FORTH radiated, the whole within a beaded circle. REMEMBER THE DEBTORS IN ILCHESTER GAOL .
　E: The same as No. 1.

15. *O*: As No. 10.
　R: The same as the obverse of No. 9.
　E: The same as No. 3.

16. *O*: As No. 10.
　R: View of a building. WEST FRONT OF NEW PUMPROOM BATH. *Ex*: HEATH . IRONMONGER &c. 1795.
　E: MANUFACTURED BY W. LUTWYCHE BIRMINGHAM.

BRISTOL.

17. *O*: The arms of the city of Bristol, within a circle. PROSPERITY TO THE CITY OF BRISTOL.
　R: A figure of Galen. I. CHESTER . DRUGGIST AND CHYMIST.
　　　　　　　　　　　　　　　Conder, 131; 7.

18. *O*: As last.
　R: A public building. EXCHANGE BRISTOL . 1796.
　　　　　　　　　　　　　　　Conder, 131; 8.

19. *O*: As last.
　R: A glass house, an ornament under. SUCCESS TO THE GLASS MANUFACTORY.　　　Conder, 131; 9.

All these pennies, with the exception of No. 2, are struck from the halfpenny dies, and, with the exception of Nos. 3 and 6, are all scarce, and some are very rare.

GLASTONBURY.

✓ 20. *O* : The remains of an ancient abbey. THE . FRONT . OF . GLASTONBURY . ABBEY . *Ex* : SOMERRE. Jacobs.

     R : A globe inscribed BRITAIN between a rose and thistle. BRITISH . PENNY . *Ex* : 1797.

     E : I PROMISE TO PAY ON DEMAND THE BEARER ONE PENNY.

                         Conder, 131 ; 10.—Virt : 209.

HALFPENNIES.

COUNTY.

✓ 21. *O* : A military trophy, &c. As on No. 1. SOMERSET YEOMANRY CAVALRY * 1796 *

     R : Three horsemen. As on No. 1. THEIR TOKEN. *Ex* : P . A . ET . F.

     E : WE PROMISE TO PAY ON DEMAND ONE HALFPENNY . ✕ .

                      Conder, 131 ; 11.—Pye, 44 ; 9.—Virt : 176.

     Rare.

BATH.

✓ 22. *O* : View of entrance to Botanic Garden. HE SPAKE OF TREES &c. As on No. 3.

     R : Shrubs on a wall, and a tree. EVEN UNTO, &c. As on No. 3.

     E : Plain (not in collar, but rounded).

                    Conder, 132 ; 12.—Pye, 5 ; 8.—Virt : 50.

22*a*.   As last, but *E* : PAYABLE AT LEEK STAFFORDSHIRE.

22*b*.   „   „   *E* : PAYABLE AT W. PARRIS DIMCHURCH . ✕ . ✕ . ✕ .

22*c*.   „   „   *E* : PAYABLE IN LANCASTER LONDON OR BRISTOL.

22*d*.   „   „   *E* : MASONIC TOKEN I. SCETCHLEY FECIT 1794 .

✓ 23. *O* : Laureate bust to right, D under . GEORGIVS III REX.

     R : Shield of arms between sprigs. VISITED BATH CITY SEPTEMBER 10th, 1789.   Conder, 133 ; 22.

✓ 24. *O* : GLOVERS LONDON SHEFFIELD & BIRMINGM WAREROOMS BATH.

     R : NO 39 MILSOM STREET in two lines in centre. LATE BATH & SOMERSET BANK

     E : PAYABLE AT NO 39 MILSOM STREET . + . + .

                    Conder, 132 ; 13.—Pye, 6 ; 2.—Virt : 50.

24*a*.   As last, but *E* : PAYABLE IN LANCASTER LONDON OR LIVERPOOL.

24*b*.   As last, but *E* : PAYABLE IN LONDON. The remainder engrailed.

24*c*.   As last, but *E* : Milled.

     Scarce. Only a few lbs. of these were struck.

25. *O*: The same as last.
  R: Shield of arms. THE ARMS OF THE CITY OF BATH.
  E: PAYABLE BY I. FOSTER LAMBERHURST.
  Very rare.

26. *O*: The same as last.
  R: Bust to left. STANHOPE NOBLE WITHOUT NOBILITY. See
    Not Local, No. 147.
  E: ADAM SIMPSON ROMNEY.

  Also very rare.

27. *O*: The arms, supporters, &c., of the city of Bath.   W. GYE
    PRINTER & STATIONER BATH 1794
  R: A female seated, instructing a boy with a key to unlock
    the prison doors. GO FORTH radiated; the whole
    within a beaded circle. REMEMBER THE DEBTORS IN
    ILCHESTER GAOL
  E: PAYABLE AT W. GYE'S PRINTER BATH ×.×
                  Conder, 132; 16.—Pye, 5; 6.

✓ 27a.   As last, but *E*: PAYABLE BY JAMES TEBAYS HASTINGS.×.
    (An artist's proof.)
    Very rare. In consequence of an omission of the " bends "
    in the arms on the obverse, and a failure in the die of
    the reverse, only a very few proofs were struck, and
    another token was produced as follows :—

✓ 28. *O*: Similar to last, but with the *bends* added on the shield
    of arms.
  R: Similar to last, but the end of the boy's robe, which
    floats over his shoulder, does not go so high; there is
    also more room at the end of legend, and a period
    and a trefoil, instead of the quatrefoil, as on
    No. 27.
  E: Same as No. 27.   Conder, 132; 15.
    Rare. This reverse die also failed, and the following
    appeared instead :—

✓ 29. *O*: and *E*: The same as last.
  R: Similar, but the boy has no robe floating over his
    shoulder, and the rays from " GO FORTH " are not so
    long.   Conder, 132; 14.—Pye, 5; 7.—Virt: 50.
    This token supplies the rev. dies of the pennies, Nos. 13 and
    14, which see.

    The rev. of No. 28 appears as an obv. with the following
    reverse :—

✓ 30. *R*: Bust to left.   IOHN HOWARD F.R.S. HALFPENNY.   See
    Not Local, No. 109.
  E: PAYABLE AT BANBURY OXFORD OR READING +

30a.   As last, but *E*: PAYABLE IN LANCASTER LONDON OR BRISTOL.
                  Conder, 225; 126.
    A very similar design occurs on the rev. of Not Local, No.
    109.

31. *O* : Bust to left, with bow and quiver.   BLADUD FOUNDER OF
        BATH   SUCCESS TO THE BATH WATERS
    R : A tea urn, IRONMONGERY BRAZIERY & CUTLERY.   *Ex* :
        F. HEATH. 1794.
    E : PAYABLE BY F : HEATH BATH.
               Conder, 132 ; 17.—Pye, 5 ; 9.—Virt : 49.
    This obv. occurs with the following reverses :—
32. *R* : A public building.   WEST FRONT OF NEW PUMPROOM
        BATH.   *Ex* : HEATH IRONMONGER &c 1795.
    E : Milled.   Conder, 133 ; 18.—Pye, 5 ; 10.—Virt : 49.
    *This is struck on both large and small flans, with
    a very considerable difference in size, the large ones
    showing a broad toothed border.*
33. *R* : A public building.   NORTH FRONT OF PUMPROOM.   *Ex* :
        HEATH IRONMONGER &c 1796.
    E : Milled.   Conder, 133 ; 19.—Virt : 100.
34. *R* : Shield of arms of the city of Bath, &c. See No. 25.
    E : PAYABLE AT ANGLESEY LONDON OR LIVERPOOL.
                     Conder, 133 ; 20.
35. *R* : Ancient walls and tower, &c.   See No. 54.
                     Conder, 133 ; 21.
    Rare.
36. *R* : View of a building.   STALL STREET BATH.   *Ex* : INDIA
        HOUSE 1794.   Conder, 134 ; 27.
37. *R* : A turnpike gate and house.   WALCOT TURNPIKE TOKEN.
        Ex : 1796 NO TRUST.
    E : PAYABLE AT WALCOT TURNPIKE BATH . × .
               Conder, 135 ; 44.—Pye, 6 ; 1.—Virt : 70.
    A few lbs. only struck.
38. *R* : A tea chest inscribed M. LAMBE & SON &c.   See No. 104
    E : PAYABLE AT ADAM SIMPSONS ROMNEY.
    *This is struck from the die of the farthing, No. 104, and is
    very rare.*
39. *R* : Bust to right. RT. HL. C. J. FOX. See Middlesex, No. 529.
    This also is very rare.
40. *O* : A camel and radiation.   TEAS COFFEE SPICES & SUGARS.
    Ex : A pentagonal star.
    R : View of the " INDIA HOUSE 1794 " within a beaded circle.
        M. LAMBE & SON TEA-DEALERS & GROCERS BATH. This is
    from the same dies as the penny, No. 6.
    E : PAYABLE BY × M. LAMBE & SON.
               Conder, 133 ; 23.—Pye, 5 ; 5.—Virt : 50.
40*a*.   As last, but *E* : PAYABLE AT 39 MILSOM STREET . × × .
40*b*.   „   „ *E* : PAYABLE AT LEEK STAFFORDSHIRE.
40*c*.   „   „ *E* : PAYABLE IN LANCASTER LONDON OR BRISTOL.
40*d*.   „   „ *E* : PAYABLE BY I. SIMMONS STAPLEHURST.
40*e*.   „   „ *E* : YORK BUILT A.M. 1223. CATHEDRAL RE-
    BUILT A.D. 1075 +

✓ 40*f*.   As last, but *E* : Milled. *These are struck in brass, and are rare.*

✓ 40*g*.   As last, but *E* : Plain (not in collar, but rounded).

✓ 41.   Similar to last, but dated 1795.
    E : PAYABLE BY M. LAMBE & SON BATH   Conder, 133 ; 25.

✓ 42.   Similar to last, but dated 1796.   Conder, 134 ; 26.

    42*a*.   As last but *E* : Plain (not in collar).

✓ 43. *O* : Perspective view of a street. BATH STREET. *Ex* : BATH.
    R : The same as No. 40.
    E : The same as No. 41.   Conder, 133 ; 24.

    43*a*.   As last, but *E* : Milled.
              This obv. occurs with the following reverses :—

44. *R* : The same as No. 41.

45. *R* : The same as No. 42.
          The edges of both, the same as No. 41.

46. *O* : Shield of arms, &c. As on No. 25.
    R : Female seated, &c. As on No. 27.
    E : PAYABLE BY I. FOSTER LAMBERHURST.
          This obv. occurs with the following reverses :—

47. *R* : Tea urn, &c. As on No. 31.

48. *R* : West front of pumproom, &c. As on No. 32.

49. *R* : India House, 1794, &c. As on No. 40.

50. *R* : India House, 1795, &c. As on No. 41.

51. *R* : GOLD SILVER OR COPPER &c. See No. 85.
          The edges of all these are the same as No. 41.

52. *R* : View of a street. BATH STREET. *Ex* ; BATH. See
          No. 43.
    E : Engrailed.   Conder, 136 ; 46.

    52*a*.   As last, but *E* : PAYABLE AT SOUTH SHIELDS AND LONDON.

    52*b*.   „   „   *E* : PAYABLE IN HULL AND IN LONDON.

✓ 52*c*.   „   „   *E* : Milled.

    52*d*.   „   „   *E* : Plain (not in collar).

✓ 53. *R*. View of a building. PRINCIPAL ENTRANCE NEW ROOMS.
          Ex : BATH.
    E : Milled.   Conder, 136 ; 48.—Pye, 6 ; 3.—Virt : 65.
              *These various combinations were made by Mr. Lambe with
              the object of giving a fictitious interest to this issue of
              tokens; they are consequently most of them rare.*

✓ 54. *O* : A crowned bust to right. ALFRED YE GREAT REFOUNDED
          BATH . A D . 900.
    R : Ancient walls and a tower. AND SURROUNDED IT WITH
          WALLS & TOWERS . X . See also No. 35.
    E : PAYNE & TURNER SILVER-SMITHS BATH .
                        Conder, 135 ; 43.—Pye, 6 ; 4.—Virt : 49.

54a.　　As last, but *E*: I PROMISE TO PAY ON DEMAND ONE HALF-
　　　　PENNY.
　　　　*This is struck from the same dies as the penny, No. 5.
　　　　A few lbs. only of this were struck.*

55.　*O*: A scroll inscribed READY MONEY ONLY within a circle.
　　　　WOOD & CO. LINEN DRAPERS &C.
　　R: Shield of arms, &c. As on No. 25.
　　E: Engrailed.　　　　　　　Conder, 135; 47.—Virt: 65.

55a.　　As last, but *E*: WILLEY SNEDSHILL BERSHAM BRADLEY.

55b.　　　　　,,　　,,　　*E*: Plain (not in collar).

56.　*O*: Same as last.
　　R: View of a street. BATH STREET. *Ex*: BATH. See No. 43.
　　E: PAYABLE AT LONDON. The remainder engrailed.

56a.　　As last, but *E*: Engrailed.　　　Conder, 136; 47.

56b.　　　　,,　　,,　　*E*: Milled.

57.　*O*: A head, front face. MINERVA PATRONESS OF BATH.
　　R: A sphinx. Badly executed.　　　Conder, 134; 28.

Bath Buildings.

58.　*O*: Front view of a chapel. *Ex*: ALL SAINTS CHAPEL.
　　R: The arms and supporters of Bath, in a sunk oval. BATH
　　　CITY TOKEN.
　　E: Plain (in collar).　　　Conder, 134; 29.—Virt: 234.

59.　*O*: Front view of chapel. ARGYLE CHAPEL.
　　R: and *E*: Same as last.　　　Conder, 134; 30.

60.　*O*: View of a street. BATH STREET. *Ex*: BATH.
　　R: and *E*: Same as last.　　　Conder, 134; 31.

61.　*O*: Front view of a building. CROSS BATH PUMP ROOM.
　　R: and *E*: Same as last.　　Conder, 134; 32.—Virt: 234.

62.　*O*: View of a church. *Ex*: FREE CHURCH.
　　R: and *E*: Same as last.　　　Conder, 134; 33.

62a.　　As last, but *E*: COVENTRY TOKEN.

63.　*O*: View of a building. *Ex*: FREE SCHOOL.
　　R: and *E*: The same as No. 58.　　Conder, 134; 34.

64.　*O*: View of a building. GENERAL HOSPITAL. *Ex*: OPEN TO
　　　PEOPLE OF ALL COUNTRIES BATH ALONE EXCEPTED.
　　R: and *E*: As last.　　　Conder, 134; 35.—Virt: 234.

65.　*O*: View of a chapel. KENSINGTON * CHAPEL *
　　R: and *E*: As before.　　Conder, 134; 36.—Virt: 234.

66.　*O*: View of a chapel. ST. MARYS above, CHAPEL below.
　　R: and *E*: As before.　　　Conder, 135; 37.

67.　*O*: A similar view of the same building. *Ex*: ST. MARYS
　　　CHAPEL.
　　R: and *E*: As before.　　-　　Conder, 135; 38.

68.　*O*: Front view of a building. PRIVATE BATHS. *Ex*: STALL
　　　STREET.
　　R: and *E*: As before.　　　Conder, 135; 40.

✔ 69. *O*: View of a bridge with houses. *Ex*: PULTENEY BRIDGE
        BATH.
     R: and *E*: As before.   Conder, 135; 39.

   70. *O*: Interior of a public building, showing ceiling, with
        INTERIOR OF NEW PUMP ROOM above it. *Ex*: BATH
        ERECTED 1796.
     R: and *E*: As before.

✔ 71. *O*: View of the same interior, but not showing ceiling.
        INTERIOR OF NEW PUMP ROOM BATH ERECTED 1796.
     R: and *E*: As before.   Conder, 135; 41.

   71*a*.   As last, but *E*: COVENTRY TOKEN.

✔ 72. *O*: View of a building. PRINCIPAL ENTRANCE NEW ROOMS.
        Ex: BATH.
     R: and *E*: As No. 58.   Conder, 135; 42.

   73. *O*: Military trophy. PRO REGE ET PATRIA ✳ ✳ BATH ASSOCIA-
        TION ✳ 1798.
     R: and *E*: As before.
        *Of these pieces Nos. 59, 60, 69, 70, and 73 are the most
        rare, No. 70 being especially so.*

BRIDGEWATER.

✔ 74. *O*: Front view of a house. I. HOLLOWAY AND SON DRAPERS
        &c. POST OFFICE. *Ex*: 1794.
     R: Part of a castle and a bridge. B.WATER HALFPENNY . FOR
        CHANGE NOT FRAUD.
     E: ON DEMAND WE PROMISE TO PAY.
                    Conder, 136; 49.—Pye, 9; 9.—Virt: 31.
        Also struck in silver.

   74*a*.   As last, but *E*: PAYABLE AT GOLDSMITHS & SONS SUDBURY.
   74*b*.   „   „   *E*: PAYABLE AT SOUTH SHIELDS AND LONDON.
   74*c*.   „   „   *E*: PAYABLE AT THE STORE OF . ✚ ✚ ✚ ✚ .
   74*d*.   „   „   *E*: PAYABLE IN LONDON. The remainder en-
        grailed.
   74*e*.   As last, but *E*: Plain (not in collar).
        This rev. appears as an obv. with the following re-
        verse :—

✔ 75. *R*: A dragoon mounted. PRO REGE ET PATRIA. *Ex*: QUEENS
        BAYS. See Norfolk, No. 47.
     E: PAYABLE IN LONDON. The remainder engrailed.

   75*a*.   As last, but *E*: Engrailed.   Conder, 136; 50.

   75*b*.   „   „   *E*: Plain (not in collar).

BRISTOL.

76. *O*: A tower and spire of a church. ONE HALFPENNY HAWKINS
BIRD.
R: Front view of a building. PAYABLE AT THE INDIA TEA
WAREHOUSE 1793.
E: Milled. Conder, 136; 51.—Pye, 10; 4.
76a. As last, but *E*: Plain (not in collar, but rounded).
*Both very rare, as after a few proofs were taken the obv.
die was altered to the following:—*
✓ 77. *O*: Similar to last, but with an inner legend added, WINE
STREET NO. 2 BRISTOL.
R: The same as last.
Conder, 136; 52.—Pye, 10; 5.—Virt: 51.
This occurs with oblique, and nearly upright milling.
.77a. As last, but *E*: Plain (rounded).
✓ 78. *O*: The arms of Bristol within a circle. PROSPERITY TO THE
CITY OF BRISTOL.
R: A figure of Galen. I . CHESTER . DRUGGIST AND CHYMIST.
Conder, 136; 53.—Pye, 10; 6.—Virt: 56.
This is from the same dies as the penny No. 17.
This obv. occurs with the following reverses:—
✓ 79. *R*: A public building. EXCHANGE BRISTOL . 1796.
E: BRISTOL FAIR TOKEN . ×.×.×.×.×.×.× .
Conder, 137; 54.—Pye, 10; 8.—Virt: 70.
80. *R*: An antique shield inscribed PRO ARIS ET FOCIS and a mili-
tary trophy. BRISTOL VOLUNTEER TOKEN 1798.
81. *R*: A glass factory. SUCCESS TO THE GLASS MANUFACTORY.
E: I PROMISE TO PAY ON DEMAND ONE HALFPENNY . × .
Conder, 137; 55.
Rare. Only a few lbs. of each of these were struck.
82. *R*: A scroll within a circle, inscribed READY MONEY ONLY.
Similar to the centre of No. 55.
83. *R*: A flame issuing from a tomb inscribed HAMPDEN &
SYDNEY. See Not Local, No. 137.
84. *R*: Bust to right. J. PRIESTLEY CITIZEN OF THE WORLD. See
Not Local, No. 137.
These three are very rare.
✓ 85. *O*: GOLD | SILVER OR | COPPER | I CAN COMMAND | VALUE ONE
| HALFPENNY | UPON | DEMAND.
R: and *E*: The same as No. 81.
Conder, 137; 56.—Pye, 10; 7.—Virt: 195.
Only a few lbs. of these were struck. See also No. 51.
✓ 86. *O*: A large bale marked N H B *No.* 1 crest, a leopard, GENE-
RAL COMMISSION & PUBLIC SALE ROOM BRIDGE STREET
BRISTOL. There is no period at end of legend, and
the *N* on the bale is *Italic*, whilst the 1 is a square
top figure.
R: A figure of Justice standing, dividing the date 17—95.
PAYABLE AT NIBLOCK & HUNTER'S.

12

87. *O*: Similar to last, but with a period at end of legend, and the 1 is a sloping figure.
    R: As last.

✔ 88. *O*: Very similar, but from a different die, which may be distinguished by the letter s in "BRISTOL" being larger than any other letter. (This will apply to all the s's.)
    R: As last.   Conder, 137; 57.—Pye, 10; 9.—Virt: 51.

✔ 89. *O*: Two men talking. (I WANT TO BUY SOME CHEAP BARGAINS.) (THEN GO TO NIBLOCK'S, IN BRIDGE STREET.)
    R: View of a bridge.   BRISTOL TOKEN 1795.

✔ 90. *O*: Very similar to last, but from a different die, which may best be distinguished by noting in this that the B of "BARGAINS" is directly under the T of "To," whilst in the former it is considerably to the left of it.
    R: Same as last.
       Conder, 137; 58.—Pye, 10; 10.—Virt: 183.
Both rare in good condition, No. 89 especially so.

CREWKERNE.

91. *O*: A man weaving in a loom.
    R: PAYABLE | ON DEMAND AT | SPARKS & GIDLEYS | LINEN & WOOLLEN | GIRTH WEB | MANUFACTORY | CREWKERNE 1797.
    E: Milled.

✔ 92. *O*: Very nearly like the last, but a portion of the treadles show behind the feet of the man and inside the loom.
    R: and *E*: The same as last.
       Conder, 316; *58.—Pye, 15; 7.
Both scarce in good condition.

DUNKIRK.

✔ 93. *O*: A fleece and a cypher *M & I* under . . SUCCESS TO THE STAPLE OF ENGLAND.
    R: Front view of a large building.   DUNKIKRE FACTORY 1795.
    E: Milled to left.
       Conder, 137; 60.—Pye, 17; 5.—Virt: 84.
Rare. In consequence of the error in spelling a second reverse die was executed as follows :—

94. *O*: Same as last.
    R: View of building as before.   DUNKIRK SOMT. FACTORY 1795.
    E: Milled in opposite direction to last.
    Also rare.

94a.   As last, but *E*: Plain (not in collar).

✔ 95. *O*: Similar to last, but without the small ornamental flourishes to the cypher.
    R: and *E*: The same as last.
              Conder, 137; 59.—Pye, 17; 6.—Virt: 84.
    See also Yorkshire, No. 51.
    Dunkirk Factory was situate in the parish of Freshford, about five miles from Bath.

YEOVIL.

✔ 96. *O*: A man weaving in a loom.
    R: *B & C* YEOVIL 1797. In three lines occupying the whole of the field.
    In good condition scarce.
              Conder, 317; *60.—Pye, 50; 4.

FARTHINGS.

BATH.

✔ 97. *O*: A tea-chest inscribed M. LAMBE & SON GROCERS BATH SPICES TEAS SUGARS COFFEES.
    R: Front view of a public building. STALL STREET BATH.
    Ex: INDIA HOUSE + 1794 +
              Conder, 137; 61.—Pye, 6; 6.—Virt: 125.
98. *O*: The same as last.
    R: A monogram cypher *L L.* A BATH FARTHING TOKEN * 1795.
    E: Milled. *Mostly struck in brass.*
✔ 98a. As last, but *E*: Plain (not in collar).
              Conder, 138; 62.— Pye, 6; 7.—Virt: 125.
✔ 99. *O*: The same as last.
    R: A cypher *M L & S.* PAYABLE ON DEMAND . 1796.
              Conder, 138; 63.—Pye, 6; 8.
✔ 100. *O*: The same as last.
    R: A camel and rays of sun. *Ex*: 1797.
              Conder, 138; 64.—Pye, 6; 9.
✔ 101. *O*: A crowned bust to left, with bow and quiver. BLADUD FOUNDED BATH.
    R: Bladud driving his swine. THROUGH HIS SWINE. *Ex*: 1794.   Conder, 138; 65.—Pye, 6; 10.
✔ 102. *O*: The same as last.
    R: Front view of a building. WEST FRONT OF NEW PP. ROOM BATH. *Ex*: HEATH IRONMONGER &c. 1795.
              Conder, 138; 66.—Pye, 6; 11.
103. *O*: A tea-chest, &c. Same as No. 97.
    R: Bust of Bladud, &c., as on obverse of No. 101.
    These varieties were issued by Mr. Lambe for the reason assigned in a note to No. 53; Nos. 98, 99, 100, and 103 are rare, the latter especially so.

104. *O*: The same as last.
    R: A balance, with the Persian word (Adel) "Justice,"
        between the scales.

        *This is from the die for the half-pice of Bombay. Very
        rare.*

        This obverse die was also used for the halfpenny,
        No. 38.

105. *O*: A cypher *M L & S*, &c. As on rev. of No. 99.
    R: Shield of arms of the city of Bath; from the centre of
        No. 25.
    E: Milled.

106. *O*: The same as last.
    R: A female standing holding a pole upon which is a cap
        of Liberty; on her right is an altar with a heart in
        flames, and on her left a pedestal supporting a balance.
        EQUALITY, LIBERTY, FRATERNITY.

    These last two pieces are exceedingly rare.

Staffordshire.

PENNIES.

LICHFIELD.

✓ 1. *O*: Bust to left. RICHARD GREENE COLLECTOR OF THE LICHFIELD MUSEUM DIED JUNE 4 1793 AGED 77.

    R: An antique door and porch. WEST PORCH OF LICHFIELD CATHEDRAL. *Ex*: 1800.

    E: PENNY TOKEN PAYABLE BY RICHARD WRIGHT LICHFIELD.

                                 Pye, 35*; 2.

    Very rare. Private token; only six dozen struck.

STAFFORD.

2. *O*: The arms of the borough of Stafford (a castle and four lions). STAFFORD 1801.

    R: A cypher *W H* and a Staffordshire knot. PENNY. Curved bases to the letters.

    E: PAYABLE BY HORTON AND COMPANY.

3. *O*: Similar to last, but the lions are higher up and nearer to legend.

    R: and *E*: The same as last.

4. *O*: Similar, but the lions are farther from the castle and quite under the first and last letters of legend.

    R: The knot differs, in the end to right being under the loop.

✔ 5.   Similar to No. 2, but dated 1803.

    This is another instance in which tokens of the 19th century have, from their intimate connection with the present series, been included in this work. See the halfpenny, No. 17.

TAMWORTH.

✓ 6. *O*: View of a castle. TAMWORTH CASTLE EAST VIEW 1799.

    R: View of a building. TOWN HALL REBUILT BY THOMAS GUY. *Ex*: TAMWORTH 1701.

    E: PENNY TOKEN | PAYABLE AT THE | HOUSE OF | IOHN HARDING | CALICO PRINTER | TAMWORTH.   Pye, 46; 6.

    Very rare. Six impressions in silver and four dozen in copper only were taken when the dies failed.

6a.   As last, but *E*: Plain (in collar).

    Sharp says, only three impressions were struck with a plain edge.

HALFPENNIES.

LEEK.

v   7. *O*: A caduceus, supported by a large bale of goods, lying
across a chest. LEEK COMMERCIAL HALFPENNY 1793.
The top of caduceus points to first limb of R in
" COMMERCIAL " and the bottom to the 3 in date. The
1 of date is curved.

   R: Two hands united, and an olive branch. ARTE FAVENTE
NIL DESPERANDUM

   E: PAYABLE AT LEEK STAFFORDSHIRE

Conder, 139 ; 1.—Pye, 26 ; 6.—Virt: 68.

   8. *O*: Similar to last, but the top of caduceus comes between
the R and C and the bottom to the 9.

   R: Same design and legend as before, but the letters much
smaller.

   E: As last.

   9. *O*: Similar, the top of caduceus as before between the R and
C, but the bottom comes to the 3. There is a flaw
running through the first part of the word
" HALFPENNY."

   R: and *E*: The same as last.

   9*a*.   As last, but *E*: Plain (not in collar).
Both these are very rare.

v 10. *O*: Similar to No. 7, but the 1 in date is square and the
3 much smaller.

   R: Differs slightly from No. 8 ; there are not so many
berries on the olive under the hands (8 as against 10).

   E: As before.

v 10*a*.   As last, but *E*: Milled.   These are on a larger flan.

   11. *O*: Similar to preceding; the top of caduceus points to last
limb of R, the bottom to the Y.

   R: and *E*: The same as No. 10.

   11*a*.   As last, but *E*: BIRMINGHAM LIVERPOOL OR LONDON.

   12. *O*: Similar, but the top of caduceus points to centre of R,
and the bottom to the period.

   R: and *E*: The same as No. 10.

Conder, 139 ; 2.— Pye, 26 ; 7.

The obv. of No. 10 occurs with the following reverse :—

   13. *R*: Figure of Justice standing. FOR CHANGE NOT FRAUD. *Ex*:
1794.   See Suffolk, No. 20.

   E: PAYABLE BY THOMAS BALL SLEAFORD.

v 13*a*.   As last, but *E*: Plain (not in collar).

Conder, 139 ; 3.—Virt: 101.

The rev. also of No. 10 occurs as obv. with the following
reverse :—

v 14. *R*: The same as last.

   E: Milled.

Conder, 224 ; 119.

LICHFIELD.

✓ 15. *O*: Bust to left, a small ornament under. DR. SAML. IOHNSON.
    R: A laurel wreath. LITCHFIELD TOKEN. MDCCXCVI.
                         Conder, 139; 4.—Virt: 71.
    This obv. occurs with the following reverse :—
✓ 16. *R*: A figure of Britannia seated.   * * RULE BRITANIA * *
        Ex: 1797. See Middlesex, No. 751.
    E: PAYABLE IN LONDON. The remainder engrailed.
    See also Norfolk, No. 9; and Warwickshire, No. 31.

STAFFORD.

✓ 17. *O*: The arms of Stafford. The same as on No. 2. STAFFORD
        1797.
    R: A cypher *W. H.* and a Staffordshire knot. HALFPENNY.
    E: PAYABLE BY HORTON AND COMPANY + + +
17*a*.   As last, but *E*: Plain (not in collar).
18. *O*: Similar to last, but the lions are a little higher, and the
        letters of legend do not spread out to the edge so far
        as the lions do.
    R: and *E*: The same as last.   Conder, 139; 5.
18*a*. As last, but *E*: PAYABLE AT GLOCESTER . . . × .

TAMWORTH.

✓ 19. *O*: A view of Tamworth castle and church. CHURCH AND
        CASTLE. *Ex*: TAMWORTH.
    R: An ornamental cypher *I. B.* DEUS NOBIS FIDUCIA. *Ex*:
        HALFPENNY TOKEN MDCCXCIX.   Pye, 46; 5.
    *Very rare. A few impressions only in silver, and six dozen
    in copper were taken, also a few in tin.*

TIPTON.

✓ 20. *O*: View of a church. TIPTON HALFPENNY.
    R: An anchor and cable. PAYABLE . . IN . . STAFFORDSHIRE .
        1797.
    E: Engrailed.   Conder, 139; 6.
    Rare.

WOLVERHAMPTON.

✓ 21. *O*: A barrel and two bunches of grapes.
    R: *Wines* | And Spirits | WHOLESALE *and* | Retail by | T.
        BEVAN | WOLVERHAMPTON. In six lines, the top and
        bottom ones being curved.
                 Conder, 140; 7.—Pye, 49, 3.
    *Very rare. Six dozen impressions only were taken when the
    dies failed.*

FARTHINGS.

LICHFIELD.

∨ 22. *O* : Shield of arms of the city of Lichfield between ornaments.
   R : PAYABLE ON | WHIT-MONDAY | AT THE | GREENHILL | BANK.
   In five lines, the bottom one curved.

∨ 23.   There is a variety of this from different dies, and struck
           upon a thicker flan; this may be identified by its
           having no period at end of legend on the reverse.
                    Conder, 140 ; 8.—Pye, 27 ; 1.—Virt: 174.

   Very rare, the latter especially so.

∨ 24. *O* : The same as No. 21.
   R : S. BARKER | DOZENER | SADLERS STRT. | WARD. | 1794. In
         five lines..   Conder, 140 ; 9.—Pye, 27 ; 2.

   *Very rare. Only a few specimens struck in tin, and fewer
   still in copper.*

STAFFORD.

∨ 25. *O* : A reduced copy of No. 17.
   R : A cypher *W H* and a Staffordshire knot. HALF HALF-
         PENNY.
   E : Milled.   Conder, 140; 10.—Virt: 219.
   This also is very rare.

Suffolk.

PENNIES.

BUNGAY.

1. *O*: Remains of an ancient fortress. BUNGAY HALFPENNY. *Ex*:
    BIGODS CASTLE.

    R: Figure of Justice standing. FOR CHANGE NOT FRAUD.
    Ex: 1794.

    E: DOUBLE TOKEN PAYABLE BY S. PRENTICE. ×.×.×.
    Conder, 141 ; 1.—Virt: 126.

   1a.   As last, but *E*: Engrailed.

2. *O*: and *E*: The same as last.

    R: A figure of Justice, standing on a pedestal. FOR THE USE
    OF TRADE. Conder, 141 ; 2.—Virt: 126.

   2a.   As last, but *E*: Engrailed.

3. *O*: Remains of an ancient fortress. BUNGAY HALFPENNY 1796.

    R: and *E*: The same as No. 2. Conder, 141 ; 3.—Virt: 125.
    These are struck from the halfpenny dies of Nos. 20-22.

4. *O*: Remains of an ancient tower. BUNGAY . TOWER . SUFFOLK.
    Ex: JACOBS.

    R: A globe inscribed BRITAIN between a rose and a thistle.
    BRITISH PENNY. *Ex*: 1797.

    E: I PROMISE TO PAY ON DEMAND THE BEARER ONE PENNY ×
    Conder, 141 ; 4.—Virt: 218.

BURY.

5. *O*: Bust to left in cocked hat. CHARLES MARQUIS CORNWALLIS.

    R: Figure of Fame, standing between implements of war.
    HIS FAME RESOUNDS FROM EAST TO WEST.

    E: VALUE ONE PENNY AT P. DECKS POST OFFICE BURY 1794.
    Conder, 141 ; 5.—Pye, 11 ; 5.—Virt: 127.

6. *O*: An ancient gateway. Over the entrance ABBEY GATE BURY.

    R: An open book. PAYABLE AT RACKHAMS CIRCULATING LIBRAY.
    ANGEL HILL BURY.

    *Struck from the dies of the halfpenny, No. 27, and is very
    rare.*

HOXNE.

7. *O*: A light horseman standing leaning against his horse.
    PRO ARIS ET FOCIS.

    R: A castle in a garter crowned. HOXNE & HARTSMERE SUFFOLK
    LOYAL YEOMANRY CAVALY.

    E: GOD SAVE THE KING AND CONSTITUTION.

   7a.   As last, but *E*: Plain. Conder, 142 ; 6.
    This is from the dies of the halfpenny, No. 31.

IPSWICH.

✓ 8. *O*: Bust to left, in a cap, with a small tassel, or button on
top. A small cypher *I M* under the bust. CARDINAL
WOLSEY BORN AT IPSH. 1471.
R: View of an ancient gateway. JAS. CONDER . IPSWICH .
1795. *Ex*: WOLYS. GATE.
E: Plain (in collar).
Conder, 142 ; 7.—Pye, 24 ; 5.—Virt: 88.
*Very rare. Six impressions in silver and four in copper only
taken; there were also six struck in tin after the die
failed.*

✓ 9. *O*: A similar bust, but without the tassel. A small *M*.
under the bust. CARDINAL WOLSEY BORN AT IPSWICH
1471.
R: and *E*: The same as last.
Conder, 142 ; 8.—Pye, 24 ; 6.—Virt: 88.
Rare. Of this there were six silver, and 200 copper impressions.

✓ 10. *O*: The same as last.
R: A cypher *I M C*. CONDERS IPSWICH PENNY 1797.
Conder, 142 ; 11.

✓ 11. *O*: The same as last.
R: PAYABLE | AT | CONDER'S | DRAPERY | WAREHOUSE | IPSWICH |
1796. In seven lines.
E: I PROMISE TO PAY ON DEMAND THE BEARER ONE PENNY ✕
Conder, 142 ; 9.—Pye, 24 ; 7.
Rare.

✓ 12. *O*: View of an ancient building. TOWN HALL IPSH. *Ex*
FORMERLY ST. MILDRED'S CHURCH.
R: Same as No. 10.
E: The same as last.   Conder, 142 : 10.—Pye, 24 : 8.
Rare.

✓ 13. *O*: View of gateway, &c. As on *R*: of No. 8.
R: Same as last.   Conder, 142 ; 12.

WOODBRIDGE.

✓ 14. *O*: A front face bust. THOS. SEKFORD ESQ. FOUNDED WOOD-
BRIDGE ALMSHOUSES 1587.
R: Shield of arms between palm branches, and the motto,
ORATIONES . ET . ELEEMOS . ASCENDUNT . IN . MEMORIAM .
CORAM . DEO . within a beaded circle . AT WHOSE
EXPENSE COUNTY MAPS WERE FIRST ENGRAVED 1574.
E: PUBLISHED BY R. LODER 1796 . ✕ .
Conder, 142 ; 13.—Pye, 49 ; 4.—Virt: 148.

HALFPENNIES.

BECCLES.

✓ 15. *O*: South porch of the church. B'ECCLESIÆ.
   R: View of a bridge. F S U on a label under it. COMMUNI-
      TATE AUCTA 1795.
   E: PAYABLE AT BECCLES SUFFOLK / * / * / * /
                     Conder, 143; 14.—Pye, 7; 1.—Virt: 43.
15a.   As last, but *E*: Inscribed as last, and the remainder
       obliquely milled.
15b.   As last, but *E*: PAYABLE IN LANCASTER LONDON OR BRISTOL.
15c.   „   „   *E*: WARLEY CAMP HALFPENNY MDCCXCIV × × ×
15d.   „   „   *E*: Plain (not in collar).

BLYTHING.

16. *O*: A mounted yeoman. LOYAL SUFFOLK YEOMANRY. *Ex*:
       FIRST TROOP.
    R: A castle. SUFFOLK 1794 within a garter crowned.
       BLYTHING HUNDRED HALFPENNY.
    E: GOD SAVE THE KING AND CONSTITUTION . × × .   Pye, 9; 7.

    *This obverse die failed after about twelve impressions had
    been taken, which necessitated the making of a fresh
    one as follows:—*

✓ 17. *O*: Similar to last, but does not show the gender of the
       horse, and the sword points to the L of "SUFFOLK,"
       whereas previously it pointed to the O.
    R: and *E*: Same as last.   Conder, 143; 15.
    Also struck in silver.

17a.   As last, but *E*: CAMBRIDGE BEDFORD AND HUNTINGDON ×.×
17b.   „   „   *E*: WE PROMISE TO PAY THE BEARER ONE CENT.
17c.   „   „   *E*: Milled.
17d.   „   „   *E*: Plain (not in collar).

BUNGAY.

18. *O*: Bust to right. T. MILLER * BOOKSELLER * BUNGAY *
    R: Books and MSS., above them a beehive radiated.
       INDUSTRY . ENTERPRISE . STABILITY . CONTENT   1795.
    E: Plain (in collar).
                     Conder, 143; 16.—Pye, 11; 3.—Virt: 61.
    Very rare. Only 21 impressions taken, when the dies broke.

✓ 19. *O*: A hand holding a scroll which is inscribed, "we promife
       to pay the Bearer on DEMAND one HALFPENNY." In
       five lines. BUNGAY 1795.
    R: A figure of Justice standing on a pedestal. FOR THE USE
       OF TRADE.
    E: S. PRENTICE   S. DELF   M. ABEL.
                     Conder, 143; 17.—Pye, 11; 4.—Virt: 30.

19*a*.   As last, but *E* : s. PRENTICE   s. DELL   M. ABEL.

19*b*.   „   „   *E* : PAYABLE IN SUFFOLK-STREET HAY-MARKET.

19*c*.   „   „   *E* : Plain (not in collar).

✓ 20. *O* : Remains of an ancient fortress. BUNGAY HALFPENNY.
            Ex : BIGODS CASTLE.

    R : A figure of Justice standing. FOR CHANGE NOT FRAUD.
            Ex : 1794.

    E : Plain (not in collar, but rounded).
                    Conder, 143 ; 18.—Pye, 11 ; 2.—Virt : 30.

20*a*.   As last, but *E* : PAYABLE AT BIRMINGHAM LONDON OR BRISTOL.

20*b*.   „   „   *E* : PAYABLE ✕ AT ✕ CRONEBANE ✕ OR ✳ IN ✳
            DUBLIN ✕ ✳ ✕

20*c*.   As last, but *E* : PAYABLE IN DUBLIN OR LONDON.

20*d*.   „   „   *E* : PAYABLE IN LANCASTER LONDON OR BRISTOL.
            *See also Herefordshire, No. 5 ; Staffordshire, Nos. 13 and
            14 ; and Westmoreland, No. 5.*

21. *O* : The same as last.
    R : The same as No. 19.
    E : PAYABLE BY SAMUEL PRENTICE . ✕ . ✕ .

21*a*.   As last, but *E* : PAYABLE BY N. TODD DENTON NORFOLK.

✓ 21*b*.   „   „   *E* : Milled. *These are on large and small
            flans.*   Conder, 143 ; 19.

21*c*.   As last, but *E* : Plain (not in collar).

✓ 22. *O* : Remains of an ancient fortress as before, the date 1796
            above it. BUNGAY HALFPENNY.

    R : and *E* : The same as No. 21.   Conder, 144 ; 20.

✓ 22*a*.   As last, but *E* : The same as No. 21*a*.
                            Conder, 144 ; 21.—Virt : 55.

22*b*.   „   „   *E* : Milled over " SAMUEL PRENTICE."

22*c*.   „   „   *E* : The same as No. 21*c*. *This is on a
            very large flan.*

BURY.

✓ 23. *O* : Shield of arms of Bury St. Edmunds, crest a wolf.
            SUCCESS TO THE PLOUGH & FLEECE ❖ The head of the
            wolf is much nearer the E of " THE " than the P of
            " PLOUGH."

    R : A cypher *P D* above a crown, between palm and laurel
            branches. THE COMMERCE OF BRITAIN.

    E : PAYABLE AT P. DECKS POST OFFICE BURY . ✕ ✕ .
            A flaw is observable to left of shield, and the die failed
            after a very few pieces had been struck necessitating
            the making another, as follows :—

24. *O*: A very close copy of the preceding but the wolf's head is about equi-distant.
   R: and *E*: The same as last.
                   Conder, 144; 22.—Pye, 11; 9.—Virt: 29.
24*a*.   As last, but *E*: PAYABLE AT IOHN FINCHAM'S SUFFOLK. Struck over some other inscription, most probably the same as No. 23.
24*b*.   As last, but *E*: IOHN HARVEY OF NORWICH .×× .
24*c*.   „   „   *E*: PAYABLE IN LONDON BRISTOL & LANCASTER.
24*d*.   „   „   *E*: CURRENT EVERY WHERE
24*e*.   „   „   *E*: Plain (not in collar).
✔ 25. *O*: The same as No. 24.
   R: PAYABLE | AT | JAMS. GOERS | IRONMONGER | BURY. In five lines, the top and bottom curved.
                   Conder, 144; 23.—Pye, 11; 10.—Virt: 29.
   Also struck in silver.

✔ 26. *O*: Arms and crest as on No. 23. PAYABLE AT MICHAEL APSEYS.
   R: A tea kettle, and a Bath stove. SUCCESS TO TRADE.
   E: Milled.   Conder, 144; 24.—Pye, 11; 6.—Virt: 29.
26*a*.   As last, but *E*: PAYABLE IN DUBLIN OR LONDON .+.+.
26*b*.   „   „   *E*: THIS IS NOT A COIN BUT A MEDAL.+.+.+.+.
26*c*.   „   „   *E*: Plain (rounded, not in collar).
✔ 27. *O*: An ancient gateway. Over the entrance ABBEY GATE BURY.
   R: An open book. PAYABLE AT RACKHAMS CIRCULATING LIBRAY. ANGEL HILL BURY.
   E: OR AT LEATHERDALES .× . HARLESTON NORFOLK.
                   Conder, 144; 25.—Pye, 11; 7.—Virt: 28.
27*a*.   As last, but *E*: PAYABLE IN LANCASTER LONDON OR BRISTOL.
27*b*.   „   „   *E*: MASONIC HALFPENNY TOKEN MDCCXCIV.× .× .
27*c*.   „   „   *E*: PAYABLE BY HENRY OLIVERS +
✔ 27*d*.   „   „   *E*: Milled.
27*e*.   „   „   *E*: Plain (not in collar).
   The dies of this piece were used for the penny, No. 6.
✔ 28. *O*: An arm and hand holding a hammer. GOING, A GOING. 1795.
   R: A figure of Fame. PAYABLE AT CHARLES GUEST'S. *Ex*: AUCTIONEER BURY.
   E: Milled.   Conder, 144; 26.—Pye, 11; 8.—Virt: 29.
28*a*.   As last, but *E*: Plain (not in collar).

HAVERHILL.

✔ 29. *O*: A man weaving in a loom. HAVERHILL MANUFACTORY.
   R: A cypher *I F* within an oval, crest a wolf's head. PRO BONO PUBLICO 1794.
   E: PAYABLE AT IOHN FINCHAMS SUFFOLK.
                   Conder, 144; 27.—Pye, 22; 4.—Virt: 23.
   Also struck in silver.

29*a*.   As last, but *E* : PAYABLE AT CLACHAR & CO'S CHELMSFORD ESSEX +

29*b*.   As last, but *E* : PAYABLE IN HULL AND IN LONDON— × × —

29*c*.   ,,   ,,   *E* : PAYABLE AT SOUTH SHIELDS AND LONDON . × × .

29*d*.   As last, but *E* : Plain (not in collar).

✓ 30. *O* : The same as last.

      R : A shuttle and plough. SUCCESS TO THE PLOUGH & SHUTTLE. See Norfolk, No. 18.

      E : The same as No. 29*b*.   Conder, 145 ; 28.

30*a*.   As last, but *E* : Milled.

HOXNE.

✓ 31. *O* : A dismounted yeoman leaning against his horse. PRO ARIS ET FOCIS.

      R : A castle within a garter. 1795 HOXNE & HARTSMERE SUFFOLK LOYAL YEOMANRY CAVALY.

      E : PAYABLE BY THOS. TALLANT HOXNE ×   Conder, 145 ; 29.

✓ 31*a*.   As last, but *E* : GOD SAVE THE KING AND CONSTITUTION . +.

                    Conder, 145 ; 30.—Pye, 23 ; 4.—Virt : 30.

      Also struck in silver.

31*b*.   As last, but *E* : PAYABLE IN DUBLIN OR LONDON.

31*c*.   ,,   ,,   *E* : Milled to right.

31*d*.   ,,   ,,   *E* : Milled to left.

31*e*.   ,,   ,,   *E* : Plain (not in collar).

      These dies were used for the penny, No. 7.

IPSWICH.

✓ 32. *O* : Arms, supporters, crest, and motto of the town of Ipswich.

      R : A man ploughing, and a ship sailing. GOD PRESERVE THE PLOUGH & SAIL ✳

      E : PAYABLE AT ROBERT MANNINGS IPSWICH . × × .

                    Conder, 145 ; 31.—Pye, 24 ; 10.—Virt : 10.

32*a*.   As last, but *E* : Plain (not in collar).

✓ 33. *O* : An ancient market cross. IPSWICH CROSS. *Ex* : 1794.

      R : PAYABLE AT CONDER'S DRAPERY WAREHOUSE IPSWICH. In six lines.

      E : Milled.   Conder, 145 ; 32.—Pye, 24 ; 4.—Virt : 24.

      Also struck in silver.

33*a*.   As last, but *E* : The same as No. 29.   (FINCHAM.)

33*b*.   ,,   ,,   *E* : The same as No. 36.   (GOLDSMITH.)

33*c*.   ,,   ,,   *E* : PAYABLE AT I. IORDANS DRAPER GOSPORT.

33*d*.   ,,   ,,   *E* : WILLEY SNEDSHILL BERSHAM BRADLEY.

33*e*.   ,,   ,,   *E* : CURRENT EVERY WHERE

33*f*.   ,,   ,,   *E* : ON DEMAND WE PROMISE TO PAY

33*g*.   ,,   ,,   *E* : WE PROMISE TO PAY THE BEARER ONE CENT.

33*h*.   ,,   ,,   *E* : Plain (not in collar).

34. *O*: Bust to left, a small *M* under.   CARDINAL WOLSEY BORN
     AT IPSWICH 1471.
     R: Similar to preceding, but with the date 1796 added in a
         seventh line, at the bottom.
     E: Milled.   Conder, 145; 33.

34a.   As last, but *E*: Plain (not in collar).
     This is from the same dies as the penny, No. 11, and is
     likewise rare.

LOWESTOFT.

35. *O*: Bathing machines in the water, and ships at sea.
     LOWESTOFT TOKEN.   SEA BATH (RP) 1795.
     R: Men in a boat fishing, and ships at a distance.   SUCCESS
         TO THE FISHERIES.
     E: Milled.   Conder, 145; 34.—Pye, 35; 10.—Virt: 31.

SUDBURY.

36. *O*: Shield of arms of Sudbury, crest a talbot's head between
         two ostrich feathers, the head almost touches the F
         and s in legend.   MAY THE TRADE OF SUDBURY FLOURISH.
     R: PRO BONO | PUBLICO | 1793. In three lines occupying the
         entire field, the 1 in the date comes under the B in
         "PUBLICO."
     E: PAYABLE AT GOLDSMITH & SONS SUDBURY . × × ×.
                         Conder, 146; 35.—Pye, 45; 8.

36a.   As last, but *E*: PAYABLE AT GOLDSMITHS. The remainder
         engrailed.   Conder, 146; 36.

36b.   As last, but *E*: ON DEMAND WE PROMISE TO PAY.

36c.   „   „   *E*: Plain (not in collar).

     *Rare. The obverse die soon gave signs of failure, which
     necessitated the making of a fresh one, as follows :—*

37. *O*: Shield of arms and crest as before, but the talbot's head
         is farther from the " OF " and nearly under the s of
         "SUDBURY."
     R: and *E*: The same as No. 36.   Virt: 68.

38. *O*: and *E*: As last.
     R: Similar to preceding, but the 1 of date comes under
         the U in " PUBLICO."

38a.   As last, but *E*: Plain (not in collar).

Surrey.

PENNIES.

GODSTONE.

✓ 1. *O*: An ancient ruin and trees. GODSTONE TOWER . SURRY.
  Ex: JACOBS.
  R: A globe inscribed BRITAIN between a rose and thistle.
  BRITISH . PENNY . 1797.
  E: I PROMISE TO PAY ON DEMAND THE BEARER ONE PENNY ×
  Conder, 147; 1.

GUILDFORD.

✓ 2. *O*: An ancient fortress in ruins. GUILDFORD . TOWER . SURRY.
  Ex: JACOBS.
  R: and *E*: The same as last. Conder, 147; 2.—Virt: 210.

LAMBETH.

✓ 3. *O*: View of palace and trees. LAMBETH . PALACE . SURRY.
  Ex: JACOBS.
  R: and *E*: The same as last.   Conder, 147; 3.
✓ 4. *O*: A man standing, smoking a pipe, and holding a mug,
  and a keg. SR. GEORGE COOK . MAYOR OF GARBAT .
  ELECD. AUGT. 24·96.
  R: SR. G. COOK | FRUITERER | GREENGROCER | & OYSTER | MER-
  CHANT | STANGATE | LAMBETH. In seven lines, with a
  bunch of turnips at top, a cabbage at bottom, and a
  bunch of radishes on either side.
  E: ON DEMAND WE PROMISE TO PAY ONE PENNY.
  Conder, 147; 4.—Virt: 130.
  4a. As last, but *E*: VALUE ONE PENNY AT P. DECKS POST OFFICE
  BURY 1794.   Virt: 131.
  See halfpenny, No. 15.
✓ 5. *O*: As last.
  R: A man seated on the ground gnawing a bone. FRENCH
  LIBERTY.   Virt: 131.
  E: The same as No. 1.
  5a. As last, but *E*: Plain (not in collar).
  See halfpenny, No. 17.

HALFPENNIES.

BERMONDSEY.

✓ 6. *O*: View of a church. ST. MARY-MAGDALEN . BERMONDSEY. *Ex*:
  BUILT . 1680 JACOBS.
  R: A cypher *P S Co.* in a beaded circle. DEDICATED TO
  COLLECTORS OF MEDALS & COINS.
  Conder, 148; 10.—Virt: 86.

✔ 7. *O*: An ancient building. BERMONDSEY PRIORY. *Ex*: JACOBS.
    R: Similar to last, but with the date 1797 added below the
        cypher.   Conder, 148; 11.—Virt: 232.
  8. *O*: T T between two keys. SPA . GARDEN . BERMONDSEY.
    R: Two clarionets and a French horn, with a flaming heart
        in the centre. 1797.
    E: SKIDMORE HOLBORN LONDON.   Conder, 148; 12.
  9. *O*: T. KEYS | BERMONDSEY | SPA | GARDEN. | 1786. In five
        lines occupying the field.
    R: The same as last.   Conder, 148; 13.
 10. *O*: The same as No. 8.
    R: The same as obverse of No. 9.
    All rare.

CROYDON.

✔ 11. *O*: A cypher *D G*. HALFPENNEY . PAYBLE . AT . GARRAWAYS .
    CROYDON.
    R: A teapot. THE BEST TEAS IN CROYDON. 1797.
        Conder, 148; 14.—Pye, 15; 8.—Virt: 197.
✔ 12. *O*: Similar to last, but the spelling of "HALFPENNY" and
    "PAYABLE" corrected.
    R: Similar to last; the teapot is not quite so large, nor so
        near the legend.   Pye, 15*; 7.
    Rare.

GUILDFORD.

✔ 13. *O*: The arms of Guildford (a castle and leopard). GUILDFORD
    HALFPENNY.
    R: A three-quarter figure of Bishop Blaize, and a woolpack.
    SUCCESS TO THE WOOLEN MANUFACTORY.
        Conder, 148; 15.—Pye, 21; 10.—Virt: 22.
    The rev. of No. 13 also occurs as an obv. with the
    following reverse :—
 14. *R*: An anchor, cable and cap of Liberty. LIBERTY PEACE
    COMMERCE.   Conder, 269; 47.
    See also Anglesea, Nos. 224 and 236; Cambridgeshire,
    No. 22; and Middlesex, No. 733.

LAMBETH.

✔ 15. *O*: A man smoking, &c. From the same die as the penny,
    No. 4.
    R: SR. G. COOK, &c. From the same die as the penny, No. 4.
    E: Plain (not in collar).   Conder, 149; 17.
 15*a*.   As last, but *E*: EAMES HOLLAND & ANDREWS PETERS-
    FIELD — × —
 15*b*.   As last, but *E*: Milled.
    This obv. occurs with the following reverses :—
 16. *R*: The arms of London, &c. See Middlesex, No. 341.

17. *R*: A man seated on the ground, &c. See Middlesex, No. 591.

                        Conder, 272; 74.

     The rev. of No. 15 appears as an obv. with the following reverses :—

18. *R*: The arms of London, &c. As No. 16.   Conder, 284; 205.

19. *R*: A crown radiated, &c.   See Not Local, No. 123.

                        Conder, 284; 204.

     These are all rare.

     See also Middlesex, No. 342; and Dublin, No. 23.

ROTHERHITHE.

20. *O*: View of a church and houses.   ST. MARY'S ROTHERHITHE BUILT . 1739.   *Ex*: JACOBS.

     R: The same as No. 6.   Conder, 149; 18.—Virt: 175.

SOUTHWARK.

21. *O*: View of a church. CHRIST . CHURCH SURRY . BUILT . 1737. *Ex*: JACOBS.

     R: The same as No. 7.   Conder, 149; 19.—Virt: 198.

22. *O*: View of a church. ST. JOHN'S SOUTHWARK . BT. 1732. *Ex*: JACOBS.

     R: As last.   Conder, 149; 20.—Virt: 199.

23. *O*: View of a church. ST. OLIVE'S SOUTHWARK . BT. 1739. *Ex*: JACOBS.

     R: The same as No. 6.   Conder, 149; 21.

24. *O*: View of a church. ST. SAVIOUR'S SOUTHWARK . 1539. *Ex*: JACOBS.

     R: The same as No. 7.   Conder, 149; 22.

25. *O*: View of a church. ST. THOMAS SOUTHWARK. *Ex*: JACOBS.

     R: The same as No. 6.   Conder, 149; 23.

FARTHINGS.

LAMBETH.

26. *O*: A wheatsheaf and sickle between two doves.   1796.

     R: Denton Engraver ❖ & . Printer ❖ 7 . Mead ❖ ❖ Row ❖ near the ❖ ❖ Asylum ❖ Lambeth.

              Conder, 150; 24.—Virt: 173.

     This obverse is struck from the halfpenny die of Essex, No. 38.

27. *O*: Remains of an ancient fortress.

     R: The same as last.   Conder, 150; 25.

     This obv. is from the halfpenny die of Aberdeen.

28. *O*: The Prince of Wales' feathers and motto.

     R: The same as last.

     This obv. is from the halfpenny die of Hertfordshire, No. 2.

29. *O*: A deformed dwarf. SIR JEFFERY DUNSTAN 1795. See Middlesex, No. 756.

R: The same as last.   Conder, 305; 421.—Virt: 173.

This obv. occurs also with the following reverses struck from halfpenny dies:—

30. *R*: A crown, &c. in a radiated circle; from Hertfordshire, No. 2.   Conder, 248; 28.—Virt: 157.

31. *R*: Britannia seated holding scales, &c.; from Middlesex, No. 265.   Conder, 305; 423.—Virt: 157.

32. *R*: A cart unloading into a ship, &c.; from Northumberland, No. 25.   Conder, 305; 424.—Virt: 133.

33. *R*: A crown in a radiated circle; from Not Local, No. 123.   Conder, 305, 422.

𝔖𝔲𝔰𝔰𝔢𝔵.

PENNY.

BATTLE.

✓ 1. *O*: An ancient building and trees. BATTEL . ABBEY . SUSSEX.
Ex: JACOBS.
R: A globe inscribed BRITAIN between a rose and thistle.
BRITISH . PENNY. *Ex*: 1797.
E: I PROMISE TO PAY ON DEMAND THE BEARER ONE PENNY. ✕
Conder, 151; 1.—Virt: 219.

HALFPENNIES.

BATTLE.

✓ 2. *O*: Remains of an ancient abbey behind trees. HALFPENNY
Ex: 1796.
R: BATTLE | PROMISSORY | HALFPENNY | PAYABLE | IN . SUSEX. In
five lines.
E: Milled.   Conder, 151; 2.—Virt: 155.
Rare.

BRIGHTON.

✓ 3. *O*: Bust to right. GEORGE PRINCE OF WALES. The forehead
in a line with the E.
R: The Prince of Wales' crest and motto. HALFPENNY 1794.
No period.
E: BRIGHTON CAMP HALFPENNY . ✕ . ✕ . ✕ . ✕ .
Conder, 151; 3.—Pye, 9; 10.—Virt: 76.
*The drawing of the obv. of this piece in Pye's plate is
not accurate; there is nothing just like it.*

4. *O*: Similar to last, but the line of forehead is between the N
and C.
R: and *E*: The same as last.
Very rare.

✓ 4a. As last, but *E*: BRIGHTON CAMP HALFPENNY MDCCXCIV
✕ . ✕ .   Conder, 151; 4.

✓ 5. *O*: The same as No. 4.
R: Similar to No. 3, but from a fresh die, with a period at
end of legend.
E: The same as No. 3.

✓ 6. *O*: Similar to No. 4, but without period at end of legend.
R: Similar to No. 3, but dated 1795.
E: PAYABLE AT LONDON OR BRIGHTON.   Conder, 151; 5.
See also Essex, Nos. 35-37; and Not Local, Nos. 159-165.

✓ 7. *O*: An officer standing, and distant view of a camp.
     BRIGHTON.
     R: Soldiers besieging a city. HALFPENNY.
                         Conder, 151 ; 6.—Virt : 45.
     This obv. occurs with the following reverses :—
✓ 8. *R*: Ships at sea, and trophies of war under. *Ex* : 1795.
                         Conder, 152; 7.—Virt: 4.
✓ 9. *R*: Heart in hand. HONOUR, &c. See Middlesex, No. 516.
                         Conder, 152; 8.—Virt: 45.
     Both rare.
     The rev. of No. 7 appears as an obv. with the following
     reverse :—
✓ 10. *R*: Ships at sea, &c. As No. 8.   Conder, 218 ; 70.
     See also Middlesex, Nos. 526 and 632.
✓ 11. *O*: HONOR | THE | KING. In three lines in the centre.
     PAYABLE AT W ., MIGHELLS.
     R: In the centre the date 1796. BRIGHTELMSTONE * HALF-
     PENNY *   Conder, 152; 9.—Pye, 10; 1.—Virt : 159.
     In fine condition rare.
  12. *O* : The same as last.
     R : Bust to right. THOMAS SEYMOUR. *This rev. will be found
     also amongst the Imitation Regal.* Conder, 231; 176.
  13. *O*: The same as *R*: of No. 11.
     R: Profile bust to left. SHAKESPEAR. See Not Local, No.
     143.

CHICHESTER.

✓ 14. *O* : A front face of Queen Elizabeth with crown and sceptre.
     QUEEN ELIZABETH.
     R: View of Chichester Cross. CHICHESTER HALFPENNY.
     Ex : 1794.
     E : PAYABLE AT DALLYS CHICHESTER.
                         Conder, 152 ; 10.—Pye, 14 ; 4.—Virt: 94.
     Also struck in silver.
  14*a*.   As last, but *E* : WILLEY SNEDSHILL BERSHAM BRADLEY.
  14*b*.   „   „   *E* : Plain (not in collar).
  14*c*.   A proof of this obv. die occurs with *E* : PAYABLE IN
     LONDON LIVERPOOL OR BRISTOL +
  15. *O*: and *E* : The same as last.
     R : Similar to last, but from a different die, which may be
     recognized by the last letter of " CHICHESTER " being
     farther from the cross, and there is no period.
     *This must not be confounded with flawed impressions of the
     R : die of No. 14, which sometimes appear to have no
     period at end of legend.*
  15*a*.   As last, but *E* : Plain (not in collar).
     The obv. of No. 14 occurs with the following reverse :—
  16. *R*: Figure of Britannia seated. RULE BRITANNIA. *Ex* : 1795.
     See Hampshire, No. 10.
     E : EMSWORTH HALFPENNY PAYABLE BY IOHN STRIDE.

16*a*.   As last, but *E* : PAYABLE IN LONDON. The remainder
          engrailed.   Conder, 213 ; 28.

16*b*.   WE PROMISE TO PAY THE BEARER ONE CENT.
          See also Middlesex, No. 346 ; and Norfolk, No. 10.

17. *O* : Bust to left.   IOHN HOWARD F.R.S. PHILANTHROPIST.
    R : The same as No. 14.
    E : PAYABLE IN LONDON. The remainder engrailed.
          This piece is exceedingly rare, possibly unique.

✔ 18. *O* : Very similar to last, but from a different die.
      R : The sun and moon over a castle.   CHICHESTER AND
            PORTSMOUTH HALFPENNY. *Ex* : 1794.
      E : PAYABLE AT SHARPS PORTSMOUTH AND CHALDECOTTS
            CHICHESTER.   Conder, 42 ; 17.

✔ 19. *O* : Similar to last, but from a different die, in which the
            edge of frill differs from the preceding and which
            has an elongated dot at end of legend.
      R : and *E* : The same as last.
            A very similar token, but reading "PORTSMOUTH AND
            CHICHESTER HALFPENNY," *will be found under Hamp-
            shire, Nos. 32—34.*

EASTBOURNE.

✔ 20. *O* : View of a house.   FISHER'S LIBRARY AND LOUNGE 1796.
      R : PROSPERITY | TO | THE | GENTRY | WHO VISIT | EAST-BOURN.
            In five lines, with an ornament above and below.
      E : CELEBRATED FOR PURE AIR & SEA BATHING . ✚ . ✚ .
                              Conder, 152 ; 11.—Pye, 18 ; 1.—Virt : 180.

EAST GRINSTEAD.

✔ 21. *O* : The Freemasons' arms, crest, supporters, and motto.
            PRO BONO PUBLICO.
      R : A cypher *I H B*, a pair of scales above, and the date
            1795 below.   EAST GRINSTEAD HALFPENNY.
      E : PAYABLE AT I ✚ H BOORMAN . ✕ .
                              Conder, 152 ; 13.—Pye, 18 ; 2.—Virt : 194.
21*a*   As last, but *E* : PAYABLE IN LANCASTER LONDON OR BRISTOL.

FRANT.

✔ 22. *O* : A cypher *G R*; crest, a lamb.   FOR THE PUBLIC GOOD.
      R : Shield of arms.   SUSSEX HALFPENNY TOKEN. The date
            1794 upon a label.
      E : PAYABLE BY G. RING FRANT. ✚ ✚ ✚ ✚
                              Conder, 152 ; 12.—Pye, 45, 9.—Virt : 36.
            The crosses on the edge of some of these pieces, owing
            to a failure in the dies, appear in places as raised,
            instead of incuse impressions.

HASTINGS.

▾ 23. *O*: A sloop sailing, at bottom sprigs of leaves. SUCCESS &
SAFETY·ATTEND THE ENDEAVOUR.

   R: Shield of arms suspended by a ribbon and between
   sprigs of palm and laurel. HASTINGS HALFPENNY
   1794. The second blade of palm is just beyond the A.

   E: PAYABLE BY JAMES TEBAYS HASTINGS.
   Conder, 153; 14.—Pye, 22; 3.

23a. As last, but *E*: PAYABLE BY W. MYNS GOUDHURST.
   *The reverse die failed, which caused a new one to be
   fabricated as follows :—*

▾ 24. *O*: and *E*: The same as No. 23.

   R: Very similar to preceding, but may be distinguished
   by noticing that the second blade of the palm
   comes to the first limb of the A in "HALFPENNY."
   The ribbon is also much nearer to the legend, almost
   touching the s and H. Conder, 153; 15.—Virt: 3.

24*bis*. A very close imitation of preceding.
   E: Plain (not in collar).

HORSHAM.

▾ 25. *O*: Laureate bust to right. LONG . LIVE . THE . KING.
   R: An anchor and cable. M . PINTOSH . HORSHAM . 1791.
   E: Milled. Conder, 153; 16.—Virt: 76.

▾ 25a. As last, but *E*: SKIDMORE HOLBORN LONDON.
   This obv. occurs with the following reverses :—

26. *R*: View of a street, and spire of a church. See Yorkshire,
   No. 11. Conder, 268; 40.

   E: As No. 25a.

27. *R*: Two busts. LOUIS . XVI ET . M . ANTIONETTE, &c. See Not
   Local, No. 95. Conder, 278; 144.

   E: Milled.

28. *R*: Bust in cocked hat. MAY THE FRENCH, &c. See Not Local,
   No. 117. Conder, 282; 183.

   E: As No. 25a.
   The rev. of No. 25 appears as an obv. with the following
   reverses :—

29. *R*: View of a church in ruins. DESTROY' BY FIRE, &c. See
   Middlesex, No. 399.

▾ 30. *R*: A cypher I. O. M. &c. See Yorkshire, No. 11.
   Edges of both the same as No. 25a.
   See also Buckinghamshire, No. 15; and Middlesex,
   Nos. 380, 402, 406, and 694.

NORTHIAM.

✓ 31. *O*: Arms between laurel branches. FOR THE CONVENIENCE OF SOCIETY *

     R: A cypher *I F*, crest a wheatsheaf. HALFPENNY TOKEN PAYABLE AT . 1794.

     E: PAYABLE AT IOHN FOLLER'S NORTHIAM .✕.
               Conder, 153 ; 17.—Pye, 38 ; 7.—Virt: 6.

✓ 32. *O*: Arms between palm and laurel branches. UNANIMITY IS THE BOND OF SOCIETY.

     R: A cypher *E G*, crest a squirrel. NORTHIAM HALFPENNY . 1794.

     E: PAYABLE AT G. GILBERTS NORTHIAM .✕.✕.✕.✕.✕.
               Conder, 153 ; 18.—Pye, 38; 6.—Virt: 6.

RYE.

✓ 33. *O*: Two sugar loaves, a chest inscribed FINE TEAS, and a pair of scales. G. BENNETT . GROCER . RYE . SUSSEX . 1796.

     R: A cypher *G B*. FOR . THE . USE . OF . TRADE.

     E: Milled over SKIDMORE HOLBORN LONDON.
               Conder, 154; 21.—Virt: 176.

     This rev. appears as an obv. with the following reverses :—

34. *R*: A figure of Minerva. TRUTH FOR MY HELM, &c. See Middlesex, No. 394.

✓ 35. *R*: Bust in cocked hat. As No. 28.

     E: The same as No. 33.   Conder, 282 ; 185.

     See also Middlesex, Nos. 381, 412 and 457.

     These are all very rare.

WINCHELSEA.

36. *O*: Very similar to No. 3, but not from the same die.

     R: The same as No. 3.

     E: PAYABLE AT RICHARD MAPLESDENS WINCHELSEA . ✕ . ÷

     This Richard Maplesden was the issuer of Nos. 3—6, of which this would appear to be the original impression. It is very rare.

✓ 37. *O*: A beehive and bees, within a beaded circle. INDUSTRY THE .SOURCE OF CONTENT. There is a quatrefoil at end of legend, the four parts of which are nearly equal.

     R: Shield of arms, suspended by a ribbon, between palm branches. WINCHELSEA HALFPENNY . 1794.

     E: The same as last.

37a.   As last, but *E* : PAYABLE IN LANCASTER LONDON OR BRISTOL. *Rare. This obverse die failed after a few impressions only had been taken, and the following appears to have been made to take its place :—*

v 38. *O* : Similar to last, but the quatrefoil at bottom is much wider, the rose bush also is different, and there are more bees (26 in this, to 22 in the former).

   R : and *E* : The same as No. 37.

                              Conder, 154; 22.—Pye, 49; 2.—Virt: 46.

Warwickshire.

HALFCROWN.

BIRMINGHAM.

v 1. *O*: A female seated, giving alms to an old man and a boy, a child kneeling by her side.

    R: A cypher *B W H*, 1788 over it. TWO SHILLINGS AND SIXPENCE.   Conder, 320; 11*.—Pye, 8; 1. This occurs in silver, copper, brass, and white metal. *Pye says that only 6 dozen impressions of this piece were taken.*

v 1*a*.   The same as preceding, but countermarked with a **W** on both sides.

EIGHTEENPENCE.

v 2. *O*: A beehive and bees. INDUSTRY HAS ITS SURE REWARD. See Cambridgeshire, No. 10.

    R: 1s. 6D., marked by a punch.

SHILLINGS.

v 3. *O*: Bust to left. ADML. LD. NELSON . VICTORY AT THE NILE AUGUST . 1 . 1798.

    R: 1s, marked by a punch.
    These two latter pieces are placed by Sharp to the 19th century, although it does not appear upon what grounds; the obverse of No. 2 is certainly of the 18th.

  4. *O*: A beehive and bees. INDUSTRY HAS ITS SURE REWARD. Similar to Cambridgeshire, No. 34, but not from that die.

    R: 1799 1s, in two lines, occupying the field.
    The date upon this one lends authority to the opinion that these tokens belong to the 18th century. These are all rather scarce, especially the last.

PENNIES.

COUNTY.

v 5. *O*: View of Cæsar's Tower, Kenilworth. FIRMIM IN VITA NIHIL. *Ex*: MDCCXCVI.

    R: A cypher *P K*. WARWICKSHIRE PROMISSORY PENNY. upon a raised rim.

    E : I PROMISE TO PAY ON DEMAND THE BEARER ONE PENNY.
                                  Conder, 160; 1.

BIRMINGHAM.

✓6. *O*: Presentation of colours to troops. COLOURS PRESENTED TO THE BIRM. ASSOCIATIONS 4 IUNE 1798.

R: A long row of gibbets with men hanging on them. END OF BUNEPART AND THE FRENCH ARMY.

✓ 7. *O*: Bust to left (Demosthenes). SOCIETY FOR FREE DEBATE INSTITUTED IN BIRMINGHAM 1789.

R: TO RAISE THE GENIUS AND TO MEND THE HEART.

8. *O*: St. Andrew with his cross. AMOR PATRIÆ within a border of thistles.

R: A thistle in a shield, crowned. NEMO ME IMPUNE LACESSET upon a ribbon. BIRMINGHAM CALEDONIAN SOCIETY . 1789. The whole within a border of thistles.

✓ .9. *O*: Bust to right, with a hat on. THE BIRMINGHAM POET.

R: BRITONS BEHOLD | THE BARD OF FREEDOM | PLAIN & BOLD | WHO SINGS AS DRUIDS | SUNG OF OLD. In five lines within an oak wreath.

E: MANUFACTURED BY W. LUTWYCHE BIRMINGHAM.
Conder, 160 ; 2.

10. *O*: Antique bust to left. WILLIAM PITT EARL OF CHATHAM. I. G. HANCOCK SCULP AGED YEARS.

R: Blank. Pye, 12 ; 5.
Artist's proof in tin, of which only 4 were struck.

✓ 11. *O*: The bust last described, with wig and drapery added. The legend as last. The blank space filled in with the figure 8.

R: THIS | UNPARALLED | PRODUCTION | OF EARLY | GENIUS | WAS STRUCK UNDER | THE INSPECTION | OF | GEO. BARKER | 1800. In ten lines. Pye, 12 ; 6.

In consequence of the misspelling of the word " UNPAR-ALLELED " and a mistake in the age of the artist, only 8 impressions of this were taken.

✓ 12. *O*: As last, but the legend under the bust is replaced by BORN 1708 DIED 1778 on a ribbon.

R: A beehive and bees. THE WORK | OF | IOHN | GREGORY HANCOCK | AGED | NINE YEARS | 1800. In seven lines, with two laurel branches under. PENNY TOKEN FOR EXCHANGE.

E: BY GEORGE BARKER BIRMINGHAM . × . Pye, 12 ; 7.
Very rare; 6 specimens in copper, and 12 in tin.

✓ 13. *O*: Female bust to right. DIVA BRITANNIÆ. FAUTRIX ARTIUM.

R: Centre legend similar to last; no beehive or laurel branches. UTILE DULCI FOR EXCHANGE.

E: BY GEORGE BARKER BIRMINGHAM MDCCC. Pye, 12 ; 8.
Very rare; only 2 dozen struck.

13*a*. A proof of the obv. die occurs with *E*: The same as No. 5.

✔ 14. *O*: A man behind a counter holding scales. PENNY TOKEN
1798.

R: BN. JACOB | AUCTIONEER | IRONMONGER &c | WELCH CROSS |
BIRMINGHAM. In five lines, with a hand holding an
auctioneer's hammer between the fourth and fifth.
Pye, 12; 9.
Only 9 dozen of these were issued.

✔ 15. *O*: A lion sleeping in a cave. NEMO ME IMPUNE LACESSET.
Ex: 1796 in a sunk oval.

R: A cypher *P K* within a wreath of flowers, in which is
entwined a ribbon inscribed PROMISSORY PENNY TOKEN.
This reverse also occurs at Yorkshire, No. 3.

E: The same as No. 5.   Conder, 206; 39.—Virt: 146.

✔ 16. *O*: Shield of arms, crest a stag's head. JUNGANTUR LEXET
JUSTICIA. *Ex*: MDCCXCV.

R: A cypher *T W* (Welch). BIRMINGHAM PROMISSORY TOKEN.
On a raised border.

E: ON DEMAND I PROMISE TO PAY THE BEARER ONE PENNY.
Conder, 160; 3.—Pye, 8; 2.
Rare.   Private token; 6 dozen only struck.

17. *O*: A mounted yeoman at speed. WARWICKSHIRE YEOMANRY.
HANCOCK. *Ex*: ENROLLED JUNE 25 . 1794.

R: PROMISSORY | PENNY TOKEN | ISSUED BY | THOMAS WELCH |
SECOND TROOP | 1799. In six lines.

E: (ARMED TO PROTECT | OUR LIVES PROPERTY) (AND CONSTITU-
TION | AGAINST FOREIGN) (AND DOMESTIC | ENEMIES).
Divided into three compartments by military
trophies.   Pye, 47; 7.
With this edge only 3 impressions taken.

✔ 17a.   A last, but *E*: ARMED TO " PRESERVE " &c. instead of
" PROTECT."
With this edge 2 dozen impressions were taken.

17b.   As last, but *E*: Plain (in collar).
Of this, 2 dozen also were struck.

18. *O*: As last.
R: Similar legend to last, but the letters are a different
size, and there is a fasces and laurel branch crossed
above the legend.

E: The same as No. 17a.   Pye, 47; 8.
With this edge only 4 impressions were taken.

18a.   As last, but *E*: ON DEMAND I PROMISE TO PAY THE BEARER
ONE PENNY
An artist's proof, and with this edge probably unique.

✔ 18b.   As last, but *E*: Plain (in collar).
About 2 dozen with plain edge were struck.

✔ 19. *O*: Bust to left. THE WORK OF JOHN GREGORY HANCOCK AGED
9 YEARS . **+** . FROM A MODEL BY I. G. HANCOCK SEN.

R: TO | ENCOURAGE | A RARE INSTANCE | OF GENIUS | THIS |
COIN WAS STRUCK | FOR T. WELCH | BIRMINGHAM | 1800.
In nine lines.

E: PENNY TOKEN PAYABLE ON DEMAND × ×   Pye, 12; 4.
*Very rare, only 3 dozen struck. A proof of the unfinished
obv. die occurs with E: The same as* 18*a.*

✔ 20. *O*: An obelisk partly covered with ivy.   CRESCIT IN
IMMENSVM. Within a circle of pellets.

R: A cypher *T. W.* (Wyon). A bouquet in a sunk circle
over it. PROMISSORY PENNY TOKEN 1796.

E: The same as No. 5.   Virt: 145.

COVENTRY.

21. *O*: View of a church. *Ex*: ST. MICHAELS CHURCH.

R: View of interior. *Ex*: THE CHANCEL.

E: COVENTRY TOKEN.   Conder, 160; 4.

✔ 21*a*. As last, but *E*: Plain (in collar).
This is also struck in silver.

✔ 22. *O*: Front face bust (Dr. Holland). PHILEMON HOLLAND M.D.
DIED 1636 AGED 85.

R: View of interior of school. FREE SCHOOL COVENTRY.

E: PENNY TOKEN PAYABLE BY E. W. PERCY COVENTRY ×
    Pye, 15*; 4.
*Of these 6 were struck in silver, and 3 dozen in copper;
there were also 6 proofs in tin, on which the name is
spelt* HOLLOND.

23. *O*: and *E*: The same as last.

R: The same design as last, but with three boys playing
marbles; the date 1801 in *Ex*: instead of "FREE
SCHOOL COVENTRY."   Pye, 15*; 5.
*Extremely rare, as the die broke when only 6 impressions
had been taken.*

✔ 24. *O*: and *E*: The same as last.

R: An open book supported by two others which are lettered
BRITANNIA and CYROPÆDIA. The open book is inscribed, " *With one Sole Pen I wrote this Book, Made
of a gray Goose Quill. A Pen it was when I it took A
Pen I leave it still.*" Before the book is an inkstand
with a pen in it. *Ex*: 1801 I. G. H.   Pye, 15*; 6.
Of these there were 15 *impressions bronzed, and* 3 *unbronzed;
there were also* 4 *unfinished proofs in tin.*

HALFPENNIES.
COUNTY.

✔ 25. *O*: Bust of Shakespeare. WARWICKSHIRE. A trefoil after
legend.

R: A female seated, supporting a cornucopia, part of a ship
in the distance. HALFPENNY. *Ex*: 1791.

∨ 26.   Similar to preceding, excepting that the fruit hangs over the lower edge of the cornucopia, whereas in the former it is contained within it.   Conder, 161; 5.

∨ 27. *O*: Similar to last, but from smaller die, and there is a period at end of legend instead of a trefoil. There are eight buttons on the coat, the previous ones having only six.

     R: Similar, but from smaller die; the head of female and the fruit in cornucopia both touch the legend, and there is less of the ship visible.

     E: Plain (in collar).

∨ 28.   Similar to last, but the period after legend on *O*: is quite close to the last letter.   Pye, 47; 9.—Virt: 119.
     This is very rare.

∨ 29. *O*: Similar to preceding, but from a different die.

     R: Vulcan seated at work. HALFPENNY. *Ex*: 1792.

     E: PAYABLE IN ANGLESEY LONDON OR LIVERPOOL . ✕ .

                                 Conder, 161; 6.

BIRMINGHAM.

∨ 30. *O*: A figure of a boy standing, leaning upon a screw. BIRMINGHAM HALFPENNY. *Ex*: 1793.

     R: Shield bearing four hedgehogs, crest a hedgehog. INDUSTRY HAS ITS SURE REWARD.

     E: CURRENT EVERY WHERE.

                   Conder, 163; 20.—Pye, 8; 3.—Virt: 65.
     Also struck in silver.

∨ 30*a*.   As last, but *E*: PAYABLE AT CLOUGHER OR IN DUBLIN.

30*b*.   „   „   *E*: PAYABLE AT EDINBURGH GLASGOW & DUMFRIES.

30*c*.   As last, but *E*: PAYABLE IN LONDON.   The remainder engrailed.

30*d*.   As last, but *E*: PAYABLE IN LONDON BRISTOL & LANCASTER.

30*e*.   „   „   *E*: AT GEORGE EDWARD SARGEANT'S PORTSEA.

30*f*.   „   „   *E*: PAYABLE AT THE STORE OF.   The remainder engrailed.

30*g*.   As last, but *E*: Milled.

30*h*.   „   „   *E*: Plain (not in collar).
     This obv. occurs with the following reverses:—

∨ 31. *R*: Bust to left. DR. SAML. IOHNSON. See Staffordshire, No. 15.

     E: PAYABLE IN LONDON.   The remainder engrailed.

                                 Conder, 163; 22.

∨ 32. *R*: Ship under sail. SUCCESS TO THE COAL TRADE. See Durham, No. 4.

     E: The same as No. 31.

✓ 33. *R*: Britannia seated. RULE BRITANNIA. *Ex*: 1795. See
     Hampshire, No. 10.
   E: Milled.
✓ 34. *R*: A female standing, supporting a rudder, &c. LIBERTY
     & COMMERCE. *Ex*: 1794. This is from a New York
     token.   Conder, 163; 21.
   E: The same as No. 31.
✓ 35. *R*: Three men hanging on a gibbet. NOTED ADVOCATES FOR
     THE RIGHTS OF MAN 1796. See Not Local, No. 129.
   E: Engrailed.   Conder, 163; 23.
35a.   As last, but *E*: Plain (rounded).
✓ 36. *R*: A WAY | TO PREVENT | KNAVES | GETTING | A TRICK. In five
     lines. See Not Local, No. 129.
   E: Engrailed.   Conder, 268; 45.
     The rev. of No. 30 appears as an obv. with the following
     reverses:—
✓ 37. *R*: Britannia as No. 33.
✓ 38. *R*: Ship in full sail. PRO BONO PUBLICO. *Ex*: 1794. See
     Hampshire, No. 22.
   E: CURRENT EVERY WHERE.
38a.   As last, but *E*: Plain (not in collar).
                                            Conder, 228; 149.
39. *R*: A dragoon mounted. PRO REGE ET PATRIA &c. See
     Norfolk, No. 47.
   E: CURRENT EVERY WHERE.
39a.   As last, but *E*: EMSWORTH HALFPENNY PAYABLE BY
     IOHN STRIDE.
✓ 39b.   As last, but *E*: The same as No. 31.
39c.   „   „   *E*: WILLEY SNEDSHILL BERSHAM BRADLEY.
✓ 39d.   „   „   *E*: WE PROMISE TO PAY THE BEARER ONE
     CENT.   Conder, 234; 205.

Allin's.

✓ 40. *O*: A man holding a flag, and supporting a shield, inscribed
     ALLIN'S | PANORAMA | GRAND | EXHIBITION | ADMITE. |
     1s. In six lines. PEACE AND GOOD WILL TO ALL MEN.
   R: CHEAP | CLOTHES | & | YORK SHOE | WAREHOUSE | WHOLE-
     SALE | & RETAIL. In eight lines in the centre.
     I ALLIN HAY-MARKET BIRMINGHAM . 1796.
   E: Milled.   Conder, 161; 7.—Pye, 8; 8.—Virt: 159.

Alston's.

✓ 41. *O*: A public building. BIRM. POOR HOUSE HALFPENNY
     TOKEN. *Ex*: PAYABLE THERE.
   R: A beehive and bees. FOR THE USE OF THE PARISH. *Ex*:
     I. *Alston . Fecit* 1796.
   E: Engrailed.   Conder, 163; 25.—Pye, 8; 6.—Virt: 44.
41a.   As last, but *E*: Plain (not in collar).

Barker's.

42. *O* : A shield of arms. LEGI REGI FIDELIS.
     R : An ornamental cypher *G. B.* 1797 under. BIRMINGHAM
         HALFPENNY FOR EXCHANGE.
     E : PAYABLE BY GEORGE BARKER.

                                 Conder, 317 ; *7.—Pye, 9 ; 1.
     Very rare. Only 3 known with edge inscribed. There
     were 3 dozen altogether, of which a few are silver.

✔ 42a.   As last, but the *E* : Plain (in collar).

43. *O* : Arms as before, crest an armed warrior, *G H B*
         under. BIRMINGHAM HALFPENY.
     R : A figure of Justice, in a sunk oval. FACTA ÆQUATO
         EXAMINE PENDIT MDCC XCVII at the sides.
     E : PAYABLE ON DEMAND.   Pye, 8 ; 9.
     Only 15 in copper were struck, of which 3 only have the
     edge inscribed, and 12 in tin.

✔ 43a.   As last, but *E* : Plain (in collar).

✔ 44.   As last, but LIBRAT in place of PENDIT on *R*.

                                    Conder, 318 ; *7.
     Also very rare ; 24 impressions only taken.

45. *O* : Head of Mercury to left. FURTUM INGENIOSUS AD OMNE .
         BIRMINGHAM HALFPENNY.
     R : Ruins of a pyramid and a fallen statue. Three hands
         clasped, FŒDUS above them, SIC OMNIA under. *Ex* :
         MIHI SORTE DATUM MDCCXCIX.
     E : PAYABLE BY GEORGE BARKER + +   Pye, 12 ; 11.

✔ 45a.   As last, but *E* : Plain (in collar).
     These latter are struck in white metal.
     Both very rare. Only 12 impressions of each were taken.

Biggs'.

✔ 46. *O* : Bust to left in cocked hat. GENERAL ELLIOT. A small
         ornament under bust.
     R : A fleur-de-lis. BIRMINGHAM HALFPENNY. 1792.
     E : PAYABLE AT HENRY BIGGS MOORE STREET.

                       Conder, 161 ; 8.—Pye, 7 ; 5.—Virt : 9.

✔ 46a.   As last, but *E* : Plain (not in collar). These are
     smaller and thinner than the former.

✔ 47. *O* : Bust to right. DR. SAMUEL JOHNSON. A small ornament
         under the bust.
     R : Three lions rampant. PROMISSORY . HALFPENNY . PAYABLE .
         AT.
     E : PAYABLE AT HENRY BIGGS MOORE STREET.   Pye, 7 ; 9.
     Extremely rare with this edge, only 6 being known.

✔ 47a.   As last, but *E* : BIRMINGHAM W. HAMPTON OR LITCHFIELD.
                           Conder, 162 ; 18.—Virt : 10.
     Pye says that a great quantity of No. 46 being sent in for
     payment just as No. 47 was being issued, the edge of
     the latter was altered to 47a.

Birmingham Coining & Copper Co.

48. *O*: A female seated on a rock, holding a fasces.
   BIRMINGHAM COINING AND COPPER COMPANY. *Ex*: 1794.
   The fasces is directly under the D of "AND."
R: A stork standing upon a cornucopia. HALFPENNY
   PAYABLE AT.
E: BIRMINGHAM REDRUTH & SWANSEA.
✔ 48a. As last, but *E*: PAYABLE AT LONDON LIVERPOOL OR BRISTOL.
   Conder, 162; 16.—Virt: 64.
✔ 49. *O*: Similar to last, but the fasces is a little to left of the D.
R: The end of cornucopia is nearer to the legend, and higher up, and the two leaves branching out of cornucopia embrace the second limb of the letter H.
E: M. ABEL   S. PRENTICE   S. DELL.
49a. As last, but *E*: PAYABLE AT ANGLESEY LONDON OR LIVERPOOL.
49b. „ „ *E*: PAYABLE IN ANGLESEY LONDON OR LIVERPOOL.
49c. „ „ *E*: PAYABLE AT BANBURY OXFORD OR READING.
49d. „ „ *E*: PAYABLE IN DUBLIN OR AT BALLYMURTAGH.
49e. „ „ *E*: PAYABLE AT IOHN FOLLARS NORTHIAM.
49f. „ „ *E*: PAYABLE IN LANCASTER LONDON OR BRISTOL.
49g. „ „ *E*: PAYABLE IN LANCASTER LONDON OR LIVER-POOL.
49h. As last, but *E*: PAYABLE IN SUFFOLK BATH OR MANCHESTER.
49i. „ „ *E*: Milled.
49k. „ „ *E*: Plain (not in collar).
50. *O*: Similar to last, but the fasces is farther from legend, and the foot of the figure touches and cuts off part of the last letter of the legend.
R: Similar to last, but the end of the cornucopia is more pointed, and the two leaves before mentioned embrace the first limb of the letter H.
E: PAYABLE AT BECCLES SUFFOLK / */ */ */ */
50a. As last, but *E*: PAYABLE IN DUBLIN OR AT BALLYMURTAGH.
✔ 50b. „ „ *E*: PAYABLE IN LANCASTER LONDON OR BRISTOL.
50c. „ „ *E*: PAYABLE IN LANCASTER LONDON OR LIVER-POOL.
50d. As last, but *E*: PAYABLE IN SUFFOLK LONDON OR LIVERPOOL.

Birmingham Company.

✔ 51. *O*: A female seated, holding fasces as before. BIRMINGM
   COMPANY. *Ex*: 1793.
R: Similar to preceding.
E: BIRM. LIVERPOOL OR LONDON.   Conder, 162; 15.
✔ 51a. As last, but *E*: LIVERPOOL QR LONDON.
51b. „ „ *E*: PAYABLE IN LONDON BRISTOL & LANCASTER.
51c. „ „ *E*: Plain (not in collar).
14

Mining & Copper Co.
1791.

✓ 52. *O*: Female with fasces as before. BIRMINGHAM MINING AND
COPPER COMPANY. *Ex*: 1791. The point of the
laurel wreath touches the A of "AND," the fasces is
under the N and D. There is a small W (for Wyon)
under the rock, and a period at end of legend.

 R: A stork upon a cornucopia as before; the head of the
stork comes immediately under the letter P in
" PAYABLE."

 E: BIRMINGHAM REDRUTH & SWANSEA.
Conder, 161; 9.—Pye, 7; 3.—Virt: 64.

53. *O*: and *E*: The same as last.
 R: The head of the stork comes midway between the Y and
the P; the end of the cornucopia comes higher (about
the middle of the B in " PAYABLE ").

54. Similar to last, but the fasces comes under the A and N,
and the point of laurel wreath comes midway
between the G and the A.

✓ 55. *O*: Similar to last, but without the small W under the rock
on which the female is sitting.
 R: Similar to last, excepting that the end of the cornucopia
comes higher up, reaching to midway between the A
and the B.

 E: As before.

✓ 56. Similar to preceding, but the point of laurel comes
directly at the end of the letter G, the fasces being
more under the letter A; there is no period at end of
legend.

✓ 57. Similar, but the point of laurel comes midway between
the letters G and A, somewhat like No. 54, but without the small W, or the period at end of legend.

✓ 58. Similar, but the point of laurel comes to the centre of
the letter G, and the fasces comes under the A.
There is no small W, nor period.

 All these, from Nos. 52 to 58, are included in Conder
under one number. There are other variations of
die, too minute to specify.

1792.

✓ 59. *O*: Similar to preceding, the point of laurel being midway
between the G and the A, and the fasces comes under
the A and the first limb of the N. *Ex*: 1792.

 R: As before, the first limb of the H being between the two
leaves.

 E: As No. 52.   Conder, 161; 10.

✔ 59a. As last, but with *E* : ANGLESEY LONDON OR LIVERPOOL.

59b. ,, ,, *E* : PAYABLE IN HULL AND IN LONDON.

✔ 60. Similar, but the second limb of the H comes between the two leaves.

✔ 61. Similar, but the two leaves touch one each of the two limbs of the H.

✔ 62. As before, but the second leaf does not quite touch the H.

63. Similar to No. 59, except that the head of the stork comes under the P. As on No. 52.

✔ 64. Similar to No. 62, but the fasces comes more under the letter N, quite to the second limb.

64a. As last, but *E* : PAYABLE AT COALBROOKE DALE AND KETLEY.

✔ 65. *O* : Similar to last, excepting that the point of laurel comes quite near the letter A.

    R : As before, but the first limb of the letter H touches the second of the two leaves.

✔ 66. Similar, but the first limb of the H comes between the two leaves.

✔ 67. Similar to No. 64, but the two leaves point one each to the limbs of the letter H.

✔ 68. Similar, but the end of the cornucopia comes higher, quite opposite the B, whereas in the previous ones it only came midway between the B and the L.

✔ 69. *O* : Similar to No. 65, excepting that the fasces almost touches the D, the point of laurel coming between G and A.

    R : As before, but one single leaf comes below the first limb of the H, and the cornucopia is shorter, only just reaching to the end of the letter L.

    E : As No. 52. Conder, 162 ; 11.

70. Similar, but the cornucopia is longer, coming to the end of the letter R.

70a. As last, but *E* : PAYABLE IN ANGLESEY LONDON OR LIVER-POOL.

✔ 70b. As last, but *E* : PAYABLE AT BIRMINGHAM BRIGHTON or LIVERPOOL. Conder, 162 ; 12.

✔ 70c. As last, but *E* : PAYABLE AT LONDON LIVERPOOL OR ANGLE-SEY.

70d. As last, but *E* : Plain (not in collar).

✔ 71. *O* : Similar to No. 65, but the 1 of date joins the *Ex :* line.

    R : Similar to No. 68, but with a single leaf at centre of H.

    E : The same as No. 70a.

72 *O*: As before, excepting that the point of laurel comes
between the G and A, and the fasces comes under the D.

   R: There are three leaves; the centre one points between
the two limbs of the H.

   E: As No. 52.

✓ 72*a*.   As last, but *E*: PAYABLE IN ANGLESEY LONDON OR LIVER-
POOL.

✓ 72*b*.   As last, but *E*: PAYABLE AT BIRMINGHAM BRIGHTON or
LIVERPOOL.

72*c*.   As last, but *E*: PAYABLE AT LONDON LIVERPOOL OR
ANGLESEY.

72*d*.   As last, but *E*: WILLEY SNEDSHILL BERSHAM BRADLEY.

72*e*.   ,,   ,, *E*: Plain (not in collar).

73.   Similar, but the second limb of the H comes between the
two leaves.

73*a*.   As last, but *E*: PAYABLE IN ANGLESEY LONDON OR LIVER-
POOL.

73*b*.   As last, but *E*: PAYABLE IN LANCASTER LONDON OR BRISTOL.
                                    Conder, 162; 13.

73*c*.   ,,   ,, *E*: PAYABLE AT LEEK STAFFORDSHIRE.

73*d*.   ,,   ,, *E*: PAYABLE AT LONDON OR ANGLESEY.

73*e*.   ,,   ,, *E*: PAYABLE ‖‖‖ AT ‖‖‖ LONDON ‖‖‖ ANGLE-
SEY ‖‖‖

73*f*.   As last, but *E*: Engrailed.

✓ 74. *O*: Similar, but the point of the laurel is under the A, and
the fasces come under the D.

   R: As No. 66.

   E: As No. 52.

1793.

✓ 75. *O*: As before, but the legend in much smaller letters, date
in *Ex*: 1793. The point of the laurel wreath is
under the A, and the fasces under the D.

   R: Similar to the previous ones, but the fruit differently
disposed.

   E: BIRMINGHAM, LIVERPOOL, OR LONDON.

75*a*.   As last, but *E*: BIRM LIVERPOOL OR LONDON.

75*b*.   ,,   ,, *E*: PAYABLE AT LEEK STAFFORDSHIRE.

✓ 76. *O*: Similar to last, but the point of the laurel comes between
the G and A, and the fasces is under the N and D.

   R: The end of cornucopia comes to the centre of B, whereas
in No. 75 it comes barely to it.

   E: The same as No. 75.

76*a*.   As last, but *E*: The same as No. 75*a*.

76*b*.   ,,   ,, *E*: Plain (not in collar).

      These are included in Conder, 162; 14.

77. *O*: Similar to preceding, but the legend in much larger
letters, and the date in *Ex*: so far as can be distinguished appears to be 1771. Design most like No.
69.

   R: As before.

   E: PAYABLE AT LONDON OR ANGLESEY.

77*a*.   As last, but *E*: Plain (not in collar).

Metal and Copper Co.

✓ 78. *O*: Female with fasces as before. METAL AND COPPER COM-
PANY HALFPENNY. *Ex*: 1795.

   R: A stork upon a cornucopia. SUCCESS TO TRADE & COM-
MERCE ⁑

   E: PAYABLE IN ANGLESEY LONDON OR LIVERPOOL . ✕ .

                                 Conder, 6 ; 42.

78*a*.   As last, but *E*: PAYABLE IN HULL AND LONDON . ✕ ✕ .

*This is placed by Conder to Anglesea on account of its
edge, but this appears the more appropriate position for
it.*

See also Lancashire, Nos. 65, 73 and 82.

Bissett's.

79. *O*: View of interior of a temple. BISSETTS MUSEUM &
FANCY PICTURE MANUFACTORY.

   R: Ornaments of spar, &c. ALABASTER SPAR & PETRIFACTION
WAREHOUSE. *Ex*: BIRMINGHAM. Conder, 164 ; 31.

*Very rare. This obv. die appears to have failed when only
a very few impressions had been taken, upon which the
following was executed to take its place :—*

✓ 80. *O*: Similar to last, but with pictures hanging round the side
of the temple.

   R: The same as last.

          Conder, 164 ; 30.—Pye, 8 ; 7.—Virt. 25.

80*a*.   As last, but *E*: PAYABLE AT BANBURY OXFORD OR READING.

Clarke's.

✓ 81. *O*: Britannia crowning with laurel a bust of Geo. III., placed
upon a pedestal which is inscribed JUSTA PRÆMIA,
the whole being within a sunk oval. BIRMINGHAM
HALFPENNY.

   R: An oak tree, and ships at sea. Upon a raised rim
BRITANNIÆ TUTAMEN. *Ex*: MDCCXCV.

   E: PAYABLE AT THE HOUSE OF JOHN CLARKE BULL STREET +

          Conder, 164 ; 32.—Pye, 8 ; 4.—Virt : 161.

*A flaw in the obv. die gives in some impressions of this
piece the idea of a landscape at the back of the pedestal.
Rare ; only 36 struck.*

Donald and Co.

∨ 82. *O* : DONALD & CO. | STOCKING | MANUFACTURERS | WHOLESALE & | RETAIL. In five lines within an oval formed of leaves. HALFPENNY PAYABLE AT.

R : A beehive and bees, within a circle of leaves. NO. 29 BULL STREET BIRMINGHAM 1792. Conder, 163; 24.

For another token issued by the same firm, and two trial pieces likewise, see Nottingham, Nos. 2—6.

Hallan's.

∨ 83. *O* : Dealer in CHINA and staffordshire : ware in all its BRAnches : NO. 2 BUll ring BI. In three circles with a dove and olive branch in the centre.

R : halfpenny | payable at th | e.intelligence | office FOR MAS | ters and serv | ants KEPT by | WM HALLEN | 1792. In eight lines.

Conder, 164 ; 33.—Pye, 7 ; 10.—Virt : 71.

There are recent counterfeits of this piece, which may be recognized by their very inferior workmanship. The genuine pieces are rare.

∨ 84. *O* : Bust to left, 1795 under it. WILLIAM HALLAN BIRMINGHAM. The legend begins and ends with a sprig.

R : A teapot, cream jug, &c. DEALER . IN . GLASS . AND . STAFFORDSHIRE . WARE.

E : Milled. Conder, 164 ; 34.—Pye, 8 ; 5.—Virt : 71.

These also are rare.

85. *O* : The same as last.

R : The same as the obv. of No. 83.

Exceedingly rare, if not unique.

This obv. occurs with the following reverses :—

∨ 86. *R* : Bust to left. DAVID GARRICK, ESQR. See Middlesex, No. 156.

E : Milled. Conder, 280 ; 159.

∨ 87. *R* : A guillotine and part of a house. HALFPENNY. See Middlesex, No. 375.

E : SKIDMORE HOLBORN LONDON.

∨ 88. *R* : Ruins of a church. DESTROY'D BY FIRE &c. See Middlesex, No. 399.

E : The same as last.

89. *R* : Bust of Geo. III. LONG LIVE THE KING. See Sussex, No. 25.

E : The same as last. Conder, 280 ; 161.

∨ 90. *R* : A cypher, *I O M* &c. See Yorkshire, No. 11.

See also Middlesex, No. 365.

The rev. of No. 83 appears as an obv. with the following reverse :—

∨ 91 : *R* : Bust of Garrick. The same as No. 86.

Conder, 179 ; 150.

These varieties are mostly rare.

Hickman's.

✓ 92. *O* : Bust to left. IOHN HOWARD F R S
    R : A cypher *H H*. BIRMINGHAM PROMISSORY HALFPENNY 1792.
    E : PAYABLE AT H HICKMANS WAREHOUSE BIRMINGHAM.
                        Conder, 164 ; 35.—Pye, 7 ; 4.—Virt : 90.

92a.   As last, but *E* : Plain (not in collar).
    Pye's engraving shows no button hole to the coat, and in a note to pl. 7 he says :—" There is another die with two button holes." All the author has seen when properly struck, and unworn, have two button holes.

93. *O* : A rose and thistle. QUIS NOS SEPARABIT.
    R : The same as last.
    E : PAYABLE AT THE SHOP OF DUNHAM & YALLOP GOLDSMITHS.
                            Conder, 164 ; 36.

    Very rare.
    The obv. of No. 92, with a very similar reverse, has already appeared as a " Westminster Halfpenny." See Middlesex, No. 752.

Kempson's Buildings.

✓ 94. *O* : Side view of a chapel. ASHTED CHAPEL ERECTED. Date in *Ex* : 1790.
    R : Shield of arms. P. KEMPSON MAKER OF BUTTONS . MEDALS &c. BIRMINGHAM. No period after Kempson.
                        Conder, 165 ; 38.—Virt : 158.

95.   As last, but with an inner legend on rev. round the shield of arms which reads, TWENTY SEVEN PUBLIC BUILDINGS PUBLISHED 1796.

96. *O* : As last.
    R : Shield of arms, a star on either side. BIRMINGHAM ARMS. I. OTTLEY MEDALIST.
    E : COVENTRY TOKEN and a wavy line.

97. *O* : A public building. BARRACKS ERECTED. *Ex* : 1793.
    R : P. Kempson, &c. As on No. 94, but with a period after KEMPSON and the M of "MAKER" and B of " BIRMINGHAM " are farther apart.
                        Conder, 165 ; 39.—Virt : 156.

✓ 98. *O* : As last.
    R : P. Kempson, &c. As on No. 94.

99. *O* : As last.
    R : I. Ottley, &c. As on No. 96.

100.*O* : View of a chapel. ST. BARTHOLOMEWS CHAPEL.
    R : P. Kempson, &c. As on No. 94.
                        Conder, 165 ; 40.—Virt : 87.

✓ 101.*O* : As last.
    R : P. Kempson, &c. As on No. 97.

102. *O*: As last.
  R: I. Ottley, &c. As on No. 96.

∨ 103. *O*: A large building. BLUE SCHOOL ERECTED 1724.
   R: P. Kempson, &c. As No. 94.
             Conder, 165; 41.—Virt: 157.

104. *O*: As last.
  R: P. Kempson, &c. As No. 95.
  E: The same as No. 96.

105. *O*: As last.
  R: I. Ottley, &c. As on No. 96.

∨ 106. *O*: A different view of the same building. BLUECOAT
   CHARITY SCHOOL. *Ex*: ENLARGED 1794.
   R: P. Kempson, &c. As on No. 97.
             Conder, 165; 42.—Virt: 54.

107. *O*: As last.
  R: I. Ottley, &c. As on No. 96.

∨ 108. *O*: A large building. THE NEW BRASSWORKS 1796.
   R: P. Kempson, &c. As on No. 94.
             Conder, 165; 43.—Virt: 97..

∨ 109. *O*: As last.
   R: P. Kempson, &c. As on No. 97.

110. *O*: As last.
  R: I. Ottley, &c. As on No. 96.

∨ 111. *O*: A building. NEW BREWERY ERECTED, 1792.
   R: P. Kempson, &c. As on No. 94.
             Conder, 165; 44.—Virt: 157.

112. *O*: As last.
  R: I. Ottley, &c. As on No. 96.

∨ 113. *O*: A public building. FREE SCHOOL.
   R: P. Kempson, &c. As on No. 97.
             Conder, 165; 45.—Virt: 44.

114. *O*: As last.
  R: I. Ottley, &c. As on No. 96.

∨ 115. *O*: A public building. GENERAL HOSPITAL ERECTED, 1779.
   R: P. Kempson, &c. As No. 94.
             Conder, 165; 46.—Virt: 54.

∨ 116. *O*: As last.
   R: P. Kempson, &c. As on No. 97.

117. *O*: As last.
  R: I. Ottley, &c. As on No. 96.

∨ 118. *O*: A large building. HOTEL ERECTED MDCCLXXII.
   R: P. Kempson, &c. As on No. 94.
             Conder, 165; 47.—Virt: 109.

119. *O*: As last.
  R: I. Ottley, &c. As No. 96.

∨ 120. *O*: Side view of a chapel. ST. JOHNS CHAPEL DERITEND.
   R: P. Kempson, &c. As on No. 97.
             Conder, 165; 48.—Virt: 90.

ᵛ 121. *O*: View of a church. ST. MARTIN'S CHURCH.
    R: P. Kempson, &c. As No. 97.
                    Conder, 165; 49.—Virt: 66.

122. *O*: As last.
    R: I. Ottley, &c. As No. 96.

ᵛ 123. *O*: Side view of a chapel. ST. MARY'S CHAPEL ERECTED 1774.
    R: P. Kempson, &c. As on No. 95.
                    Conder, 166; 50.—Virt: 66.

ᵛ 124. *O*: As last.
    R: P. Kempson, &c. As No. 97.

125. *O*: As last.
    R: I. Ottley, &c. As on No. 96.

126. *O*: View of an ancient building. THE OLD MEETING DE-
    STROYED, 1791.
    R: P. Kempson, &c. As on No. 94.
                    Conder, 166; 51.—Virt: 97.

ᵛ 127. *O*: As last.
    R: P. Kempson, &c. As No. 97.

128. *O*: As last.
    R: I. Ottley, &c. As No. 96.

ᵛ 129. *O*: A public building. OLD MEETING AS REBUILT IN 1794.
    R: P. Kempson, &c. As on No. 97.
                    Conder, 166; 52.—Virt: 84.

130. *O*: As last.
    R: I. Ottley, &c. As on No. 96.

ᵛ 131. *O*: View of a building. NEW MEETING BURNT IN 1791.
    R: P. Kempson, &c. As No. 94.
                    Conder, 166; 53.—Virt: 97.

ᵛ 132. *O*: As last.
    R: P. Kempson, &c. As No. 97.

133. *O*: As last.
    R: I. Ottley, &c. As on No. 96.

ᵛ 134. *O*: View of a building. MEETING PARADISE STRT. ERECTED
    1786.
    R: P. Kempson, &c. As on No. 94.
                    Conder, 166; 54.—Virt: 156.

135. *O*: As last.
    R: I. Ottley, &c. As No. 96.

ᵛ 136. *O*: View of a building. NAVIGATION OFFICE. Date in *Ex*:
    MDCCXCVI.
    R: P. Kempson, &c. As on No. 97.
                    Conder, 166; 55.—Virt: 84.

137. *O*: As last.
    R: I. Ottley, &c. As on No. 96.

ᵛ 138. *O*: View of a building. NEW JERUSALEM TEMPLE ERECTED
    1790.
    R: P. Kempson, &c. As No. 94.
                    Conder, 166; 56.—Virt: 156.

139. *O*: As last.
    R: I. Ottley, &c.   As on No. 96.

✓ 140. *O*: View of an ancient building.   OLD CROSS ERECTED 1702.
    R: P. Kempson, &c.   As on No. 94.
                          Conder, 166 ; 57.—Virt : 102.

141. *O*: As last.
    R: P. Kempson, &c.   As on No. 95.

142. *O*: As last.
    R: I. Ottley, &c.   As on No. 96.

✓ 143. *O*: View of a chapel.   ST. PAUL'S CHAPEL.
    R: P. Kempson, &c.   As on No. 94.
                          Conder, 166 ; 58.—Virt : 97.

✓ 144. *O*: As last.
    R: P. Kempson, &c.   As No. 97.

145. *O*: As last.
    R: I. Ottley, &c.   As on No. 96.

✓ 146. *O*: View of a church.   ST. PHILIP'S CHURCH.
    R: P. Kempson, &c.   As on No. 94.
                          Conder, 166 ; 59.—Virt : 44.

✓ 147. *O*: As last.
    R: P. Kempson, &c.   As on No. 97.

148. *O*: As last.
    R: I. Ottley.   As on No. 96.

✓ 149. *O*: View of a large building.   SOHO MANUFACTORY ERECTED
        1764.
    R: P. Kempson, &c.   As on No. 94.
                          Conder, 166 ; 60.—Virt : 155.

✓ 150. *O*: As last.
    R: P. Kempson, &c.   As on No. 95.
    E: As on No. 95.

151. *O*: As last.
    R: I. Ottley, &c.   As on No. 96.

✓ 152. *O*: View of a building.   BIRMINGHAM THEATRE 1795.
    R: P. Kempson, &c.   As on No. 94.
                          Conder, 166 ; 61.—Virt : 98.

✓ 153. *O*: As last.
    R: P. Kempson, &c.   As No. 97.

154. *O*: As last.
    R: I. Ottley, &c.   As No. 96.

✓ 155. *O*: View of an ancient building.   WELCH CROSS.
    R: P. Kempson, &c.   As on No. 94.
                          Conder, 166 ; 62.—Virt : 102.

✓ 156. *O*: As last.
    R: P. Kempson, &c.   As on No. 97.

157. *O*: As last.
    R: I. Ottley, &c.   As No. 96.

✓ 158. *O*: View of a large building.   BIRMM. WORKHOUSE ERECTED
        1733 ENLARGED 1794.
    R: P. Kempson, &c.   As on No. 94.
                          Conder, 167 ; 63.—Virt : 5.

159. *O*: As last.
  R: I. Ottley, &c. As on No. 96.

v 160. *O*: View of a public meeting. LIBRARY AS BUILDING
  DECEMR. MDCCXCV.
  R: P. Kempson, &c. As on No. 95.
  Conder, 167 ; 64.—Virt : 158.

161. *O*: As last.
  R: I. Ottley, &c. As on No. 96.

v 162. *O*: Bust to right. GEORGIVS III DEI GRATIA.
  R: P. Kempson, &c. As on No. 97.
  Conder, 165 ; 37.—Virt : 54.
  *A set of these buildings was struck in silver, and a set of
  those with Ottley rev. in tin, also a few in brass.*

Lutwyche's.

v 163. *O*: A figure of Justice seated, holding in one hand a
  pair of scales, and with the other pouring forth
  medals from a cornucopia. On an oval behind is
  inscribed ENGRAVING & DIE SINKING. Legend—
  MEDALS AND PROVINCIAL COINS. *Ex*: DEA PECUNIA.
  R: A coining press. LUTWYCHE'S MANUFACTORY. *Ex*:
  BIRMINGHAM.
  E: Milled.   Conder, 167 ; 65.—Pye, 8 ; 10.—Virt : 59.

163*a*.   As last, but *E* : Blundered letters.

v 163*b*.   „   „   *E* : Plain (in collar).
  This obv. occurs with the following reverse :—

v 164. *R*: Bust of George III. and Queen Charlotte. LONG MAY
  THEY REIGN OVER A GRATEFULL PEOPLE. See Not
  Local, No. 54.   Conder, 213 ; 25.
  See also No. 305 ; and Hampshire, No. 59.

Pye's.

v 165. *O*: A cypher *C. P.* 1797 under. BIRMINGHAM HALFPENNY
  FOR EXCHANGE.
  R: Female seated beside boring tools, pouring medals from
  a cornucopia. A beehive on a stand in front. THE
  SUPPORT OF BRITAIN.
  E: Plain (in collar).   Pye, 9 ; 2.
  Rare.   Private token ; 3 dozen only struck.

Skidmore's.

v 166. *O*: A cypher *P. S.* in an ornamented circle, a small ornament
  over. BIRMINGHAM HALFPENNY 1792.
  R: Bust in cocked hat. GENERAL ELLIOT.
  This obv. occurs with the following reverses :—

220   WARWICKSHIRE.   *Halfpennies.*

✓ 167. *R* : Two busts, &c. See Not Local, No. 90.
    E : Milled.

   168. *R* : Bust to left. MAY THE FRENCH &c. See Not Local,
    No. 117.
    E : Milled.   Conder, 282; 181.
    The rev. of No. 166 appears as an obv. with the
    following reverses :—

   169. *R* : MUR'D BY THE FACTIOUS &c. See Not Local, No. 90.
    E : Milled.

   170. *R* : An anchor and cable, &c. See Not Local, No. 117.
    E : Milled.
    See also Devonshire, No. 5 ; and Middlesex, Nos. 366
    and 382.
    All these varieties are exceedingly rare.

COVENTRY.

1792.

✓ 171. *O* : Lady Godiva on horseback. PRO BONO PUBLICO. The
    triangular dot at the end of the legend just touches
    the horse's tail. *Ex* : 1792.
    R : Elephant and castle. (The arms of the city.) COVENTRY
    HALFPENNY.
    E : PAYABLE AT THE WAREHOUSE OF ROBERT REYNOLDS & CO.
          Conder, 167; 66.—Pye, 15; 3.—Virt: 62.

✓ 172. Similar to last, but the dot at the end of legend on *R* :
    is a little farther from the elephant.
    This variety may be best distinguished by a flaw
    running obliquely through the reverse.

✓ 173. Similar to last, but the triangular dot is still farther
    away, and larger, something like a small letter Y.

✓ 174. *O* : Similar, but the legend comes lower ; the last letter o as
    well as the dot touches the horse.
    R : The same as last.
    E : NUNEATON BEDWORTH AND HINKLEY.

✓ 175. *O* : As last.
    R : Similar, but no dot at the end of legend.
    E : As No. 171.

✓ 176. *O* : Similar to No. 174, but without dot at end of legend.
    R : and *E* : As last.

✓ 177. *O* : Legend in smaller letters, and some distance from horse
    at end.
    R : As No. 172. The same flaw being observable.
    E : As No. 171.

1793.

✓ 178. *O*: Godiva, as before; head of figure close to second o of
　　　　BONO, period close to last letter of legend. Date in
　　　　Ex: 1793.

　　R: Elephant and castle, no period at end of legend. N and
　　　　Y nearly touch tail of elephant, and there is a
　　　　protuberance about the centre of the tail.

　　E: PAYABLE AT BIRMINGHAM LONDON OR BRISTOL.

　　　　　　　　　　　　　　　　　　Conder, 167; 67.

178*a*.　　As last, but *E*: PAYABLE IN BEDWORTH HINKLEY OR
　　　　NUNEATON.

178*b*.　　As last, but *E*: PAYABLE AT NUNEATON HINKLEY |||| OR ||||
　　　　BEDWORTH.

178*c*.　　As last, but *E*: PAYABLE ✕ AT ✕ CRONEBANE ✕ OR ✱ IN ✱
　　　　DUBLIN ✱ ✱ ✱

178*d*.　　As last, but *E*: PAYABLE IN LANCASTER LONDON OR
　　　　BRISTOL.

178*e*.　　As last, but *E*: Milled.

✓ 179. *O*: Similar to last, but the head is near to the P in PUBLICO,
　　　　and the period is farther from end of legend.

　　R: As No. 178.

　　E: Milled to right.

179*a*.　　As last, but *E*: Milled to left.

✓ 179*b*.　　　„　　„　*E*: Plain (not in collar).

　　　　　　　　　　　　　　　　　　Conder, 167; 68.

180. *O*: Similar; the head of figure comes under second o of
　　　　BONO, the legend is more spread, and there is no
　　　　period at the end.

　　R: As No. 178.

　　E: PAYABLE AT CRONEBANE OR IN DUBLIN.

180*a*.　　As last, but *E*: PAYABLE AT NUNEATON BEDWORTH OR
　　　　HINKLEY.

180*b*.　　As last, but *E*: PAYABLE IN LANCASTER LONDON OR
　　　　BRISTOL.

180*c*.　　As last, but *E*: Milled to right.

✓ 180*d*.　　　„　　„　*E*: Milled to left.　　Conder, 167; 69.

181. *O*: As last.

　　R: The legend is higher up, the last letter only coming
　　　　near the elephant, which has no protuberance on its
　　　　tail as before in No. 178.

　　E: PAYABLE IN BEDWORTH HINKLEY OR NUNEATON.

181*a*.　　As last, but *E*: PAYABLE AT BEDWORTH NUNEATON OR
　　　　HINKLEY.

✓ 181*b*.　　As last, but *E*: PAYABLE AT NUNEATON BEDWORTH OR
　　　　HINKLEY.

181*c*.　　As last, but *E*: PAYABLE AT NUNEATON |||| HINKLEY ||| OR
　　　　||| BEDWORTH.

181*d*.　　As last, but *E*: PAYABLE AT LONDON OR ANGLESEY.

✓ 182. *O* : As last.

  R : Similar to last, but the tuft at end of elephant's tail touches the hind leg, which it does not in former.

  E : PAYABLE AT NUNEATON ||| HINKLEY ||| OR ||| BEDWORTH.

182*a*. As last, but *E* : Milled.

 183. *O* : As last.

  R : Similar, but the legend is higher, the Y being quite clear of the elephant, and the right-hand corner of the castle comes to the first part of the L in HALFPENNY.

  E : As No. 181.

✓ 183*a*. As last, but *E* : As No. 181*d*.

 183*b*. As last, but *E* : Plain (not in collar).

✓ 184. *O* : As last.

  R : Similar to last, but there is a branch of a tree lying beneath the elephant.

  E : As last.   Conder, 167 ; 69.

✓ 185. *O* : Similar to preceding.

  R : An ancient cross. COVY. CROSS upon its base. COVENTRY HALFPENNY.

  E : PAYABLE AT THE WAREHOUSE OF THO & ALEX HUTCHISON.
  Very rare.

1794.

✓ 186. *O* : Lady Godiva on horseback. PRO BONO PUBLICO. **Date** in *Ex* : 1794.

  R : An ancient cross. COVY. CROSS upon its base. COVENTRY HALFPENNY.

  E : PAYABLE AT THE WAREHOUSE OF ROBERT REYNOLDS & CO.
      Conder, 167 ; 70.—Pye, 15 ; 3.—Virt : 62.

1795.

✓ 187. *O* : Lady Godiva, as before. PRO BONO PUBLICO. **Date** in *Ex* : 1795.

  R : Elephant and castle. COVENTRY HALFPENNY.

  E : PAYABLE IN LANCASTER LONDON OR BRISTOL.
  Very rare.

✓ 188. *O* : As last.

  R : and *E* : As No. 186.

 188*a*. As last, but *E* : PAYABLE AT THE WAREHOUSE OF THOMAS CLACKE.

✓ 189. *O* : Similar to last, but without the elongated dot after legend.

  R : As last.

  E : Milled.   Conder, 168 ; 71.

  This latter is by far the largest piece of the series.

Varieties.

190. *O*: Lady Godiva on horseback. PRO BONO PUBLICO. Date in *Ex*: 1792.
   R: A public building. EAST INDIA HOUSE. See Lancashire, No. 76.   Conder, 223; 112.

191. *O*: As last, but dated 1794.
   R: Arms, crest a crank, &c. See Wicklow, No. 21.
   E: PAYABLE IN LONDON LIVERPOOL OR BRISTOL.
   Conder, 223; 113.

192. *O*: An elephant and castle.
   R: St. Andrew and his cross, &c. See Lothian, No. 16.
   E: PAYABLE AT THE WAREHOUSE OF ROBERT REYNOLDS & CO.
   Conder, 168; 72.

193. *O*: An ancient cross. As the reverse of No. 186.
   R: Crowned bust to left. IOHN OF GAUNT DUKE OF LANCASTER ∗ See Lancashire, No. 4.
   E: PAYABLE AT LIVERPOOL OR BRISTOL.

194. *O*: As last.
   R: A head in profile. STANHOPE NOBLE WITHOUT NOBILITY.
   E: PAYABLE AT ADAM SIMPSONS ROMNEY.

The reverse of this piece forms the obverse of the Not Local token, No. 147, and the edge, with the exception of the name of the town, belongs to Chesham, Buckinghamshire. It is very rare, if not unique.

Kempson's Buildings.

195. *O*: An ancient building. BABLAKE HOSPITAL. *Ex*: FOUNDED 1506.
   R: Shield of arms and crest. P. KEMPSON FECIT. at sides of shield. THE ARMS OF COVENTRY 1797.
   E: COVENTRY TOKEN and a wavy line.
   Conder, 168; 74.—Virt: 205.

196. *O*: As last.
   R: A bust to left. GEORGE FREDERICK HANDEL.
   E: Plain (in collar).   Conder, 168; 75.

197. *O*: A public building. THE BARRACKS. *Ex*: ERECTED 1794.
   R: (Arms, &c.) and *E*: As No. 195.   Conder, 168; 76.

198. *O*: As last.
   R: (Bust of Handel) and *E*: As No. 196.

199. *O*: Remains of an ancient building and houses. REMAINS OF CATHEDRAL. *Ex*: ERECTED 1043.
   R: (Arms, &c.) and *E*: As No. 195.
   Conder, 168; 77.—Virt: 188.

200. *O*: As last.
   R: (Bust of Handel) and *E*: As No. 196.
   Conder, 168; 78.

201. *O*: View of a gateway and houses. COOK STREET. *Ex*: GATE.
R: (Arms, &c.) and *E*: As No. 195.
Conder, 169 ; 79.—Virt: 191.

202. *O*: As last.
R: (Bust of Handel) and *E*: As No. 196.
Conder, 169 ; 80.

203. *O*: An ancient cross. COVENTRY CROSS * ERECTED 1544 TAKEN DOWN 1771.
R: (Arms, &c.) and *E*: As No. 195.
Conder, 169 ; 81.—Virt: 205.

204. *O*: As last.
R: (Bust of Handel) and *E*: As No. 196.
Conder, 169 ; 82.

205. *O*: View of a public building. COUNTY . HALL. *Ex*: ERECTED. 1784.
R: (Arms, &c.) and *E*: As No. 195.   Conder, 169 ; 83.

206. *O*: As last.
R: (Bust of Handel) and *E*: As No. 196.

207. *O*: A large building. DRAPERS HALL. *Ex*: ERECTED 1775.
R: (Arms, &c.) and *E*: As No. 195.   Conder, 169 ; 84.

208. *O*: As last.
R: (Bust of Handel) and *E*: As No. 196.

209. *O*: An ancient building. FORDS HOSPITAL. *Ex*: FOUNDED 1529.
R: (Arms, &c.) and *E*: As No. 195.
Conder, 169 ; 85.—Virt: 227.

210. *O*: As last.
R: (Bust of Handel) and *E*: As No. 196.
Conder, 169 ; 86.

211. *O*: An ancient building. FREE SCHOOL. *Ex*: OLD FRONT TAKEN DOWN 1794.
R: (Arms, &c.) and *E*: As No. 195.
Conder, 169 ; 87.—Virt: 195.

212. *O*: As last.
R: (Bust of Handel) and *E*: As No. 196.
Conder, 169 ; 88.

213. *O*: A different view of the same building. FREE SCHOOL. *Ex*: NEW FRONT 1797.
R: (Arms, &c.) and *E*: As No. 195.   Conder, 169 ; 89.

214. *O*: As last.
R: (Bust of Handel) and *E*: As No. 196.

215. *O*: View of an ancient gateway and houses. GREY FRIARS GATE. *Ex*: TAKEN DOWN 1781.
R: (Arms, &c.) and *E*: As No. 195.
Conder, 170 ; 90.—Virt: 186.

216. *O*: As last.
R: (Bust of Handel) and *E*: As No. 196.
Conder, 170 ; 91.

217. *O*: Remains of a church enclosed with trees. GREY FRIARS
     STEEPLE. *Ex*: ERECTED 1234.
     R: (Arms, &c.) and *E*: As No. 195.
                              Conder, 170; 92.—Virt: 189.

218. *O*: As last.
     R: (Bust of Handel) and *E*: As No. 196.
                              Conder, 170; 93.

219. *O*: View of a church. ST. JOHNS CHURCH. *Ex*: ERECTED
     1350.
     R: (Arms, &c.) and *E*: As No. 195.
                              Conder, 170; 94.—Virt: 186.

220. *O*: As last.
     R: (Bust of Handel) and *E* · As No. 196.
                              Conder, 170; 95.

221. *O*: An ancient building. ST. MARY HALL.
     R: (Arms, &c.) and *E*: As No. 195.
                              Conder, 170; 96.—Virt: 206.

222. *O*: As last.
     R: (Bust of Handel) and *E*: As No. 196.
                              Conder, 170; 97.

223. *O*: View of an ancient gateway and houses. MILL LANE
     GATE.
     R: (Arms, &c.) and *E*: As No. 195.
                              Conder, 170; 98.—Virt: 187.

224. *O*: As last.
     R: (Bust of Handel) and *E*: As No. 196.
                              Conder, 170; 99.

225. *O*: An ancient gateway and houses. SPON GATE. *Ex*:
     TAKEN DOWN 1771.
     R: (Arms, &c.) and *E*: As No. 195.
                              Conder, 170; 100.—Virt: 185.

226. *O*: As last.
     R: (Bust of Handel) and *E*: As No. 196.
                              Conder, 171; 101.

227. *O*: View of a church. TRINITY CHURCH.
     R: (Arms, &c.) and *E*: As No. 195.
                              Conder, 171; 102.—Virt: 187.

228. *O*: As last.
     R: (Bust of Handel) and *E*: As No. 196.
                              Conder, 171; 103.

229. *O*: An ancient gateway in ruins. WHITEFRIARS GATE.
     R: (Arms, &c.) and *E*: As No. 193.
                              Conder, 171; 104.—Virt: 188.

230. *O*: As last.
     R: (Bust of Handel) and *E*: As No. 196.
                              Conder, 171; 105.

✔ 231. *O* : An ancient building with a tree in front. WHITEFRIARS.
   Ex : FOUNDED 1342.
 R : (Arms, &c.) and *E* : As No. 195.
       Conder, 171 ; 106.—Virt: 195.

✔ 232. *O* : As last.
 R : (Bust of Handel) and *E* : As No. 196.
        Conder, 171 ; 107.
This bust of Handel is taken from a token of Hardingham of Norwich; see Norfolk, No. 36. There are three different dies used, for "Arms" rev., No. 213 occurs with all, and No. 215 with two of them. Those with rev. "Arms" are also struck in silver.

Nickson's.

✔ 233. *O* : A three-quarter figure in cap and gown, holding a book, by the side of the figure WYON, the artist's name, in small letters. JOHN HALES FOUNDED.
 R : End view of an ancient building. THE FREE SCHOOL COVENTRY. *Ex* : ANNO 1545.
 E : COVENTRY HALFPENNY PAYABLE BY JOHN NICKSON 1799 + +
         Pye, 15* ; 3.
Very rare. Private token ; 6 specimens in silver and 6 dozen in copper.

✔ 234. *O* : Similar, but with a tassel added to the cap, and a deed with two seals instead of the book.
 R : and *E* : The same as last.   Pye, 15* ; 2.
Very rare. Only 15 impressions were taken.

Sharp's.

235. *O* : A figure seated, leaning upon a sword, and holding a shield. CIVITAS COVENTRIÆ. *Ex* : MDCCXCVII.
 R : The house wherein the figure of Peeping Tom is placed, with the King's Head Inn adjoining.
 E : COVENTRY HALFPENNY PAYABLE BY THOMAS SHARP. (In raised letters). Conder, 318 ; 73.—Pye, 15 ; 5.
Of this extremely rare piece only 6 impressions were taken as the rev. die was not approved of.

✔ 236. *O* : and *E* : The same as last.
 R : Similar, but the execution different, and in *Ex*: MEMORIÆ GODIVÆ. Conder, 168 ; 73.—Pye, 15 ; 6.
Very rare. Private token ; only about 4 dozen struck, some of which are in silver, and others in white metal.

237. *O* : As the rev. of No. 235.
 R : An unfinished proof of the rev. of No. 236 with no legend in *Ex*.
 E : As before, only part being struck up. (This is in tin.)
Exceedingly rare. Only 2 specimens known.
There are also artist's proofs in tin, of both obv. and rev. of No. 236.

MERIDEN.

⌄ 238. *O* : An archer shooting. FOR . THE . PRIZE ARCHERY
  R : The Prince of Wales' crest, radiated, over a bow,
    quiver, horn, &c. MERIDEN TOKEN 1796
                Conder, 171 ; 108.—Virt : 163.
    Rare.

⌄ 239. *O* : The same as last.
  R : A dove flying with an olive branch, &c. See Middlesex,
    No. 456.   Conder, 210 ; 3.
    This also is rare.
    See also Buckinghamshire, No. 10.

NEWTON.

⌄ 240. *O* : A pack, marked "WOOL." NEWTON HALFPENNY PAYABLE
    BY JOHN WEBB 1796.
  R : Shield of arms, crest an arm holding an arrow,
    between branches of oak.
  E : Plain (in collar).   Conder, 171 ; 109.—Pye, 38 ; 4.
    *Very rare. Only about 4 dozen struck before the dies
    broke.*

NUNEATON.

⌄ 241. *O* : The Lady Godiva. As on No. 174. Date in *Ex* : 1792.
  R : The Grocer's arms, supporters, &c. HALFPENNY, 1792.
    See Lancashire, No. 76.
  E : NUNEATON BEDWORTH AND HINKLEY.
                Conder, 171 ; 110.—Virt : 62.

241*a*.   As last, but *E* : PAYABLE AT NUNEATON BEDWORTH OR
    HINKLEY.

STRATFORD.

242. *O* : Bust of Shakespeare to left. STRATFORD PROMISSORY
    HALFPENNY.
  R : STRUCK | IN HONOR AND | TO PERPETUATE | THE MEMORY
    OF | SHAKESPEARE | BORN APRIL 1564 | DIED APRIL
    | 1616.
  E : Engrailed. (Conder says, "A carved oak leaf
    engrailed.")   Conder, 172 ; 112.—Virt : 120.
    With this edge, very rare.

⌄ 242*a*.   As last, but *E* : Milled.

242*b*.   „   „   *E* : Plain (not in collar). This is struck
    in white metal.
    This obv. occurs with the following reverses :—

⌄ 243. *R* · T. SPENCE BOOKSELLER, &c. See Middlesex, No. 528.
                Conder, 294 ; 308.
                    15 *

244. *R*: A pair of breeches on fire. PANDORAS BREECHES. See Middlesex, No. 522. Conder, 289; 259.

245. *R*: "Little Turnstile Halfpenny." See Middlesex, No. 527. Conder, 294; 309.

The rev. of No. 245 appears as an obv. with the following reverses:—

246. *R*: T. SPENCE, &c. The same as No. 243.

247. *R*: Pandora's breeches. As No. 244. Conder, 289; 260.

248. *R*: Little Turnstile. As No. 245. Conder, 300; 379.

WILLEY.

249. *O*: Bust of Mr. Wilkinson to right, in a plain coat, without collar. There are four buttons on the coat, and four on the waistcoat. I. G. HANCOCK . F. in minute characters under the bust. IOHN WILKINSON IRON MASTER.

R: Blank. Pye, 48; 2.

This is an artist's proof, and possibly unique.

Barge, 1788.

250. *O*: Bust to right. The coat has a turned down collar and there are four buttons on it, but only two on the waistcoat. IOHN WILKINSON IRONMASTER.

R: A two-masted sailing barge. The date in *Ex*: 1788.

E: WILLEY SNEDSHILL BERSHAM BRADLEY.
Conder, 172; 118.—Pye, 48; 6.—Virt: 117.

251. *O*: and *E*: The same as last.

R: A very similar design, but not from the same die. FINE SILVER. *Ex*: 1788.

Note.—*This piece, as its reverse legend denotes, is struck in silver, and was issued by Mr. Wilkinson in 1788 at the value of 3s 6d. About 100 impressions were taken. There is a specimen in the British Museum struck in copper. In a letter dated July 14, 1787, Mr. John Wilkinson says: "Yesterday week my iron boat was launched. It answers all my expectations and has convinced the unbelievers, who were 999 in 1000. It will be only a nine days' wonder and afterwards a Columbus's Egg."*

Barge, 1792.

252. *O*: A close imitation of No. 250, but with only three buttons on coat, and none on waistcoat.

R: Barge, as before. Date in *Ex*: 1792.

E: PAYABLE IN ANGLESEY LONDON OR LIVERPOOL. The N's inverted. Conder, 6; 45.

Most probably a counterfeit, but rare.

Forge, 1787.

✔ 253. *O*: Similar to No. 249, but with three buttons only on coat, and three on waistcoat.

R: Interior of forge, showing a semi-circular window at back. Date in *Ex*: 1787.

E: Unless expressly stated to the contrary, it may be taken for granted that all the edges are the same as No. 250.

Conder, 172 ; 114.—Pye, 48 ; 4.—Virt: 116.

Rare. A few impressions only were taken.

✔ 254. *O*: Similar to last, but from a different die; the buttons on coat are very large.

R: Interior of forge, without window. Curved 1 and 7's in date. Pye, 48; 5.

255. Similar to preceding, but no period at end of legend.

✔ 256. Similar to No. 254, but the final letter of legend nearly touches the coat. There is a period, which is above the line.

✔ 257. Similar to last, but without the period.

✔ 258. Similar to No. 256, but the 1 in the date is straight.

Conder, 172 ; 115.

✔ 259. *O*: Similar to No. 254, but more hair under the bust, reaching almost to buttons.

R: Interior of forge as before. The 1 in date is curved and the 7's straight.

✔ 260. *O*: Similar to No. 255.

R: Same as last.

✔ 261. *O*: Similar to No. 256.

R: Same as last. Conder, 172 ; 116.

✔ 262. *O*: Similar to No. 254.

R: Similar to No. 259, excepting that it has a neat scroll or chain border instead of the beaded rim which is on all the others. Pye, 48; 3.

Very rare. A few specimens only.

✔ 263. *O*: A very poor imitation of the preceding.

R: Forge, as before. *Ex*: 1787, the 8 being much longer than any of the other figures.

E : PAYABLE AT ANGLESEA LONDON OR LIVERPOOL.

Conder, 6 ; 43.

Forge, 1788.

✔ 264. *O*: Similar to No. 256.

R: Interior of forge. Date in *Ex*: 1788.

✔ 265. *O*: Similar to No. 257.

R: The same as last. Conder, 172 ; 117.

Forge, 1790.

266. *O* : Bust to right. The coat has a turned down collar, and
its surface is ribbed; there are three buttons on the
coat, but no waistcoat shows. There is no period at
end of legend.

    R : Interior of forge. Date in *Ex* : 1790. Both the 1 and
7 are straight.

266*a*.   As last, but this mark ∞ on edge between " BRADLEY "
and " WILLEY."

267. *O* : Similar to preceding, but with a little final curl to hair
under bust, and the bottom roll of the wig is broken
into three divisions.

    R : The same as last.   Conder, 172 ; 119.—Pye, 48 ; 7.

268. *O* : Bust, as before. The surface of the coat smooth, turned
down collar, four buttons, and three on waistcoat.
There is a period at end of legend.

    R : Interior of forge. Date in *Ex* : 1790. Curved 1 and
straight 7.

269. *O* : Similar to last, but the final letter of legend touches
the bust. No period.

    R : Interior of forge. Date in small figures; the top of
the 1 is pointed, the 7 straight.   Conder, 172 ; 120.

Forge, 1792.

270. *O* : Similar to No. 266.

    R : Interior of forge. Date in *Ex* : 1792.
                                     Conder, 173 ; 124.

271. *O* : Bust, as before. Coat smooth, three buttons, no waistcoat, period at end of legend.

    R : Interior of forge. Work coarse, figures of date large,
the 1 pointed at top.

    E : PAYABLE IN ANGLESEY LONDON OR LIVERPOOL. The N's
retrograde.   Conder, 6 ; 44.

271*a*.   As last, but *E* : PAYABLE AT NUNEATON BEDWORTH OR
HINKLEY.   Conder, 172 ; 111.

Forge, 1793.

272. *O* : Bust, as before. Coat ribbed, turned down collar ribbed
at different angle to coat. There are four buttons
on coat, two on waistcoat. The last letter of legend
touches bust ; no period.

    R : Interior of forge. Date in *Ex* : 1793. There are two
pairs of bands on top beam, the left-hand pair being
very close to support. One small bolt on left hand
upright and two larger ones on right hand.
                                      Conder, 173 ; 126.

272*a*.   As last, but *E* : PAYABLE AT GOLDSMITH & SONS SUD-
BURY × ×

✓ 273. *O*: The same as last.

R: Differs from preceding in left-hand bands being farther from support, the flames also different.

✓ 274. *O*: Differs from preceding in letters of legend being larger, and placed differently, the letter o in "IRON" at junction of hair and forehead, whereas in the former it is the i that is so.

R: The same as last.

✓ 275. *O*: Differs in the letters of legend being much smaller, and closer together. The final letter is some distance from bust.

R: The same as last.

✓ 276. *O*: The same as No. 266.

R: Similar, but the figures of date larger and better formed than previous ones, flat top to the 1 and 3.

Tokens ✓ *Also struck in silver.*

276a. As last, but *E*: WILLEY SNEDSHILI, &c.

276b. „ „ *E*: PAYABLE IN ANGLESEY LONDON OR LIVERPOOL.

276c. As last, but *E*: PAYABLE AT THE HOUSE OF GILBERT SHEARER & CO:

276d. As last, but *E*: Plain (not in collar). This is on a small flan.

277. *O*: Similar to No. 266.

R: Pointed top to 1 in date, two pairs of bands, as No. 272, three small bolts on left-hand upright, and two large ones on right-hand one.

277a. As last, but *E*: The same as No. 276b.

277b. „ „ *E*: PAYABLE AT ANGLESEA LONDON OR LIVERPOOL.

277c. As last, but *E*: PAYABLE AT BIRMINGHAM BRIGHTON OR LIVERPOOL.   Conder, 164; 28.

✓ 277d. As last, but *E*: PAYABLE AT THE WAREHOUSE OF THOMAS CLARKE.

277e. As last, but *E*: PAYABLE AT MACCLESFIELD LIVERPOOL OR CONGLETON.

277f. As last, but *E*: I PROMISE TO PAY ON DEMAND ONE HALFPENNY. ✕.

277g. As last, but *E*: Plain (not in collar). This is on a small flan.

278. *O*: Bust, as before. Coat smooth, three buttons, no waistcoat, hair long, a period at end of legend.

R: The same as last.

278a. As last, but *E*: M. ABEL   S. PRENTICE   S. DELL.
   Conder, 241; 265.

278b. „ „ *E*: PAYABLE AT IOHN CROW COPPERSMITH ✕.✕

✔ 278c.   As last, but E : PAYABLE IN LANCASTER LONDON OR BRISTOL.
                                                    Conder, 57 ; 18.

278d.   „   „ E : PAYABLE AT LONDON. ✝ . ✝ . ✝ . ✝ .

278e.   „   „ E : PAYABLE AT LONDON OR DUBLIN.

278f.   „   „ E : MASONIC TOKEN I SCETCHLEY FECIT . 1794.

✓ 279. O : The same as last.
        R : Similar, but with three pairs of bands on hammer beam,
             and the pivot on which it works is shown.
        E : PAYABLE BY THOMAS BALL SLEAFORD.

280. O : Bust, as before. Coat smooth, turned down collar, four
           buttons on coat, two on waistcoat, no period.
      R : The same as No. 273.

280a.   As last, but with an annulet between each word on E :
           thus :—WILLEY O SNEDSHILL O, &c.

280b.   As last, but E : PAYABLE IN LONDON BRISTOL &
           LANCASTER.

281. O : Bust, as before. Coat smooth, turned down collar, two
           buttons on coat, no waistcoat, no period at end of
           legend.
      R : Similar to No. 279, but from a different die, and the
           pivot of hammer is not shown.
      E : PAYABLE AT BIRMINGHAM BRIGHTON OR LIVERPOOL.
                                                    Conder, 164; 28.

Forge, 1795.

✓ 282. O : The same as No. 266.
        R : Interior of forge.   Date in Ex : 1795.   The figures are
             close together.

✓ 283. O : Similar to No. 272, but the final letter of legend does
             not touch bust.
        R : The figures of date are more spread than last, and the
             smoke is different.

Vulcan, 1790.

✓ 284. O : Bust different to any preceding. Coat smooth, three
             buttons, no waistcoat, no period after legend.
        R : Figure of Vulcan seated at work, holding a rod on an
             anvil. HALFPENNY. Ex : 1790.
             The two-masted barge is seen in the distance, and
             several varieties will be marked by it. In this
             instance the period after legend is above the pennant
             on foremast.

✓ 285. O : The same as last.
        R Similar, but the period is just below the pennant.

✓ 286. Similar, but the final letter of legend is lower, nearly opposite the end of rod on anvil, the figures of date are close together.

✓ 286*bis.* Similar, but the final letter of legend is quite opposite the rod, and the date is more spread.

✓ 287. Similar, but the final letter of legend is lower still, touching the pennant on foremast.

Conder, 173 ; 121.—Pye, 48, 8.—Virt: 117.

There is no obv. nearly like Pye's engraving, and No. 285 is the nearest rev. to it.

✓ 288. *O*: Bust, as before. Coat smooth, two buttons, a period at end of legend.

R: Similar to No. 284 ; but although the final letter comes down to the rod on anvil, the period is above the pennant on foremast. The bowsprit is much shorter than usual.

Vulcan, 1791.

✓ 289. *O*: Bust, as before. Coat smooth, three buttons, no period.

R: Vulcan seated. Date in *Ex*: 1791. The period is above the pennant on foremast.

✓ 290. *O*: Similar, but the end of legend is farther from the bust, and there is a period.

R: The period is immediately above the pennant, touching it.

Conder, 173 ; 122.

✓ 291. *O*: The same as last.

R: The period is immediately below the pennant.

✓ 292. *O*: Bust, as before. Coat smooth, *no buttons*, a period at end of legend.

R: Similar to last, but the period is a little farther below the pennant.   Pye, 48 ; 9.

Very rare. The buttons on the coat omitted in mistake.

✓ 293. *O*: Bust, as before. Coat ribbed, three buttons, no period.

R: The two masts are very close together, the period is above both pennants. A flaw comes across the first N of " HALFPENNY."

E: PAYABLE IN ANGLESEY LONDON OR LIVERPOOL . × .

293*a.* As last, but *E*: PAYABLE IN DUBLIN OR AT BALLYMURTAGH.

293*b.* As last, but *E*: MANUFACTURED BY W. LUTWYCHE BIR-MINGHAM.

✓ 294. *O*: Similar to last, but with a period at end of legend.

R: Similar, but no flaw in HALFPENNY.

E: PAYABLE AT LONDON . + . + . + .   Conder, 91; 181.

294*a.* As last, but *E*: PAYABLE IN LANCASTER LONDON OR BRISTOL.

✓ 294*b.*   „   „   Milled.

295. *O*: Bust, as before. Coat smooth, three buttons. First three letters of legend are under bust.

    R: The same as No. 293.

295*a*.   As last, but *E*: PAYABLE AT BANBURY OXFORD OR READING +

295*b*.   As last, but *E*: PAYABLE AT DUBLIN OR LONDON.

296. *O*: Similar to No. 293, but the final letter of legend touches bust.

    R: Vulcan seated. Date in *Ex*: 1791. No period after " HALFPENNY."

    E: PAYABLE AT LONDON LIVERPOOL OR BRISTOL.

296*bis*. *O*: Similar to No. 255.

    R: The same as last.

    E: PAYABLE IN LONDON LIVERPOOL OR BRISTOL.

Vulcan, 1792.

297. *O*: Bust, as before. Coat smooth, three buttons, the hair under the bust shorter and thicker than before.

    The letters of legend much smaller than usual, a period at end.

    R: Vulcan at work, a barge in the distance. Date in *Ex*: 1792.   Conder, 173 ; .125.—Pye, 48 ; 10.

298. *O*: The same as last.

    R: The foremast of barge is lower and has not so much rigging ; but this piece may best be identified by a flaw near the P of " HALFPENNY," which gives the appearance of a crest to Vulcan.

299. *O*: Similar to No. 297, but the legend is more spread and approaches the bust more nearly.

    A flaw runs across the chin and collar of this piece.

    R: Nearly the same as No. 297.

300. *O*: Bust, as before. Coat smooth, three buttons, hair long, first two letters of legend under bust.

    There is a period at end of legend, the letters of which are larger again.

    R: Vulcan at work, the hammer midway between the P and E. The pennant touches the period.

300*a*.   As last, but *E*: PAYABLE AT BECCLES SUFFOLK /*/*/*/*/

300*b*.   ,,   ,,   *E*: BRIGHTON CAMP HALFPENNY MDCCXCIV.

300*c*.   ,,   ,,   *E*: PAYABLE IN LANCASTER LONDON OR BRISTOL.

                                         Conder, 57 ; 17.

300*d*.   ,,   ,,   *E*: PAYABLE AT LEEK STAFFORDSHIRE.

300*e*.   ,,   ,,.   *E*: PAYABLE BY I. SIMMONS STAPLEHURST.

300*f*.   ,,   ,,   *E*: WARLEY CAMP HALFPENNY MDCCXCIV.

300*g*.   ,,   ,,   *E*: Plain (not in collar). Struck on a large flan.

✔ 301. *O*: Similar to last, but buttons are closer together; the legend does not commence under bust.
    R: The same as last.
    E: PAYABLE AT NUNEATON BEDWORTH OR HINKLEY.
                                 Conder, 172 ; 111.

✔ 302. *O*: The same as No. 263.
    R: A poor imitation of the preceding pieces.
    E: PAYABLE AT ANGLESEA LONDON OR LIVERPOOL.
                                 Conder, 7 ; 46.

    See also Cheshire, No. 50.

Vulcan, 1793.

303. *O*: A close copy of No. 297.
    R: Vulcan seated, barge in distance. Date in *Ex*: 1793.
    HALFPENNY. The 3 is square topped.
    E: PAYABLE IN ANGLESEY LONDON OR LIVERPOOL . + .
303*a*.   As last, but *E*: PAYABLE AT LONDON CORK OR BELFAST.
303*b*.   ,,   ,,   Plain (not in collar).
    See also Anglesea, No. 229 ; and Middlesex, No. 255.

Mining Tools.

✔ 304. *O*: The same as No. 293. (The flaw in legend on left hand.)
    R: A female seated, holding mining tools. HALFPENNY.
    Ex: 1790.   Conder, 242 ; 267.
✔ 305. *O*: A poor copy of No. 268.
    R: Similar to last, but dated 1794.   Conder, 242 ; 268.
    There are many slight variations of die in these pieces especially noticeable in Nos. 255, 256, 274, 275, and 277.

Varieties.

✔ 306. *O*: A close copy of No. 264.
    R: A figure of Justice, &c. See No. 163.
                              Conder, 242 ; 266.
    The obv. of No. 304 occurs with the following reverses :—
✔ 307. *R*: A cypher, *H. M. Co.*, &c. See Dublin, No. 26.
                              Conder, 242 ; 271.
✔ 308. *R*: A female seated, holding a harp, &c. See Dublin, No. 39.   Conder, 242 ; 270.
✔ 309. *R*: A harp crowned. * NORTH * * WALES * (*This reverse will be found in the imitations of Regal Coins*).
                              Conder, 158 ; 36.
    The obv. of No. 305 occurs with the following reverses :—
✔ 310. *R*: A cypher, &c. As No. 307.   Conder, 242 ; 272.
✔ 311. *R*: A female, &c. As No. 308.   Conder, 242 ; 269.

WILKENSON.

Vulcan, 1790.

312. *O*: Bust to right. Coat smooth, three very small buttons.
IOHN WILKENSON IRONMASTER.
   R: Vulcan at work. Something like No. 288, but not
the same die. Date in *Ex*: 1790.
   E: Milled.

Vulcan, 1791.

313. *O*: Bust, as before. Very similar to No. 284. IOHN
WILKENSON IRONMASTER.
   R: Vulcan at work. Nearly like No. 292, but not the same
die. Date in *Ex*: 1791.
   E: WILLEY SNEDSHILL BERSHAM BRADLEY.
313a. As last, but *E*: WILLEY SNEDSHILL BRADLEY BERSHAM.
✓ 313b.   ,, ,, *E*: WILLEY BRADLEY SNEDSHILL BERSHAM.
313c.   ,, ,, *E*: WILLEY BRADLEY BERSHAM SNEDSHILL.
313d.   ,, ,, *E*: WILLEY BERSHAM BRADLEY SNEDSHILL.
313e.   ,, ,, *E*: BIRMINGHAM W. HAMPTON OR LITCHFIELD.
                 Conder, 163; 27.
There is a slight variation of obv. die.

Forge, 1792.

✓ 314. *O*: Similar to last, but the final letter of legend touches
the bust, no period.
   R: Interior of forge. Nearly like No. 277. Date in *Ex*: 1792.
   E: PAYABLE IN ANGLESEA LONDON OR LIVERPOOL. The N's
retrograde.

Forge, 1793.

315. *O*: and *R*: Similar to No. 276, but name spelt WILKENSON.
   E: WILLEY SNEDSHILL BERSHAM BRADLEY.
✓ 315a. As last, but *E*: BIRMINGHAM LIVERPOOL OR LONDON.
315b.   ,, ,, *E*: PAYABLE AT LEEK STAFFORDSHIRE.
315c.   ,, ,, *E*: CURRENT EVERYWHERE.

WILKISON.

Barge, 1792.

✓ 316. *O*: Similar to No. 271, but the final letter of legend touches
bust. IOHN WILKISON IRONMASTER.
   R: The same as No. 252.
   E: PAYABLE IN ANGLESEY LONDON OR LIVERPOOL. The N's
retrograde.   Conder, 7; 49.
316a. As last, but *E*: PAYABLE IN LONDON OR LIVERPOOL.

Forge, 1787.

317. *O*: and *R*: Similar to No. 254, but the work is rather coarser, and the name, as before, WILKISON.

    E: WILLEY SNEDSHILL BERSHAM BRADLEY.

318. *O*: Similar to last, but poorer work, the letters of legend larger, the final letter touches bust.

    R: Similar to last, but poorer work.

    E: The same as last.

v 318*a*.   As last, but *E*: IN ANGLESEY LONDON OR LIVERPOOL. The N's retrograde.   Conder, 7; 47.

319. *O*: Similar to No. 269.

    R: and *E*: The same as No. 318.

v 319*a*.   As last, but *E*: The same as No. 318*a*. Conder, 7; 48.

Forge, 1792.

320. *O*: and *R*: The same as last, but dated 1792.

    E: PAYABLE IN ANGLESEY LONDON OR LIVERPOOL.

320*a*.   As last, but *E*: PAYABLE AT BIRMINGHAM BRIGHTON OR LIVERPOOL.

320*b*.   As last, but *E*: PAYABLE AT DUBLIN CORK OR BELFAST.

320*c*.   ,,   ,,   *E*: PAYABLE AT LONDON OR ANGLESEY.

320*d*.   ,,   ,,   *E*: PAYABLE AT LONDON CORK OR BELFAST.

v 320*e*.   ,,   ,,   *E*: Plain (not in collar).

Forge, 1794.

320*bis*.   Similar to last, but dated 1794.

Vulcan, 1792.

v 321. *O*: Similar to No. 290, but inferior work, and the name mispelt WILKISON.

    R: Vulcan seated at work.   Date in *Ex*: 1792.

    E: PAYABLE IN ANGLESEY LONDON OR LIVERPOOL. The N's retrograde.   Conder, 7; 50.

321*a*   As last, but *E*: PAYABLE IN BEDWORTH HINKLEY OR NUNEATON.

321*b*.   As last, but *E*: PAYABLE IN LONDON OR ANGLESEY.

322. *O*: Similar to No. 268, with the above exception.

    R: The same as last.

    E: PAYABLE × AT × CRONEBANE × OR × IN × DUBLIN × × ×

                            Conder, 198; 27.

v 322*a*.   As last, but *E*: PAYABLE‖‖AT‖‖LONDON‖‖OR‖‖ANGLESEY.

322*b*.   ,,   ,,   *E*: PAYABLE AT BIRMINGHAM LONDON OR BRISTOL.

323. *O* : Similar to No. 297, with the above exception.
   R : The same as last.
   E : The same as No. 322*b*.
323*a*.   As last, but *E* : PAYABLE IN LANCASTER LONDON OR BRISTOL.
324. *O* : Bust, similar to No. 268. IOHN WILKISON IORN MASTER.
   R : The same as last.
   E : Engrailed.

Vulcan, 1793.

325. *O* : The same as No 322.
   R : Vulcan at work. Date in *Ex* : 1793. The period touches
      just above the mizen pennant.
   E : The same as No. 313.
325*a*.   As last, but *E* : The same as No. 318*a*.
✓ 325*b*.   ,, ,, *E* : The same as No. 320*a*.
✓ 325*c*.   ,, ,, *E* : The same as No. 321*a*.
✓ 326. *O* : The same as No. 323.
   R : Similar to last, but the period is higher, and there are
      knobs on the ends of the yards or crosstrees of the
      barge.
   E : The same as No. 321.   Conder, 7 ; 51.
326*a*.   As last, but *E* : PAYABLE AT LONDON CORK OR BELFAST.
326*b*.   ,, ,, *E* : Plain (not in collar).
                 Conder, 242 ; 275.

Mining Tools.

✓ 327. *O* : The same as No. 322.
   R : Female holding mining tools. HALFPENNY. *Ex* : 1794.
            Conder, 242 ; 268.
✓ 328. *O* : A poor copy of No. 297. And the name misspelt
      WILKISON.
   R : The same as last.   Conder, 242 ; 274.

    Note.—Before finally quitting this exceedingly interest-
    ing series, we will notice two very singular tokens
    which appear to be connected with it, as follows:—
329. *O* : An indented impression of one of the Wilkinson busts
      (No. 295 ?).
   R : A man at table writing, a woman seated by him holding
      a lighted candle, a clergyman behind, &c. See
      Cheshire, No. 44.
   E : PAYABLE IN LONDON LIVERPOOL OR BRISTOL.
             Conder, 112 ; 347.
    This is an artist's proof of this rare rev. of which only
    two are known; it is engraved by Conder on Pl. 1 of
    his work.

330. *O* : A profile bust to right, being a rude imitation of those
preceding. IRON MASTER.

   R : AND HE | SAID LET US | MAKE PEN- | NYS AFTER | MY OWN | IMAGE. In six lines.

   E : PAYABLE AT MACCLESFIELD LIVERPOOL OR CONGLETON.

This was intended to satirize the presumption on the
part of Mr. Wilkinson in venturing to place his
portrait on these coins, a feeling which further found
vent in the following, which appeared in the *London
Magazine* for 1787 :—

EPIGRAM ON MR. WILKINSON'S COPPER MONEY.

In Greece and Rome your men of parts,
Renoun'ed in arms, or famed in arts,
On splendid coins and medals shone,
To make their deeds and person's known ;
So Wilkinson, from this example,
Gives of himself a matchless sample ;
And bids the iron monarch pass
Like his own metal, wrapt in *brass !*
Which shows his modesty and sense,
And how, and where, he made his pence* ;
As iron when 'tis brought in taction,
Collects the copper by attraction.
So this in him 'twas very proper
To stamp his brazen face on *copper !*

   * *The tokens were first issued as pence, but were soon
called in and re-issued as halfpence.*

FARTHINGS.

BIRMINGHAM.

✓ 331. *O* : Bust to right, a small cross under. DR. SAMUEL IOHNSON.

   R : Three lions. PROMISSORY HALF HALFPENNY PAYABLE AT .

   E : Milled.   Conder, 250 ; 49.

✓ 332. *O* : A female seated upon a rock, holding a fasces. COPPER COMPANY. *Ex* : 1791.

   R : A stork standing upon a cornucopia of flowers. FARTHING.

   E : Milled.   Conder, 247 ; 22.

✓ 332*a*.   As last, but *E* : plain (not in collar).

333. *O* : and *R* : Struck from the halfpenny dies of No. 48, on
a farthing size flan, which show no legend on either
side.

334. *O* : The same as No. 332.

   R : MAY A | FLOWING | TRADE FOLLOW | A SPEEDY AND | HONOR-
ABLE | PEACE | 1796.

   E : Milled.   Conder, 247 ; 23.

✓ 334*a*.   As last, but *E* : Plain (not in collar).

✓ 335. *O*: Bust to left in cocked hat, a small cross under. GENERAL
 ELLIOT.
  R: A fleur de lis. BIRMINGHAM HALF HALFPENNY.
  E: Milled.   Conder, 174; 129.

✓ 336. *O*: Bust to left. IOHN HOWARD. F.R.S.
  R: A cypher, *H. H.* BIRMINGHAM PROMISSORY FARTHING. *1792*.
  E: H. HICKMANS WAREHOUSE BIRMINGHAM.
                Conder, 174; 130.—Pye, 9; 3.—Virt: 127.

✓ 336*a*.   As last, but *E*: plain (not in collar).

✓ 337. *O*: A figure standing on a pedestal, upon an oval
 is DIE SINKR.—PROVINCIAL COINS & MEDALS. *Ex*:
 & ENGRAVER.
  R: A coining press. LUTWYCHES MANUFACTORY BIRMINGHAM.
                Conder, 174; 131.—Pye, 9; 4.—Virt: 127.

STRATFORD.

✓ 338. *O*: Bust of Shakespeare. STRATFORD PROMISSORY HALF
 HALFPENNY.
  R: STRUCK | IN HONOR AND | TO PERPETUATE | THE MEMORY OF
 | SHAKESPEARE | BORN APRIL 1564 | DIED APRIL | 1616.
  E: Milled.   Conder, 174; 132.

Westmoreland.

PENNIES.

KENDAL.

1. *O*: A cypher *R & D*, crest a lion. KENDAL.
   R: Figure of Justice standing. FOR CHANGE NOT FRAUD.
   Ex: 1794.
   E: ON DEMAND WE PROMISE TO PAY ONE PENNY.
   Conder, 175; 1.
1a. As last, but *E*: Plain (not in collar).
   *Rare. This reverse is also found upon the Suffolk penny
   No. 1, and is struck like that from the Halfpenny dies.*
2. *O*: As last.
   R: T. HALL | CITTY ROAD | NEAR | FINSBURY SQUARE | &c.
   See Middlesex, No. 26.
   E: MANUFACTURED BY W LUTWYCHE BIRMINGHAM
   Conder, 175; 2.
3. *O*: Remains of an ancient fortress. KENDAL . CASTLE .
   WESTMORLAND. *Ex*: Jacobs.
   R: A globe inscribed BRITAIN between a rose and thistle.
   BRITISH . PENNY. *Ex*: 1797.
   E: I PROMISE TO PAY ON DEMAND THE BEARER ONE PENNY.
   Conder, 175; 3.

HALFPENNIES.

KENDAL.

4. *O*: A cypher *R & D*, crest a lion. KENDAL.
   R: A female with mining tools, similar to the Macclesfield
   tokens. HALFPENNY. *Ex*: 1794.
   E: PAYABLE IN LANCASTER LONDON OR BRISTOL.
   Conder, 175; 7.—Pye, 25; 1.
   *This reverse was the first used for this token, but after a
   few specimens only had been struck, it was determined
   to change it for the one next following.*
5. *O*: As last.
   R: A figure of Justice standing. FOR CHANGE NOT FRAUD.
   Ex: 1794.
   E: PAYABLE AT BANBURY OXFORD OR READING ×
   Conder, 175; 4.—Pye, 25; 2.—Virt: 33.
5a. As last, but *E*: PAYABLE IN LANCASTER LONDON OR BRISTOL.
   *This reverse, like the No. 1 penny, is also found upon
   Herefordshire, No. 5; and Suffolk, No. 20.*
6. *O*: As last.
   R: A man-of-war sailing. THE GUARD & GLORY OF BRITAIN.
   See Not Local, No. 54.
   E: PAYABLE IN DUBLIN OR AT BALLYMURTAGH.

 6*a*.   As last, but *E*: M. ABEL   S. PRENTICE   S. DELL.
✔ 6*b*.   ,,   ,,   *E*: PAYABLE IN DUBLIN OR LONDON.
✔ 6*c*.   ,,   ,,   *E*: Plain (not in collar).   Conder, 175; 5.
✔ 7.   *O*: As last.
      R: A man-of-war sailing.   THE WOODEN WALLS OF OLD
           ENGLAND.   See Not Local, No. 55.   Conder, 175; 6.
✔ 8.   *O*: As last.
      R: Arms and motto SIC DONEC.   SUCCESS TO NAVIGATION.
           See Lancashire, No. 80.

𝔚iltshire.

HALFPENNIES.

COUNTY.

✔ 1. *O*: A horseman galloping. WILTSHIRE YEOMANRY CAVALRY. *Ex*: 1794.

R: Three horsemen mounted, one carrying a flag. THEIR TOKEN. *Ex*: P. A. ET. F. (For "Pro Aris et Focis.")

E: Milled.   Conder, 176; 1.—Pye, 49; 1.—Virt: 73. *Rare.*

DEVIZES.

✔ 2. *O*: Shield of arms. THE ARMS OF THE TOWN OF DEVIZES ✳

R: A stag. I. BASTER . DEVIZES WILTS. *Ex*: 1796.

E: BREECHES AND GLOVE MANUFACTORY . ✕ . ✕ . ✕

✔ 2a.   As last, but *E*: Milled over PAYABLE IN ANGLESEY LONDON OR LIVERPOOL.

In some of these pieces the inscription predominates, in others the milling.

✔ 2b.   As last, but *E*: Milled without any inscription.
    Conder, 176; 2.—Pye, 16; 3.—Virt: 87

✔ 2c.   „   „   *E*: Plain (not in collar).

HOLT.

✔ 3. *O*: A figure of Fame standing, blowing a trumpet. HOLT . WILTSHIRE MINERAL WATERS ✳ DISCOVER'D 1688.

R: SOLD | AT THE | SPA HOUSE | HOLT | BY D. ARNOT | PROPRIETOR. In six lines in the centre within a beaded circle. & BY INO. GRIFFITHS NO. 27 ST. ALBANS STREET LONDON ✳

E: Milled.   Conder, 176; 3.—Pye, 23; 1.—Virt: 67.

✔ 3a.   As last, but *E*: Plain (not in collar).

✔ 4. *O*: As last. .

R: A building, SPA HOUSE above NEAT LODGINGS | B | under, the whole within a beaded circle.   SOLD BY JNO GRIFFITHS NO 27 ST. ALBANS STREET LONDON ✳
    Conder, 176 : 4.—Pye, 23; 2.—Virt: 100.

✔ 5. *O*: As *R*: of last, excepting with HOLT | SPA HOUSE above the building, and NEAT LODGINGS | ✳ ✳ ✳ | HOLT WATER below.

R: As No. 3.   Conder, 176; 5. *Rare.*

The obv. of No. 3 occurs with the following reverse:—

✔ 6. *R*: Bust to right. ✳ HE FEELS HIS PEOPLES WANTS & RELIEVES THEM ✳ See Not Local, No. 63. Conder, 248; 202.

The obv. of No. 5 occurs with the following reverses:—

7. *R*: A beggar receiving alms. I WAS HUNGRY &c. See Gloucestershire, No. 22.   Conder, 281; 171.

16 ✳

8. *R*: TO THE ILLUSTRIOUS DUKE OF BEAUFORT &c. See Gloucestershire, No. 22. Conder, 281; 172.
9. *R*: The same as No. 6. Conder, 284; 203.
10. *R*: A pair of scales, 3½lb.-1s WORTH OF BREAD &c. See Not Local, No. 67. Conder, 293; 296.
11. *R*: A pair of scales, 6½lb.-1s WORTH OF BREAD &c. See Not Local, No. 68. Conder, 294; 301.

SALISBURY.

12. *O*: A head in profile to left. PAYABLE . AT SALISBURY.
   R: A cypher *W. G. M.* the date 1791 under. HALFPENNY above.
   E: Milled. Conder, 176; 6.—Virt: 73.
12a. As last, but *E*: Plain (not in collar).
   This obv. occurs with the following reverses :—
13. *R*: Ruins of a church. DESTROY'D BY FIRE &c. See Middlesex, No. 399.
   E: SKIDMORE HOLBORN LONDON Conder, 292; 280.
13a. As last, but *E*: Milled.
14. *R*: A cypher *I. O. M.* between sprigs, &c. See Yorkshire, No. 11.
   E: SKIDMORE HOLBORN LONDON. Conder, 291; 278.
15. *R*: MUR'D BY THE FACTIOUS &c. See Not Local, No. 90.
16. *R*: An anchor and cable. IN COMMEMORATION OF THE &c. See Not Local, No. 117.
   E: Milled. Conder, 291; 279.
17. *R*: Bust to left in cocked hat. MAY THE FRENCH EVER KNOW &c. See Not Local, 117.
   See also Middlesex, No. 367.
   The rev. of No. 12 appears as an obv. with the following reverses :—
18. *R*: Bust to left. MAY THE FRENCH &c. See Not Local, No. 117.
   E: Milled. Conder, 282; 180.
19. *R*: The same as No. 16. Conder, 278; 140.
   See also Essex, No. 28; and Middlesex, Nos. 384 and 390.
20. *O*: View of a church. CATHEDRAL CHURCH OF SARUM.
   R: The Grocers' Arms, supporters, &c., the date 1796 under. FINE TEAS &c.
   E: PAYABLE AT I & T SHARPES SALISBURY— × —
     Conder, 176; 7.—Pyc, 44; 1.—Virt: 175.
20a. As last, but *E*: PAYABLE AT I. IORDANS DRAPER GOSPORT.
20b. As last, but *E*: Plain (not in collar).

𝔚orcestershire.

PENNIES.

COUNTY.

✓ 1. *O*: A dove standing upon a harp, between olive branches. PEACE LOVE AND HARMONY.
   R: A cypher *M.S.*, within a circle of leaves. PENNY . PAYABLE . IN . WORCESTERSHIRE.
   E: I PROMISE TO PAY ON DEMAND THE BEARER ONE PENNY.
                               Conder, 177; 1.
   Rare.

DUDLEY.

✓ 2. *O*: Ruins of an ancient building. PART OF DUDLEY PRIORY.
     Ex: 1797. Jacobs.
   R: A cypher *E. D.*, between sprigs of laurel. E . DAVIES . NAIL . FACTOR . DUDLEY.
   E: As last.   Conder, 177; 2.
✓ 3. *O*: A different view of the same building. DUDLEY . PRIORY.
   R: and *E*: As last.   Conder, 177; 3.
✓ 4. *O*: Part of an ancient fortress. THE . CHAPPLE . IN . DUDLEY . CASTLE.
   R: and *E*: As last.   Conder, 177; 4.
✓ 5. *O*: A different view of the same building. TOWER . OF . DUDLEY . CASTLE . 1797.
   R: and *E*: As last.   Conder, 177; 5.
   See also Middlesex, No. 80.
   All these pennies are rare.

EVESHAM.

✓ 6. *O*: View of the Abbot's Tower and Evesham Church. EVESHAM PENNY.
   R: A cypher *T T* between sprigs of laurel. PAYABLE BY above, and JUNE . 6 . 1796 . under.
   E: As No. 1.   Conder, 178; 6.—Pye, 19; 4.
   Rare; private token, only 60 *impressions, of which three were struck in gold.*

HALFPENNIES.

DUDLEY.

7. *O*: A distant view of Dudley castle, trees in foreground. DUDLEY TOKEN. *Ex*: JAMES.
   R: A shepherd lying under a tree. *Ex*: 1790.
   E: Milled.

7*a*.   As last, but *E* : PAYABLE IN LONDON. The remainder engrailed.

✔ 7*b*.   As last, but *E* : Plain (not in collar).
                        Conder, 178 ; 7.—Virt : 59.
     This obv. occurs with the following reverses :—

✔ 8.   *R* : THOS. SPENCE SIR THOS. MORE THOS. PAINE &c.   See Middlesex, No. 511.
     E : PAYABLE IN LONDON. The remainder engrailed.
                        Conder, 274; 101.

8*a*.   As last, but *E* : Milled.
8*b*.   „   „   *E* : Plain (not in collar).
9.   *R* : Britannia seated, &c. See Middlesex, No. 512.
                        Conder, 275; 105.

✔ 10.   *R* : A caduceus, &c. See Middlesex, No. 513.
     E : SPENCE × DEALER × IN × COINS × LONDON ×
                        Conder, 275 ; 109.

✔ 11.   *R* : A cat, &c. See Middlesex, No. 514.
     E : As last.   Conder, 275 ; 110.
11*a*.   As last, but *E* : Milled.
12.   *R* : Three citizens armed, &c. See Middlesex, No. 515.
     E : SPENCE ✱ DEALER ✱ IN ✱ COINS ✱ LONDON ✱
                        Conder, 275; 106.

✔ 13.   *R* : Heart and hand, &c. See Middlesex, No. 516.
     E : Same as No. 8.
13*a*.   As last, but *E* : Plain (not in collar).
                        Conder, 274; 102.

✔ 14.   *R* : A Highlander, &c. See Middlesex, No. 517 ; and also Lothian, No. 13.
     E : Same as No. 12.   Conder, 275; 108.
15.   *R* : A Lion dismayed, &c. See Middlesex, No. 519.
     E : As last.   Conder, 274; 103.

✔ 15*a*.   As last, but *E* : The same as No. 8.
✔ 16.   *R* : ODD FELLOWS, &c. See Middlesex, No. 520.
     E : As No. 10.   Conder, 275 ; 104.
17.   *R* : AFTER THE REVOLUTION, &c. See Middlesex, No. 523.
                        Conder, 275; 107.

✔ 18.   *R* : Soldiers besieging a city, &c. See Middlesex, No. 526 ; and also Sussex, No. 7.   Conder, 178; 8.

✔ 19.   *R* : Two boys at a Turnstile, &c. See Middlesex, No. 527.
                        Conder, 275 ; 111.

HAGLEY.

✔ 20.   *O* : An arbour, and trees, beside the water, a man angling.
     Ex : HAGLEY TOKEN.
     R : A snail, a tree, and a bridge in the distance. A SNAIL MAY PUT HIS HORNS OUT.
     E : Plain (not in collar).   Conder, 178 ; 9.—Virt : 87.
20*a*.   As last, but *E* : SPENCE × DEALER × IN × COINS × LONDON ×

✔ 21. *O*: As last.
   R: A shepherd under a tree. As No. 7.
   E: Plain (not in collar).   Conder, 178; 10.
21*a*.   As last, but *E*: SPENCE × DEALER × IN × COINS × LONDON ×
21*b*.   „   „   *E*: PAYABLE AT YORK.
   These are all rare.
   The two preceding reverses are commonly found mixed with Spence's "mules." See also Cambridgeshire, No. 33.

KIDDERMINSTER.

✔ 22. *O*: A wool pack between palm branches. PAYABLE | AT . T .
    SANTER | KIDDERMINSTER in three lines above.
   R: Shield of arms dividing the date 17-91, between laurel branches. HALFPENNY. Conder, 178; 11.—Virt: 63.
   This obv. occurs with the following reverses:—
23. *R*: Two busts. LOUIS . XVI ET M . ANTOINETTE, &c. See Not Local, No. 91.   Conder, 283; 194.
24. *R*: Bust to left in cocked hat. MAY THE FRENCH EVER KNOW &c. See Not Local, No. 117.
   E: Milled.
   The rev. of No. 22 appears as an obv. with the following reverses:—
✔ 25. *R*: Bust of DAVID GARRICK, &c. See Middlesex, No. 156.
    Conder, 222; 102.
✔ 26. *R*: A guillotine, &c. See Middlesex, No. 375.
   E: SKIDMORE HOLBORN LONDON.
27. *R*: MUR'D BY THE FACTIOUS, &c. See Not Local, No. 90.
   E: Milled.
28. *R*: An anchor and cable. IN COMMEMORATION OF, &c. See Not Local, No. 117.
   E: Milled.   Conder, 265; 21.
   See also Middlesex, Nos. 368, 369, 383, 385, and 407.

STOURBRIDGE.

✔ 29. *O*: View of a church. BRIRLEY . HILL . TOKEN ....
   R: A cypher *R A* within a circle of leaves. R . ASTIN . MALSTER STOURBRIDGE 1797.
   E: Engrailed.   Conder, 178; 12.—Virt: 195.
   Rare.

WORCESTER.

✔ 30. *O*: Laureate bust to right. W. A. & CO. under. GEORGIVS III DEI GRATIA.
   R: A shield crowned, inscribed WORCESTER . AUGUST . 6 . 7 & 8 . in four lines. M . B . F . ET . H . REX . F . D . B . ET . L . D . S . R . I . A . T . ET . E . 1788.
    Conder, 179; 14.

31. *O*: Bust as before. I . B under it.   Legend as last.
   R: A crown radiated, above musical instruments. WORCES-
      TER AUGUST . 6 . 1788.   Conder, 179 ; 15.

✓ 32. *O*: Bust as before, DAVIES under it.   Legend as before.
   R: A crown (not radiated), above musical instruments.
      WORCESTER . AUGUST . 6 . 1788.   Conder, 179 ; 13.

33. *O*: As last.
   R: Similar, but AUGUST 6 7 8 1788.

34. *O*: Bust as before, I . H & co under it.   Legend as before.
   R: A crown radiated. WORCESTER, AUGUST, 6 . 7 . & 8 .
      1788.
   The edges of all these are scalloped.

FARTHINGS.

DUDLEY.

✓ 35. *O*: A pair of scales above a chest. FINE TEAS   THOS. JONES.
     Ex: 1796.
   R: An anchor. DUDLEY within a circle of leaves.
                 Conder, 179 ; 16.
   Very rare.

WORCESTER.

✓ 36. *O*: Laureated bust to right. GEORGIUS III DEI GRATIA. Under
     the bust C. I.
   R: A cornucopia, musical instruments, book, &c., lying upon
     an altar. WORCESTER AUGUST . 6 . 1788.
                 Conder, 318; 17.

37. *O*: Bust as before, but with W. A. & co under.
   R: Similar to No. 30.

38. *O*: Bust as before, but with DAVIES under.
   R: Similar to No. 33.
   These all have scalloped edges.

𝔜𝔬𝔯𝔨𝔰𝔥𝔦𝔯𝔢.

PENNIES.

BOLTON.

✓ 1. *O*: View of an ancient fortress. BOLTON CASTLE YORKSHIRE.
R: An urn between scythes and sprigs of laurel, an arrow, skull, and hour-glass under. TIME DESTROYS ALL THINGS 1797.

? *E*: ON DEMAND IN LONDON LIVERPOOL OR ANGLESEY.

Conder, 180 ; 1.

A specimen of this very rare piece, struck on a Spanish dollar, is in the British Museum.
See also Middlesex, No. 11.

BOWES.

✓ 2. *O*: Remains of an ancient fortress. BOWES . CASTLE.
R: A globe inscribed BRITAIN between a rose and thistle. BRITISH . PENNY. *Ex*: 1797.
E: I PROMISE TO PAY ON DEMAND THE BEARER ONE PENNY.

Conder, 180 ; 2.

FOUNTAINS ABBEY.

✓ 3. *O*: View of an abbey and trees. FOUNTAINS ABBEY NEAR RIPPON YORKSHIRE IN ITS PRESENT STATE THE FINEST RUIN IN BRITAIN. *Ex*: P. KEMPSON FECIT. An ornament at the bottom.
R: A cypher *T . K*, within a wreath of flowers, entwined is a ribbon inscribed PROMISSORY PENNY TOKEN.

Conder, 180 ; 3.

This rev. also occurs on a Birmingham penny. See Warwickshire, No. 15.

GISBOROUGH.

✓ 4. *O*: Remains of an ancient abbey. RUINS . OF . GISBOROUGH . ABBEY. *Ex*: YORKSH. JACOBS.
R: and *E*: As No. 2. Conder, 180 ; 4.

MALTON.

✓ 5. *O*: Bust to right. THE RT. HONBLE. EDMUND BURKE, M.P: MALTON PENNY 1798. The name of the artist "*Westwood*" in script characters upon the truncation of the bust.
R: A figure of Fame flying, blowing a trumpet. BRITISH ORATOR above, DIED JULY 9. | 1797 AGED | 68. in three lines under, between branches of laurel.
E: Plain (in collar).

SHEFFIELD.

6. *O*: The cap of liberty on a pole between oak branches.
PRO PATRIA on a label across the pole. SHEFFIELD
CONSTITUTIONAL SOCIETY.

   R: An oval shield inscribed BRITAIN between four flags
inscribed AMERICA HOLLAND FRANCE POLAND. Date
at sides 17—92. UNITE & BE FREE   TO PERSEVERE
IS TO CONQUER. The tops of the flag-poles of Poland
and Holland are broken.

   E: The same as No. 1.   Conder, 181; 5.

✓ 6a.   As last, but *E*: The same as No. 2.
6b.   „   „   *E*: ON DEMAND WE PROMISE TO PAY-THE BEARER
ONE PENNY ✕
6c.   As last, but *E*: PAYABLE IN LONDON LIVERPOOL OR
ANGLESEY.
6d.   As last, but *E*: Plain (not in collar).
This obv. occurs with the following reverses :—
7. *R*: Laureate bust of William III., &c. See Not Local, No.
14.
8. *R*: A lion rampant, supporting a shield, &c. See Not
Local, No. 14.   Conder, 264; 5.
See also Middlesex, Nos. 14 and 17; and Anglesea, Nos.
125 and 127.

YARUM.

✓ 9. *O*: Remains of an ancient fortress. YARUM . CASTLE . YORKSH.
Ex : JACOBS.

   R: and *E* : Same as No. 2.   Conder, 181; 6.
All these pennies are rare, especially No. 1.

HALFPENNIES.

COUNTY.

✓ 10. *O*: Bust to right. PAY . THE . BEARER . ONE . HALFPENNY .
1796.

   R: A cypher *B. S. Co.* BENⵟ. SMITH & CO. IRON REFINERS
YORKSHIRE.

   E: COVENTRY TOKEN.
10a.   As last, but *E*: Plain (not in collar). Conder, 318; *6.
Very rare.

BEDALE.

11. *O*: View of a street and spire of a church. *Ex* : 1792.

   R: A cypher *I O M*, between branches of laurel. JAMES .
METCALF * BEDAL . YORKSH. *

   E: Milled.
✓ 11a.   As last, but *E*: SKIDMORE HOLBORN LONDON.
11b.   „   „   *E*: Plain (not in collar).
Conder, 318; 7.—Virt: 17.

The rev. of No. 11 appears as an obv. with the following reverses :—

12. *R*: Arms between laurel branches. HALFPENNY 1791. See Worcestershire, No. 22.

    E: SKIDMORE HOLBORN LONDON.   Conder, 268 ; 43.

13. *R*: Two busts. LOUIS XVI ET M. ANTOINETTE &c., the date at the sides. See Not Local, No. 95.

    E: The same as last.

13*a*.   As last, but *E*: Milled.   Conder, 268 ; 42.

✓ 14. *R*: Bust in cocked hat. MAY THE FRENCH &c. See Not Local, No. 117.

    E: The same as No. 12.

✓ 14*a*.   As last, but *E*: Milled.

    See also Essex, Nos. 18 and 29; Middlesex, Nos. 163, 370, 371, 386, 403, and 408; Sussex, Nos. 26 and 30; Warwickshire, No. 90; and Wiltshire, No. 14.

BEVERLEY.

✓ 15. *O*: Three balls suspended, the lower one divides the date 17—97. I . GREEN . PAWNBROKER . BEVERLEY.

    R: MONEY | LENT | ON PLATE | WEARING | APPAREL | &c. In six lines, between sprigs of leaves.

    E: Plain (not in collar).   Conder, 181 ; 8.—Virt : 182.

15*a*.   As last, but *E*: PAYABLE IN DUBLIN OR LONDON.

15*b*.   „   „   *E*: PAYABLE AT I. DENNIS LONDON.

15*c*.   „   „   *E*: PAYABLE AT LONDON OR DUBLIN.

15*d*.   „   „   *E*: Milled.

    Many of these pieces have been struck upon other tokens, the first impressions showing through on most of them more or less.

HUDDERSFIELD.

16. *O*: View of a public building. EAST INDIA HOUSE.

    R: The Grocers' arms, supporters, &c. HALFPENNY 1792.

    E: PAYABLE AT IOHN DOWNINGS HUDDERSFIELD.

    Very rare. This is from the same dies as Lancashire, No. 76.

✓ 17.   Similar to preceding, but dated 1793.

                Conder, 181 ; 9.—Pye, 23 ; 5.—Virt : 110.

17*a*.   As last, but *E*: LONDON BRISTOL AND LIVERPOOL.

17*b*.   „   „   *E*: Plain (not in collar).

HULL.

✓ 18. *O*: An equestrian statue of William III. GULIELMUS TERTIUS REX. *Ex*: MDCLXXXIX.

    R: Shield of arms between sprigs of oak, with seven acorns to the right hand, and eight to the left. HULL HALFPENNY. The date 1791 above the shield.

    E: PAYABLE AT THE WAREHOUSE OF IONATHAN GARTON & CO.. X.

                Conder, 181 ; 10.—Pye, 23 ; 6.—Virt : 57.

19. *O*: and *E*: As last.
   R: Similar to last, but there are eight acorns on each side.

20. *O*: The baton in the king's hand is more elevated, and the
       horse's ear touches the letter ɪ.
   R: and *E*: As last.

21. *O*: and *E*: As last.
   R: Differs from preceding in several minor details. The
       first 1 in date comes under the centre of the letter
       ʜ, whereas in the former ones it came to the outer
       part of it, and there is also a small thorn-like
       projection after the double acorns on left sprig
       which does not appear in this.

22.   An unfinished artist's proof of the obverse die occurs
       with *E*: PAYABLE AT THE WAREHOUSE OF THOS. &
       ALEXR. HUTCHISON . × .

23. *O*: Similar to *R*: of preceding, but the sprigs of oak are
       different and the 1's in date are curved.
   R: A ship sailing, at the bottom sprigs of leaves. See
       Hampshire, No. 44.
   E: PAYABLE IN HULL AND IN LONDON.
                    Conder, 182; 11.—Pye, 23; 7.—Virt: 57.

23*a*.   As last, but *E*: PAYABLE AT LEEK STAFFORDSHIRE.
23*b*.   „   „   *E*: PAYABLE AT GOLDSMITH & SONS SUDBURY.
       This obv. occurs with the following reverses:—

24. *R*: A ship sailing. PRO BONO PUBLICO 1794. See Hamp-
       shire, No. 22.
   E: CURRENT EVERY WHERE.   Conder, 182; 14.

24*a*.   As last, but *E*: PAYABLE IN LONDON BRISTOL & LANCASTER.
24*b*.   As last, but *E*: Milled.
24*c*.   „   „   *E*: Plain (not in collar).

25. *R*: A figure of Hope, &c.   See Norfolk, No. 24.
   E: PAYABLE IN HULL AND IN LONDON.   Conder, 182; 12.

26. *R*: St. Andrew with his cross, &c.   See Lothian, No. 32.
   E: PAYABLE IN LONDON BRISTOL & LANCASTER.
                    Conder, 182; 13.—Virt: 20.

LEEDS.

Birchall's.

27. *O*: Shield of arms between branches of oak, crest a lion
       rampant and an oak-tree. LEEDS COMMERCIAL HALF-
       PENNY.
   R: A fleece. PROSPERITY TO THE WOOLLEN MANUFACTORY 1795.
   E: PAYABLE BY SAMUEL BIRCHALL.
                    Conder, 182; 16.—Pye, 26; 5.—Virt: 95.

27*a*.   As last, but *E*: PAYABLE IN ANGLESEY LONDON OR LIVER-
       POOL. × .   Conder, 182; 17.
       This specimen is struck upon a larger blank and shows
       the whole of the dotted rim.

27*b*.   As last, but *E*: ARMIS TUTERIS BRADLEY WILLEY.

27c.   As last, but *E* : Plain.
      Rare. Private token, only a small number struck.

Brownbill's.

28. *O* : A bust of Bishop Blaze. SUCCESS TO THE YORKSHIRE
      WOOLEN MANUFACTORY.
   R : A view of the Leeds Cloth Hall with other houses in
      the distance. LEEDS HALFPENNY. *Ex* : 1793.
   E : Milled.
      Exceedingly rare, if not unique.
29. *O* : As last, but the bishop is holding a wool-comb.
   R : As last, but the country in the distance is quite bare.
   E : PAYABLE AT THE SHOP OF H. BROWNBILL SILVERSMITH.

      Conder, 182 ; 18.
      Very rare; the reverse die failed after only a few
      impressions had been taken.
30. *O* : As last.
   R : Similar, but with trees showing in the distance. A flaw
      runs diagonally across the *R* : of this piece from the
      date to the end of "LEEDS."
   E : PAYABLE AT H. BROWNBILLS SILVERSMITH.
31. *O* : As last.
   R : Similar to No. 30, but the arrangement of the trees is
      somewhat different and there is no flaw in the die.
      NOTE. The top of the wool-comb on the *O* : of these
      pieces is in a line with the letter U of "MANUFACTORY"
      and the teeth reach down to the end of the letter R.
32. *O* : As before, the top of the comb is in a line with the letter
      U, but the teeth only come down to the letter O.
   R : Slightly differs in arrangement of trees from any of the
      preceding.
33. *O* : As before, but the top of the comb is parallel with the
      first part of the letter F, and the teeth come down to
      the first limb of the letter R. There is a flaw at the
      top of the comb by which this piece may be readily
      identified.
   R : Differs slightly from the preceding.
33a.   As last, but *E* : PAYABLE AT THE HOUSE OF GILBERT
      SHEARER & CO.
34. *O* : As No. 33, but the comb is farther from the legend, and
      there is no flaw, and the teeth come to the second
      limb of R.
   R : Again slightly different.
35. *O* : As before, the top of the comb is in line with F, but
      the teeth come down to the Y.
   R : Nearly like No. 31.
36. *O* : As before, the top of the comb in line with F, the
      teeth come to last limb of R.
   R : Very nearly as last, but there is a flaw at LE of "LEEDS"
      which will identify it.

37. *O*: As before, the top of comb comes between the F and A, the teeth come down to the Y.
 R: Slightly different.

∨ 38. *O*: As before, the top of comb at an acute angle to the legend and in line with the letter A.
 R: This is nearly like No. 34.
 There are slight differences in all the reverses, but the different varieties will be best discovered by studying the obverses.
 The edges of all from No. 30 onwards with the exception of No. 33a are alike, and all are included under Conder, 182; 19.—Pye, 26; 4.—Virt: 191.

∨ 39. *O*: As rev. of preceding.
 R: A wheatsheaf. PEACE PLENTY & LIBERTY. See Cambridgeshire, No. 17.

Paley's.

∨ 40. *O*: A whole-length figure of Bishop Blaze, and a lamb. ARTIS NOSTRÆ CONDITOR. The Bishop is holding a wool-comb, which is under the TR and nearly touches the S of "NOSTRÆ."
 R: Shield of arms, crest and owl. LEEDS HALFPENNY 17 91.
 E: PAYABLE AT THE WAREHOUSE OF RICHARD PALEY.
 Conder, 183; 20.—Pye, 26; 3.

∨ 41. *O*: Similar, but the comb is farther from the S, more under the R, and parallel with the legend. The small scroll at the termination of the crozier also is a trifle smaller.
 R: As before, but the owl's head is a little nearer the A in legend, almost touching.
 E: As last.

∨ 42. *O*: As before, but the comb only reaches to the centre of T and goes to the end of R. The tip at end of crozier is very small.
 R: and *E*: The same as last.

∨ 43. *O*: Similar, but the corner of comb touches the foot of T, standing out away from legend. The scroll of crozier is larger, and the period at end of legend is midway between R and lamb.
 R: Similar to No. 40, but the head of owl is rather farther from legend.
 E: The same as last.

∨ 44. *O*: Similar to No. 43, but the period is nearer to end of legend and farther from the lamb. The left side of the foot of the letter T is broken off.
 R: and *E*: as last.

∨ 45. *O*: As last.
 R: and *E*: As No. 41.

✔ 46. *O*: Similar, but the corner of comb touches the first limb of
the R.
R: and *E*: As before.   A crack in the die is usually seen
running through the word " NOSTRÆ."

✔ 47. *O*: Similar, but the comb nearly touches the T and R, and
stands away from the legend nearly at right angle.
R: Similar to No. 40.
E: PAYABLE IN LONDON LIVERPOOL OR BRISTOL.
Conder, 183; 21.

✔ 48. *O*: Three-quarter figure of Bishop Blaze, holding a cup
and book. SUCCESS TO THE WOOLEN MANUFACTORY.
R: The same as No. 41.
E: PAYABLE IN ANGLESEY LONDON OR LIVERPOOL.
Conder, 183 ; 22.
This obv. is altered from the Exeter die, the comb being
converted into a cup, which has occasioned a failure
across that part of the die. See also Shropshire,
No. 22.
The obv. of No. 47 occurs with the following reverses:—

49. *R*: Bust to left of " JOHN OF GAUNT ;" a star under the bust.
See Lancashire, No. 4.

50. *R*: A different bust, without the star.   See Lancashire,
No. 17.

✔ 51. *R*: A fleece, *M & I* under. SUCCESS TO THE STAPLE OF ENGLAND.
See Somersetshire, No. 93.
E: PAYABLE AT THE WAREHOUSE OF THOMAS CLACKE.
Conder, 218 ; 71.

51*a*.   As last, but *E*: PAYABLE IN LANCASTER LONDON OR BRISTOL.
See also Cheshire, No. 55; Lancashire, Nos. 27, 63, and
72 ; and Wicklow, No. 39.
The rev. of No. 41 appears as an obv. with the
following reverse:—

✔ 52. *R*: Bust of John of Gaunt. As No. 50.
E: The same as No. 48.   Conder, 183 ; 23.

52*a*.   As last, but *E* : PAYABLE IN LIVERPOOL OR BRISTOL.

SHEFFIELD.

✔ 53. *O*: A head in profile with a hat on. YORKSHIRE HALFPENNY
1793.
R: Shield of arms, crest on elephant's head. PAYABLE IN
SHEFFIELD.
E: Engrailed.   Conder, 183 ; 24.—Pye, 50 ; 9.—Virt: 9.

53*a*.   As last, but *E*: Milled.

✔ 53*b*.   „   „   *E* : Plain (not in collar).

✔ 54. *O*: Three men working at an anvil. SUCCESS TO TRADE.
Ex: 1794.
R: Shield of arms, between sprigs of oak. PEACE THROUGH-
OUT THE GLOBE.
Conder, 239 ; 241.—Pye, 44; 4.—Virt: 11
In good condition rare.

✓ 55. *O*: Four hands crossed. LOVE PEACE AND UNION. 1794.
    R: Eight arrows crossed, a ribbon with forked ends in the
centre, between two arrow-heads. HALFPENNY .
PAYABLE AT IOHN HANDS SHEFFIELD.
    E: Engrailed.   Conder, 183 ; 25.—Pye, 44 ; 6.—Virt : 9.

✓ 56.   Similar to last, but quatrefoils instead of arrow-heads,
and the ribbon ends differently.
                     Conder, 183 ; 26.—Pye, 44 ; 5.
    Rare.

✓ 57. *O*: Cap of liberty, &c. SHEFFIELD CONSTITUTIONAL SOCIETY.
    R: An oval shield between four flags, &c. UNITE & BE FREE
TO PERSEVERE IS TO CONQUER.
    E : PAYABLE AT MACCLESFIELD LIVERPOOL OR CONGLETON . ✕ .
                     Conder, 183 ; 27 or 28.

57*a*.   As last, but *E* : PAYABLE AT CRONEBANE LODGE OR IN
DUBLIN . ✕ .
    This is struck from the same dies as the penny No. 6.

YORK.

✓ 58. *O*: View of a cathedral. *Ex* : YORK . 1795.
    R: View of a castle and drawbridge. CLIFFORD'S TOWER A.D.
1100.
    E : YORK BUILT A . M . 1223 . CATHEDRAL REBUILT A.D. 1075.
                Conder, 184 ; 29.—Pye, 50 ; 8.—Virt : 43.
58*a*.   As last, but *E* : PAYABLE IN DUBLIN OR LONDON.
58*b*.   „   „   *E* : PAYABLE IN LANCASTER LONDON OR LIVER-
POOL.
58*c*.   As last, but *E* : FEAR GOD AND HONOUR THE KING.
✓ 58*d*.   „   „   *E* : Plain (in collar).
    Rare with this edge.
    This obv. occurs with the following reverses :—
✓ 59. *R*: A mounted dragoon. PRO REGE, &c. See Norfolk, No. 47.
    E : The same as No. 58*c*.   Conder, 184 ; 31.
✓ 60. *R*: A female holding a pole with a cap of liberty on it.
      .   LIBERTY & COMMERCE 1795. This is the rev. of a
New York token.
    E : The same as last.   Conder, 184 ; 30.
    The rev. of No. 58 appears as an obv. with the following
reverses :—
✓ 61. *R*: Britannia seated. RULE BRITANNIA 1795. See Hampshire, No. 10.
    E : The same as last.   Conder, 184 ; 33.
✓ 62. *R*: Bust to left. IOHN HOWARD, &c. See Hampshire, No. 32.
    E : The same as last.   Conder, 184 ; 32.
✓ 63. *O*: The Prince of Wales' arms, supporters, crest, and motto.
    R : B. HOBSON | IRONMONGER | & | CUTLER | YORK. In five
lines upon a shield. Conder, 184 ; 34.—Pye, 50 ; 7
    This piece is struck in brass.

✔ 64. *O* : Roman bust to left. CONSTANTINE THE GREAT . BORN AT
      YORK . A.D. 271.
   R : Shield of arms, between oak branches. YORK HALFPENNY .
      1796.
   E : PAYABLE AT YORK .×. .×. .×. .×. .×.
                  Conder, 184; 35.—Pye, 50; 6.—Virt: 101.
      Rare, only 200 *impressions taken.*
✔ 65. *O* : A female crowned, seated, holding a sword and shield,
      within a border of leaves. *Ex* : EBORACUM.
   R : A cap of liberty, sword, and scales, intermixed with
      sprigs of laurel. LIBERTAS . JUSTITIA . PAX. ✠ YORK
      MDCCXCV. ✠
   E : Plain (in collar).
                  Conder, 184; 36.—Pye, 50; 5.—Virt: 101.
      Rare, only 200 *impressions taken.*

17

𝔚𝔢𝔩𝔰𝔥 𝔗𝔬𝔨𝔢𝔫𝔰

issued in

North and South Wales

Anglesea   .   .

Carmarthen

Carnarvon   .   .

Glamorgan   .   .

Pembroke   .

North Wales.

HALFPENNIES.

1. *O*: A Druid's head within an oak wreath, containing 29 acorns, there is a sprig departing from the main branch both in front and behind bust, and there are two acorns just *below* the junction at the back of bust.

R: A cypher *R N G*, the date 1793 above. NORTH WALES HALFPENNY. There is a quatrefoil or cross between the beginning and end of legend.

E: CHAMBERS . LANGSTON HALL & CO. × × × ×

1a. As last, but *E*: PAYABLE IN HULL AND IN LONDON

✓ 1b. As last, but *E*: PAYABLE IN LONDON BRISTOL & LANCASTER — × —

1c. As last, but *E*: WILLEY SNEDSHILL BERSHAM BRADLEY.

✓ 1d. „ „ *E*: CURRENT EVERY WHERE.
 Conder, 155; 3.—Virt: 104.

1e. „ „ *E*: Engrailed.

1f. „ „ *E*: Plain (not in collar).

2. *O*: The same as last.

R: Similar to last, but the first stroke of *R* projects farther, almost reaching the foot of 7, the quatrefoil or cross is shorter and with squarer ends.

E: CAMBRIDGE BEDFORD . AND HUNTINGDON . × . ×

✓ 2a. As last, but *E*: PAYABLE AT THE WAREHOUSE LIVERPOOL

2b. As last, but *E*: The same as No. 1b.

✓ 3. *O*: Similar to No. 1, but the two acorns are *above* the junction of sprig behind bust, and the acorn between sprig and branch in front of bust has a longer stem.

R: The same as No. 1.

E: PAYABLE IN HULL AND IN LONDON — × × —

3a. As last, but *E*: PAYABLE AT IOHN FINCHAMS SUFFOLK. The remainder engrailed.

4. *O*: The same as last.

R: The top of first stroke of *R*, approaches the foot of 7 similar to No. 2; but the quatrefoil and bottom flourish are different. A flaw runs through "NORTH."

E: PAYABLE AT LEEK STAFFORDSHIRE.

✓ 4a. As last, but *E*: PAYABLE IN LONDON BRISTOL & LANCASTER.
 Conder, 155; 5.—Pye, 47; 2.

4b. „ „ *E*: Engrailed.

17.*

5. *O*: A different bust, within a similar wreath, but containing 30 acorns, 14 to left, and 16 to right.
   R: A harp between sprigs of oak, the date 1793 above. NORTH WALES HALFPENNY. The cross comes above the space between the 7 and 9. There are 6 acorns on each sprig.
   E: Engrailed.

✓ 6. *O*: Similar to last, but the wreath has 31 acorns, 15 to left, and 16 to right.
   R: Similar, but the cross comes above the 7. There are 7 acorns in left sprig, 6 in right.
   E: PAYABLE AT LONDON OR ANGLESEA.
   Conder, 155; 6.—Pye, 47; 3.—Virt: 105.

6*a*.   As last, but *E*: PAYABLE AT LONDON OR ANGLESEY *

6*b*.   „   „   *E*: Coarse oblique milling.

✓ 7. *O*: The same as last.
   R: Similar, but the cross comes above the 9. There are 6 acorns on left sprig, and 5 on right.
   E: Engrailed.

✓ 8. *O*: Similar number of acorns, but 14 to left, and 17 to right.
   R: The same as last.
   E: The same as No. 6*a*.   Conder, 156; 8.

✓ 8*a*.   As last, but *E*: PAYABLE IN BEDWORTH HINKLEY OR NUNEATON.

8*b*.   As last, but *E*: Plain (not in collar, and on thin flan).

✓ 9. *O*: Bust similar to No. 1, in a wreath without branching sprigs, 24 acorns, 12 on each side.
   R: and *E*: The same as No. 6.   Conder, 155; 7.

✓ 10. *O*: Bust similar to No. 5, in a wreath without side branches, 25 acorns, 13 to left, 12 to right.
   R: The same as No. 7.
   E: PAYABLE AT ANGLESEA LONDON OR BRISTOL.
   Conder, 156; 9.

✓ 11. *O*: A laureated bust to right, sprigs of oak below. PRO BONO PUBLICO.
   R: A harp between sprigs of oak, the date 1794 above. NORTH WALES HALFPENNY.
   Conder, 156; 10.—Pye, 47; 4.—Virt: 107.
   Good impressions are rare.
   The rev. of No. 2 occurs as an obv. with the following reverse :—

✓ 12. *R*: Britannia seated. RULE BRITANNIA * * *Ex*: 1797. See Middlesex, No. 751.
   E: PAYABLE IN LONDON. The remainder engrailed.
   For many other so-called North Wales Halfpennies, see the Imitation of Regal Coins.

FARTHINGS.

✓ 13. *O*: A laureate bust to right. NORTH WALES FARTHING. A
triangular stop after legend.
R: The Prince of Wales' crest.   Conder, 159; 47.

✓ 14. *O*: The same as last.
R: The Prince of Wales' crest, in a shield between sprigs of
flowers. PRO BONO PUBLICO 1793.
E: Milled.   Conder, 159; 45.—Pye, 47; 5.—Virt: 161.

✓ 14*a*.   As last, but *E*: Plain (rounded). These are struck on
large flans, showing a broad-toothed rim, and on small
flans, showing no rim.

✓ 15. *O*: Similar to last, but has a dot at end of legend instead of
triangular stop.
R: Similar, but legend, date, and sprigs all rather larger.

✓ 16. *O*: Similar, but with a triangular stop (or trefoil), and two
dots after legend.
R: The same as No. 14.

✓ 17. *O*: Similar, but without any stop after legend, the point of
laurel comes to E of "WALES."
R: Nearly like No. 15, but the leaves and flowers on sprigs
differently arranged.

✓ 18. *O*: Similar to last, but point of laurel comes after the s of
"WALES."
R: The same as No. 14.
These are on smaller flans than the last, and usually
have a flaw running across lower part of bust.

✓ 19. *O*: Bust and legend as before. There is a small quatrefoil
under bust, and no period after legend.
R: Similar to preceding, but dated 1794. Conder, 159; 46.

✓ 20. *O*: Bust rather smaller, no quatrefoil under, but a period
after legend.
R: Similar to last, but sprigs of laurel instead of flowers.

✓ 21. *O*: The same as No. 19.
R: Similar to preceding, but dated 1795.
These are struck on large flans, showing a wide-toothed
margin, and on small flans, not showing margin.

South Wales.

FARTHINGS.

✓ 22. *O*: A laureate bust to left. SOUTH WALES FARTHING.
R: The Prince of Wales' crest on shield, between sprigs of
flowers. PRO BONO PUBLICO.   Conder, 159; 51.

23. *O*: Similar to last, but with a triangular stop instead of quatrefoil.

   R: Similar, but with date above shield, 1793, and a triangular stop after legend. The figure 3 is square topped.

   E: Milled.

✓ 23*a*.   As last, but *E*: Plain (not in collar, but rounded).

✓ 24. *O*: Similar to last, but with a dot at end of legend.

   R: Similar, but the sprig is different, and no stop after legend.

   E: Milled.   Conder, 159; 50.

✓ 24*a*.   As last; but *E*: Plain.

25. *O*: Similar to last, but without stop of any kind after legend.

   R: Similar to preceding, but the 3 in date is round topped, the sprig has only 2 flowers on each side.

   E: Milled.

✓ 26. *O*: Similar to last, but the laurel points to right of s in "WALES," no stop.

   R: Similar, but the sprigs larger, with 4 flowers on each side.   Conder, 159; 49.

✓ 27. *O*: The same as last.

   R: Similar, but the sprigs are of oak with 2 acorns on each side.

28. *O*: Similar to last, with a small sprig under the bust.

   R: The same as No. 26.

        Conder, 159; 48.—Pye, 47; 6.—Virt: 161.

✓ 29. *O*: The same as last.

   R: Britannia seated. FARTHING. *Ex*: 1793.

         Conder, 317; *51.

The obv. of No. 24 occurs with the following reverses:—

✓ 30. *R*: Beehive and bees. INDUSTRY HAS ITS SURE REWARD. See Cambridgeshire, No. 34.

✓ 31. *R*: A cornucopia and olive branch. FARTHING. 1793. See Not Local, No. 220.

32. *R*: A naval crown above a harp. COMMERCE PROTECTED. See Not Local, No. 240.

Anglesea.

PENNIES.

1784.

✔ 1. *O*: A Druid's head in profile, encircled with an open wreath of oak. There are 22 acorns in wreath, 11 on each side.

R: A cypher *P M Co*. WE PROMISE TO PAY THE BEARER ONE PENNY . 1784. Date above the cypher.

E: ON DEMAND IN LONDON LIVERPOOL OR ANGLESEY. ×.×.

Conder, 1; 1.

In good condition, rare.

The early date of this piece, together with its inferior workmanship, leaves little doubt as to its being only an imitation of the genuine Anglesea Pennies. See also Nos. 68, 114, and 121.

1787.

✔ 2. *O*: A different head to last, the wreath also is different and much better work. There are only 10 acorns in the wreath, 4 on left side and 6 on right.

R: A monogram cypher, *P. M. Co.* ornamented. WE PROMISE TO PAY THE BEARER ON DEMAND ONE PENNY *

E: EDW. HUGHES . THO. WILLIAMS . IOHN . DAWES + PARIS . LODGE . Conder, 3; 19.—Pye, 1; 1.

Very rare, a few proofs only were struck.

2a. As last, but *E*: Plain (in collar).

Struck also in silver, with plain edge; and in tin.

✔ 3. *O*: A close copy of last (by Westwood). There are only 5 acorns on right side of wreath.

R: Very similar to last, but the top of the *P* does not touch the first stroke of the *M*.

E: The same as No. 2. Conder. 310; *19.—Virt: 122.

✔ 4. *O*: A different, and larger, head than before, the wreath terminates with an acorn on either side. There are 31 acorns in wreath, 18 on left, and 12 on right, and 1 under the tie in the centre. A failure in the die will be noticed, extending from the point of hood to edge.

R: The cypher *P M Co*. with the date 1787 below it, and a large D enclosing a 1 above. Legend the same as No. 1.

Edge of this, and all future ones, excepting where specially mentioned to the contrary, the same as No. 1. Conder, 3; 14.—Pye, 1; 2.

Rare. Only a few proofs struck.

Also struck in silver.

5. *O*: Similar to last, but the head is in lower relief, and there
is a border or hem to the hood. The wreath has
19 acorns, 9 on left hand and 10 on right; the left
hand terminates with 1 acorn, the right with 2.

R: The same as last.   Conder, 309; *14.
Very rare.

✔ 6. *O*: Head in higher relief than last, hood bordered, wreath
has 20 acorns, 10 on each side, and it terminates
with leaves instead of acorns.

R: The same as last.   Conder, 3; 15.
Very rare.
Also struck in silver.

6a.   As last, but *E*: ON DEMAND IN LONDON LIVERPOOL & ANGLE-
SEY. ×.   Pye, 1; 4.
With this edge exceedingly rare.
Nos. 4-6 occur both struck in collar and not in collar.

7. *O*: Head similar to No. 4, the wreath has 22 acorns, 12 on
left, and 10 on right.

R: The same as last.
E: As No. 1 (in collar).
This also is very rare.

ᵛ 8. *O*: Different head to any preceding, a small w (for "Wilson")
on the truncation of neck; there is a border of small
acorns outside the wreath. See *post*, No. 116.

R: A poor copy of No. 4.   Conder, 3; 16.

8a.   As last, but *E*: Plain (not in collar).
Plain edge very rare.

ᵛ 9. *O*: The same as No. 7.

R: The cypher and legend as No. 1, the date 1787 above
cypher. The 1 straight, the 7's curved.
                        Conder, 1; 3.—Pye, 1; 3.
This and the following are both struck in collar.

9a.   As last, but *E*: Plain (in collar).

✔ 10. *O*: Similar head, the wreath has 19 acorns, 9 to left, 10 to
right.

R: Similar to last, but the 1 as well as 7's of date is
curved.

11. *O*: Similar head, wreath very different, having 25 acorns,
13 on left, 12 on right; there is a cluster of 3 acorns
on either side the tie of wreath, and an acorn at the
termination of each branch.

R: The same as last.   Pye, 2; 6.

✔ 12. *O*: A head resembling the Cornish Druid, being much
larger than any preceding, within a wreath containing 24 acorns, 12 on each side; there is a cluster
of 3 acorns on left of ribbon, and 4 on right.

R: The cypher and legend as before, the date above the
cypher, the 1 and 7's straight.

12a.   As last, but *E*: Plain (in collar).
These are all very rare. No. 11 is probably unique.

1787. Thick Wreath with Curved 7.

13. *O*: Druid's head, encircled with a very thick wreath of oak, one acorn only by the ribbon which ties the wreath, on the left hand side at bottom. There is a border to the hood.

　R: The cypher and legend as before, date above cypher, the 1 straight, the 7's curved.　　Conder, 2; 11.

14. Similar to last, but the 1 is also curved. The 1 comes between the N and Y, and the dot is over the space between the 7 and 8, the bottom flourish ends over the H of "THE."

15. Similar, but the 1 comes just under the foot of Y.

16. Similar, but the 1 comes to second limb of N, and the dot is just over the 8. The bottom flourish ends above the E of " THE."

17. *O*: Druid's head in thick wreath as before, but with *two* acorns, one on each side *above* ribbon, and a projecting acorn just in front of the hood.

　R: The same as No. 13.　　Pye, 1; 5.

18. Similar to last, but *R*: The same as No. 14.

19. The 1 is quite to the right of the Y, and the dot comes above the first 7.

20. The figures of date are very close together, and in a straight line, clear of legend.

21. *O*: Similar to No. 17, but without the projecting acorn by the front of hood.

　R: The same as No. 15.

22. *O*: The same as last.

　R: The same as No. 19.

23. Similar to last, but the date comes closer to beginning of legend, the 7 almost touches the W.

24. The 1 is under the first limb of N, and the dot comes over the 8.

25. *O*: Druid's head in thick wreath, with *two* acorns, both being *below* ribbon.

　R: The same as No. 14.

26. *O*: Druid's head in thick wreath with *two* acorns, one acorn *above* to right, one *below* to left.

　R: Cypher and legend as before, the 1 of date comes under first limb of N. The dot over second 7.

27. *O*: Druid's head in thick wreath, *three* acorns by ribbon, one to right above, and one on each side below. There is a projecting acorn four leaves from ribbon on left hand side.

　R: The same as last.

28. *O*: Similar to last, but with the acorn only two leaves from ribbon, and not projecting.

　R: The same as No. 14.

29. *O*: The same as last.

　　R: The 1 of date straight and comes just under foot of Y, the dot is over the first 7.

30. *O*: Druid's head in thick wreath, *four* acorns by ribbon, on the inside of wreath to left there are three leaves, an acorn, two leaves, an acorn, two leaves, and a third acorn.

　　R: The same as No. 24.

31. 　　Similar, but the 1 comes between the N and Y, the dot is over the 8.

32. 　　Similar, but the 1 comes just under foot of Y, the figures of date are close together.

33. *O*: Similar to No. 30, but on the inside of left wreath there are :—three leaves, an acorn, four leaves, and another acorn, the acorn by point of hood being omitted.

　　R: Similar to last, but the figures of date not quite so close together. A flaw runs across the lower part of cypher.

34. *O*: Similar to last, but arrangement on inside of wreath to left as follows :—Three leaves, an acorn, three leaves, and another acorn.

　　R: Similar, but the figures of date quite close together, so as to clear the legend.

35. *O*: Similar to preceding, but with two leaves, an acorn, three leaves, and another acorn.

　　R: The same as No. 19. (The 1 to right of Y.)

36. 　　Similar, but the *R*: as No. 23. (The 7 almost touches the W.)

37. 　　Similar, but the *R*: as No. 31. (The 1 between N and Y.)

38. 　　Similar, but the *R*: as No. 32. (The 1 under foot of Y.)

39. 　　Similar, but the *R*: as No. 34.

40. *O*: Similar to preceding, but the arrangement on inside of wreath to left, as follows: a leaf, an acorn, leaf, acorn, two leaves, and a third acorn.

　　R: The same as No. 19. (The 1 to right of Y.)

41. 　　Similar, but the *R*: as No. 26. (The 1 under first limb of N.)

42. 　　Similar, but the *R*: as No. 31. (The 1 between the N and Y.)

1787. Thick Wreath. Straight 7.

43. *O*: The same as No. 17. (Two acorns above.)

　　R: The cypher and legend as before, the 1 and 7's straight, the 1 under first limb of N.

44. 　　Similar, but the 1 comes between the N and Y, the figures of date are close together, and a small flaw connects the 1 and 7.

45. Similar, but the dot comes exactly over the 8, the end of bottom flourish comes above the H.
46. Similar to last, but the flourish ends above the E.
47. Similar, but the figures of date much more spread, the 1 directly under the Y and the dot comes over the first 7.
48. *O*: The same as No. 25. (Two acorns below.)
   R: The same as last.
49. Similar, the 1 comes under the second limb of N. There is a border of acorns instead of dots.
   Conder, 3; 12.
50. *O*: The same as No. 28. (Three acorns.)
   R: The 1 is curved, the 7's straight, the 1 comes quite to right of Y, the dot over 7.
▼ 51. Similar, the 1 comes under the second limb of N, the beginning and end of legend are close together.
52. Similar, but the 1 comes under foot of Y, and the flourish of P nearly touches " BEARER." Pye, 2; 1.
53. *O*: The same as No. 35. (Four acorns.)
   R: The same as No. 49. Pye, 2; 7.

1788.
Long-topped P. Curved 7. No double acorns.

54. *O*: Druid's head in a thin wreath, there is no border to the hood, 22 acorns in wreath, 11 on each side, a border of acorns outside wreath.
   R: The cypher and legend as usual, a long top to the P, the 1 is curved, and touches the foot of the Y. There is a border of acorns. Conder, 2; 4.
55. *O*: Similar to last, but only 20 acorns, 10 on each side.
   R: Similar, but the top of the 1 touches the second limb of the N.
56. *O*: Similar to last, but only 19 acorns, 10 to left and 9 to right.
   R: The same as No. 54.
57. *O*: Similar, 9 acorns to left and 10 to right.
   R: The same as last.
58. *O*: Similar to last, but not from the same die.
   R: Very nearly like No. 54, but the beginning and end of legend approach nearly together and there is an upright acorn for a stop.
59. *O*: Similar to last, but only 18 acorns, 9 on each side.
   R: Similar, the top of 1 comes between N and Y.
60. *O*: Similar, but only 17 acorns, 9 to left and 8 to right, arranged thus :—Left, four pairs and one single. Right, one pair, two singles and two pairs.
61. *O*: The same number of acorns as last, arranged thus:—Left, two pairs, single, again two pairs. Right, pair, two singles, and two pairs.
   R: The same as No. 54.

62. *O*: The same number of acorns, arranged thus :—Left, as No. 60. Right, two pairs, one single, pair, and two singles.
   R: The same as last.
63. *O*: Similar, but 8 to left and 9 to right.
   R: The same as last.
64. *O*: Similar, but only 16 acorns, 8 on each side.
   R: The same as last.
65. *O*: Similar, but only 14 acorns, 7 on each side.
   R: The same as No. 59.

1788.
Curved 7. With double acorns.

66. *O*: Druid's head in thin wreath with 24 acorns, 12 on each side.
   R: The same as No. 59.
67. *O*: Similar, but only 23 acorns, 12 to left and 11 to right.
   R: The same as No. 54.   Pye, 1 ; 7.
68. *O*: Similar, but only 22 acorns, 11 on each side.
   R: The same as No. 59. The design and execution of this piece closely resemble that of No. 1.
69. *O*: Similar, but only 21 acorns, 11 to left and 10 to right, arranged thus :—Left, pair, 2 singles, double, 2 pairs, and another single. Right, 2 pairs, double and single together, pair, and 2 singles.
   R: The same as last.
70. *O*: The same number of acorns, arranged thus :—Left, 2 pairs, single, double and single together, pair, and another single. Right, pair, 2 singles, double and single together, another single, and a pair.
   R: The same as No. 54.
71. *O*: Similar, but only 20 acorns, 11 to left, 9 to right, arranged thus :—Left, pair, 2 singles, double and single together, another single, and a pair. Right, pair, 2 singles, double and single together, and another pair.
   R: The same as last.
72. *O*: The same number of acorns, arranged thus :—2 pairs, single, double and single together, another single, and a pair. Right, pair, 2 singles, double and single together, and a pair.
   R: The same as last.
73. *O*: Similar to preceding ; there are 22 acorns, 10 to left and 12 to right.
   R: The same as No. 59.
74. *O*: There are 21 acorns, 10 to left and 11 to right, arranged thus :—Left, pair, single, double, single, and 2 pairs. Right, pair, single, double and single together, another single, and 2 pairs.
   R: The same as No. 54.

75. *O*: The same number of acorns, arranged thus:—Left, 2
pairs, single, double and single together, and 2
singles. Right, pair, single, pair, double and single
together, single, and another pair.

  ·*R*: The same as last.

76. *O*: There are 19 acorns, 10 to left, 9 to right.

  R: The same as last.

77. *O*: There are 20 acorns, 9 to left and 11 to right.

  R: The same as No. 55.

78. *O*: There are 19 acorns, 9 to left and 10 to right.

  R: The same as No. 54.

79. *O*: There are 17 acorns, 8 to left and 9 to right, and in
addition there is an acorn terminating the branch
on either side.

  R: The same as No. 59.

1788.

Long-topped P. Straight 7. No double acorns.

▼ 80. *O*: Druid's head in a thin wreath, with 23 acorns, 12 to left
and 11 to right, no double acorns.

  R: The cypher and legend as before, the 1 curved the 7
straight, the 1 comes under second limb of N.

Pye, 1; 6.

Rare, these only occur as proofs, gilt, silver, and copper.

81. *O*: Similar to last, but only 20 acorns, 10 on each side.

  R: The 1 comes between the N and Y.

82. *O*: Similar, but only 19 acorns, 10 to left and 9 to right.

  R: The 1 and 7 are both straight, there is a dash instead of
a dot between beginning and end of legend. The
workmanship of this is coarse.

▼ 83. *O*: A different wreath to any preceding, with 27 acorns, 13
to left and 14 to right, the leaves are as much like
laurel as oak. Ribbed border instead of acorns.

  R: The 1 and 7 both straight, a large dot between beginning and end of legend, and ribbed border instead of
acorns.

1788.

Straight 7. With double acorns.

84. *O*: Wreath contains 24 acorns, 13 to left and 11 to right,
double acorns on inside of wreath, both before, and
behind, head.

  R: The 1 curved, the 7 straight, the 1 under the foot of Y,
but does not touch it. Acorn borders on both
sides.

▼ 85. *O*: Similar to last, but with 12 acorns on each side.

  R: The 1 and 7 both straight, the 1 comes between the N
and Y. An acorn as stop.

86. *O*: A poor copy of last, with the same number of acorns, but may be distinguished by noticing the second leaf on each side has a very long stalk, the acorns also have long stems.

    This may be rather a copy of No. 122.

   R: Similar to last, but the 1 comes under the second limb of N. There is a ribbed border instead of acorns on both sides.

87. *O*: There are 22 acorns in wreath, 10 to left and 12 to right.

   R: The same as No. 81.

88. *O*: Similar, but only 19 acorns, 10 to left and 9 to right.

   R: The 1 and 7 straight, the 1 under the N and the 7 under the Y. There is no division between the beginning and end of legend. This is of very coarse workmanship. The *P* can scarcely claim a long top, as it ends at the foot of the 7.

1788.

Short-topped P. Curved 1. Straight 7.

89. *O*: Druid's head in thin wreath, 25 acorns, 12 to left and 13 to right, arranged thus:—Left, 2 singles, 2 pairs, double and single together, pair, and another single, Right, 3 singles, 2 pairs, double and single together, pair, and another single.

   R: Cypher and legend as before, but the end of the top of *P* not nearly so long, the 1 curved, the 7 straight, the 1 comes under foot of Y. Of very fine workmanship.

90. *O*: The same number of acorns, arranged thus:—Left, pair, single, pair, double and single together, and 2 pairs. Right, 3 pairs, double and single together, and 2 pairs. The nearest acorn to end of branch on left is *inside*.

   R: Similar to last, but the 1 comes under second limb of N.

                       Pye, 1; 8.

91. *O*: The same as last.

   R: Similar, but the 1 comes between the N and Y.

92. *O*: Differs from No. 90 principally in the *outside* of the last pair of acorns being nearest the end.

   R: Similar to last, but not from the same die.

93.   Similar, but the last pair of acorns are just level.

94. *O*: The same as last.

   R: The same as No. 90.

95. *O*: Wreath contains 24 acorns, 12 on each side, arranged thus:—Both sides alike. Pair, single, pair, double and single together, and 2 pairs.

   R: The same as No. 90.

96. *O*: The same number of acorns, arranged thus :—Left, as
   last. Right, 3 pairs, double and single together,
   pair, and another single.
   R: Similar to last, but not from the same die.
97. *O*: The same number of acorns, arranged thus:—Left, pair,
   single, double and single together, and 3 pairs.
   Right, as left.
   R: The same as last.
98. *O*: Wreath contains 23 acorns, 12 to left and 11 to right.
   R: The same as No. 91.
99. *O*: Wreath contains 23 acorns, 11 to left and 12 to right.
   R: The same as No. 90.
100. *O*: Wreath contains 22 acorns, 11 on each side.
   R: The same as last.
   A silver proof, and probably unique.

1788.

Short-topped P. Straight 1 and 7.

101. *O*: The same as No. 90.
   R: Cypher and legend as before, the 1 and 7 both straight,
   the 1 comes under the *first* N of " PENNY."
102. *O*: The same as last.
   R: Similar to No. 90, excepting that the 1 is straight, not
   curved, it is under the second limb of the second N.
103. *O*: The same as last.
   R: Similar to No. 91, with the same exception, the 1 is
   under the space between N and Y.
104. *O*: Similar to preceding, but with only 24 acorns, 12 on
   each side. The same as No. 95.
   R: Similar, but the 1 comes under the first limb of the
   second N.
105. *O*: The same as last.
   R: The same as No. 102.
106. *O*: The same as last.
   R: The same as No. 103.
107. *O*: The same as last.
   R: Similar to No. 102, but without dot between beginning
   and end of legend.
108. *O*: The same number of acorns, arranged thus :—Left, as
   No. 95. Right, 3 pairs, double and single together,
   pair, and another single.
   R: The same as No. 102.
109. *O*: The wreath has only 23 acorns, 12 to left and 11 to
   right.
   R: The same as last.
110. *O*: The same as last.
   R: The same as No. 103.

111. *O*: Druid's head in wreath, with 24 acorns, 12 on each side, arranged both sides alike, thus:—Pair, single pair, double and single together, and 2 pairs.

   R: Similar to No. 103, but with an acorn on a long stem as a stop, between beginning and end of legend.

112. *O*: Druid's head in a different wreath to any previous, the leaves mostly double and on long stems, there are 15 or 17 acorns, but it is struck so badly as to leave them in doubt.

   R: Very like No. 104, but the figures of date closer together.   Pye, 2; 2

   Pye in his note to this plate says—"This was not so well executed as the rest, and was therefore rejected. Only 2 in copper and 1 in tin known to exist."

P. M. S.

113. *O*: Druid's head in wreath containing 24 acorns, 12 on each side. Similar to No. 94, but finer work. A ribbed border instead of acorns.

   R: A cypher *P M S*. Legend as before, date 1788 above cypher.

113*a*. As last, but *E*: Plain.

1789.

114. *O*: Druid's head in thin wreath, 22 acorns, 11 on each side. The design and execution of this piece is very similar to that of Nos. 1 and 68.

   R: Cypher and legend as usual, date 1789 above cypher, the 1 and 7 both curved.

115. *O*: Druid's head in thin wreath, differs considerably from last, and very nearly resembles No. 83, both in design and execution.

   R: Cypher and legend as usual, date 1789 above cypner, the 1 and 7 both straight. A ribbed border on both sides instead of acorns.   Conder, 2; 8.

116. *O*: Druid's head resembling that on the Cornish halfpenny, within a wreath, under the ribbon of which is the letter w (for Westwood).

   R: A monogram cypher, inscribed "PARYS MINES COMPANY." A sprig of oak above. WE PROMISE TO PAY THE BEARER ON DEMAND ONE PENNY . 1789.   Conder, 310; *19. A fine toothed border on both sides.

116*a*. As last, but *E*: Plain (in collar). *Very rare with edge inscribed; with edge plain, more so.*

1790.

117. *O*: A different Druid's head, in a thin wreath, with a
border of small acorns.

  R: The usual cypher, with the date 1790 below. The 1
is curved. ANGLESEA * MINES * PENNY.

  E: PAYABLE * IN * LONDON * OR * ANGLESEY.

117*a*. As last, but *E*: Without the stars. Pye, 2; 3.
*Very rare with either edge. Pye says " only 3 impressions
known."*

v 118. *O*: A very close copy of the preceding, with a small w on
truncation of neck (for Wilson).

  R: Similar to last, but the letters of legend are larger and
cypher differs slightly, and the 1 is straight.

  E: PAYABLE IN ANGLESEY OR LONDON . X.

  Conder, 3; 17.—Pye, 2; 4.—Virt: 122.

118*a*. As last, but *E*: The same as No. 117*a*.
Both very rare.

v 118*b*. As last, but *E*: Plain (not in collar). Conder, 3; 18.
With plain edge, not so rare.

119. *O*: The same as last.

  R: A poor copy of the reverse of No. 2.
Rare.

  See also Nos. 8 and 124 for this obv.; for the rev. see
also Nos. 127 and 128, and Middlesex, No. 15.

120. *O*: A Druid's head in thin wreath, with 21 acorns, 10 to
left and 11 to right.

  R: Cypher and legend as usual, the date 1790 above
cypher and touching legend.

v 121. *O*: The same number of acorns, but differently arranged,
11 to left and 10 to right.

  R: The same as last. Conder, 2; 9.

  These two pieces resemble closely in design and execution
Nos. 1, 68, and 114.

1791.

v 122. *O*: Druid's head in thin wreath, with acorn border, very
nearly like No. 90.

  R: Cypher and legend as usual, the date 1791 above cypher,
the 1 and 7 both straight.

  Conder, 2; 10.—Pye, 2; 5.

Fine impressions rare.

Various.

123. *O*: The same as No. 6.

  R: The cypher *P M Co.* no date, SUCCESS TO THE ANGLESEY
MINERS.

  E: Coarsely milled. (Conder says " Engrailed.")

  Conder, 310; *15.

18

The obv. of No. 118 occurs with the following reverses :—

124. *R* : A cypher *D. A. R.* &c.   See Middlesex, No. 12.
125. *R* : Cap of Liberty between oak branches, &c.   See Yorkshire, No. 6.
✓ 126. *R* : A lion rampant, &c.   See Not Local, No. 14.
Conder, 264; 6.
The rev. of No. 59 appears as an obv. with the following reverse :—
126*bis*. *R* : Two hands united, &c.   See Staffordshire, No. 7.
E : WE PROMISE TO PAY THE BEARER ONE PENNY.
The rev. of No. 119 appears as an obv. with the following reverses :—
127. *R* : Oval shield and flags, &c.   See Yorkshire, No. 6.
✓ 128. *R* : Laureate bust of William III. &c.   See Not Local, No. 14.   Conder, 264; 7.

HALFPENNIES.
1787.

✓ 129. *O* : A Druid's head within a wreath of oak.   (Copied from the penny, No. 2, by Westwood.)
R : A monogram cypher *P M Co.* ornamented.   WE PROMISE TO PAY THE BEARER ON DEMAND HALFPENNY ✱
E : EDW . HUGHES . THO . WILLIAMS . IOHN . DAWES . PARIS . LODGE +   Conder, 7; 53.
✓ 130.   The same as last, but the legend reads :—ONE HALFPENNY.
Conder, 7; 52.
Both very rare, although only copies.
✓ 131. *O* : A Druid's head encircled with an open wreath of oak.
R : A monogram cypher inscribed " PARYS MINES COMPANY." The date 1787 under.   THE ANGLESEY MINES HALFPENNY.
E : PAYABLE IN ANGLESEY LONDON OR LIVERPOOL . X .
Conder, 310 ; ✱19.
This also is by Westwood and very rare.

1788.

✓ 132. *O* : A different Druid's head within a wreath of oak. Upon the single fold of the hood or cowl, covering the forehead, is a sprig of oak.
R : An inscribed monogram cypher *P M Co.* with the date 1788 under.   HALFPENNY.
E : PAYABLE IN ANGLESEY AT GREENFIELD OR IN LONDON X X (in collar).   Conder, 8; 54.—Pye, 3; 5.
Exceedingly rare, a few proofs only struck.
132*a*.   As last, but *E* : Inscribed but not in collar, the piece being therefore much expanded.
132*b*.   As last, but *E* : Plain (not in collar).
A few proofs were struck, in copper and tin, of the unfinished die, without the sprig of oak.

✓ 133. *O* : A Druid's head, very similar to that on the Cornish
halfpenny, within a *thick* wreath of oak.

   R : A cypher, *P M Co.* the date 1788 above it.   THE
ANGLESEY MINES HALFPENY . . .

   E : PAYABLE IN ANGLESEY LONDON AND LIVERPOOL . × .

Pye, 3 ; 4.

Very rare.
Sharp says this was rejected on account of error in spelling
" HALFPENNY."

1788.
27 Acorns.

✓ 134. *O* : Druid's head in a thin wreath of oak containing 27
acorns, 13 to left and 14 to right, there are double
and single acorns together next to the tie of wreath
on right.

   R : Similar to last, the word HALFPENNY spelt correctly, and
only one dot at end of legend. The 1 comes under the
first limb of the second N.

   E : The same as No. 131, and all the following, unless
expressly stated to the contrary.

  135. *O* : The same as last.

   R : Similar, but the 1 is closer to the first N than to second.

✓ 136. *O* : The same number of acorns, but on the right there are
2 single acorns, and then a double and single together:
on the left an acorn without any stem springs from
the branch leaf stem.

   R : The 1 comes under the second limb of the second N.

✓ 137. *O* : Similar to last, but the acorn on left has a short stem,
and the double acorn in front of bust springs with a
very short stem from the top of a leaf.

   R : The 1 comes under first limb of second N.

  138. *O* : Very similar to last, but the double acorn before
mentioned has a long stem, and is quite clear of the
leaf, the double acorn at back also has a longer stem.

   R : The same as last.

  139. *O* : The same as last.

   R : The same as No. 136.

✓ 140. *O* : Similar to No. 136, but the acorn has a short stem and
lies along the leaf stem, which itself is much longer and
springs from the main branch close to tie of wreath.

   R : The 1 comes under the centre of the second N.

  141. *O* : Similar to last, but the acorn stem is longer, and there
is a bud or spur at the base of the leaf stem.

   R : The same as No. 137.

✓ 142. *O* : The second acorn on left springs from the main branch,
and the leaf stem just above it.

   R : The 1 comes under the second limb of the *first* N.

  143. Similar, but the 1 comes under the first limb of *second* N.

18 *

144. Similar, but the 1 comes under the second limb of second N.
145. Similar, but the 1 comes under the space between the N and the Y.

1788.
26 Acorns.

146. O: Wreath contains 26 acorns, 13 on each side, the leaf stem on left is very short and lies close alongside the main branch.
 R: Similar to last, but not from the same die.
✔ 147. O: The leaf stem is longer and bows out more from the main branch.
 R: The same as No. 137.?
✔ 148. O: The leaf stem is much longer and leaves the main branch close to tie of wreath, and has an acorn on it close to the leaf.
 R: The 1 comes under the second limb of the second N.
149. O: The leaf stem is nearly as long as last, but has no acorn on it.
 R: The 1 comes under the first limb of the second N.
149a. As last, but struck on much smaller flans, and E: PAYABLE IN LANCASTER LONDON OR BRISTOL.
150. O: The wreath has 26 acorns, 12 to left and 14 to right.
 R: The 1 comes under the space between the two N's.
✔ 151. Similar to last, but the figures of date are much closer together, the 1 comes under the first limb of the second N.

-28-'93-

1788.
25 Acorns.

✔ 152. O: The wreath contains 25 acorns, 12 to left and 13 to right, arranged thus:—Left, pair, single, 2 pairs, double and single together, and another pair. Right, double and single together, single, pair, double and single together, and 2 pairs.
 R: The same as No. 148.
✔ 153. O: The same number of acorns, arranged thus:—On left, pair, single, pair, double, single, and 2 pairs. Right, 3 pairs, double and single together and 2 more pairs, but chiefly noticeable from the wreath being more remote from the border than in any other specimen.
 R: Similar to No. 145.
 Several varieties will now be described with the same number of acorns, and with nearly the same arrangement, as last, but differing chiefly in the buds or spurs on the long leaf stem under the bust on either side.

v **154.** *O*: Similar to last, but the wreath much nearer the border; there are two spurs on the left hand leaf stem, one pointing inwards and one outwards. A flaw running from the second to the third acorn on the left outside of wreath will distinguish this.

    R: The same as No. 149.

155. *O*: One spur only on leaf stem to left, a flaw runs *through* second outside acorn on left.

    R: The 1 comes under the second limb of the first N.

v **156.** *O*: Similar to No. 154; but has a single acorn close to point of hood, a spur comes out of leaf stem on left which appears to cross main stem and carry the second acorn on outside.

    R: The 1 is under the first limb of the second N.

v **157.** *O*: The leaf and main stem on either side have a spur opposite each other, and all pointing inwards.

    R: Similar to last.

158. *O*: The same as last.

    R: The 1 is under the space between the two N's.

159. *O*: Similar to last, but there are two projecting hairs in the beard which touch the wreath.

    R: Similar to No. 156.

160. *O*: Similar to No. 157, but not from the same die, may be distinguished by a flaw on the field at the back of the head.

    R: The 1 is under the second limb of the first N. .

161. *O*: The same as last.

    R: The same as No. 149.

162. *O*: The spur on inside of leaf stem to left is below the bust, all others have been in front of it, otherwise very similar to No. 156.

    R: Similar to No. 156.

v **163.** *O*: Similar to No. 157 on the left, but on the right the spur on leaf stem points outwards nearly touching at its tip a spur from the main stem pointing inwards.

    R: The same as No. 156.

164. *O*: The same as last.

    R: The same as No. 158.

165. Similar to No. 163 on the right, but on the left there are no spurs, but two very slight protuberances, both inside the loop made by the two stems.

    R: The same as No. 158.

166. *O*: Similar on the left to No. 157, but on the right the spurs point outwards, that on the main stem being very slight.

    R: Similar to No. 156.

167. *O*: Similar on the left to No. 162, on the right the spur on leaf stem points inwards and that on the main stem points outwards.

    R: The same as last.

278   ANGLESEA.   *Halfpennies.*

168. *O*: The leaf stems are short and have no spurs on either side.
    R: The same as last.
169. *O*: The leaf stems are longer than in the last, that on the left has a slight protuberance, that on right an acorn, the veins of the leaves do not show. (Apparently an unfinished die.)
    R: The 1 comes under the centre of the second N.
    E: PAYABLE AT ANGLESEY LONDON OR LIVERPOOL . ✕.
169*a*. As last, but *E*: PAYABLE IN LANCASTER LONDON OR BRISTOL.
169*b*. As last, but *E*: LONDON LIVERPOOL OR MONTROSE . ✕.
169*c*. „ „ *E*: Plain (not in collar).
These three last are on small thin flans.
170. *O*: The same as No. 157.
    R: Has an acorn as a stop, lying horizontally, pointing to end of legend. The 1 is under the centre of the second N.
171. *O*: The same as No. 159.
    R: Has an acorn as before, but pointing to beginning of legend. The 1 is under the space between the two N's.
172. *O*: The same as No. 160.
    R: Similar to last, but the 1 is under the first limb of the second N.
173. *O*: The leaf stem on either side has two spurs opposite each other.
    R: Similar to last, but the 1 is under the second limb of the second N.
174. *O*: The same as No. 155.
    R: The acorn in this instance presents more the appearance of a tadpole.

1788.

24 Acorns.

175. *O*: Bust in wreath containing 24 acorns, 12 on each side, arranged thus: pair, single, pair, double and single together, and 2 pairs.
    R: Has an acorn with a stem lying horizontally, as a stop, pointing to the beginning of the legend. The 1 is under the foot of the Y.
    Also struck in silver.
176. *O*: Very similar to last, but not from the same die.
    R: There is a dot as stop instead of acorn. The 1 is under the second limb of the second N.
177. *O*: The same as last.
    R: Similar, but the 1 is under the space between the N and Y.
178. *O*: The same as last.
    R: Similar, but the 1 is under the foot of the Y.

178.*bis*.

v 179. *O*: The same number of acorns arranged thus : left same
as last, right 3 pairs, double and single together,
pair, and another single.
R: The 1 is under the centre of the second N.

1788.
23 Acorns.

v 180. *O*: Wreath contains 23 acorns, 12 to left and 11 to right.
There are spurs on the leaf stems on both sides
pointing inwards.
R: The 1 is under the first limb of the second N.
181. *O*: The same as last.
R: The 1 is under the *second* limb of the second N.
v 182. *O*: Similar to No. 180, excepting that there are no spurs
or buds on the leaf stems.
R: The same as No. 180.
There are many other variations of die in Nos. 134-182,
too minute for description, which may be discovered
upon a close inspection of both obverse and reverse.
They are included in Conder, 4; 20-23.—Pye, 3;
2 & 3.—Virt. 103.
183. *O*: A similar bust to preceding, within a wreath containing
23 acorns, 11 to left and 12 to right, surrounded with
a cable border.
R: Blank.
E: Beautifully engrailed.   Pye, 3; 1.
An artist's proof, and most likely unique.

1789.

v 184. *O*: and *E*: The same as No. 132.
R: Inscribed monogram cypher as No. 132, date 1789
under. HALFPENY ON DEMAND.
                Conder, 8; 55.—Pye, 3; 5.
*Exceedingly rare, only a very few proofs were struck,
because of the mistake in spelling "* HALFPENNY.*" See
also No. 133.*

1789.
25 Acorns.

185. *O*: Druid's head in an oak wreath containing 25 acorns,
12 to left and 13 to right.
R: The cypher *P M Co.* with the date 1789 above it. THE
ANGLESEY MINES HALFPENNY. An acorn with a stem
lies above the date pointing to the end of legend.
v 186. *O*: Similar, although not from the same die. The leaf
stems are short, and have a small spur or bud on
each pointing inwards.
R: There is an upright acorn as a stop. The 1 is under
the second limb of the second N.

187. *O*: The same as last.
    R: The 1 is under the foot of the Y.

✓ 188. *O*: The same as last.
    R: The acorn stop is more˜like a semi-colon; the 1 is
        under the second limb of the second N.

✓ 189. *O*: The leaf stems are longer, that on the left has two
        spurs pointing inwards, that on the right two spurs
        and an acorn.
    R: An upright acorn as stop, as before. The 1 is under
        the first limb of the second N.

190. *O*: Similar to last, but not from the same die.
    R: The same as No. 186.

1789.
24 Acorns.

191. *O*: Wreath contains 24 acorns, 12 on each side, the leaf
        stems long and nearly straight and with scarcely
        any protuberance upon them.
    R: The same as No. 189.

192. *O*: Similar to last, but the leaf stem on left has three
        small spurs, and that on the right is very much bent.
    R: The same as last.

193. *O*: Similar, but not from the same die.
    R: The 1 comes just to the left of the foot of the Y.

✓ 194. *O*: Similar on the left to last, the leaf stem on right is
        nearly straight and has four spurs.
    R: The 1 is under the centre of the second N.

195. *O*: Similar, but both leaf stems are long and nearly
        straight, that on the left has two small spurs upon
        it, and that on the right four.
    R: The 1 is under the second limb of the second N.

196. *O*: The leaf stem to left as last, that on right has two
        spurs, one pointing in, the other out, nearly
        opposite. A flaw runs diagonally across the piece.
    R: The 1 is under the first limb of the second N.

197. *O*: Similar to last, but only one spur on leaf stem to
        right, pointing inwards.
    R: The same as last.

198. *O*: The same as last.
    R: The same as No. 195.
        All these from No. 185 onwards are included under
        Conder, 4 ; 24, and Pye, 3 ; 6.

✓ 199. *O*: Druid's head in wreath with 24 acorns, but differently
        arranged on the right thus :—pair, single, double
        and single together, and three pairs.
    R: The 1 is curved, and is under the foot of Y. Acorn
        stop as before.
    E: BIRMINGHAM REDRUTH & SWANSEA.   Conder, 4 ; 25.

199*a*. As last, but *E* : PAYABLE AT LONDON . LIVERPOOL OR BRISTOL.

199*b*. As last, but *E* : Plain (not in collar).

1790.

200. *O* : Druid's head in oak wreath containing 18 acorns, 9 on each side.

R : The usual cypher and legend, date 1790 above, a dot between the beginning and end of legend.

E : PAYABLE IN ANGLESEY OR LONDON. The remainder engrailed.

Very rare, only a few proofs known to exist. This is said by Pye to be an imitation of the following, but there can be no doubt as to its being genuine, as it has the same obv. as Pye, 3 ; 8. See No. 206.

✓ 201. *O* : A bust very similar to the Cornish Druid in an oak wreath containing 19 acorns, 8 to left and 11 to right. The hood is worked with fine parallel lines.

R : and *E* : The same as last. Conder, 4 ; 28.—Pye, 3 ; 7.
Exceedingly rare.
These two are struck in collar.

202. *O* : The same bust as last, with a hem added to edge of hood, in a wreath containing 24 acorns, 10 to left and 14 to right, a spray springs from the tie to right, under the bust.

R : An incuse impression of the Macclesfield halfpenny. See Cheshire, No. 18.

E : PAYABLE AT MACCLESFIELD LIVERPOOL OR CONGLETON . ✕ .

203. *O* : The same bust, but with a fringe added to edge of hood, in a much thicker wreath containing 15 acorns, 8 to left and 7 to right. The wreath appears to be unfinished.

R : and *E* : Blank.

✓ 204. *O* : A good imitation of No. 201 (by Westwood). There are 22 acorns in the wreath, 11 on each side, and a spray springs from the tie to right nearly like No. 202.

R : Similar to No. 200, but not from the same die.
E : PAYABLE IN ANGLESEY LONDON OR LIVERPOOL . ✕ .

Conder, 4 ; 27.

205. *O* : A very different and inferior bust in a wreath containing 16 acorns, 8 on each side ; there is a small w (for Wilson) on the truncation-of neck.

R : The cypher *P M Co.* date 1790 *below* it. ANGLESEY . MINES . HALFPENNY. An acorn border on both sides.

E : PAYABLE ✕ IN ✕ LONDON ✕ OR ✕ ANGLESEY. ✕

1791.

206. *O* : and *E* : The same as No. 200.

R : Similar, but dated 1791. The final 1 in date is under the first limb of the Π in " THE."

Conder, 5 ; 29.—Pye, 3 ; 8.

207. *O* : and *E* : The same as No. 200.

R : Similar to last, but the final 1 is under the space between the T and H of " THE."

These are struck in collar.

208. *O* : A smaller bust than last, in a wreath containing 21 acorns

R : and *E* : The same as last.

209. *O* : A Druid's head with a Roman nose, in a very thin wreath containing 18 acorns.

R : The usual cypher and legend, with the date 1791 above cypher, and an acorn with a bent stem as a stop, pointing to the commencement of legend.

E : PAYABLE IN ANGLESEY OR LONDON . ×.

Conder, 5 ; 30.—Pye, 3 ; 9.

Rare, only a few proofs struck.

210. *O* : The same as last.

R : Similar to last, but with an upright acorn for a stop.

E : PAYABLE IN LONDON LIVERPOOL OR BRISTOL +

Conder, 6 ; 37.

211. *O* : The same as No. 205.

R : The cypher *P M Co.* with the date 1791 below it. ANGLESEY MINES HALFPENNY. The top of the *P* curves round and almost touches the *M*. An acorn border on both sides.

E : PAYABLE × IN × LONDON × OR × ANGLESEY. × Conder, 5 ; 31.

212. *O* : and *E* : The same as last.

R : Similar to last, but coarser work ; it may be recognized by noticing that the top of the *P* is nearly straight and only projects a short distance, also that the last down stroke of the *M* follows exactly the same curve as the *C*.

212*a*. As last, but *E* : Without the cross after OR.

212*b*. 　　„　　„　　*E* : Plain (not in collar).

213. *O* : A close copy of No. 205, but without the small w ; the acorns are smaller.

R : Similar to No. 211, but not from the same die.

E : The same as No. 211. Conder, 5 ; 32.

214. *O* : A bust similar to No. 205, within a wreath containing 15 acorns, 7 to left and 8 to right.

R : A cypher *P M Co.* ANGLESEY MINES HALFPENNY 1791. Acorn border as before.

E : PAYABLE IN LONDON. The remainder engrailed.

214*a*. As last, but *E* : Engrailed with a wavy line and dots.

1792.

∨ 215. *O*: A bust resembling No. 201, but the drapery about the shoulders different; in a wreath containing 28 acorns, 14 on each side, there are 3 acorns on each side of tie of wreath.

R: A monogram cypher *P M Co.* the date 1792 under, and a sprig of oak over it. THE ANGLESEY MINES HALFPENNY.

E: ARMIS TUTERIS MORIBUS ORNES . × .   Conder, 5; 36. *Exceedingly rare pattern by Westwood.*

216. *O*: A bust, the same as last, in a wreath containing 15 acorns, 7 to left and 8 to right; there is no tie to the wreath, and there are two very large leaves about the centre of each side.

R: Blank.

E: PAYABLE AT MACCLESFIELD LIVERPOOL OR CONGLETON . × . *An artist's proof, possibly unique.*

1794.

217. *O*: Druid's bust in a wreath containing 25 acorns, very similar to No. 164.

R: The usual cypher, date 1794 above it. THE ANGLESEY MINES HALFPENNY. With an acorn stop after legend.

E: BIRMINGHAM REDRUTH & SWANSEA.

∨ 217*a*.   As last, but *E*: Plain (rounded).

∨ 218. *O*: Druid's head in a wreath, containing 22 acorns, 11 on each side, of very poor workmanship.

R: The cypher and date as last. THE ANGLESEY MINES HALFPENNY.

E: PAYABLE IN ANGLESEY LONDON OR LIVERPOOL . × .

218*a*.   As last, but *E*: Plain (rounded).   Conder, 5; 35.

Varieties.

219. *O*: The same as No. 200.

R: The Cornish Druid. See Cornwall, No. 2.

E: PAYABLE AT THE GEORGE & BLUE BOAR LONDON. *Exceedingly rare, if not unique.*

220. *O*: The same as No. 138.

R: An open book, &c. See Middlesex, No. 436.

The obv. of No. 205 occurs with the following reverses:—

∨ 221. *R*: Struck from the die of the penny, No. 119.

Conder, 273; 83.

∨ 222. *R*: A wheatsheaf, &c. See Cambridgeshire, No. 17.

Conder, 273; 86.

∨ 223. *R*: Arms of London, &c. See Middlesex, No. 729.

Conder, 273; 84.

∨ 224. *R*: Arms of Guildford, &c. See Surrey, No. 13.

Conder, 149; 16.

∨ 225. *R*: Anchor and cap of Liberty, &c. See Not Local, No. 123.

Conder, 273; 85.

The obv. of No. 209 (?) occurs with the following reverses :—

✔ 226. *R*: T. SPENCE BOOKSELLER, &c. See Middlesex, No. 528.
Conder, 273 ; 87.

✔ 227. *R*: Pandora's Breeches, &c. See Middlesex, No. 522.
Conder, 289 ; 257.

✔ 228. *R*: Turnstile Halfpenny. See Middlesex, No. 527.
Conder, 220 ; 91.

✔ 229. *R*: A woolpack, &c. See Shropshire, No. 18.
E: PAYABLE IN ANGLESEY LONDON OR LIVERPOOL. ×.
Conder, 6 ; 39.

✔ 230. *R*: Arms, crest, a windlass, &c. See Wicklow, No. 21.
E: The same as last. Conder, 6 ; 40.

✔ 230*a*. As last, but *E*: PAYABLE IN LONDON LIVERPOOL OR BRISTOL.
The obv. of No. 214 occurs with the following reverse:—

✔ 231. *R*: Britannia seated, &c. See Hampshire, No. 10.
E: PAYABLE IN LONDON. The remainder engrailed.
Conder, 220 ; 90.

The obv. of No. 218 occurs with the following reverses :—

✔ 232. *R*: Vulcan seated, 1793, &c. See Warwickshire, No. 303.
E: The same as No. 229. Conder, 5 ; 34.

✔ 232*a*. As last, but *E*: AN ASYLUM FOR THE OPPRESS'D OF ALL NATIONS. ×.

233. *R*: Female leaning on anchor, &c. See Dublin, No. 6.
Conder, 228 ; 157.

The rev. of No. 199 appears as an obv. with the following reverse :—

234. *R*: Bust of George Prince of Wales, &c. See Not Local, No. 159. Conder, 4 ; 26.

The rev. of No. 212 appears as an obv. with the following reverses :—

235. *R*: The Cambridge Druid, &c. See Cambridgeshire, No. 10.
E: The same as No. 231.

✔ 235*a*. As last, but *E*: The remainder crosses and dots.
235*b*.   „   „   *E*: Plain (rounded). Conder, 311 ; 51.

✔ 236. *R*: Bishop Blaize and woolpack. See Surrey, No. 13.
Conder, 265 ; 12.

237. *R*: A helmed bust to right, &c. See Not Local, No. 101.

Paris Miners.

✔ 238. *O*: Druid's bust in oak wreath, containing 26 acorns similar in arrangement to No. 145.
R: A cypher *P M Co.*, with the date 1791 above it. THE PARIS MINERS HALFPENNY. The 1's in date are flat-topped.
E: PAYABLE AT BIRMINGHAM LONDON OR BRISTOL.
Conder, 8 ; 57.

238*a.*   As last, but *E*: PAYABLE × AT × CRONEBANE × OR ✳ IN ✳ DUBLIN × ✳

✓ 239.   *O*: and *E*: The same as No. 238.

      R: Similar to preceding, but the figures of date are shaped differently, the 1's are sloping at the top.

239*a.*   As last, but *E*: The same as No. 238*a*, but without the stars and crosses.

240.   *O*: A similar Druid's bust in a wreath, containing 24 acorns, 12 on each side, similar to No. 175.

      R: Similar to last, but the figures of date are closer together.

      E: The same as No. 238.

240*a.*   As last, but *E*: The same as No. 238*a*.

✓ 240*b.*   „   „   *E*: PAYABLE IN LANCASTER LONDON OR BRISTOL.   Conder, 8; 56.

240*c.*   As last, but *E*: PAYABLE IN LANCASTER LONDON OR LIVERPOOL.

240*d.*   As last, but *E*: PAYABLE IN LONDON. The remainder engrailed.

240*e.*   As last, but *E*: PAYABLE AT I + DENNIS LONDON .×.

240*f.*   „   „   *E*: PAYABLE AT RICHARD MAPLESDEN'S WIN-CHELSEA .×.+.

240*g.*   As last, but *E*: PAYABLE IN SUFFOLK — BATH OR MANCHESTER .×.

✓ 241.   *O*: A similar Druid's bust in a wreath containing 22 acorns, 11 on each side.

      R: Similar to last, but not from the same die.

      E: PAYABLE AT ANGLESEA LONDON LIVERPOOL. The N's retrograde.

✓ 242.   *O*: A different Druid's head, similar to that on the North Wales halfpenny, No. 5 ; in a wreath containing 22 acorns.   ℣

      R: The same as No. 239.

      E: The same as No. 238.   Conder, 8; 58.

242*a.*   As last, but *E*: The same as No. 238*a*.

✓ 243.   *O*: The same as last.

      R: The cypher *P M Co* with the date 1791 above it, and above the date four acorns in a line. PARIS MINERS HALFPENNY.

      E: The same as No. 238.   Conder, 8; 59.

243*a.*   As last, but *E*: Plain (not in collar).

      The rev. of No. 238 appears as an obv. with the following reverses :—

244.   *R*: Profile bust of " J. PRIESTLEY, CITIZEN OF THE WORLD." See Not Local, No. 137.

245.   *R*: Profile bust of " STANHOPE NOBLE WITHOUT NOBILITY." See Not Local, No. 147.

Promissory.

᷉ 246. *O*: The same Druid's head in a wreath containing 25
acorns, 13 to left and 12 to right. This is the same
as North Wales, No. 10.

   R: The cypher *P M Co* with the date 1791 above it.
PROMISSORY HALFPENNY.

   E: PAYABLE AT ANGLESEA LONDON OR BRISTOL.

✓ 246*a*.   As last, but *E*: The same as No. 238.

Conder, 220 ; 84.

247. *O*: A different bust in a wreath containing 24 acorns, 12
on each side. This is from the same die as North
Wales, No. 9.

   R: A cypher *P M C* with the date 1793 above.
PROMISSORY HALFPENNY.

   E: The same as No. 246.

✓ 247*a*.   As last, but *E*: LONDON ///////// ANGLESEA ////// OR //////
BRISTOL ////// The N's retrograde.

247*b*.   As last, but *E*: Milled.   Conder, 220 ; 85.

✓ 248. *O*: A Druid's head in a wreath having side branches, and
containing 31 acorns. This is from the same die as
North Wales, No. 6.

   R: The cypher *P M Co*, the date 1793 above. PAY THE
BEARER ONE HALFPENNY.

   E: PAYABLE AT LONDON OR ANGLESEY.

248*a*.   As last, but *E*: Engrailed.   Conder, 220 ; 86.

✓ 249. *O*: A similar Druid's head in a wreath containing 23
acorns.

   R: The cypher *P M Co*. PAY THE BEARER ONE HALFPENNY.
1794 ⁘

   E: PAYABLE IN LANCASTER LONDON OR BRISTOL.

Conder, 220 ; 87.

✓ 250. *O*: The same as No. 247.

   R: A cypher *R. M. Co.*, otherwise as No. 246.

   E: Milled to right.

✓ 250*a*.   As last, but *E*: Milled to left.   Conder, 220 ; 88.

✓ 251. *O*: The same as No. 248.

   R: and *E*: The same as last.   Conder, 220 ; 89.

FARTHINGS.

✓ 252. *O*: A Druid's bust in a thin wreath of oak, containing 26
acorns.

   R: The cypher *P M Co.*, the date 1788 above. THE
ANGLESEY MINES FARTHING.

Conder, 8; 60.—Virt: 121.

✓ 253. *O* : A Druid's bust within a wreath of oak, containing 24 acorns.

       R : The cypher *P M Co*, the date 1788 above it. THE ANGLESEY MINES HALF HALFPENNY.

       E : Milled.   Conder, 9; 61.—Virt : 208.

✓ 254. *O* : The same as last.

       R : Similar to last, but dated 1789, and with an upright acorn as stop at end of legend.

       E : Milled.   Conder, 9; 62.

255. *O* : The same as last.

       R : Similar, but dated 1791, and a dot instead of the acorn stop.

       E : Milled.   Conder, 9; 63.

✓ 256. *O* : A Druid's head in a wreath, containing 16 acorns.

       R : and *E* : The same as last.   Conder, 9; 64.

       The obv. of No. 252 occurs with the following reverses :—

✓ 257. *R* : The royal cypher *G R*. FARTHING. 1793.

       Conder, 247 ; 25.

✓ 258. *R* : A female seated by a harp. HIBERNIA. See Dublin, No. 184.

       E : Milled.   Conder, 247 ; 26.

✓ 259. *R* : A man on a gibbet. THE END OF PAIN. See Not Local, No. 233.   Conder, 307 ; 440.

260. *O* : A Druid's head.

       R : The cypher *P M Co*.

       This is struck from the halfpenny dies of No. 211.

       The rev. of No. 252 appears as an obv. with the following reverses :—

✓ 261. *R* : Bust to left. ROBERT ORCHARD 1796. See Middlesex, No. 760.

       E : Milled.   Conder, 305 ; 428.

262. *R* : Two men working in a forge; from the die of the halfpenny. Middlesex, No. 361.

       E : The same as last.   Conder, 303; 401.

✓ 263. *R* : Pandora's Breeches, &c. See Middlesex, No. 806.

       Conder, 303 ; 408.

✓ 264. *R* : MAY THE KNAVE OF JACOBIN CLUBS, &c. See Not Local, No. 233.

✓ 265. *R* : An open book, inscribed THE WRONGS OF MAN, &c. See Not Local, No. 235.

       E : Milled.   Conder, 303 ; 405.

✓ 266. *R* : A man hanging. THE END OF P ☾ T &c. See Not Local, No. 237.

       E : The same as last.   Conder, 306 ; 437.

Carmarthenshire.

HALFPENNIES.

CARMARTHEN.

1. *O*: Interior of ironworks. IOHN MORGANS IRONWORKS 1792. Upon a label, CAERMARTHEN.

    R: Blank.

    E: PAYABLE AT LONDON BRISTOL AND CAERMARTHEN . ✕ .

Pye, 13 ; 2.

    Very rare, only a few proofs struck, the die rejected.

2. *O*: Similar to last, CAERMARTHEN IRON WORKS 1792. *Ex*: IOHN MORGAN.

    R: and *E*: The same as last. Conder, 21 ; 2.—Pye, 13 ; 1.

    Very rare, the die broke.

3. *O*: Similar to last, but with much more work in the roof, and the back of the archway filled in with brickwork. IRONWORKS AT CAERMARTHEN. *Ex*: HALFPENNY.

    R: and *E*: The same as last.   Pye, 13 ; 3.

    Exceedingly rare. Pye says "only 3 known."

4. *O*: Similar to last. CAERMARTHEN IRON WORKS. *Ex*: HALF-PENNY.

    R: and *E*: The same as last.   Pye, 13 ; 4.

    This is also exceedingly rare, as the die broke. Pye says "only 6 known."

5. *O*: Similar to No. 3, but from different dies. Legend the same as last.

    R: Interior of a forge. KIDWELLY WHITLAND BLACKPOOL AND CWMDWYFRON FORGES. *Ex*: I. MORGAN. The exergue line comes to the E of "KIDWELLY" and F of "FORGES."

    E: PAYABLE IN LONDON . BRISTOL & CARMARTHEN . ✕ .

6. *O*: Similar to last, but without the brickwork in archway, the lower beam of roof comes to the A of "CAERMAR-THEN," whereas in the former it came to the M.

    R: Similar to last, but the exergue line comes to L and O. There are several other differences, but this will be sufficient to distinguish it by.

    E: The same as last.

Conder, 21 ; 1.—Pye, 13 ; 5.—Virt : 75.

6a. As last, but *E*: The same as last, but without the dot after LONDON.

6b. As last, but *E*: Has a dot after IN . and a dot and dash after LONDON . —

6c. As last, but *E*: Plain (not in collar).

Carnarbonshire.

HALFPENNY.

BANGOR.

✓ 1. *O* : A harp crowned, and R D V in an ornamental circle. NORTH WALES TOKEN 1797.

    R : *Sth* . *R* and 4 within a circle of leaves. S. ROBERTS . IRON-MONGER . BANGER . . . .

    E : Milled.   Conder, 312 ; 1.

    Very rare.

To Sept . 11- 1893 .

Glamorganshire.

HALFPENNIES.

GLAMORGAN.

✓ 1. *O* : Bust to left. JESTYN . AP . GWRGAN . TYWYSOG . MORGANWG
- - - 1091 - - -
R : Britannia seated with spear and shield, a pedestal
behind her entwined with laurel. Y. BRENHIN . AR .
GYFRAITH . *Ex* : . 1795.
E : Plain in collar.   Pye, 21 ; 2.
Very rare, only a few impressions taken as the dies broke.

✓ 2. *O* : Similar to last, but without the little dashes by side of
date, and no pellet on crown.
R : Similar to last, but with a crown upon the pedestal, and
no dots by the side of date.
E : GLAMORGAN HALFPENNY. In raised letters.
Conder, 36 ; 1.—Pye, 21 ; 3.—Virt : 52.
There are varieties of edge, in which from one to four
leaflike ornaments follow the inscription.

SWANSEA.

✓ 3. *O* : View of a castle. SWANSEA HALFPENNY. 1796.
R : A key. JOHN VOSS DRAPER, &c.
E : PAYABLE ON DEMAND. The remainder engrailed.
Conder, 36 ; 2.—Pye, 46 ; 1.—Virt : 31.

𝔓embrokeshire.

FARTHING.

ST. DAVIDS.

∨ 1. *O*: Laureated bust to right, sprigs of leaves and a star
under. MEDALLION OF ST. DAVID.

R: The Prince of Wales' crest on a shield, between sprigs
of oak. PRO BONO PUBLICO 1793.

Conder, 126; 1.—Virt: 162.

This reverse also appears on the North and South
Wales farthings, which see.

Scotch Tokens

issued in the following Counties :—

Aberdeenshire .	.		.	.
Angusshire (now Forfar)		.	.	
Argyleshire	.	.	.	.
Ayrshire	.	.	.	.
Dumfriesshire .		.	.	
Fifeshire	.		.	.
Invernesshire .				
Kinrosshire	.	.		.
Kirkcudbrightshire				.
Lanarkshire	.	.	.	
Linlithgowshire			.	.	.
Lothian	.	.	.	.	.
Perthshire	.	.	.	.	.
Renfrewshire .				.	.
Roxburghshire .		.	.	.	.

Aberdeenshire.

HALFPENNY.

ABERDEEN.

✔ 1. *O*: An ancient fortress, encircled with a wreath of leaves.
   R: A cypher *J. B.* ABERDEEN TOKEN 1797.

Conder, 10; 1.—Virt: 181.

Rare private token.

Angusshire (now Forfarshire).

SHILLINGS.

DUNDEE.

1. *O*: An ancient ruin. DUNDEE SHILLING PAY'LE. BY J. WRIGHT JUNR. 1797. *Ex*: BROUGHTY CASTLE.

   R: An armed Highlander. FROM THE HEATH COVER'D MOUNTAINS OF SCOTIA WE COME. *Ex*: The arms, supporters and motto of Dundee in a sunk oval.

   Conder, 11 ; 1.

2. *O*: An ancient cross, W-DES at the sides. DUNDEE SILVER MEDAL PRICE ONE SHILLING. *Ex*: CROSS TAKEN DOWN 1777.

   R: The same as last. Conder, 11 ; 2.

   These are rare, as only a few proofs in silver and copper were struck.

PENNIES.

DUNDEE.

3. *O*: Large buildings. PUBLIC WAREHOUSES ON THE QUAY SHIPPING OF THIS PORT 8800 TONS REGR. *Ex*: Arms, &c., in oval as before. WRIGHT JUN—DES.

   R: A public building. DUNDEE PENNY 17—97. *Ex*: TOWN HOUSE FOUNDED 1732.

   E: PAYABLE ON DEMAND BY THO.S WEBSTER JUN.R.

   Conder, 11 ; 3.—Pye, 16 ; 6.—Virt: 216.

   Also struck in silver.

4. *O*: A front face bust. DUNDEE PENNY 1798 ADML. LD. DUNCAN BORN HERE 1731 DEFEATD. THE DUTCH FLEET 1797.

   R: Adam and Eve with the serpent in the garden of Eden. 23000 INHABITANTS IN DUNDEE VID. STATISTICAL ACCOUNT BY R. SMALL D.D. *Ex*: BE FRUITFULL AND MULTIPLY GEN . I . 28. Conder, 311 ; *3.

   Rare, private token.

HALFPENNIES.

BRECHIN.

5. *O*: View of a church with two towers. *Ex*: CHURCH.

   R: A building with a water wheel. EAST MILL BRECHIN 1801.

   E: PAYABLE BY SMITH AND WILSON × × × Pye, 12 ; 10.

   Rare, as the obv. die soon failed; upon which a fresh one was executed as follows.

✓ 6. *O*: Similar to last, but from the new die, with the legend
      added, PAYABLE BY SMITH AND WILSON.
  R: The same as last.
  E: Plain (in collar).
      *This is one of the few places in which it has been thought
      advisable to admit tokens of the 19th century.*

DUNDEE.

✓ 7. *O*: View of a harbour, with a ship alongside a quay.
      COMMERCE AUGMENTS DUNDEE. *Ex*: Arms, supporters,
      and motto. DEI DONUM. At the sides, WRIGHT DELIN.
  R: View of an ancient tower. DUNDEE HALFPENNY . 1795.
      Ex: OLD TOWER FOUNDED 1189.
  E: PAYABLE AT THE WAREHOUSE OF ALEXR. MOLISON . × .
                          Conder, 11 ; 4.—Pye, 16 ; 4.
      Also struck in silver.
✓ 8. *O*: Shield of arms, crest, and supporters, DEI DONUM above,
      PRUDENTIA ET CANDORE below. PAYABLE AT W. CROOMS.
      HIGH STREET DUNDEE.
  R: SELLS | WHOLESALE | WOOLEN & LINEN | DRAPERY GOODS |
      WATCHES &c &c | CHEAP. In six lines.
  E: Plain in collar. Conder, 12 ; 5.—Pye, 16 ; 10.—Virt: 67.
✓ 9.   Similar to last, but without period on *O*: at the end of
      legend.
      Also struck in silver.
✓ 10.   Very close copy of No. 8; but not struck in a collar, and
      not from the same dies.
  11. *O*: Same as last.
  R: The letters are larger and differently arranged, the c of
      " CHEAP " comes under the A of " WATCHES," whereas
      in the former it came under the T.
      This latter is rare.
✓ 12. *O*: A public building, I . W . I . DESIGN in small letters
      under. the whole within a sunk oval. DUNDEE
      HALFPENNY 1796 above, INFIRMARY FOUNDED 1794
      below.
  R: Slightly different design to *O*: of No. 7. MARE ET
      COMMERCIUM COLIMUS.
  E: Engrailed, with a waved line and dots.
                          Conder, 12 ; 6.—Pye, 16 ; 5.—Virt : 189.
      Also struck in silver.
  13.   A poor copy of No. 12, with edge milled.
                          Conder, 311 ; *6.
✓ 14. *O*: A public building. DUNDEE HALFPENNY 1797. *Ex*: TOWN
      HOUSE FINISHED 1734.
  R: View of a glass manufactory. GLASS WORKS WEST CONE
      FOUNDED 1788. *Ex*: WRIGHT DES.
  E: PAYABLE BY IOHN PILMER CHURCH LANE × ×
                          Conder, 12 ; 7.—Pye, 16 ; 8.—Virt : 197.
      Also struck in silver.

14*a*.   As last, but *E* : Plain.

✓ 15. *O* : An ancient fortress. DUNDEE HALFPENNY 1797. *Ex* : DUDHOPE CASTLE FOUND'D. 1660, CONVERTED INTO BARRACKS 1794.

     R : A man working flax. FLAX-HECKLING above, W : DES : below, within a circle. 3336 TONS FLAX & HEMP IMPORTED HERE IN 1796 ; VALUE . L.160.128 – *

     E : Plain in collar.

                  Conder, 12 ; 8.—Pye, 16 ; 9.—Virt : 206.
     Also struck in silver.
     There are at least four different dies issued for the obverse of this piece, the variations being chiefly observable in the shrubs in front of the Castle.

✓ 16. *O* : View of a church. DUNDEE HALFPENNY 1797. ST. ANDREW'S CHURCH FOUND'D. 1772.

     R : A ruin. COWGATE PORT * THE LAST REMAINS OF OUR ANCIENT WALLS * *Ex* : WRIGHT JUNr. DES, a star under.

     E : PAYABLE AT THE WAREHOUSE OF ALEXR. SWAP & CO.

                  Conder, 12 ; 9.—Pye, 16 ; 7.—Virt : 214.
     Also struck in silver.

16*a*.   As last, but *E* : PAYABLE IN LONDON, the remainder engrailed.

FORFAR.

✓ 17. *O* : A castle. PAYABLE ON DE = MAND BY JOHN STEELE. *Ex* : WRIGHT DES.

     R : Distant view of a town from the water. HALFPENNY. *Ex* : FORFAR 1797.

     E : .+.+.+.+.+.
     Also struck in silver.

✓ 18.   Similar to last, but the first letter of legend does not quite touch the castle, which it does in the former. Pye, 20 ; 3 ; is not quite like either.

                  Conder, 12 ; 10.

MONTROSE.

19. *O* : A distant view of a town and bridge from the water. MARE DITAT. *Ex* : MONTROSE.

     R : A woman spinning. SURE ARE THE REWARD'S OF INDUSTRY. *Ex* : 1796.

     E : Plain (not in collar).   Conder, 13 ; 12.—Pye, 37 ; 6.
     Very rare ; these dies were rejected as being too small. This piece may be identified by having no period at end of legend on rev : and by the right hand top of spinning wheel rail coming to the s of " INDUSTRY," whereas in the next it touches the R.

✓ 20.   The same device as last, but on a larger scale.
          E : PAYABLE BY I. BISSETT & SON MONTROSE.
                              Conder, 13 ; 11.—Virt : 165.
20a.   As last, but *E* : LONDON LIVERPOOL OR MONTROSE.
20b.   „   „   *E* : PUBLISHED BY JOS. DANL. & INO. BOULTER.
20c.   „   „   *E* : Milled.   Pye, 37 ; 4.
✓ 21. *O* : and *R* : Similar to No. 20, but with date in *Ex* : on *O* :
          and MONTROSE on *R* : There is no period after legend
          on *O* :
          E : Same as No. 20a.
✓ 22. *O* : Shield of arms, supporters, crest, &c. MONTROSE HALF-
          PENNY 1799.
          R : View of a building. MONTROSE LUNATIC HOSPITAL ERECTED
          BY SUBSCRIPTION 1781.
          E : PAYABLE BY ANDREW NICOL TOBACCONIST ✕   Pye, 37 ; 5.
✓ 23.   Similar to last, but the M of "MONTROSE" on *R* : nearly
          touches the second chimney, whilst in the former it
          barely reaches so far as the first.
          *In addition to this variety, there are at least three
          slight variations of obverse die noticeable in the size
          and position of eagle's wing and tail in the crest.*

FARTHINGS.

DUNDEE.

✓ 24. *O* : A pair of scales above a small cypher, *M & Co.* PAYABLE
          ON DEMAND DUNDEE.
          R : A sentinel on duty, the breech of a cannon on one side,
          and part of a fort on the other.
                    Conder, 13 ; 13.—Pye, 17 ; 4.—Virt : 135.
✓ 25. *O* : A horse and cart, with two packages marked DR and TR.
          SIC ITUR AD OPES. *Ex* : WRIGHT DES.
          R : A large building. ✱ ✱ DUNDEE FARTHING ✱ ✱ 17 96 *Ex* :
          TRADES ALL.
                    Conder, 13 ; 14.—Pye, 17 ; 1.—Virt : 196.
          Rare, only a few lbs. struck.
✓ 26.   Similar to last, but dated 1797, and without the stars
          before and after legend on *R* :
                              Conder, 13 ; 15.—Pye, 17 ; 2.
          Very rare, as the dies soon failed.
✓ 27.   Similar to No. 25, but TRADES HALL in *Ex* : on *R* : and
          dated 1797.
                    Conder, 13 ; 16.—Pye, 17 ; 3.—Virt : 196.
          Also struck in silver.

PENNIES.

ARGYLE HOUSE.

1. *O*: An ancient building. ARGYLE-HOUSE . SCOTLAND . on a raised rim. *Ex*: JACOBS.

   R: A cypher *T* . *G* between palm branches. BRITISH PENNY 1797.

   E: I PROMISE TO PAY ON DEMAND THE BEARER ONE PENNY.

   Conder, 311; 1.

   Exceedingly rare; only 3 specimens known.

INVERARY.

2. *O*: A view of an ancient fortress. INVERARY CASTLE on a raised rim. *Ex*: JACOBS.

   R: and *E*: As last. Conder, 14; 1.

   Also very rare.

Ayrshire.

HALFPENNIES.

v 1. *O*: Bust in armour. GULLIELMUS VALLÛS.
   R: A female figure seated, supporting a shield. SCOTIA
   REDIVIVA. *Ex*: 17 *C F* 97.
   Conder, 235; 213.—Pye, 4; 7.
   Also struck in silver.
   The initials in cypher *O. F.* are for Col. Fullerton, by
   whom also the following token was issued, as well
   as a half-crown, shilling, and sixpence in silver.

2. *O*: Bust of the Prince of Wales. GEORGIUS P. S. S. C. D.
   1799.
   R: The British arms on four shields crosswise. BR . L . PR .
   E . REG . SCO . PR . ET . SEN . GR . DUX.

v 3. *O*: Profile of Adam Smith.
   R: A female seated mourning over antique military
   trophies.
   Very rare, only a few proofs. Also struck in silver.

4. *O*: As No. 2.
   R: A female dropping herbs into a still. HYGEIA PREPARING.
   VELNO'S VEGETABLE SYRUP.
   This is the reverse of a London Token (Swainson's).
   *These tokens are all rare, Nos. 3 and 4 especially so; of
   No. 1, there were 576 impressions taken, of which four
   were in silver. The dies of No. 2 are still in existence,
   and recently impressions have been taken from them.*

FARTHING.

KILMARNOCK.

5. *O*: The date 1786 in the centre. KILMARNOCK . BLIND .
   COALL.
   R: Blank.

𝔇umfriesshire.

FARTHING.

SANQUHAR.

1. *O*: JOHN HALLIDAY TEA WINE & SPIRIT MERCHT.
   R: DEALER IN SEEDS STATIONARY &C. SANQUHAR.

𝔉𝔦𝔣𝔢𝔰𝔥𝔦𝔯𝔢.

PENNY.

KIRKCALDY.

✔ 1. *O* : Bust to right. THE PENNY OF SCOTLAND (1 . oz) 17 97.
Ex : 'ADAM SMITH L.L.D. F.R.S BORN AT KIRKALDY 1723.
The artist's name WYON in minute letters on the
truncation of the bust.
R : Agricultural implements, bales, &c., on a wharf, ships
in the distance. WEALTH OF NATIONS. *Ex* : Two
thistles, BOOG JUNr. DES. P. KEMPSON FECIT.
E : Plain in collar. Conder, 207 ; 46.

HALFPENNY.

BURNT ISLAND.

✔ 2. *O* : A cypher *B V Co.* under it a carboy between a rose
and a thistle.
R : BURNT | -ISLAND | VITRIOL | COMPY. | 1797. In five lines
within a garter radiated on which is inscribed NEMO
ME IMPUNE LACESSIT.
E : Milled. Conder, 313 ; 1.—Pye, 12 ; l.

FARTHINGS.

ANSTRUTHER.

3. *O* : ROBERT TAYLOR WINE & SPIRIT ✶ DEALER ✶
R : A fishing smack, with an anchor below. SHORE
ANSTRUTHER.

INNERKEITHIN.

4. *O* : A sugarloaf with a thistle under it. JOHN MEIKLEJOHN.
R : A ship under sail. INNERKEITHIN.

KIRKCALDY.

5. *O* : JAMES HARDIE MERCHT. KIRKALDY.
R : TEA & SUGAR WAREHOUSE.
6. *O* : P. HENDERSON ✶ LINKS ✶ KIRKCALDY.
R : TEA . COFFEE & SPIRIT WARE=HOUSE.
✔ 7. *O* : THOMAS RONALD MERCHT. ✶ KIRKALDY ✶
R : TEAS SPIRITS WINES ✶ & GROCERIES ✶

𝔍𝔫𝔟𝔢𝔯𝔫𝔢𝔰𝔰𝔥𝔦𝔯𝔢.

HALFPENNIES.

INVERNESS.

1. *O*: A rose and thistle united.   INVERNESS HALFPENNY.
   R: A cornucopia of flowers.   CONCORDIA ET FIDELITAS.
   Upon a stone at the bottom the date 1793.
   E: PAYABLE . AT . MACINTOSH INGLIS & I WILSON'S.
   Conder, 47 ; 1.—Pye, 24 ; 1.—Virt: 19.

✓ 1a.   As last, but *E*: without the I before WILSON.

1b.   „   „   *E*: without the dot after PAYABLE.

✓ 2. *O*: Similar to last, but the date 1794 added at bottom.
   R: Similar to last, but instead of the date, the stone is
   inscribed CLACH NA CUDDEN.
   E: The same as No. 1a.
   Conder, 47 ; 2.—Pye, 24 ; 2 .—Virt: 19.

✓ 3.   Similar to last, but dated 1795.   Conder, 47 ; 3.

✓ 4.   Similar to last, but dated 1796.

   Rare.

𝕶inrossshire.

PENNY.

LOCH LEVEN.

∀ 1. *O*: A castle in ruins, and trees, upon an island, within a circle. LOCH LEVEN PENNY 1797 ✱ Q. MARY IMPRISONED IN THE ISLE AND CASTLE. A.D. 1567 ✱ *Ex*: P . K . FECIT.

R: A girl treading linen in a tub, between two thistles. ANTIENT SCOTTISH WASHING ✱ HONI . SOIT . QUI . MAL . Y . PENSE ✱

E: Plain (in collar).   Conder, 53; 1.
Rare.

HALFPENNY.

GATEHOUSE.

⌄ 1. *O*: Crest a griffin, and motto IMPERO upon a label over it.
GATEHOUSE HALFPENNY.

R: View of a large building.   PAYABLE AT THE HOUSE OF
THOS. SCOTT & CO.   *Ex*: 1793.

Conder, 54; 1.—Pye, 21; 1.—Virt: 8.

Good impressions are rare.

𝕷anarkshire.

PENNY.

GLASGOW.

1. *O* : The arms of Glasgow. LET GLASGOW FLOURISH.
   R : A river god reclining on an urn, inscribed CLYDE, from which water is issuing. NUNQUAM ARESCERE. *Ex* : MDCCXCI. A small ornament under.
   Very rare. This is struck from the dies of the halfpenny, No. 5.

HALFPENNIES.

GLASGOW.

✓ 2. *O* : The arms of Glasgow. LET GLASGOW FLOURISH.
   R : A river god reclining on an urn, inscribed CLYDE, from which water is issuing. NUNQUAM ARESCERE. *Ex* : MDCCXCI. The initials R. D. under.
   E : PAYABLE AT THE HOUSE OF GILBERT SHEARER & CO :
   Conder, 62 ; 1.—Pye, 21 ; 4.—Virt : 19.
   Also struck in silver.

   2*a*.   Same as last, but without the colon at the end of edge inscription, and the o looks like a c.
   2*b*.   As last, but *E* : PAYABLE AT H. BROWNBILLS SILVERSMITH.
   2*c*.   „   „   *E* : Plain (in collar).

✓ 3. *O* : and *R* : Similar to last, but not such fine work and no initials under date.
   E : PAYABLE AT EDINBURGH GLASGOW & DUMFRIES — × .—
   Conder, 62 ; 2.

✓ 3*a*.   As last, but *E* : CAMBRIDGE BEDFORD AND HUNTINGDON.
✓ 3*b*.   „   „   *E* : PAYABLE IN LONDON. The remainder engrailed.
   3*c*.   As last, but *E* : PAYABLE IN LONDON BRISTOL & LANCASTER.
   3*d*.   „   „   *E* : Milled.
   3*e*.   „   „   *E* : Plain (not in collar but rounded).

✓ 4. *O* : and *R* : Similar to last, but with the initials F. A. under the date.
   E : PAYABLE IN LANCASTER LONDON OR BRISTOL.
   Conder, 62 ; 3.

   4*a*.   As last, but *E* : PAYABLE BY W. FUGGLES GOUDHURST.
   4*b*.   „   „   *E* : PAYABLE AT JOHN MATHEWS'S.
   4*c*.   „   „   *E* : PAYABLE AT JAMES ROBERTSONS.
   4*d*.   „   „   *E* : PAYABLE AT LEEK STAFFORDSHIRE.
   4*e*.   „   „   *E* : MASONIC TOKEN I. SCETCHLEY FECIT.
✓ 4*f*.   „   „   *E* : Plain (not in collar).

20

✔ 5. *O*: and *R*: Similar to last, but with a small ornament
     instead of the initials under date.
     E: PAYABLE IN LANCASTER LONDON OR LIVERPOOL.

5*a*.   As last, but *E*: PAYABLE AT SHARPS PORTSMOUTH &
     CHALDECOTTS CHICHESTER.

5*b*.   As last, but *E*: Plain (not in collar, but rounded).
     The obv. of No. 3 occurs with the following reverses:—

6. *R*: Figure of Britannia seated. RULE BRITANNIA. *Ex*: 1795.
     See Hampshire, No. 10.
     E: PAYABLE AT THE WAREHOUSE OF ALEXANDER MOLISON. ✕.

✔ 6*a*.   As last, but *E*: Milled.   Conder, 62; 4.

6*b*.   ,,   ,, *E*: Plain (not in collar, but rounded).

7. *R*: Bust to left.   IOHN HOWARD F.R.S. PHILANTHROPIST.
     See Hampshire, No. 34.
     E: PAYABLE AT THE WAREHOUSE OF ALEX.R MOLISON.
                                     Conder, 62; 5.

✔ 7*a*.   As last, but *E*: Milled.

7*b*.   ,,   ,, *E*: Plain (not in collar).
     The rev. of No. 3 also appears as an obverse with the
     following reverses:—

✔ 8. *R*: A large ship sailing. PRO BONO PUBLICO. *Ex*: 1794. See
     Hampshire, No. 22.   Conder, 218; 72.

✔ 9. *R*: The same as No. 6.
     E: PAYABLE IN LONDON. The remainder engrailed.

9*a*.   As last, but *E*: CURRENT EVERYWHERE.
                                     Conder, 218; 73.
     See also Cambridgeshire, No. 14; and Lancashire,
     No. 28.

FARTHINGS.

GLASGOW.

Anderson's.

✔ 10. *O*: ARCHD. ANDERSONS + PROVISION + WAREHOUSE.
     R: A ham over two casks. 106 KING STREET ✻ GLASGOW ✻

✔ 11.   Similar to last, but the word " PROVISION " is curved.

12.   Similar, but a small quatrefoil instead of a star before
     and after " GLASGOW."

✔ *11.bis* .

Angus'.

✔ 13. *O*: A sugar-loaf dividing the date 1780. JS. ANGUS. A
     FARTHING.
     R: " Tea Shop," in two lines in the centre of field.

14. *O*: A sugar-loaf with a ribbon on top. JAMES ANGUS A
     FARTHING.
     R: TEA SHOP above, GLASGOW, below. The centre blank.

✔ 15. *O*: The same as last.
     R: As last, with the addition of A SHIFT 1780 in the centre
     in three lines.

✓ 16.　　Similar to last, but the date is in smaller figures and there is no period after " GLASGOW" Conder, 62 ; 6.

Bilton's.

✓ 17. *O* : W. BILTON + TOBACCONIST + 630 : ARGYLE STREET.
　　R : The arms of Glasgow. LET GLASGOW FLOURISH.

Cubie & Paterson's.

✓ 18. *O* : PAYABLE | AT | CUBIE | & PATERSON'S | HEAD OF | KING STREET. In six lines, the last curved.
　　R : GLASGOW | FARTHING. In two lines, in centre of field.

Erskin's.

✓ 19. *O* : RALPH ERSKIN & COMPY. GLASGOW 1781. The last word on a ribbon in centre of field.
　　R : A ship. RALPH ERSKIN AND COMP.Y Conder, 314 ; *6.
✓ 20.　　Similar to last, but a new rev : which has no dot in COMPY, and the position of the ship is different.

Ewing's.

✓ 21. *O* : A thistle crowned, a quatrefoil below. FARTHING PAYABLE AT THE SHOP OF.
　　R : A tea-chest between two sugar-loaves. ALEX. EWING GROCER * GLASGOW * 1799.
✓ 22. *O* : The arms of Glasgow. 1799 above. FARTHING PAYABLE AT THE SHOP OF *
　　R : A hand holding a pair of scales. ALEXR. EWING GROCER * GLASGOW *

Finlayson's.

23. *O* : T : FINLAYSON 68 KING : ST. + ONE FARTHING +
　　R : The arms of Glasgow. LET GLASGOW FLOURISH.
✓ 24.　　Similar to last, but without the crosses before and after " ONE FARTHING."

Hamilton's.

✓ 25. *O* : The arms of Glasgow, a quatrefoil under. GLASGOW FARTHING PAYABLE AT.
　　R : St. Andrew and his cross. ALEXR. HAMILTON'S SNUFF SHOP. 1791.
26. *O* : Similar to last, but without the quatrefoil.
　　R : Similar, but the feet of St. Andrew are surrounded with small rocks.
✓ 27. *O* : Similar, but the fish is on the ground and the stem of the tree is plain.
　　R : Same as last. Conder, 62 ; 7.—Pye, 21 ; 6.—Virt : 137.
20 *

Kirkwood's.

28. *O*: A sugar-loaf with a ribbon on top.   JA'S KIRKWOOD A FARTHING.
    R: TEA SHOP GLASGOW.   1781.

Randolph's.

√ 29. *O*: Three canisters and a roll of tobacco.   FARTHING PAYABLE AT GEORGE RANDOLPH & CO.
    R: A negro holding a tobacco plant, a ship in the distance. TOBACCONISTS KING STREET GLASGOW. *Ex*: 1799.
    E: Milled.   Pye, 52; 6.

Retailers' Tokens.

30. *O*: The arms of Glasgow.   LET GLASGOW FLOURISH *   The bird is in the centre of top.
    R: GLASGOW RETAILERS TOKEN.   In three straight lines.
√ 31. *O*: Similar to last, but the bird is more to the left, under the s of " GLASGOW."
    R: Same as last, but with a period at end of legend.
√ 32.   Similar to last, but the legend on a ribbon, the bird under the w.
√ 33.   Similar, but the bird comes under the o.

Waterson & Co.

√ 34. *O*: A snuff jar labelled (37).   E. WATERSON & CO. TOBACCONISTS.
    R: SNUFF SHOP 193 TRONGATE + GLASGOW +

LEVEN.

√ 35. *O*: W. & G. MEIKLE . IRONMONGER . LEVEN.
    R: TEAS SPIRITS WINES * & GROCERIES *

RUTHERGLEN.

36. *O*: WM. MILLER VICTUALLER . RUTHERGLEN.
    R: TEAS SPIRITS GROCERIES &cc.

Linlithgowshire.

FARTHINGS.

BATHGATE.

1. *O*: JOHN FINLAY HOPETOWN ST. BATHGATE.
   R: DEALER IN TEAS WINES FOREIGN & BRITISH SPIRITS.

LINLITHGOW.

✓ 2. *O*: THOMAS GLEN WOOLLEN DRAPER ＊ LINLITHGOW ＊
   R: TEAS GROCERIES &c.   An ornament above and below.

✓ 3. *O*: STEPHEN MITCHELL & SON TOBACCONIST.
   R: A roll of tobacco, two leaves crossed below, and two
      pipes above. LINLITHGOW.

𝔏𝔬𝔱𝔥𝔦𝔞𝔫.

HALFPENNIES.

EDINBURGH.

✓ 1. *O*: A filtering stone. FOR FILTERING WATER. *Ex*: 1796.
   R: A bunch of grapes in a shield, between thistles.
   Conder, 221; 96.—Pye, 18*; 5.

✓ 2. *O*: A flower spray in a shield. BRITANIA RULES THE WAVES.
   R: A buck's head, the date 1796 under. LET BRITAIN
   FLOURISH. Within an ornamented border.
   Conder, 214; 29.—Pye, 18*; 6.—Virt: 203.
   There is a variety of this, the difference being very slight.

3. *O*: A tower within an oval surrounded by an ornamental
   border.
   R: Same as last.

Anderson, Leslie & Co.

✓ 4. *O*: View of a public building. EDINBURGH HALFPENNY 1797.
   PAYE. BY ANDERSON LESLIE & CO. WRIGHT DES. in small
   letters on the ground. *Ex*: UNIVERSITY OF EDINBURGH.
   R: A gardener holding a spade in one hand and a shrub
   in the other. NEU SEGNES JACEANT TERRÆ ETIAM
   MONTES CONSERERE JUVAT.
   E: Plain (in collar). Conder, 64; 5.—Pye, 18; 4.
   Very rare; the obverse die failed when only a dozen impressions had been taken, upon which the following took its place.

✓ 5. *O*: Very similar to last, but with NEW UNIVERSITY in *Ex*:
   R: and *E*: Same as last.
   Conder, 64; 4.—Pye, 18; 5.—Virt: 190.
   Also struck in silver.

Archibald's.

✓ 6. *O*: A palm branch. DITAT SERVATA FIDES. JOS. ARCHIBALD .
   SEEDSMAN . EDIN.
   R: SELLS | GARDEN, GRASS, | & FLOWER SEEDS, | FRUIT TREES |
   &c. &c. &c. In five lines.
   E: Milled. Conder, 64; 1.—Pye, 18; 8.—Virt: 193.
6a. As last, but *E*: Plain.

✓ 7. *O*: Shield of arms, dividing date 17—96. Crest a palm branch.
   DITAT . SERVATA FIDES JOS. ARCHIBALD . SEEDSMAN .
   EDIN. A group of seven dots between "JOS." and
   "DITAT."
   R: Same as last.
   E: Milled. Conder, 64; 2.—Pye, 18; 7.—Virt: 164.
8. Similar to last, but with a dot after *each* word of legend,
   and the group of seven dots comes between "FIDES"
   and "EDIN."

✓ 9. *O* : Similar to last, but larger, and a six-pointed star instead of the group of seven dots.

  R : Similar, but larger, and no commas after " GARDEN " or " GRASS."

  E : PAYABLE AT THE SHOP OF JOSEPH ARCHIBALD ✱ ✱ ✱ ✱ ✱ *There are varieties of edge with four, and with six stars after inscription.*

Campbell's.

✓ 10. *O* : A Turk's head. JAMES and a small ornament under. PAYABLE AT CAMPBELLS SNUFF SHOP.

  R : A snuff jar labelled 79, the date 1796 under. SAINT ANDREWS STREET EDINBURGH. ✱

  E : Milled.

✓ 10*a*. As last, but *E* : Plain (in collar).
        Conder, 64 ; 6.—Pye, 19 ; 7.—Virt : 19.

11. *O* : A similar Turk's head smoking a pipe, legend and artist's name as before.

  R : A snuff jar labelled 37, between two thistles, two pipes crossed above, the date 1796 under. SAINT ANDREWS STREET EDINBURGH.

  E : SPENCE × DEALER × IN × COINS × LONDON ×

11*a*. As last, but *E* : Milled.

✓ 11*b*.   „ „ *E* : Plain (not in collar). Conder, 65 ; 7.

✓ 12. *O* : Similar to last, but without artist's name and ornament under bust.

  R : Similar, stems of pipes not so long, left hand one only reaches to T of " STREET."

  E : Milled.

✓ 13. *O* : Figure of a Highlander. THE GALLANT GARB OF SCOTLAND ✥

  R : and *E* : Same as No. 11.   Conder, 65 ; 8.

  See also Spence's London.

Harrison's.

✓ 14. *O* : A cypher, *H II* with a small ornament top and bottom.

  R : An anchor dividing the date 17—96. H . HARRISON . ST . LEONARDS . EDIN. The N's retrograde.
      Conder, 65 ; 10.—Pye, 18 ; 9.—Virt : 238.

  Rare.

✓ 15. *O* : Same as last.

  R : Similar, but the letters N are formed properly, and there are no dots between the words of the legend.

Hutchison's. (1790.)

✓ 16. *O* : St. Andrew with his cross between thistles. NEMO ME IMPUNE LACESSIT. *Ex* : 1790.

  R : The arms of Edinburgh between thistles, crest an anchor. EDINBURGH HALFPENNY There are four bands on the anchor stock, and no period at end of legend.

  E : PAYABLE AT THE WAREHOUSE OF THOS. & ALEXR. HUTCHISON.

✓ 17. Similar, but from different dies, and having a period at
       end of legend on rev.

✓ 18. *O*: Similar, the right hand top corner of the cross comes to
       the centre of the letter A, the top thistle leaf on the
       right points to the period.

   R: No bands on anchor stock, the small thistle head to right
       points to the end of the first letter N, and the top
       leaf to the beginning of the second.

✓ 19. *O*: Same as last.

   R: The small thistle head to right points to the centre of
       the second N, and the top leaf to the foot of the Y.

✓ 20. *O*: The top right hand corner of cross comes to the end of
       the A, and the top thistle leaf on the *left* nearly
       touches the beginning of the N of "NEMO."

   R: The small thistle head points to beginning of second N,
       the top leaf just above foot of Y.

✓ 21. *O*: Same as last.

   R: The small thistle head points to end of first N, the top
       leaf between the N and Y.

✓ 22. *O*: Same as last.

   R: The small thistle head points to middle of second N, the
       top leaf to foot of Y.

              Conder, 65; 11 and 12.—Pye, 18; 3.—Virt: 20.

1791.

✓ 23. *O*: The top right hand corner of cross points to end of letter
       L, a flaw through the last word of legend makes it
       doubtful if there is a period at the end.   Dated
       1791.

   R: The small thistle head points to the beginning, and the
       top leaf to the end of the second N.

   24. *O*: The top right hand corner of cross points between the
       L and A, the *middle* leaf to period.

   R: The thistle bud points to end of second N, the top leaf
       between the Y and the period.

✓ 25. *O*: The top right hand corner of cross points to centre of
       the L, the period is about central between the top
       and middle leaves.

   R: Same as last.

✓ 26. *O*: Same as last.

   R: The thistle bud points to centre of second N, the top
       leaf to the period.

✓ 27. *O*: Same as last.

   R: The thistle bud points between the two N's, the top leaf
       to the foot of the Y.

✓ 28. *O*: The top right hand corner of the cross points to the
       beginning of the letter A, the top leaf just below the
       period.

   R: The thistle bud points to beginning of second N, the top
       leaf between the N and Y.

∨　29. *O* : Same as last.

　　　R : The thistle bud points to the end of second N, the top
　　　leaf between the Y and the period.　Conder, 65 ; 13.
　　　All these edges from No. 17 onwards are the same as
　　　No. 16.

∨　30. *O* : A very good copy of the preceding, but the last word of
　　　legend spelt LACESSET.　The top right hand corner
　　　of cross points to beginning of A, the middle leaf just
　　　below period.

　　　R : The thistle bud nearly touches beginning of second N,
　　　the second leaf is just below period.

　　　E : PAYABLE . AT EDINBURGH GLASGOW & DUMFRIES — × —

∨　31. *O* : The top right hand corner of cross points to centre of
　　　the L, the middle leaf touches end of E.

　　　R : and *E* : As last.

　　31*a*.　　As last, but *E* : Plain.

　　32. *O* : The top right hand corner of cross as last, the middle
　　　leaf points between T and period.

　　　R : and *E* : As last.

　　　These three are included in Conder, 65 ; 14.

∨　32*a*.　　As last, but *E* : PAYABLE IN HULL AND IN LONDON — × × —

∨　32*b*.　　　　,,　　,,　　*E* : PAYABLE IN LONDON BRISTOL & LANCASTER.

　　　　　　　　　　　　　　　　　　　　　　　Conder, 66 ; 15.

1792.

∨　33. *O* : Top right hand corner of cross points to centre of the letter
　　　L, the two top leaves are close together and both
　　　above the period.　The spelling of last word of
　　　legend correct.　Date 1792.

　　　R : The thistle bud points to beginning of first N, the top
　　　leaf to beginning of foot of the Y.

　　　E : Same as No. 16.　　　　　　　　Conder, 66 ; 16.

　　34. *O* : Top right hand of cross points between L and A, the
　　　period midway between two leaves.

　　　R : The thistle bud points to beginning of second N, the top
　　　leaf to beginning of foot of Y.

∨　35. *O* : Top right hand of cross points to end of the L, the
　　　middle leaf to the period.

　　　R : The thistle bud points to the end of second N, the *top*
　　　leaf to the period.

∨　36. *O* : Top right hand of cross points to beginning of A, the
　　　middle leaf to the period.

　　　R : The top leaf points between the N and the Y.

∨　37. *O* : Top right hand of cross as last, period between the two
　　　top leaves.

　　　R : The thistle bud points to end of second N, the top leaf
　　　to foot of Y.

38. *O* : The workmanship of this is not so good as previously, the *left* hand top of cross is above the E of "ME," which in the last pointed to the beginning of that letter, otherwise very similar.

    R : The thistle bud points between the two N's, the top leaf to the foot of the Y.

    The edges of all these are the same as No. 16.

38a.   As last, but *E* : Milled.

38b.   ,,   ,,   *E* : Plain (not in collar).

39. *O* : The right hand corner of cross points to beginning of L, the *middle* leaf is just above the period.

    R : The thistle bud points between the N and the Y, the top leaf is just below the period.

    E : PAYABLE AT THE WAREHOUSE OF THOMAS CLACKE . X X .

39a.   As last, but *E* : Milled.   Conder, 66 ; 17.

1796.

40. *O* : Similar to preceding, but dated 1796.

    R : Very nearly like No. 19.

    E : The same as No. 39.   Conder, 65 ; 9.

40a.   As last, but *E* : PAYABLE IN LANCASTER LONDON OR BRISTOL. *Both pieces are exceedingly rare.*

Varieties.

The obv. of No. 32 occurs with the following reverses :—

41. *R* : A ship sailing, &c.   See Hampshire, No. 44.

    E : PAYABLE IN LONDON BRISTOL & LANCASTER.

41a.   As last, but *E* : Engrailed.   Conder, 210 ; 1.

42. *R* : A female seated, leaning on a harp. HIBERNIA. See Wicklow, No. 48.

    E : The same as No. 41.

42a.   As last, but *E* : Plain.   Conder, 210 ; 2.

    See also Warwickshire, No. 192 ; Yorkshire, No. 26 ; Wicklow, No. 55.

Register Office.

43. *O* : View of a public building. EDINBURGH HALFPENNY 1796. Upon the ground in small letters is WRIGHT DES. *Ex* : REGISTER OFFICE FOUNDED 1774.

    R : The figure of Britannia seated, and part of a ship. BRITANNIA. Conder, 64 ; 3.—Pye, 18 ; 6.—Virt : 19. *Rare ; only about* 100 *impressions taken when the die failed.*

Sanderson's.

44. *O* : A rose and thistle surmounted by a crown. R. SANDERSON & CO. NO. 17 SOUTHBRIDGE EDINBURGH.

    R : SELLS | ALL KINDS OF | WOOLEN & LINNEN | DRAPERY GOODS | HABERDASHERY | BUTTONS WATCHES | &C | CHEAP.

        Conder, 66 ; 18.—Pye, 18* ; 3.

✔ 45. *O* : An eagle preying on snakes.   Legend same as last.
   R : The same as last.   Pye, 18* ; 2.

 46. *O* : The same as last.
   R : SELL instead of SELLS, and LINEN instead of LINNEN ;
          otherwise the same as before.   Pye, 18* ; 1.

✔ 47. *O* : Same as last.
   R : SELLS | ALL SORTS OF | WOOLLEN AND | LINEN CLOTHS |
          BREECHES STUFFS | FANCY VESTS | HATS STOCKINGS |
          GLOVES, &C. | CHEAP.

Wright's.

✔ 48. *O* : A ram.   IOHN WRIGHT HIGH STREET EDINBURGH.

   R : The same as last.   Pye, 18* ; 4.
   *Nos. 44-48 are struck in brass : they are all rare, No. 45
   especially so.*

LEITH.

✔ 49. *O* : A ship and boat sailing by a fort.   SUCCESS TO THE PORT
          OF LEITH 1796.

   R : A female seated holding a wand in one hand and a pair
          of scales in the other, a thistle behind her, packages
          and a cask in front labelled TEA and GIN ; the end of
          the wand points to the letter E of "THE."   PAYABLE
          AT THE HOUSE OF JOHN WHITE KIRKGATE . LEITH.
                    Conder, 66 ; 19.—Pye, 26 ; 10.—Virt : 210.

 50. *O* : There is a small triangular flag on the look-out of fort,
          and three arches in place of cannons.

   R : The end of wand touches the letter U of "HOUSE," the
          packages, scales, and thistle are all different, and the
          inscriptions "GIN" and "TEA" are plainer.
                    Conder, 66 ; 20.—Pye, 26 ; 9.

 51. *O* : A ship sailing, at bottom sprigs of leaves. * LEITH
          HALFPENNY.

   R : Figure of Britannia seated, holding spear and palm
          branch (?) * LEITH HALFPENNY.   *Ex* : 1797.

   E : PAYABLE IN LEITH EDINBURGH & GLASGOW + + +
                    Conder, 66 ; 21.—Pye, 35* ; 1.—Virt : 192.

 51a.   As last, but *E* : PAYABLE AT THE SHOP OF JOSEPH ARCHI-
          BALD.   Conder, 66 ; 22.

 52. *O* : Similar to last, but there is a rope hanging like a festoon
          from end of bowsprit.

   R : Similar, but the palm branch (?) has more simple points,
          and the end of legend is farther from the *Ex* : line.

   E : Same as last.

FARTHINGS.

EDINBURGH.

ᵛ 53. *O*: St. Andrew with his cross between thistles. NEMO ME
  IMPUNE LACESSIT. *Ex*: 1790.
  R: The arms of Edinburgh between thistles, crest an anchor.
  EDINBURGH HALF HALFPENNY.
  E: Milled.   Conder, 67; 23.—Virt: 209.
ᵛ 54.   Similar to last, but dated 1791.   Conder, 67; 24.
ᵛ 55.   Similar to last, but dated 1792.   Conder, 67; 25.
ᵛ 56. *O*: Similar to last.
  R: Similar, but legend reads, EDINBURGH FARTHING.
  E: Milled.   Conder, 67; 26.—Pye, 18; 10.—Virt: 135.
ᵛ 56a.   As last, but *E*: Plain.
  Rare; only 6 lbs. struck.
  An impression of this appears upon a halfpenny flan,
  the edge being inscribed: PAYABLE IN LONDON BRISTOL
  & CARMARTHEN . × .
ᵛ 57. *O*: Similar to last.
  R: FARTHING YOUNGEST SON OF FORTUNE.
  E: Milled obliquely.   Conder, 245; 1.—Pye, 52; 4.
  Very rare; engraved in Conder, 2; 4.
ᵛ 58. *O*: and *E*: The same as last.
  R: An anchor and cable. HOPEFUL FARTHING.
          Conder, 245; 2.—Pye, 52; 5.—Virt: 136.
ᵛ 59. *O*: A shield between sprigs, bearing the Prince of Wales'
  crest in first quarter, and a letter E in the third.
  R: A bird sitting on the branch of a tree. PRO BONO
  PUBLICO. *Ex*: 1796.
ᵛ 60. *O*: The same as last.
  R: PRO | BONO | PUBLICO. In three lines. *Ex*: 1796.
ᵛ 61. *O*: A crown radiated above a thistle. 1795.
  R: EDINBURGH FARTHING. A small star on either side, and a
  small ornament at bottom.
          Conder, 67; 28.—Virt: 136.
  These are all rare.

Blackie & Co.

ᵛ 62. *O*: T. BLACKIE & CO. 22 GREENSIDE * STREET *
  R: TEAS SPIRITS & WINES.
  63. *O*: WALTER BLACKIE & CO. LEITH STREET. A small ornament
  below.
  R: The same as last.

Cotton's.

ᵛ 64. *O*: GEORGE COTTON TOBACCONIST.
  R: SNUFF SHOP 12 . NORTH BRIDGE.

Dickson's.

65. *O* : DICKSON & MCDOUGAL 36 SOUTH BRIDGE ST. *
   R : TEA DEALERS AND * GROCERS *

Doig's.

66. *O* : F. DOIG LAWN MARKET EDINR.   Two ornaments.
   R : A tea chest, a basket, and two bottles.

Douglas'.

67. *O* : A D DOUGLAS EDINB.
   R : TOBACCONIST LAUN MARKET.   Two pipes crossed.
68. *O* : ALEX. DOUGLAS F.
   R : A candlestand with moulds.   CANDLEMAKER.
   (*Both Lead.*)

Flynn's.

69. *O* : A sugar-loaf with a ribbon above it, 11 below.   FLYNN
        GROCER HAMMOND LANE.
   R : A Figure of Hope.   Conder, 248 ; 31.

Galloway's.

70. *O* : ALEXR. GALLOWAY 107 WEST BOW.
   R : TEAS SPIRITS WINES & GROCERIES.
   (*In Copper, Brass, and Lead.*)

Grerar's.

71. *O* : JOHN GRERAR NO. 60 SOUTH BRIDGE AND NEWINGTON PLACE.
   R : TEAS WINES SPIRITS ALES + AND GROCERIES +

Hair's.

72. *O* : Three sugar-loaves.   GEORGE HAIR GROCER.
   R : A canister inscribed TEA with a star below.   TEA AND
      SPIRIT DEALER.   Conder, 248 ; 33.

Harrison's.

73. *O* : A coronet above two sceptres (torches ?), H-H at the
     sides, a wreath above.
   R : A bunch of flowers, with an ornament top and bottom.
                         Pye, 18* ; 7.
74. *O* : Same as last.
   R : Similar, but the ornaments at top and bottom are very
     different and have a star in the centre of each.
75. *O* : Similar to No. 72, but without the H-H and the two
     objects are more like sceptres.
   R : Similar to No. 73, but not the same die.
                         Conder, 247 ; 24.

Havens'.

76. *O* : R. HAVENS 83 SOUTH BRIDGE &c. SPIRIT WINES.
      R : LATE SHEPPARDS TEA SHOP.
77. *O* : HAVENS.
      R : 83 SOUTHBRIDGE.
      (*Lead.*)

Hendrie's.

78. *O* : A. HENDRIE GROCER EDINBURGH.   Two ornaments.
      R : A canister.   A. HENDRIES TEA & SPIRIT SHOP.

Conder, 67 ; 29.

79.   Similar to No. 78, but the bottom ornament farther
    from the legend.

Hogg's.

80. *O* : J. HOGG CANON MILLS.
      R : TEAS & SPIRITS.

Hunter's.

81. *O* : JOHN HUNTER NO. 212 COWGATE & 109 HIGH STREET.
      R : GENUINE TEAS DIRECT FROM * THE INDIA HOUSE *

Johnstone's.

82. *O* : WM. JOHNSTONE 210 * PLEASANCE *
      R : TEA & SPIRIT DEALER.
83. *O* : JAMES JOHNSTONE TOBACCONIST EDINBURGH.   Two orna-
    ments.
      R : DEALER IN FOREIGN AND FANCY * SNUFFS *
84. *O* : JOHNSTONE 100 HIGH STREET.
      R : A jar. SNUFF SHOP.
      (*Lead.*)

Kirkwood's.

85. *O* : KIRKWOOD MARKET STREET EDINBURGH.
      R : TEAS SPIRITS WINES * & GROCERIES *

Lewis'.

86. *O* : JAS. LEWIS 177 CANONGATE AND 6 MARKET ST.
      R : GROCER WINE & SPIRIT MERCHANT.   Two ornaments.

Macarra's.

87. *O* : CHARLES MACARRA 28 PORTS-BURGH.
      R : TEAS SPIRITS WINES * & GROCERIES *

McLaren's.

88. *O* : R. M'LAREN 29 * ELDER . STREET *
      R : TEA & SPIRIT DEALER.

Meikle's.

✔ 89. *O* : GEO. MEIKLE 86 GRASS MARKET.
   R : Same as No. 87.

Melrose's.

✔ 90. *O* : ANDW. MELROSE TEA & SPIRIT WAREHOUSE 301 CANON GATE.
   R : A canister labelled *tea* and a sugar-loaf.   GENUINE TEAS
      ✷ DIRECT FROM THE INDIA HOUSE ✷
✔ 91. *O* : ANDW. MELROSE & CO. 83 SOUTHBRIDGE & 301 HEAD OF .
      CANON GATE.
   R : Same as last.

Milne's.

✔ 92. *O* : JOHN MILNE 151 ✷ PLEASANCE ✷
   R : WINES TEAS SPIRITS ✷ GROCERIES &c. ✷

Mitchell's.

✔ 93. *O* : JAMES MITCHELL TOBACCONIST.
   R : A roll of tobacco and two leaves over two crossed pipes.
      CANON GATE.

Moncrieff's.

✔ 94. *O* : A tea-chest.   C. MONCRIEFF . 497 LAWNMARKET.
   R : TEAS . SPIRITS WINES . & GROCERIES.

Morris'.

95. *O* : JAS. MORRIS 4 CATHERINE STREET.   A quatrefoil below.
   R : TEAS WINES AND SPIRITS.   An ornament at top and bottom.

Morton's.

✔ 96. *O* : DAVID MORTON 96 NICHOLSON STREET ✷ EDINBURGH ✷
   R : TEAS SPIRITS WINES ✷ & GROCERIES ✷

Nicholson's.

97. *O* : A tea-chest.   D NICHOLSON GROCER & SPIRIT DEALER.
   R : UNION PLACE BROUGHTON ST. & PRESTON HOLM.

Nimmo's.

✔ 98. *O* : ROBERT NIMMO GROCER EAST MARKET STREET.
   R : GENUINE TEAS DIRECT FROM THE ✷ INDIA HOUSE ✷

Paterson's.

✔ 99. *O* : A. & J. PATERSON NO. 10 ST. JAMES'S SQUARE.
   R : TEA & SPIRIT DEALERS.

Picken's.

100. *O*: A Druid seated holding a lamp. PICKEN FISH TACKS-
　　　MAN. *Ex*: 1793.
　　R: Arms. FARTHING PAYABLE AT EDINR.　Conder, 67; 27.

Pollands'.

101. *O*: JOHN POLLANDS 41 HANOVER ST. AND 2 GREENSIDE ST.
　　　EDINR.
　　R: TEA DEALER AND GROCER.　Two small ornaments.

Reid's.

102. *O*: A pair of scales. HENRY REID BARROWFIELD ROAD +
　　　CALTON +
　　R: TEAS . SPIRITS WINES . & GROCERIES.
103. *O*: A pair of scales and two ornaments. H. REID BARROW-
　　　FIELD CALTON.
　　R: The same as last.

Reith's.

104. *O*: REITH NO. I WEST BOW * TEA DEALER & GROCER.
　　R: A tea-chest. WINES & FOREIGN SPIRITS.

Reynolds'.

✓ 105. *O*: A ship sailing. J. REYNOLDS.
　　R: Small ornaments. 8 SAINT : LEONARDS' EDINBURGH.

Robb's.

✓ 106. *O*: ALEXR. ROBB TINSMITH * CANON * GATE *
　　R: PAYABLE AT 289.　Palm branches under.

Rodgers'.

✓ 107. *O*: THOS. RODGERS 123 * CANON GATE *
　　R: TEA & SPIRIT DEALER.

Russell's.

✓ 108. *O*: ALEXR. RUSSELL WINE & SPIRIT DEALER.
　　R: INDIA TEA WAREHOUSE 106 HIGH STREET & 243 * CANON
　　　GATE *

Scuogall & Drysdale's.

109. *O*: SCUOGALL & DRYSDALE 223 HIGH ST. & 14 SO. JAMES
　　　STT. * EDINR.
　　R: TEA COFFEE & SUGAR WAREHOUSE.　Two quatrefoils.

Sinclair's.

✓ 110. *O*: D. SINCLAIR TEA DEALER 14 * TERRACE *
　　R: SPIRITS PORTER & ALES.

Smyth's.

111. *O*: CHAS. SMYTH.
    R: MARYS ABBEY.
    (*Lead.*)

Steele's.

✔ 112. *O*: JOHN STEELE'S TIN & * OIL SHOP *
    R: PAYABLE 224 * CANONGATE *

Steuart's.

✔ 113. *O*: Three sugar-loaves. STEUART . GROCER.
    R: STEUART'S WAREHOUSE EDINBURGH. A star top and
      bottom.   Conder, 67 ; 30.

Swanston's.

114. *O*: D. SWANSTON TEA & SPIRIT MERCHANT.
    R: WINES . HEAD OF BROWN STRT. PLEASANCE.

Thallon's.

✔ 115. *O*: R. THALLON 370+GALLOWGATE. +
    R: A pair of scales. SUGARS . TEAS & GROCERIES.

Thom's.

116. *O*: A jug within a circle. J. THOM + CHINA MERCHANT.
    R: COWGATE FARTHING.
    (*Lead.*)

Thompson's.

117. *O*: A ship sailing. THOMPSONS * WAREHOUSE * EDINR. *
    Legend commences at top over centre mast.
    R: A crown. THOMPSONS * WAREHOUSE * EDINR. * Legend
    commences to right of bottom.
✔ 118. *O*: As before, the D of "EDIN." directly over centre mast.
    R: As before, the N of "THOMPSONS" over centre of
    crown.
119. *O*: As before, the E of "EDIN." comes over the centre
    mast.
    R: The legend commences to left of the bottom of crown.
✔ 120. *O*: As before, the E of "WAREHOUSE" is over the centre
    mast.
    R: Nearly like No. 118.
121. *O*: P. THOMPSON 259 * HIGH STREET *
    R: An ornament. TEAS SPIRITS & GROCERIES.

Walker's.

✔ 122. *O*: A. J. & M. WALKER 5 LEITH STREET.
    R: TEAS SPIRITS & WINES.

Watt's.

✓ 123. *O*: W. WATT . GROCER . FISHER ROW.
      R: TEAS . WINES . & SPIRITS. An octagonal ornament below
        " WINES."
✓ 124. *O*: A roll of tobacco and three leaves. JOHN WATT ✻
        TOBACCONIST ✻
      R: 21 CHARLES STREET.

Wemyss'.

✓ 125. *O*: D. WEMYSS TEA DEALER 21 ✻ ABBEY ✻
      R: SPIRITS PORTER & ALES.

Williams'.

✓ 126. *O*: JAMES WILLIAMS 76 NICHOLSON STREET ✻ EDINR. ✻
      R: DEALER IN TEAS WINES . SPIRITS &c.

Winton's.

✓ 127. *O*: A roll of tobacco and leaves. JAMES WINTON ✻ TOBAC-
        CONIST ✻
      R: SNUFF SHOP ✻ 6 CATHERINE —'''— STREET ✻

Variety.

128. *O*: The same as rev. of No. 72.
      R: A wheatsheaf.

      The following lead pieces of Edinburgh may be added:—
129. *O*: A cask. JN. DICK ... GROCER ...
      R: 523 LAWN MARKET. In three lines.
130. *O*: M'KAY GROCER.
      R: EDINR.
131. *O*: A. PINKERTON & CO. GROCER.
      R: NO. 88 HIGH STREET, EDIN.
132. *O*: D. PURDIE *WEIGH HOUSE*.
      R: *EDINR*. 1800.
133. *O*: JOHN WATSON.
      R: The same as No. 130.

LEITH.

✓ 134. *O*: DAVID GRIEVE 46 KIRKGATE LEITH.
      R: TEAS SPIRITS WINES ✻ & GROCERIES ✻
✓ 135. *O*: VICTUAL COMPANY 47 GILES' STREET ✻ LEITH ✻
      R: MEAL BARLEY & FLOUR ✻ WAREHOUSE ✻ Two ornaments.
      The following are in lead:—
136. *O*: JAMES FERGUSON.
      R: STONE WAREHOUSE LEITH.

137. O : T. HENRY.
    R : NORTH LEITH.
138. O : ALEXR. MILLAR 39 ST. ANDREWS STREET LEITH.
    R : TEAS SPIRITS & GROCERIES.
139. O : WM. MILLER 1806.
    R : LEITH FARTHING.
140. O : WM. MILLER . SENIOR.
    R : LEITH . 1806.
      Some of these farthing tokens may belong to the 19th
      century (the two last certainly do), but it was thought
      best in the absence of positive proof to the contrary
      to include them.

PORTOBELLO.

141. O : ALEXR. GRIEVE GROCER * PORTOBELLO.
    R : TEAS SPIRITS PORTER & ALES.

324

Perthshire.

HALFPENNIES.

PERTH.

✓ 1. *O*: A man dragging a fishing net to the shore, a boat lying on the beach. RETE TRAHITO FAUSTE. *Ex*: WRIGHT JUNr. DES.

R: A bridge, and distant view of hills. PERTH HALFPENNY 1797. *Ex*: TAY-BRIDGE FINISH-ED 1770. The arms of Perth in a sunk circle and motto PRO REGE LEGE ET GREGE.

E: PAYABLE ON DEMAND BY JOHN FERRIER ✠ ✠ ✠ ✠
Conder, 127; 1.—Pye, 41; 5.—Virt: 216.
Also struck in silver.

✓ 2. *O*: The same as last.

R: Similar to preceding, but without the date above the hills. Conder, 316; *1.

v 3. *O*: Similar, but the rising bank at the back of the fisherman is lumpy, whereas in the former it was a regular slope.

R: The same as last.
A flaw in the obv. die of No. 2 shows the necessity for making No. 3, of which but very few were struck as the reverse die soon afterwards failed. They are both rare.

v 4. *O*: View of a church. PERTH HALFPENNY 1797. *Ex*: ST. JOHNS CHURCH. Arms and motto in a sunk circle.

R: A watermill and trees, WRIGHT DES under. 46 WATER: MILLS FOR BLEACHING . PRINTING . COTTON WORKS . CORN &c. WITHIN 4 MILES OF PERTH.
Conder, 127; 2.—Pye, 41; 6.
Rare private token; only about 6 dozen struck, some of which are in silver.
The edges of all are like No. 1, and in some instances there are only 3 or 4 crosses.

v 5. *O*: A hank of yarn and a package of dressed flax, dividing the date 17-97 PERTH . HALFPENNY .. ✕ .

R: The arms of Perth, and motto PRO REGE LEGE ET GREGE.

E: PAYABLE AT THE HOUSE OF PAT.K MAXWELL ✕ ✕
Conder, 127; 3.—Pye, 41; 4.

v 6. *O*: and *E*: The same as last.

R: The tips of the wings nearly touch "LEGE," whereas before they only reached midway between that word, and the word on either side. *Pye's engraving of the rev. is not much like either.*

v 7. *O*: Similar to No. 5, but the legend is more spread and has a star between the beginning and end of it, the package of flax also is much larger.

R: and *E*: As before. Conder, 127; 4.—Pye, 41; 3.

8. *O*: A spirit still, casks, &c. in a circle of dots. PAYABLE AT
  DAVID PETERS WINE & SPIRIT SHOP.

  R: The arms of Perth and motto PRO REGE LEGE ET GREGE
  upon a label, with a sprig of flowers at each end.
  PERTH HALFPENNY 1797.

  E: Milled diagonally.
  Conder, 127 ; 5.—Pye, 41 ; 2.—Virt: 231.

8a.   As last, but with *E* : Straight milling.

8b.   „   „   *E* : Plain (not in collar).

FARTHINGS.

PERTH.

9. *O*: An ancient tower, and vessels lying at a quay. PERTH
  FARTHING 1798. *Ex*: MONKS TOWER.

  R: A girl watering cloth, laid out bleaching. IN OUR
  VICINITY ARE THE FINEST STREAMS FOR BLEACHING IN
  BRITAIN ⁘ *Ex*: I. MENZIES DES.
  Conder, 316 ; 6.—Pye, 41 ; 9.

  Also the following pieces in lead :—

10. *O*: W . B .
  R: PERTH.

11. *O*: ROSS TEA & SPIRIT SHOP.
  R: HIGH STREET PERTH.

Renfrewshire.

PENNIES.

PAISLEY.

1. *O* : A bishop wearing a mitre and holding a pastoral staff between two shields. P. K. SCULPSIT R. BOOG . IUN . DES under, within an oval. PAISLEY PENNY * ARMS 1798 *
   R : Interior of a church. INTERIOR of the ABBEY CHURCH as REPAIRED in the ORIGINAL STILE . A . D . 1788 * *Ex* : AUSPICIO | R. B. in two lines.

✔ 2. *O* : Exterior of a church. ABBEY-CHURCH. *Ex* : FOUNDED (CIRCITER) 1160.
   R : As last.
   Both rare, the former especially so.

FARTHINGS.

PAISLEY.

✔ 3. *O* : J. COATS | & SON | BROOMLANDS.
   R : A ham suspended. HAM CURERS | & GROCERS | PAISLEY.

✔ 4. *O* : Roll of tobacco, and three leaves. PETER TAYLOR TOBACCONIST.
   R : Two pipes crossed. 215 HIGH STREET * PAISLEY *

Roxburghshire.

FARTHING.

JEDBURGH.

1. *O* : JOHN | REID | CANDLE | MAKER | JEDBURGH.
   R : DEALER IN | SPIRITS | TEAS &c. | GROCERIES.

T. Feb. 5 . 1894 –

Irish Tokens

issued in the following Counties :—

Cork	18
Drogheda	3
Dublin	210
King's County	1
Munster (province)	19
Wexford	9
Wicklow	57

Cork.

HALFPENNIES.

✔ 1. *O*: A figure of Fame flying, blowing a trumpet. The tip of the wing points to the letter F in "OF," in the legend. FOR . THE . CONVENIENCE . OF . THE . PUBLIC . 1794.

    R: A cypher *J. E. & Co.* PAYABLE . IN . CORK . OR . DUBLIN . HALFPENNY.   Conder, 186; 1.

✔ 2. *O*: Similar to last, but from different dies. The tip of the wing comes below the F in "OF."

    R: Similar to last, but the work is coarser.

    Conder, 186; 2.—Virt: 7.

✔ 3. *O*: A female seated holding a harp. FOR THE GOOD OF THE PUBLIC ✳ 1792 ✳

    R: A cypher *W. H. Co.* PAYABLE AT CORK OR DUBLIN ✳
This cypher also appears on Dublin, Nos. 166-168.

4. *O*: A female seated holding a harp. PAYABLE . IN . CORK . OR . DUBLIN. *Ex*: 1792.

    R: A cypher *H. M. Co.* DUBLIN HALFPENNY.
These two latter are rare when in good condition.
The obverse of No. 1 occurs with the following reverses :—

5. *R*: A wheatsheaf. PEACE PLENTY & LIBERTY. See Cambridgeshire, No. 17.   Conder, 276; 122.

✔ 6. *R*: Arms of Orchard. HALFPENNY 1795. See Middlesex, No. 285.   Conder, 276; 124.

7. *R*: Arms of London in an ornamental circle. See Middlesex, No. 341.

8. *R*: Man in a loom. NOTHING WITHOUT INDUSTRY. See Dublin, No. 12.   Conder, 277; 126.

9. *R*: Arms, crest a canister, &c. See Dublin, No. 18.

    Conder, 276; 125.

✔ 10. *R*: A wheatsheaf and sickle between doves. See Munster, No. 1.   Conder, 276; 123.

11. *R*: Anchor and cap of Liberty radiated. See Not Local, No. 123.   Conder, 276; 121.

12. *R*: Arms of United States. LIBERTY AND SECURITY. See Not Local, 176.

The obv. of No. 2 occurs with the following reverse :—

✔ 13. *R*: A wheatsheaf. PEACE AND PLENTY. Conder, 233; 197.

The rev. of No. 1 appears as an obv. with the following reverses :—

✔ 14. *R*: Crowned bust of "BRYEN BOIROIMBE." See Munster, No. 1.   Conder, 286; 224.

15. *R*: Wheatsheaf and sickle between doves. See Munster, No. 1.

16. *R*: Hope standing. IRISH HALFPENNY 1795. See Dublin,
No. 6.

√ 17. *R*: A female standing holding a quadrant. See Dublin,
No. 18.   Conder, 282 ; 177.

√ 18. *R*: A cypher *H S Co* between laurel branches. See Dublin,
No. 115.   Conder, 283 ; 192.

See also Middlesex, Nos. 269, 293, 296, and 343 ; and
Dublin, Nos. 106 and 120.

𝔇𝔯𝔬𝔤𝔥𝔢𝔡𝔞.

HALFPENNIES.

1. *O*: A female seated holding a harp. FOR . THE . PUBLICK .
   GOOD . . . 1792 . . .

   R: A cypher *I. M. Co.* PAYABLE AT DROGHEDA OR DUBLIN ✳
   This cypher will also be found on one of the imitations
   of the Camac series. See Dublin, No. 57.

2. *O*: Similar to last, but from a different die.

   R: A cypher *I. M. Co.* MAY IRELAND EVER FLOURISH . ✳ .

3. *O*: A female seated holding a harp. LEINSTER . ❖.
   HALFPENNY . ❖ . 1804 . ❖ .

   R: As No. 1.
   All these three are rare when in good condition.

𝔇ublin.

PENNIES.

DUBLIN.

✔ 1. *O* : TO | PREVENT | THE ABUSE OF | CHARITY, IN THE | CONSUMP-
TION OF | WHISKEY, | THIS IS GIVEN TO | THE POOR | IN
DUBLIN | F. |

   R : VALUE | ONE PENNY, IN | PROVISIONS (ONLY) | AT 168
   JAMES'S-GATE | 44 LOW KEVIN STREET | 55 UPPER-
   COOMBE | & 23 BARRACK- | STREET. | 1797.

2. *O* : A female seated holding a harp, a spade and pickaxe
   under, within a circle of leaves.

   R : A cypher *H M Co.* CAMAC KYAN AND CAMAC. ONE
   PENNY.

   E : PAYABLE IN DUBLIN OR BALLYMURTAGH.

✔ 3. *O* : A female seated holding a harp. PAYABLE AT THE PAWN-
BROKERS OFFICE BISHOP ST.

   R : A cypher *W. T. B & Co.* PENNY above, TOKEN and the
   date 1804 below. LICENSED BY ACT OF PARLIAMENT.

   These three pennies are all very rare.

HALFPENNIES.

DUBLIN.

✔ 4. *O* : A bishop's head to right, and a crosier. MAY IRELAND
FLOURISH.

   R : A ship sailing, at bottom sprigs of leaves. PAYABLE IN .
   DUBLIN CORK LIMERICK OR NEWRY.

   E : PAYABLE IN DUBLIN CORK OR DERRY.
   Conder, 192 ; 53.—Virt : 34.

   In good condition rare.

4a.   As last, but *E* : IF NEEDFULL APPLY AT THE WAREHOUSE OF
IOHN ORD.

   Very rare with this edge.

4b.   As last, but *E* : Plain (not in collar).

✔ 5. *O* : A bishop's head to right, and a crosier. PAYABLE IN
DUBLIN CORK OR LIMERICK.

   R : A ship sailing, at bottom sprigs of leaves. FOR THE
   HONOR AND USE OF TRADE *

   In good condition rare.

✔ 6. *O* : A figure of Hope standing, leaning upon an anchor.
IRISH HALFPENNY. *Ex* : 1795.

   R : A ship sailing, at bottom sprigs of leaves. NAVIGATION
   AND TRADE.

   E : PAYABLE AT DUBLIN CORK OR BELFAST . × ×.
   Conder, 192 ; 54.—Virt : 4.

6a. As last, but *E* : Plain (not in collar).
This obv. occurs with the following reverses :—

7. *R* : A full face bust.   J. LACKINGTON 1794.   See Middlesex, No. 247.   Conder, 229 ; 158.

✓ 8. *R* : Arms and crest of the United States.   LIBERTY &c.   See Not Local, No. 176.
   E : PAYABLE AT LONDON LIVERPOOL OR BRISTOL.
                                     Conder, 228 ; 154.

✓ 9. *R* : Bust to left in cocked hat.   EARL HOWE &c.   See Not Local, No. 112.
   E : PAYABLE AT LONDON OR BRIGHTON.   Conder, 228 ; 155.

✓ 10. *R* : Full face bust.   PRINCESS OF WALES.   See Not Local, No. 166.   Conder, 228 ; 156.
   See also Anglesea, No. 233; and Cork, No. 16.

11. *O* : A harp upon a rock, and a ship at sea.   GOD GRANT PEACE.
   R : Three castles between oak and palm branches.   DUBLIN HALFPENNY.
   E : PAYABLE IN DUBLIN CORK OR LIMERICK . . .
                           Conder, 192 ; 51.—Virt : 7.

✓ 11a. As last, but *E* : Plain (not in collar).

✓ 12. *O* : A man weaving in a loom.   . . . NOTHING . WITHOUT . INDUSTRY . . .
   R : Shield of arms, crest, a crowned head, between palm branches.   PAYABLE . IN . DUBLIN . NEWRY . OR . BELFAST .
   E : PAYABLE IN DUBLIN CORK OR DERRY.
                           Conder, 192 ; 55.—Virt : 108.

✓ 13.   Similar to last, but from different dies, may be identified by noticing the centre of the crown coming to the last limb of the N, whereas in the former it was under the dot.
   E : Plain (not in collar).   Conder, 192 ; 56.
   The obv. of No. 12 occurs with the following reverses:—

14. *R* : A crown radiated, &c.   See Not Local, No. 123.
                                     Conder, 285 ; 214.

15. *R* : The Prince of Wales' crest, &c.   See No. 115.

✓ 16. *R* : A cypher *H S & Co.* &c.   See No. 115.
                                     Conder, 283 ; 191.

17. *R* : Arms, crest, a windlass, &c.   See Wicklow, No. 1.
   See also Essex, No. 40; *Munster, Nos.* 7 *and* 16; *and Wicklow, Nos.* 42 *and* 47.

✓ 18. *O* : Arms, crest a canister, between laurel branches.   IRISH . HALFPENNY . TOKEN . 1796.
   R : A female standing, holding an anchor and a quadrant.   FOR . THE . GOOD . OF . TRADE.   Conder, 229 ; 159.
   For this reverse, see also No. 101; and Cork, No. 17.
   This obv. occurs with the following reverses :—

19. *R* : Arms, &c.   As No. 13.
   E : YORK BUILT A.M. 1223 CATHEDRAL REBUILT A.D. 1075.

√ 19*a*.   As last, but *E* : Plain (not in collar).

Conder, 283 ; 189.

√ 20. *R*: A cypher *H S & Co.* &c.   See No. 117.

       E: PAYABLE IN DUBLIN OR LONDON.

21. *R*: Bust of Orchard.   See Middlesex, No. 285.

Conder, 283 ; 187.

√ 22. *R*: Arms of London, &c., in an ornamental circle.   See
       Middlesex, No. 341.   Conder, 283 ; 190.

√ 23. *R*: A man with pipe and mug.   SR. GEORGE COOK &c.   See
       Surrey, No. 15.   Conder, 283 ; 188.

       See also Cork, No. 9 ; and Munster, Nos. 8 and 17.

B. O. B.

√ 24. *O*: A spinning wheel.   BY + LABOUR + ONLY + WE + PROSPER +
      R: A cypher *B O B*.   HOUSE . OF . INDUSTRY . HALFPENNY .

Brewer's.

25. *O*: The arms of France crowned, 74 under.   IOHN . BREWER .
       FRENCH . ARMS . DUBLIN.

     R: DEALER | IN . FOREIGN | WINES AND | SPIRITOUS | LIQUORS.
       In five lines.

     E: Milled.

√ 25*a*.   As last, but *E*: Plain (not in collar).

Conder, 193 ; 63.—Virt: 197.

Camac Kyan and Camac's.

√ 26. *O*: A female seated holding a harp with *six* strings, the
       head of the figure touches the letter c of "ACT."
       INCORPORATED BY ACT OF PARLIAMENT 1792.

     R: A cypher *H M Co.*   CAMAC KYAN AND CAMAC   HALFPENNY.
     E: PAYABLE IN DUBLIN OR AT BALLYMURTAGH.

Conder, 187 ; 1.—Virt: 18.

26*a*.   As last, but *E*: PAYABLE AT BANBURY OXFORD OR READING.

26*b*.   „   „   *E*: M. ABEL   S. PRENTICE   S. DELL.

26*c*.   „   „   *E*: PAYABLE AT IOHN MATHEWS'S.

26*d*.   „   „   *E*: Milled.

√ 27. *O*: The head of figure comes under, and some distance from
       the A in "ACT."   There is a period at end of legend,
       which there is not in No. 26, and there are *eight*
       strings to the harp.

     R: Differs in shape of letters in cypher, and several other
       particulars.

     E: PAYABLE AT DUBLIN CORK OR BELFAST.

27*a*.   As last, but *E*: BIRMINGHAM REDRUTH SWANSEA.

27*b*.   „   „   *E*: PAYABLE AT LONDON LIVERPOOL OR BRISTOL.

27*c*.   „   „   *E*: Plain (not in collar).

√ 28. *O*: The head of the figure comes under A similar to last,
       but there is no period, and *ten* strings to harp.

     R: Differs from both the preceding.

     E: As No. 26.

✓ 29.   Similar to last, but with *nine* strings to the harp.
✓ 30.   Similar, but *eight* strings.
✓ 31.   Similar, but *seven* strings.
✓ 32. *O*: The head of figure nearly touches the A.   There are *nine*
       strings to the harp.
   R: Differs from preceding in size and shape of cypher.
   E: PAYABLE IN DUBLIN OR BALLYMURTAGH.
32*a*.   As last, but *E*: Plain (not in collar).
·33.   Similar to last, but with *eight* strings to the harp.
34.   Similar, but *seven* strings.
35.   Similar, but *six* strings.
36.   Similar, but the head is under and nearly touches the A
      and the C.   There are *nine* strings to the harp.
37.   Similar to last, but with *eight* strings to the harp.
37*a*.   As last, but *E*: PAYABLE AT DUBLIN CORK OR BELFAST.
37*b*.   „   „   *E*: Plain (not in collar).
38. *O*: Similar to No. 36, but with *seven* strings to the harp.
   R: Differs in several minor details.
   E: PAYABLE BY S. SAVAGE BACK LANE DUBLIN. The s's are
      retrograde.
38*a*.   As last, but *E*: Plain (not in collar).
39.   Similar to No. 36, but with *six* strings to the harp.
40.   The head of figure comes under and nearly touches the
      C and T.   There are *eight* strings to the harp.
41.   The head touches the T.   There are *fourteen* strings to
      the harp.
42.   Similar to last, but with *nine* strings to the harp.
43.   The head comes under the Y of "BY."   There are *eight*
      strings to the harp.
44. *O*: As before.
   R: As before, but with a dot before and after . HALFPENNY .
   E: PAYABLE IN DUBLIN CORK DERRY OR LIMERICK.
45. *O*: As before, but with a dot between each word of the
      legend.
   R: As last.
   E: PAYABLE IN DUBLIN CORK OR DERRY.
46.   Similar to preceding, but "ACT" is spelt ATC.
47.   Similar to preceding, but the N's in legend on rev. are
      retrograde.
      To this point there has been a gradual falling off in
      point of workmanship, some being evidently only
      imitations; from this, however, all disguise is thrown
      aside, and they appear with various spellings and
      dates, but keeping a semblance of their original,
      although getting worse and worse.

Variations of Name and Date.

48. *O*: Similar to No. 32, but not from the same die.
   R: The legend reads, CALMAC RYAN AND CALMAC.
   E: The same as No. 45.

49. *O*: and *E*: The same as last.
    R: The legend reads, CANAC ROAN AND CANAC.
                                     Conder, 188 ; 11.

49*a*.   As last but *E*: PAYABLE IN DUBLIN OR BALLISHANNON.

✓ 50. *O*: Similar to No. 45, a dot between each word of legend.
                                     Conder, 189 ; 19.
    R: Legend reads, CANAC . RYAN . AND . CANAC → ✳ HALFPENNY.←
    E: As No. 44.   Conder, 188 ; 10.

51.   Similar to last, but without dots, arrowheads, or star.

52. *O*: A female as before holding a harp with seven strings.
    INDUSTRY HAS ITS SURE REWARD . 1792.
    R: Legend reads, CANAC . RYAN . AND . CANAC . HALFPENNY .
    E: PAYABLE IN DUBLIN CORK OR DERBY ○ ○ ○ ○
                                       Conder, 189 ; 18.

53.   Similar to No. 50, but without dots in any part of legend.

✓ 54. *O*: Harp has six strings, and a dot between each word of legend.
    R: Legend reads, CANAC ↓ RYAN ↓ AND ↓ CANAC . HALFPENNY.
    E: PAYABLE IN DUBLIN CORK DERRY OR LIMERICK.

55.   Similar to No. 50, but without dots, and dated 1794.

56.   Harp has eight strings, no dots in legend, dated 1799.

57. *O*: Similar to No. 32, but not from the same die.
    R: Legend reads, CANAC RONE AND CANAC.
    E: The same as No. 52.   Conder, 188 ;. 14.

57*a*.   As last, but *E*: The same as No. 49*a*.

58. *O*: Female holding harp.   INCOPORETED BY ACT OF PARLEE-
    MENT. 1792.
    R: A cypher, *I M Co*.   CAMAK KIAN AND KAMAC HALFPENNY.

59. *O*: The same as last.
    R: A cypher *W H Co*.   KAMAC KIAN AND KAMAC HALFREADY.

60. *O*: Female holding harp.   INCORPORATED BY ACT OF PARLOUR-
    MENT. 1972.
    R: A cypher *H M Co*.   CAMAK RIAN AND CAMAK HALFREADY.

61. *O*: Female holding harp.   INCORPANTNO BY . . . .
    R: A cypher *H M Co*.   KORMAC KRAN AND GRMAC.

62. *O*: Female holding harp.   INCO . . . . . . OF PARLIAMENTMENT.
    R: A cypher *H.M.W* .   CAMAC KIAN AND KAMAC HALFADY.

63. *O*: Female holding harp.   INCORPORATED BY AN AC OF BARLI-
    MENT 1792.
    R: Legend reads, CAMAC TERNER AND CARMA HALFREADY.

64. *O*: Female holding harp.   INCORPORARED BY PARLERMENT
    1792.
    R: A cypher *H.M.C* . PAYABLE AT TUME DUBLIN HALFREADY.

65. *O*: Female holding harp.   INCORPORATED BY AN ACT 1792.
    R: A cypher *H.M.Co*.   KAMUC KYAN AND KAMUC HALFPENNY.
    E: PAYABLE AT DUBLIN CORK DERRY OR LIMERICK.
                                       Conder, 188 ; 17.

65*a*.   As last, but *E*: PASSABLE EVERYWHERE.

ᵛ 66. *O*: Female holding harp. INCORPORATED BY PARLIAMENT 1793.
    R: Cypher as before. CAMAC KYAN AND CAMAC   HALFPENNY.
    E: PAYABLE IN DUBLIN CORK OR DERRY.
ᵛ 67.   Female, &c., as before. A good imitation of No. 26, but
      dated 1794.
  68. *O*: Female seated holding a harp. ＊ INCORPORATED ＊ BY ＊
    AN ＊ ACT ＊ 1795.
    R: A good imitation of No. 26.
    E: Same as No. 66.
  69.   As last, but legend on *R*: reads CAMAC RYAN AND CAMAC.
  70.   As last, but cypher *H N Co.* and legend KAMUC KEAN AND
    KAMUC.
  71.   A good imitation of No. 26, but dated 1796.

Varieties.

     The obv. of No. 39 occurs with the following reverses :—
ᵛ 72. *R*: Bust to left. SHAKESPEARE. See Not Local, No. 139.
                        Conder, 236 ; 220.
ᵛ 73. *R*: Bust to left. SHAKESPEAR. See Not Local, No. 143.
                        Conder, 236 ; 221.
  74. *R*: Head, full face. GEO. PRINCE OF WALES. See Not Local,
    No. 157.   Conder, 240 ; 249.
     The rev. of No. 26 appears as an obv. with the following
    reverses :—
✓ 75. *R*: A crowned bust. IOHN OF GAUNT &c. See Lancashire,
    No. 16.
    E: PAYABLE IN ANGLESEY LONDON OR LIVERPOOL.
                     Conder, 223; 108.
ᵛ 76. *R*: Prince of Wales, &c. As on No. 74.
    E: Milled.   Conder, 239 ; 248.
    See also No. 144; Warwickshire, Nos. 307-311; and
    Wicklow, No. 40.

Turner Camac.

  77. *O*: Female seated, holding a harp, which has *nine* strings.
    INCORPORATED BY ACT OF PARLIAMENT 1792.
    R: A cypher *H. M. Co.* TURNER CAMAC CHAIRMAN HALFPENNY.
    E: PAYABLE IN DUBLIN OR BALLYMURTAGH.   Conder, 188; 15.
  78.   Similar, but the harp has *eight* strings.
  78*a*.   As last, but *E*: Plain (not in collar).
ᵛ 79.   Similar, but the harp has *seven* strings.
  79*a*.   As last, but *E*: Plain (not in collar).
  80.   Similar, but the harp has only *six* strings.
  81.   Similar to preceding, but of ruder workmanship; the
    harp has four double strings.
  82. *O*: The same as No. 77.
    R: A cypher *H. M. Co.* TURNE CAMAC CHAIRMAN HALFPENNY.
    E: Of all, as No. 77, excepting those that are plain.
                                 22

Camac Kyan and Camac's. (*Continued.*)

✓ 83. *O*: A crowned female seated, holding a harp, which has *five* strings, before her a still, the projecting part of which points to the lower part of E in "PAYABLE." PAYABLE AT DUBLIN OR BALLYMURTAGH.

    R: A cypher *H. M. Co.* CAMAC . KYAN AND CAMAC ONE HALF-PENNY 1793.   Conder, 190 ; 32.—Virt : 18.

✓ 84.   Similar to last, but a dot after each word of the legend on *R*: excepting after "HALFPENNY" *There are several slight variations in the relative positions of the point of the still and the letter* E.

✓ 85. *O*: Similar, but there are *six* strings to the harp, one of which appears to be broken.

    R: Similar to No. 84, but the *o* of *Co* is strung upon the loop of the *C*.   Conder, 190 ; 33.

86. *O*: Under the female is a spade to left, and a pickaxe to right, the harp has six strings but is in a slightly different position to No. 85, the point of the still comes between the letters L and E.

    R: Similar to No. 85, but no dots in legend, excepting after ONE.   Conder, 190 ; 34.

✓ 87. *O*: Similar to last, but with *ten* strings to the harp, the point of still comes below the E.

    R: Similar to last, but without the *o* to *Co.* and with MOSSOP. F. in small letters just above the date.

88. *O*: Similar to No. 86, but the pickaxe is to left, and the spade to right. The point of the still comes to middle of the L.

    R: As last.   Conder, 190 ; 35.

89. *O*: Similar to No. 86, but without the spade and pickaxe.

    R: As last.

✓ 90. *O*: The same as No. 88.

    R: A cypher *H M C* CAMAC . KYAN . AND . CAMAC ONE . HALFPENNY 1793.

    E: PAYABLE IN DUBLIN OR AT BALLYMURTAGH.

90a.   As last, but *E*: Plain (in collar). Nos. 83-90 are all well designed and executed pieces, Nos. 86-88 being struck in collar.

✓ 91. *O*: A female seated holding a harp, with *thirteen* strings, the date 1794 under, within a circle of leaves.

    R: and *E*: Similar to No. 26. Conder, 190 ; 36.—Virt : 18.

✓ 92.   Similar to last, but the harp has *twelve* strings.

✓ 93.   Similar, but with only *eleven* strings to the harp.

94.   Similar to No. 92, but with a small dot immediately after date. (12 strings.)

95.   Similar to last, but the dot is larger and further from the date.

96.   Similar to last, but with eleven strings to harp.

                            Conder, 191 ; 37.

For another token with *H M Co.* see Cork, No. 4.

Cooley's.

97. *O*: An aged man resting upon an anchor, a ship at sea in the distance. SUCCESS TO COMMERCE.

   R: A beehive and bees upon a shield, a crown above, a spade on each side. PROSPERITY TO THE AGRICULTURE OF IRELAND.

   E: HALFPENNY . PAYABLE . AT . SAMUEL . COOLEYS . DUBLIN . ❋ . *Exceedingly rare, if not unique.*

Cornwell's.

✔ 98. *O*: Bust to left. ALEXR. CORNWELL.

   R: A shield, on which is "FOR TRADE." surmounted by the Prince of Wales' crest, between sprigs of leaves and dividing the date, which is 1795. Conder, 219 ; 80.

Fyan's.

✔ 99. *O*: Figure of Justice standing, holding sword and scales. FOR THE HONOR AND USE OF TRADE.

   R: A bottle labelled BRANDY, and a sugar-loaf, the date 1794 under TALBOT FYAN GROCER POOLBEG STREET DUBLIN ✳

   E: HALFPENNY PAYABLE AT DUBLIN CORK OR DERRY.

   Conder, 191 ; 41.—Virt : 1.

99*a*.   As last, but *E*: PAYABLE AT DUBLIN CORK OR DERRY. ✕.✕.

✔ 100. *O*: A female seated, leaning upon an anchor, holding a cornucopia. MAY IRELAND EVER FLOURISH.

   R: The same as last.

   E: MANUFACTURED BY W. LUTWYCHE BIRMINGHAM.

   Conder, 191 ; 42.

100*a*.   As last, but *E*: PAYABLE IN ANGLESEY LONDON OR LIVERPOOL.

100*b*.   As last, but *E*: PAYABLE AT BANBURY OXFORD OR READING.

100*c*.   „   „   *E*: Milled over various inscriptions.
   This obv. appears again on No. 143, being apparently common to both.

H.

✔ 101. *O*: *H* and a bugle horn upon a shield. PAYABLE . IN . DUBLIN . OR . BELFAST 1795.

   R: A female standing, holding a quadrant, and an anchor. FOR . THE . GOOD . OF . TRADE.

   Conder, 193 ; 59.—Virt : 15.

See also No. 18, *ante.*

102.   Differs from the preceding in the head of the figure coming under the second o of " GOOD," whereas in the former it came under the first. There are several other slight variations.

The obv. of No. 101 occurs with the following reverses :—

103. *R*: Crowned bust. IOHN OF GAUNT &c.   See Lancashire, No. 16.

104. *R*: Bust to left.   ROBERT ORCHARD.   See Middlesex, No. 285.   Conder, 274; 97.

105. *R*: A man with a pipe in his mouth.   SR. GEORGE COOK &c. See Surrey, No. 16.   Conder, 274; 100.

106. *R*: Fame flying, &c.   See Cork, No. 1.   Conder, 274; 96.

107. *R*: A cypher *H. S. Co.* &c.   See No. 115.
     Conder, 274; 95.

108. *R*: A crown radiated, &c.   See Not Local, No. 123.
     Conder, 274; 98.

The rev. of No. 102 appears as an obv. with the following reverses :—

109. *R*: A wheatsheaf, &c.   See Cambridgeshire, No. 17.
     Conder, 282; 179.

110. *R*: Arms of Orchard.   HALFPENNY 1795.   See Middlesex, No. 285.   Conder, 282; 174.

111. *R*: A man weaving in a loom, &c.   See No. 13.
     Conder, 282; 175.

112. *R*: Prince of Wales' crest, &c.   See No. 116.
     Conder, 282; 176.

113. *R*: A wheatsheaf and doves, &c.   See Munster, No. 2.
     Conder, 281; 173.

114. *R*: An anchor and cap of Liberty, &c.   See Not Local, No. 123.   Conder, 282; 178.

See also Cambridgeshire, No. 29; Munster, Nos. 3 and 9; and Wicklow, Nos. 41, 45, and 46.

H. S. Co.

115. *O*: The Prince of Wales' crest, with HALF PENNY on the ribbon instead of the motto. PAYABLE . AT . DUBLIN . CORK . OR . LIMERICK . 1794.

R: A cypher *H. S. Co.* between laurel branches.
     Conder, 193; 60.

116. *O*: Similar to last, but with HALF PENNY divided by the crest and not on the ribbon.

R: Similar, but the branches end with four dots instead of a leaf, the cypher differs slightly also.
     Conder, 193; 61.—Virt: 7.

117.   Similar to last, but of finer workmanship, and the leaves of wreath are divided whilst those of the former are entire.   Conder, 193; 62.

The obverse of No. 116 occurs with the following reverses :—

v 118. *R*: Arms of London. SCALES WEIGHTS & STEELYARDS. See Middlesex, No. 265.　　Conder, 273 ; 90.

v 119. *R*: Bust to left. ROBERT ORCHARD. See Middlesex, No. 285.　　Conder, 273 ; 91.

v 120. *R*: Fame flying, &c. See Cork, No. 1. Conder, 273 ; 89.

v 121. *R*: Arms, crest a crowned head, &c. See *ante*, No. 13.　　Conder, 273 ; 88.

v 122. *R*: A crown, &c. See *ante*, No. 108.　Conder, 273 ; 92.

v 123. *R*: Bust of Bryen Boiroimbe, &c. See Munster, No. 1.　　Conder, 286 ; 221.

v 124. *R*: Laureate bust of William III. in a wreath. See Not Local, No. 14.　　Conder, 274 ; 93.

125. *R*: Wheatsheaf and sickle between doves. See Munster, No. 1.

The rev. of No. 116 appears as an obv. with the following reverse :—

v 126. *R*: Wheatsheaf and doves, &c. See Munster, No. 1.　　Conder, 233 ; 198.

The rev. of No. 117 appears as an obv. with the following reverses :—

127. *R*: A wheatsheaf, &c. See Cambridgeshire, No. 17.　　Conder, 302 ; 391.

v 128. *R*: A wheatsheaf and doves, &c. See Munster, No. 2.　　Conder, 234 ; 199.

129. *R*: An anchor and cap of Liberty, &c. See Not Local, No. 123.　　Conder, 264 ; 11.
See also Nos. 16, 20, 107, and 112, *ante ;* Cambridgeshire, No. 30 ; Middlesex, No. 298 ; Cork, No. 18 ; and Munster, No. 10.

L. & R.

f 130. *O*: A figure of Justice standing, holding sword and scales, dividing the date, which is 17 94. The hand holding the scales is close to the letter L in "LIVE." THE LAND WE LIVE IN. - HALFPENNY.

R: A cypher *L & R* at bottom sprigs, with seven leaves on each side ; the sprigs are tied with a ribbon with a single bow. PRO ME * SI MEREAR * IN ME.

E: PAYABLE IN DUBLIN OR HAROLDS CROSS BUTTON FACTORY *　　Conder, 192 ; 46.—Virt: 1.

v 131. *O*: Similar to last, but the hand holding scales is nearer the I of "LIVE," the dress and sash differ also.

R: and *E*: Same as last.　　Conder, 192.; 47.

v 132. *O*: Similar to No. 130, but with a Maltese cross between each word of the legend.

R: and *E*: Same as last.　　Conder, 192 ; 48.

133. *O*: and *E*: Same as No. 130.
    R: Similar, but there is scarcely any bow to the tie, and there are eight leaves on each sprig.

134. *O*: Slightly different to any of the preceding; the head of the figure which has before been under the WE is now to the left of it, the dress and sash also differ.
    R: Similar, but the wreath is tied with a triple bow, and is shorter, with six leaves on each side, and the legend is more spread.
    E: Same as No. 130.

135. *O*: and *E*: Same as last.
    R: Similar to No. 134, but without the two stars in the legend, the wreath is tied with a triple bow, and there are only five leaves on each sprig.

136. *O*: Same as No. 130.
    R: and *E*: Same as last. These may all be included under Conder, 192; 49.

137. *O*: Figure of Justice standing, holding sword in left hand and scales in right. Date and legend as before.
    R: A cypher *L & R*, within a wreath of oak.
    E: Same as before.   Conder, 192; 50.—Virt: 4.
    Very rare.

M. F. W.

138. *O*: A figure of Hope standing. PROSPERITY TO IRELAND. *Ex*: 1794.
    R: A cypher *M. F. W.* INCORPORATED BY ACT OF PARLIAMENT.
    E: PAY . THE . BEARER . ONE . HALFPENNY . IN . DUBLIN.
         Conder, 192; 52.—Virt: 4.

Pantheon.

139. *O*: View of a building. *Ex*: 1799.
    R: PAYABLE AT THE PANTHEON PHUSITECHNIKON.

140. Similar in all respects, but dated 1802.

Parker's.

141. *O*: Female seated, leaning upon an anchor, and holding a cornucopia. MAY IRELAND EVER FLOURISH.
    R: A register stove. DUBLIN HALFPENNY. *Ex*: 1794.
    E: PAYABLE AT W. PARKER'S OLD BIRMINGHAM WAREHOUSE ×
         Conder, 191; 43.

141a. As last, but *E*: PAYABLE IN DUBLIN OR LONDON.
141b.   ,,   ,, *E*: PAYABLE IN LANCASTER LONDON OR BRISTOL.
141c.   ,,   ,, *E*: Milled.
141d.   ,,   ,, *E*: Plain (not in collar).
142. Similar to No. 141, but from different dies, and dated 1795, and with F. A. in small letters under the feet of the figure.

142*a*.   As last, but *E* : PAYABLE AT DUBLIN OR AT BALLY MURTAGH.

142*b*.   „   „   *E* : Same as No. 141*b*.   Conder, 191 ; 44.

142*c*.   „   „   *E* : Milled.

✓ 143.   *O* : Slightly different in several respects, no small initials under the figure, and a flaw runs through the greater part of legend.

     R : and *E* : Same as No. 142.

144.   *O* : Same as No. 142.

     R : A cypher *H M C*? &c., same as No. 26.

     E : PAYABLE IN DUBLIN OR LONDON.   Conder, 191 ; 45.

✓ 144*a*.   As last, but *E* : PAYABLE IN ANGLESEY LONDON OR LIVER-POOL.

144*b*.   As last, but *E* : Milled over an inscription.

     The obv. of these pieces is similar to that on Fyan's of No. 100, and was apparently common to both. The rev. of No. 144 belongs to the Camac series.

R. L. T. & Co.   (Pro Bono Publico.)

✓ 145.   *O* : A female seated, holding a harp with seven strings. INDUSTRY HAS ITS SURE REWARD. 1792.

     R : A cypher *R. L. T. & Co.*   PRO BONO PUBLICO. The legend on both sides in small letters.

     E : PAYABLE IN DUBLIN CORK OR LIMERICK. Conder, 189 ; 23.

145*a*.   As last, but *E* : Plain.

✓ 146.   *O* : Similar, but the harp has five strings, the legend is in large letters and an apostrophe at IT'S.

     R : and *E* : Same as No. 145.

147.   *O* : Similar to No. 145, but there is a dot after each word of legend, no apostrophe to ITS.

     R : Similar, but letters of both cypher and legend are larger.

     E : PAYABLE IN DUBLIN OR DERRY.   Conder, 189 ; 26.

147*a*.   As last, but *E* : PAYABLE IN DUBLIN CORK DERRY OR LIMERICK.   Conder, 189 ; 27.—Virt : 4.

✓ 148.   *O* : Very nearly like last, the harp has seven strings.

     R : The letters of legend are large as No. 152, with a dot after BONO.

     E : PAYABLE IN DUBLIN CORK OR DERRY o o o o

                                               Conder, 190 ; 30.

✓ 149.   *O* : Similar to No. 145, but the date is in very small figures, and low down, scarcely showing.

     R : Letters of legend very large, the o of "BONO" touches the *C* of the cypher.

     E : Same as last.

150.   *O* : Same as No. 148.

     R : and *E* : Same as last.

✔ 151. *O*: Similar, the workmanship very poor, seven strings to
harp, a dot after each word of legend, and an arrow-
head at commencement.

R: *R. L. T & Co* between two arrow-heads.   . PRO * BONO .
. PUBLICO.

E: PAYABLE IN DUBLIN CORK DERRY OR LIMRICK.

Conder, 190; 28.

✔ 152. *O*: Similar, harp has six strings.   INDUSTRY ↓ HAS . ITS .
SURE ↓ REWARD . 1792.

R: and *E*: Same as last.   Conder, 190; 129.

153. *O*: Similar, harp has seven strings.   INDUSTRY . * . HAS ↓
ITS ↓ SURE . REWARD . 1792.

R: Cypher between arrow-heads.   PRO ↓ BONO . PUBLICO.

E: Same as last.

✔ 154. *O*: Similar to No. 147, but only six strings to harp.

R: °*R L T & C* between two stars.   PRO * BONO .   . PUBLICO.

E: Same as last.

155. *O*: Same as No. 152.

R: and *E*: Same as last.

156. *O*: Same as No. 153.

R: and *E*: Same as last.

157. *O*: Similar to No. 148, but only six strings to harp.

R: Similar to last, but the *o* of *Co* in cypher is in its proper
place.

E: As last.

158. *O*: As before, six strings to harp.   INDUSTRY ↓ HAS ↓ ITS ↓
SURE ↓ REWARD . 1792.

R: Cypher as last.   PRO . BONO * PUBLICO.   .HALFPENNY.

E: Same as last.

✔ 159. *O*: As before, seven strings to harp.·   INDUSTRY HAS ITS
SURE REWARD 1792.   s's retrograde.

R: Cypher smaller.   PRO - BONO - PUBLICO - HALFPENNY. -

E: Same as last.

160. *O*: As before, six strings to harp, legend in large letters,
dot after each word.

R: Shield of arms.   LANCASTER HALFPENNY 1792.   See
Lancashire, No. 9.

E: PAYABLE IN DUBLIN OR BALLISHANNON.

✔ 161. *O*: and *E*: Same as last.

R: Shield of arms.   ASSOCIATED MINERS ARMS.   See Wicklow, No. 37.   Conder, 189; 22.

162. *O*: A rudely executed female figure seated, holding a harp
with six strings.   INCORPORATED . BY . ACT . OF . PARLIA-
MENT . 1792.

R: and *E*: Same as No. 153.

Hibernia.

163. *O* : A female seated, holding a harp. HIBERNIA. *Ex* : 1804.
   R : A ship sailing. FOR THE CONVENIENCE OF TRADE ✶
✓ 164. *O* : Similar to last, but the letters of the legend are closer
   together.
   R : FOR THE | CONVENIENCE | OF | TRADE. In four lines.

W. T. B. & Co.

✓ 165. *O* : A female seated, holding a harp. PAYABLE AT THE PAWN-
   BROKERS OFFICE BISHOP ST.
   R : A cypher *W T B & Co.*, the date 1804 under. LICENCED
   BY ACT OF PARLIAMENT ✶

FINGALL.

✓ 166. *O* : A female seated, holding a harp. FINGALL ❖ HALFPENNY
   ❖ 1804 ❖
   R : A cypher *W H Co.* PAYABLE AT SWORDS OR DUBLIN ✶
   Rare in good condition.

SWORDS.

167. *O* : The same as the rev. of last. See also Cork, No. 3.
   R : Female seated, holding a harp. FOR THE GOOD OF THE
   PUBLIC ✶ 1792 ✶
168.   Similar to last, but dated 1804.
   Both very rare, the earlier date especially so.

FARTHINGS.

DUBLIN.

Begg's.

✓ 169. *O* : A cypher *W. B.*, the date 1797 under.
   R : WM. BEGG | TALLOWCHANDLR. | 91 | MARLBROST. | DUBLIN.
   In five lines.
170. *O* : and *R* : The same as the *rev.* of last.

Bryen's.

171. *O* : Three sugar-loaves suspended. T. O. BRYEN CHURCH
   STREET DUBLIN.
   R : A canister between sugar-loaves. GROCER & TEA DEALER
   1790. Conder, 194; 65.
✓ 172. *O* : Three sugar-loaves suspended. T. O. BRYEN. | .CHURCH.
   | ST. | DUBLIN.
   R : A canister inscribed TEA between sugar-loaves.
   . GROCER & . DEALER . 1790.
   Conder, 194; 66.—Virt: 134.

∨ 173.   Similar to last, but from different dies, and J. O. BRYEN &c.

∨ 174.   *O* : The same as No. 172.

        R : A cask between a bottle and a glass.   DEALER IN WHISKEY.   Conder, 194; 67.

∨ 175.   *O* : The same as last.

        R : A bowl inscribed WHISKEY, a bunch of grapes above, two pipes crossed below.   DEALER IN CANDLES.

                  Conder, 194; 68.—Virt: 165.

Camac's.

∨ 176.   *O* : A female seated, holding a harp.   INCORPORATED BY ACT OF PARLIAMENT.   1792.

        R : A cypher *H M Co.*   TURNER CAMAC CHAIRMAN . FARTHING.

                  Conder, 194; 64.

Hutton's.

∨ 177.   *O* : A coronet.   MAXL. HUTTON . NO. . 101.

        R : Six griffins' heads, a cross below, with a lozenge on either side.   JAMES'S STREET.   Conder, 322; *44.

∨ 178.   *O* : The same as last.

        R : Similar, but without the lozenges by side of cross, and no *fleur-de-lis* before and after legend.

        See also a leaden piece, No. 200.

Murphy's.

∨ 179.   *O* : M. MURPHY. | NO. 8 | WOOD ST. | DUBLIN. | 1796.   In five lines.

        R : The same as No. 172.   Conder, 194; 69.

        This obv. occurs with the following reverses ;—

∨ 180.   *R* : A cask, &c., as No. 174.   Conder, 194; 70.

∨ 181.   *R* : A bowl, &c., as No. 175.   Conder, 194; 71.

∨ 182.   *R* : Two heads.   WE THREE BLOCKHEADS BE 1795.   See Middlesex, No. 753.   Conder, 303; 403.

Miscellaneous.

∨ 183.   *O* : Bust to left laureated.   DAVID . GARRICK . ESQr. 1792.

        R : PAYABLE |. IN DUBLIN or | LONDON 1792.

        E : Milled.   Conder, 194; 72.—Virt: 134.

∨ 184.   *O* : A female seated, holding a harp.   HIBERNIA.

        R : A laureated bust to left.   GOD SAVE THE KING.   See Not Local, No. 187.

        E : Milled.

        This obv. occurs with the following reverses :—

∨ 185.   *R* : Bust to left.   ROBERT ORCHARD.   See Middlesex, No. 760.   Conder, 305; 429.

∨ 186.   *R* : Pandora's breeches, &c.   See Middlesex, No. 803.

                  Conder, 303; 407.

   187.   *R* : Bust of ADML. MACBRIDE.   See Not Local, No. 216.

                  Conder, 250; 54.

188. *R* : An open book, &c.   See Not Local, No. 232.
                                          Conder, 303 ; 406.
189. *R* : End of *P* ☊ *T*, &c.   See Not Local, No. 235.
                                          Conder, 306 ; 438.
190. *R* : A cypher *P. S. Co* from a halfpenny die.   See Middle-
           sex, No. 413.   Conder, 214 ; 34.
191. *R* : A dove and olive branch, also from a halfpenny die.
           See Middlesex, No. 454.   Conder, 214 ; 35.
     The edges of all these are milled.

Percival's.

192. *O* : Similar to No. 176, but not from the same die.
     R : A monogram cypher *A P*.   ANN PERCIVAL DUBLIN.

Leaden Tokens.

In addition to the foregoing there were several leaden
tokens for a farthing issued in Dublin towards the
close of the 18th century as follows :—

193. *O* : ASHLEY | BLUE BOAR | FRANS. ST.   In three lines within
           a raised border.
     R : Blank.
194. *O* : JOHN BOSHELL.   And a flower.
     R : NO. 83 | CHURCH | ST.   In three lines.
195. *O* : P. BYRNE NO. 28.
     R : CH. STRT.
196. *O* : C. COLGAN.
     R : NO. 11 THOMAS ST.
197. *O* : EDWARD DUNN.   And a rose.
     R : NO. 13 DORSET STREET.
198. *O* : WILLIAM FAY.
     R : 114 JAMES'S ST.
199. *O* : PETR. FLEMING.   And a flaming urn.
     R : NO. 101. CH. ST.
200. *O* : Four small crosses between a double circle.   MAXL.
           HUTTON.
     R : 101 JAMES STREET.   And a bird.
201. *O* : THOS. LEONARD.   And a flower.
     R : NO. 41 BRITAIN ST.   And a flower.
202.   Similar to last, but with a pellet instead of a flower on
           both *O* : and *R* :
203. *O* : A lion rampant.   I. LYON and a trefoil below.
     R : 27 FISHERS LANE. within a circle.
204. *O* : A harp.   MORN. MC.DONOUGH *
     R : NO. 14 * BRUNSWICK * ST.
205. *O* : JOHN MC.GRANE.   And two flowers.
     R : NO. 10 BOOT LANE.   And three flowers.
206. *O* : A sprig in the centre.   PAT ROONEY.
     R : NO. 101 CH. ST.   With a scroll under the bottom line.
207. *O* : R . SIMMONS BARRACK S*T*
     R : GROCERIES WINES SPIRITS

208. *O* : J. T. NO. 32.   (For John Taylor.)
  R : 32 in the centre.   UPPER CHURCH: ST. *

209. *O* : TYRRELL NO. 9 T. C.   (For Thomas Court.)
  R : Blank.   This is an octagonal piece.

210. *O* : ROBT. WHITE.
  R : 106 PILL LANE.
   This also occurs counter-marked *R. W.* in script
   characters.

349

King's County.

THIRTEENPENCE.

CHARLEVILLE.

✓ 1. *O*: Arms and supporters, &c., of the Earl of Charleville. CHARLEVILLE above, FOREST below. INDUSTRY SHALL PROSPER . 1802.

R: PAYABLE AT | TULLAMOORE | FIRST TUESDAY | IN EACH | MONTH. in five lines, a sprig above and below. ONE SHILLING AND ONE PENNY.

Munster.

HALFPENNIES.

1. *O* : A crowned head in profile, and sceptre. BRYEN BOIROIMBE
   KING OF MUNSTER.
   R : A wheatsheaf and sickle, between two doves. PEACE
   AND PLENTY HALFPENNY.
   E : PAYABLE IN DUBLIN CORK OR DERRY.
1a. As last, but *E* : Plain (not in collar).   Conder, 195 ; 1.
2. *O* : Similar, but the front point of crown touches the K of
   " KING," and there is a circle of very fine dots outside
   legend.
   R : Similar, but the wheatsheaf is farther from legend, and
   the tail of the dove to right is below the Y in " HALF-
   PENNY," whereas in the former it was above.   There
   are several other minor distinctions.
   E : Milled.
2a. As last, but *E* : Plain (not in collar).   Conder, 195 ; 2.
   It may also be noted that No. 2 is better struck and
   finer work than No. 1.
   The obv. of No. 1 occurs with the following reverse :—
3. *R* : *H* and a bugle horn, &c.   See Dublin, No. 101.
                              Conder, 193 ; 57.—Virt : 1.
   The obv. of No. 2 occurs with the following reverses:—
4. *R* : A wheatsheaf. PEACE PLENTY & LIBERTY. See Cambridgeshire, No. 17.   Conder, 286 ; 223.
5. *R* : Bust of " ROBERT ORCHARD." See Middlesex, No. 286.
                              Conder, 286 ; 227.
6. *R* : Orchard's Arms.   See Middlesex, No. 285.
                              Conder, 286 ; 228.
7. *R* : Man weaving in a loom, &c.   See Dublin, No. 13.
   E : PAYABLE AT THE WAREHOUSE LIVERPOOL.
7a. As last, but *E* : Plain (not in collar). Conder, 286 ; 226.
8. *R* : Arms, crest a canister.   See Dublin, No. 19.
   E : PAYABLE IN DUBLIN OR LONDON.
8a. As last, but *E* : Plain (not in collar). Conder, 286 ; 225.
9. *R* : *H* and a bugle horn, &c.   See Dublin, No. 101.
                              Conder, 193 ; 58.
10. *R* : Anchor and cap of Liberty, &c.   See Not Local, No. 123.
                              Conder, 286 ; 222.
11. *R* : A crown radiated, &c.   See Not Local, No. 123.
   The rev. of No. 2 appears as an obv. with the
   following reverses :—
12. *R* : The arms of London. SCALES WEIGHTS, &c. See Middlesex, No. 265.   Conder, 302 ; 399.
13. *R* : Bust of Orchard, as No. 5.

✓ 14. R: A fat man at table. ENGLISH SLAVERY. See Middlesex,
  No. 591. Conder, 276; 118.
✓ 15. R: A lean man on the ground. FRENCH LIBERTY. See
  Middlesex, No. 591. Conder, 279; 147.
  16. R: A man weaving, &c. As No. 7.
  17. R: Arms, crest a canister. As No. 8.
  18. R: An anchor, &c. As No. 10.
✓ 19. R: A crown, &c. · As No. 11. Conder, 285; 211.
  See also Cambridgeshire, No. 31; Middlesex, Nos. 270,
    294, and 344; Cork, Nos. 10, 14, and 15; and Dublin,
    Nos. 113, 123, and 128.

Wexford.

HALFPENNIES.

ENNISCORTHY.

✓ 1.   *O*: A castle by the sea, having a gateway with portcullis, the latter being formed of seven perpendicular bars, with one horizontal one running through from side to side, the whole within a sunken oval. PAYABLE AT THE BANK OF R. W. ENNISCORTHY.

      R: A monogram *R. W.*, upon a shield suspended from the branch of a tree, with a landscape in the distance. A.D. 1800.

✓ 2.   Similar to last, but the left-hand bar of portcullis is disconnected and the horizontal bar does not run through.

✓ 3.   Similar to No. 1, but with six perpendicular bars only.

✓ 4.   Similar to last, but the horizontal bar does not run through and the perpendicular bar on left hand is disconnected, the same as on No. 2.

      There are several variations of Nos. 3 and 4 too minute to specify.

✓ 5.   *O*: A cypher *R. W.*, crest a peacock. FOR CHANGE above, the date 1800 below.

      R: PAYABLE | AT | WOODCOCK'S | BANK | ENNISCORTHY in five lines, the top and bottom ones curved.

✓ 6.   Similar to last, but the apostrophe is on the top of the s and touching it, the bottom line of the legend is more spread, the Y touching the s.

✓ 7.   Similar, but instead of an apostrophe there is a pear-like drop midway between the K and s.

  8.   Similar to No. 5, but the top of the crest touches the first limb of the letter H in "CHANGE."

✓ 9.   Similar to last, but instead of the apostrophe there is a small annulet.

      In Nos. 8 and 9, the centre line of legend on *R*: is more spread out than in the former ones, coming quite to the edge of the coin. There are several variations in Nos. 5-9 too small to specify.

See also Middlesex, No. 238.

𝔚𝔦𝔠𝔨𝔩𝔬𝔴.

HALFPENNIES.

CRONEBANE.

Irish Mine Co. 1789.

✓ 1. *O*: A bishop's head in profile, and a crosier tied with a bow of ribbon, the end of the upper one comes just under the Y of "HALFPENNY." CRONEBANE HALFPENNY.

  R: Shield of arms, crest a windlass, the handle of which nearly touches the second limb of R, the date 1789 is divided by the shield, the 1 of date comes level with middle of T. ASSOCIATED IRISH MINE COMPANY.

  E: PAYABLE AT CRONEBANE LODGE OR IN DUBLIN . ✕ .

2. *O*: Similar to last, but the upper ribbon comes to the centre of the foot of the Y.

  R: The bend of the handle of windlass touches the first limb of the R, the 1 in date to lower part of T.

✓ 3.   Similar to last, but the handle touches the second limb of the R.

4.   Similar to last, but the 1 in date comes above the foot of the T.

5. *O*: The upper ribbon comes to the top of the Y.

  R: Handle as in No. 3, the 1 of date comes to centre of foot of the T.

6. *O*: The ends of ribbon come one on either side of foot of the Y.

  R: The top of the 1 in date comes level with the second limb of A.

✓ 7.   Similar, but the 1 comes between the A and the T.

8.   Similar, but the end of the upper ribbon touches the Y.

9.   Similar, but the top of the 1 comes to lower part of foot of the T.

10.   Similar, but the top of the 1 comes to middle part of foot of the T.

11.   Similar, but the top of the 1 comes to top part of foot of the T.

12.   Similar to No. 10 in most respects, but the foot of the letter Y in "HALFPENNY" being gone makes it look like a V.

13. *O*: The end of upper ribbon comes to the last limb of N and the bottom one to the Y.

  R: The handle touches second limb of R, and the 1 of date comes to lower part of T.

23

14. *O*: Same as last.
     R: Similar, but tho handle touches the first limb of R, the top of the 1 comes to middle of the T.

15. *O*: Same as last.
     R: The handle touches second limb of R, the 1 comes to top part of T.
     There is a flaw runs through the latter part of " ASSOCIATED."

16. *O*: The crosier is quite different to any others, being plain at the end, and the ribbons hang one on either side of the handle.
     R: The handle is farther from the legend, the top of the 1 in date comes to the middle of the T.
     All these have the same edge as No. 1.

17. *O*: and *R*: very nearly like No. 9, but not the same dies.
     E: Plain (not in collar).
     This is of exceptionally fine workmanship, and a bronze proof.

18. *O*: A poor imitation of No. 1, the crosier touching the bishop's nose.
     R: Similar to preceding, but the 1 of date comes to first limb of A, and the 9 opposite the o.
     E: Plain (not in collar).
     All these are included in Conder under 196; 1.—*Virt:* 34. *There are several other variations of die too minute to specify.*

19. *O*: Similar to the last, but the crosier does not quite touch.
     R: " MINE " and " COMPANY " are joined so as to form one word, the top of 1 comes to middle of T.
     E: PASSABLE EVERY WHERE . .   Conder, 196 ; 2.

20. *O*: A bishop's head in profile.   CRONEBANE HALFPENNY.
     R: and *E*: Same as No. 1.   Conder, 196 ; 3.

1793.

21. *O*: Similar to No. 1, the crosier has a bow but no ribbons hanging down.
     R: Similar, but dated 1793.
     E: PAYABLE IN LONDON LIVERPOOL OR BRISTOL.

21a.   As last, but *E*: Milled.   Conder, 197 ; 12.
     See also Anglesea, No. 227.

Miners' Arms (No date).

22. *O*: Similar to No. 1, but without a period at end of legend.
     R: Shield of arms, crest a windlass. ASSOCIATED IRISH MINERS ARMS.
     E: PAYABLE AT DUBLIN CORK OR BELFAST . ✕ ✕.

23.   Similar to last, but with a period at end of legend. The end of the top ribbon points to the middle of foot of the Y.

24.   Similar to last in having period, but the end of the upper ribbon comes quite closely between the foot of the Y and the period. There is a flaw just above the R of " IRISH " on these pieces.

∨ 24a.   As last, but *E* : PAYABLE IN ANGLESEY LONDON OR LIVERPOOL.

24b.   As last, but *E* : PAYABLE IN HULL AND IN LONDON.

24c.   ,,   ,,   *E* : PAYABLE AT LONDON LIVERPOOL OR BRISTOL.

24d.   ,,   ,,   *E* : Plain (not in collar).

These are all included in Conder under No. 10, on page 197.

∨ 25.   *O* : A poor copy of No. 23.

     R : Similar, but the left handle of windlass is broken.

     E : PAYABLE IN DUBLIN CORK OR DERRY.   Conder, 197 ; 11.

Miners' Arms, 1789.
Without Crosier. Straight 1.

26.   *O* : A bishop's head in profile. CRONEBANE HALFPENNY There is no period.

     R : Shield of arms, crest a windlass, 17-89, the 1 straight, pointed at top, flat at bottom. Legend as No. 22.

     E : PAYABLE ✕ AT ✕ CRONEBANE ✕ OR ✱ IN ✱ DUBLIN ✕ O ✕

                                                  Virt : 34.

26a.   As last, but *E* : PAYABLE AT THE BLACK HORSE TOWER HILL.

Y 26b.   As last, but *E* : PAYABLE AT BIRMINGHAM LONDON OR BRISTOL.   Conder, 197 ; 9.

26c.   As last, but *E* : PAYABLE IN LANCASTER LONDON OR BRISTOL.

26d.   ,,   ,,   *E* : PAYABLE BY THOMAS BALL SLEAFORD.

26e.   ,,   ,,   *E* : PAYABLE BY I. SIMMONS STAPLEHURST.

26f.   ,,   ,,   *E* : Plain (not in collar).

With Crosier. Straight 1.

27. *O* : A bishop's head as before, with crosier, the ends of ribbon come one to foot of Y, and one to period.

     R : Same as No. 26.

     E : PAYABLE IN DUBLIN OR LONDON +.+

27a.   As last, but *E* : Same as No. 26c.

                                     Conder, 196 ; 7.—Virt : 34

27b.   ,,   ,,   *E* : PAYABLE IN LANCASTER LONDON OR LIVERPOOL.

27c.   As last, but *E* : Plain (not in collar).

28. *O* : Similar to last, excepting that the end of the lower ribbon hangs down straight, whereas in the preceding one it curls round towards the period.

     R : The top of the 1 in date is flat, and comes to the middle of the A.

     E : PAYABLE AT ANGLESEA LONDON OR BRISTOL.

                                         Conder, 196 ; 6.

29. *O*: The end of upper ribbon touches lower part of Y, the
other hangs down straight, below the period.
R: Same as last.
E: Same as No. 26.
29*a*.   Same as last, but *E*: without the ornaments between
the words.
∨ 29*b*.   Same as last, but *E*: Same as No. 26*b*.

With Crosier. Curved 1.

∨ 30. *O*: As before, but the crosier comes quite upon the period,
both ends of ribbon above the Y.
R: The 1 of date is curved, the 9 of date comes to the ʙ,
the handle touches the ɪ.
E: PAYABLE AT CLOUGHER OR IN DUBLIN – × × –
31. *O*: The crosier nearly touches the period, the ends of
ribbon on each side of the foot of Y.
R: Similar to last, but there is a flaw at the first and last
letters of legend by which it may be distinguished.
E: Same as last.
31*a*.   As last, but *E*: PAYABLE IN HULL AND IN LONDON.
∨ 31*b*.   „   „   *E*: PAYABLE IN LONDON BRISTOL & LANCASTER.
Conder, 196 ; 4.
31*c*.   „   „   *E*: Plain (not in collar).
32.   Similar in all respects, but the shading of the arms
scarcely shows.   Conder, 196 ; 5.
32*a*.   As last, but *E*: Same as 31*a*.
32*b*.   „   „   *E*: Same as 31*b*.
32*c*.   „   „   *E*: AT EDWARD SARGEANTS PORTSEA.
33. *O*: Similar to No. 35, but the period is farther from the
crosier, and the ends of ribbon do not nearly reach
to the letter Y.
R: and *E*: Same as No. 31.
34. *O*: The period is farther still from the crosier, and the
ends of ribbon shorter. There is usually a flaw
under the bust by which this may be recognized.
R: The handle comes just under, but does not touch the
first limb of the ʀ, the 1 of date comes between the
ɪ and ᴀ, and the 9 by the s.
E: Same as No. 30.
∨ 34*a*.   As last, but *E*: CURRENT EVERY WHERE.
34*b*.   „   „   *E*: Engrailed.
34*c*.   „   „   *E*: Milled.   Conder, 196 ; 8.
34*d*.   „   „   *E*: Plain (not in collar).

1794.

∨ 35. *O*: Similar to No. 26, but from different die.
R: As before, but dated 17—94.
E: PAYABLE AT DUBLIN CORK OR BELFAST . × × .
Conder, 197 ; 13.

1795.

✓ 36. *O*: Similar, but from different die, and not so well executed as last.

    R: As before, but dated 17—95. The 5 almost touches the A of "ARMS."

    E: PAYABLE IN DUBLIN CORK OR DERRY . . . Conder, 197 ; 14.

✓ 37. *O*: Similar to last, but with a period after "CRONEBANE." and none after "HALFPENNY"

    R: Similar to last, but the 5 is opposite the s of "MINERS."

    E: PAYABLE IN DUBLIN OR IN BALLISHANNON + +

                                       Conder, 197 ; 16.

Varieties.

The obv. of No. 1 occurs with the following reverses:—

38. *R*: PAYABLE AT THE RESIDENCE OF, &c. See Middlesex, No. 277.   Conder, 198 ; 26.

✓ 39. *R*: Bishop Blaze and lamb. See Yorkshire, No. 47.

    E: PAYABLE AT LIVERPOOL OR BRISTOL.   Conder, 198 ; 25.

The obv. of No. 18 occurs with the following reverses:—

40. *R*: A cypher *H M Co.* &c. See Dublin, No. 26.

    E: PAYABLE IN DUBLIN DERRY OR LIMRICK.   Conder, 197 ; 17.

✓ 41. *R*: *H* and a bugle horn, &c. See Dublin, No. 101.

42. *R*: Arms, crest, a crowned head, &c. See Dublin, No. 12.

    E: PAYABLE IN DUBLIN CORK OR DERRY.   Conder, 198; 20.

42*a*. As last, but *E*: Plain (not in collar).

The obv. of No. 26 occurs with the following reverse:—

✓ 43. *R*: Figure of Justice. FOR CHANGE NOT FRAUD. See Suffolk, No. 20.

The obv. of No. 29 occurs with the following reverse:—

44. *R*: The same as last.

    E: PAYABLE IN LANCASTER LONDON OR BRISTOL.

                                     Conder, 198 ; 23.

45. *O*: Bust similar to No. 26, CRONEBANE NEW + MINE ✱

    R: The same as No. 41.

✓ 46. *O*: A very different bust, in very high relief.

    R: The same as No. 41.   Conder, 197; 19.

✓ 47. *O*: The same as last.

    R: The same as No. 42.   Conder, 198 ; 21.

48. *O*: Very similar to No. 33, but from a different die.

    R: Female seated holding a harp. HIBERNIA. *Ex*: A small ornament.

    E: PAYABLE IN LONDON BRISTOL & LANCASTER.

✓ 48*a*. As last, but *E*: Engrailed. Conder, 198 ; 24.—Virt: 35.

The rev. of No. 22 appears as an obv. with the following reverses :—

✓ 49. *R*: Dove with olive branch, &c. See Middlesex, No. 203.

50. *R*: Bust of Earl Howe, &c. See Not Local, No. 112.

The rev. of No. 28 appears as an obv. with the following
reverses :—

✔ 51. *R*: Ship in full sail, &c. See Durham, No. 4.
  E: PAYABLE IN LONDON.   The remainder engrailed.
                                   Conder, 229 ; 162.

  52. *R*: Bust of Earl Howe, &c. See Hampshire, No. 9.
  E: CURRENT EVERY WHERE.

  52*a*.   As last, but *E*: Plain (not in collar). Conder, 225 ; 129.

✔ 53. *R*: Bust of John of Gaunt, &c. See Lancashire, No. 14.
  E: PAYABLE IN LONDON BRISTOL & LANCASTER.
                                   Conder, 222 ; 103.

  54. *R*: Dove with olive branch. As No. 49. Conder, 235 ; 209.

  55. *R*: St. Andrew with his cross, &c. See Lothian, No. 16.
                                   Conder, 229 ; 160.

The rev. of No. 34 appears as an obv. with the following
reverse :—

✔ 56. *R*: Hibernia, &c. The same as No. 48.
  E: PAYABLE AT THE WAREHOUSE LIVERPOOL × × ×
                                   Conder, 229 ; 161.

And this rev. appears as an obv. with the following
reverse :—

✔ 57. *R*: Bust of John of Gaunt, &c. The same as No. 54.
  E: The same as No. 52.   Conder, 222 ; 104.
  See also Lancashire, No. 70; Warwickshire, No. 191;
  and Dublin, Nos. 17 and 161.

Not Local.

UNDER this heading will be placed all those pieces which show no name of issuer or place of issue, whether on obverse or reverse; some may bear such upon their edge, but in every case where this occurs the attribution is false, and arises doubtless from the tokens having been struck on flans already bearing an inscription upon them. Pye says in a note to plate 51, upon which he figures some of this series: "These were sold in small quantities to any person who would purchase them."

There are also described here some pieces which were in all probability originally made as medalets, but from the scarcity of small change came into use as tokens, the majority of them appearing in such condition as to show evident signs of having been in circulation.

Not Local.

TWOPENCE.

1. *O* : A trooper standing, leaning against his horse, within an
    inner circle. LOYAL YEOMAN. PRO REGE LEGE ET PATRIA.
   R : I PROMISE | TO PAY TO THE HON:BLE. | GEO: YEOMAN OR
    BEARER | THE SUM OF TWOPENCE | ON THE PERFECT
    ESTABLISHMENT OF | PEACE & UNANIMITY | FOR KING
    LORDS | AND COMMONS | *John Bull.* In ten lines.
    OLD ENGLAND 2 . MARCH . 1798 . ENTD. JAS. LOYAL.
    incused on a raised rim.
    This piece is exceedingly rare.

PENNIES.

British.

✔ 2. *O* : Laureate bust to right, D.F. under it.   GEORGIUS III. DE .
    GR . MA . BR . FR . ET HI . REX.
   R : A serpent entwined around an altar, the centre leg of
    tripod is in front, an olive branch and ball lying upon
    the ground. FELICITAS PUBLICA ✱ *Ex* : SAL . REG .
    REST . 1789.
✔ 3. *O* : The same as last.
   R : Similar to last, but the centre leg of tripod is behind.
✔ 4. *O* : Similar bust, DROZ . F . under it.   GEORGIVS III . D . G .
    MAG . BR . FR . ET HIB . REX.
   R : The same as last.   Conder, 199 ; 2.
✔ 5. *O* : A very different bust, GEORGIVS . . III . D . G . REX .
    within an ornamental border.
   R : A cypher *T G*, palm branches crossed under. BRITISH
    PENNY . 1797 . upon a raised rim.
   E : I PROMISE TO PAY ON DEMAND THE BEARER ONE PENNY ✕
                                      Conder, 200 ; 8.
    This is the reverse of Middlesex, No. 25. See also
    No. 17.
6. *O* : Bust to left, C . I . 1789 under it.   GEORGIVS III. REX.
   R : A crowned harp between sprigs of laurel upon an island,
    radiated   Conder, 200 ; 3.
7. *O* : The same as last.
   R : A crown between a rose and thistle upon an island,
    radiated. On a label, TO TRANSPORT TURNED A PEOPLE'S
    FEARS. *Ex* : MDCCLXXXIX.   Conder, 200 ; 4.
8. *O* : The same as last.
   R : LOST TO BRITANNIA'S HOPES BUT TO HER PRAYERS RESTORED.
                                      Conder, 200 ; 6.

✓ 9. *O*: A similar bust to the last, but turned to the right.
GEORGIUS . III DEI . GRATIA .

R: A crown within a garter, radiated. KING & CONSTITUTION.

10. *O*: As last, but on a smaller blank.

R: Similar, but the radiation touches the " & " at a different place.

✓ 11. *O*: Bust to right between G III, the date 1788 and C . I . under it. GOD SAVE THE KING.

R: WHEN | WE FORGET | HIM. | MAY GOD FORGET | US! | Thurlow. In six lines. *Ex*: RESTORED TO HEALTH MARCH . 1789.

✓ 12. *O*: The same as last.

R: Bust to right (of William III) between W III The date 1688 under. CENTENARY OF THE GLORIOUS REVOLUTION.

✓ 13. *O*: A small laureate bust of William III, the date 1688 under.

R: Britannia seated. IN . COMMEMORATION . OF . THE . REVOLU-TION. JACOBS.   Conder, 206; 41.

✓ 14. *O*: Bust and date as last, a thick wreath of oak added.

R: A Lion rampant supporting the English shield. REVOLUTION PENNY.   Conder, 207; 42.

15. *O*: Bust of William III., and date 1688 as before. CONSTI-TUTIONAL * CLUB *

R: Blank.

✓ 16. *O*: A larger and very different bust. WILLIAM . III . OF . BLESSED . MEMORY.

R: BRITONS | NEVER | WILL BE | SLAVES. Within a circle of leaves. REVOLUTION . JUBILEE . NOVR. IV. 1788.
    Conder, 207 ; 43.

17. *O*: Bust to left. * DUKE * OF * * YORK *

R: and *E*: The same as No. 5.   Conder, 200; 9.

Cabbage Society.

✓ 18. *O*: A cauliflower. CABBAGE SOCIETY *

R: A star formed of six leaves. PURIM * 1796 *
Su edge .   Conder, 201; 11.

There are two smaller sizes of similar design, dated 1780, *struck in brass, which were not issued as tokens.*

Fox.

See Middlesex, Nos. 145-148.

France (Map of).

✓ 19. *O*: A MAP OF THE PRESENT STATE OF FRANCE. France divided by serpents, the Land in mourning, Throne upside down, Honor under foot, Law and Justice, bubbles, Fire in every corner, &c.

R: MAY MONARCHY FLOURISH AND ANARCHY PERISH EVER-LASTINGLY.

Greatheads.

✔ 20. *O*: Three men in a cart under a gallows. WRONG HEADS-
RIGHT HEADS GREAT HEADS. *Ex*: MEETING AT WARWICK
MAY 31 1797.

     R: AS IF FROM TEMPLE BAR SOME HEAD WAS CUT, AND ON
REBELLING TRUNK THE FACE WAS PUT.

Conder, 203; 22.

Howard.

✔ 21. *O*: Bust to left, W. MAINWARING . FECIT under it. IOHN
HOWARD . F . R . S .

     R: HAUD ULLI | MORTALIUM SUMMA | ERGA HUMANUM GENUS |
BENEVOLENTIA | SECUNDUS. In five lines. *Ex*: OBT.
JAN . 20 . 1790 ÆT . 55.   Conder, 204; 25.

Howe.

✔ 22. *O*: Bust to left, a laurel wreath under . ADMIRAL EARL HOWE.

     R: THE MEMORABLE | VICTORY GAINED OVER | THE FRENCH
FLEET | JUNE . 1 . 1794. In four lines with a laurel
wreath under.   Conder, 204; 26.

Johnson.

✔ 23. *O*: Bust to left. THOMAS IOHNSON.

     R: BELLA ! HORRIDA BELLA ! in a circle of leaves. SCIENCE
AND INTREPIDITY. *Ex*: 1789.   Conder, 205; 29.

Lion and Lamb.

✔ 24. *O*: A Lion and Lamb lying down together. UNANIMITY. TO .
ALL . MANKIND.

     R: A Dove with olive beneath. PEACE AND PLENTY. *Ex*:
1797.

Loggerheads.

✔ 25. *O*: A cart under a gallows, three men hanging. THE END
OF THREE LOGGERHEADS.

     R: AS IF FROM NEWGATE CELLS THREE FELONS LED, AND ON THE
NEW DROP TY'D TILL DEAD, DEAD, DEAD. Conder, 205; 30.

Nelson.

✔ 26. *O*: Bust to left. ADMIRAL . SR. HORATIO NELSON K.B.

     R: IN . MEMORY . OF . THE . ACTION . OFF . THE . NILE . AUGT.
1 . 1798. TAKEN . 9 SAIL OF THE LINE 3 DESTROYED.

     E: I PROMISE TO PAY ON DEMAND THE BEARER ONE PENNY ×

26*a*.   As last, but *E*: Plain (in collar).

Paine.

ᵛ 27. *O*: Bust to right. THOMAS PAINE.
   R: Æsop's fable of the mountain in labour. THE MOUNTAIN
       IN LABOUR. *Ex*: 1793.   Conder, 205; 34.

Perrins.

ᵛ 28. *O*: Bust to right. ISAAC PERRINS.
   R: BELLA! HORRIDA BELLA! in a circle of leaves. STRENGTH
       AND MAGNANIMITY. *Ex*: 1789.   Conder, 205; 35.

Pitt.

29. *O*: Bust to right, 1789 under. THE RIGHT HON. W. PITT.
   R: THE SUPPORTER OF THE CONSTITUTION OF GREAT BRITAIN.
                                            Conder, 206; 36.
30. *O*: The same as last.
   R: Similar to last, but with a small lion at end of legend.
ᵛ 31. *O*: A slightly different bust, c . I and 1789 under it. THE
       RIGHT HONBLE. WILLM. PITT.
   R: The same as No. 29.
32. *O*: The same as last.
   R: The same as No. 30.   Conder, 206; 37.

Romaine.

ᵛ 33. *O*: Three-quarter bust to left. REVD. WILLM. ROMAINE . M . A.
   R: BUT I TRUSTED IN THEE O LORD I SAID THOU ART my GOD.
       PSALM . 31 . 14. *Ex*: OB : JULY . 26 . 1795 Æ 81 YEARS.
                                            Conder, 207; 44.
ᵛ 34. *O*: Three-quarter bust to right. REVD. W. ROMAINE . M . A .
       I. M. F.
   R: Figure of Faith standing, pointing upward. THE JUST
       SHALL LIVE BY HIS FAITH. *Ex*: D . JULY 26 . 1795 .
       A . 81.   Conder, 207; 45.

Sedition.

ᵛ 35. *O*: The monster Sedition flying, with four imps. OUR FOOD
       IS SEDITION.
   R: A snake in the grass, a radiation above. NOURISHED TO
       TORMENT. *Ex*: JULY 11 . 1791.   Conder, 207; 47.

Sheridan.

ᵛ 36. *O*: Three-quarter bust to left. R. B. SHERIDAN ESQ . M P.
   R: RESISTLESS | WIT WHOSE | POINTED DART | PIERCES COR-
       RUPTI- | -ONS DASTARD | HEART, in six lines, with
       laurel and palm branches under. Conder, 208; 48.

Slave.

37. *O* : A chained Negro in supplication. AM I NOT A MAN AND A
       BROTHER.
   R : WHATSOEVER | YE WOULD THAT | MEN SHOULD DO | UNTO
       YOU, DO YE | EVEN SO TO | THEM.   Conder, 208; 49.
✓ 38.   Similar, but from different dies, the legend on rev. reads
       DO " TO " YOU, &c.

Thurlow.

✓ 39. *O* : Bust to left in a cocked hat.   EDW . LORD THUR-LOW.
   R : The same as No. 11.   Conder, 208 ; 50.
✓ 40. *O* : The same as last.
   R : The same as the *O* : of No. 29.   Conder, 208 ; 51.

Uncharitable Monopolizer.

✓ 41. *O* : A man's head trying to swallow the world. "TAKE NOT
       WHAT WAS MADE FOR ALL," &c.   THE UNCHARITABLE
       MONOPOLIZER WILL STARVE THE POOR.
   R : An open hand dropping coins into other outstretched
       hands, and an eye radiated above "WELL DONE."
       THE CHARITABLE HAND COME . ALL . YE . DISTRESSED *

Washington.

✓ 42. *O* : Bust to left.   GEORGE WASHINGTON.
   R : Arms and crest of the United States.   LIBERTY AND
       SECURITY.
   E : AN ASYLUM FOR THE OPPRESS'D OF ALL NATIONS ✕ : ✕
43. *O* : Bust to right.   . GEORGE WASHINGTON .
   R : Arms and crest of the United States.   . LIBERTY AND
       SECURITY .   Date 17-95 divided by shield.
   E : The same as last.

Willis.

✓ 44. *O* : Three-quarter bust to left.   DOCTOR WILLIS.
   R : BRITONS REJOICE YOUR KING'S RESTORED . 1789.
                                           Conder, 209; 60.
       *Most of these pieces are struck also in tin, and several of
       them occur only in that metal, and Nos. 2, 3, 4, 12, 16,
       34, 40, and 44, are also struck in silver.*

HALFPENNIES.

British.

✓ 45. *O* : Laureate bust to right.   GEORGIVS . III REX.
   R : LOST TO BRITANNIA'S HOPE BUT TO HER PRAYERS RESTOR'D
       1789. At bottom sprigs of laurel and palm.
                                           Conder, 211; 14.

✓ 46. *O*: The same as last.

　　　R: JEHOVAH HEARD BRITANNIA'S PRAYER, AND SAV'D HER
　　　　　FAVORITE KING . 1789.　An eye radiated above.

　　　This is in white metal.

✓ 47. *O*: Laureate bust to right, I H & CO under.　GEORGIVS III
　　　　　DEI GRATIA.

　　　R: JEHOVAH HEARD BRITANNIA'S PRAYER AND RESTORED HEALTH
　　　　　TO HER KING . MARCH . 1789.　In nine lines.

　　　E: Scalloped.

　　　This is in brass.

　 48. *O*: The same as last.

　　　R: THE GENERAL THANKSGIVING FOR HIS MAJESTY HAPPY
　　　　　RECOVERY CELEBRATED AT ST. PAULS APRIL . 23 . 1789.
　　　　　In nine lines.

　　　E: Scalloped.

✓ 49. *O*: Similar to last, but with W A & CO under bust.

　　　R: A crown between branches of laurel.　HAIL BRITAIN .
　　　　　HEAVEN RESTORES YOUR KING . 1788.G

　　　E: Milled.　　　　　　　　　　　　　Conder, 211 ; 15.

　 50. *O*: Laureate bust to right.　GEORGIVS III D G REX.

　　　R: A MEMBER OF THE BRITISH SENATE 1797.　In a circle of
　　　　　dots.

　　　E: Milled.　　　　　　　　　　　　　Conder, 212 ; 20.

　 51. *O*: The same as last.

　　　R: A crown and sceptre lying on a cushion in the clouds,
　　　　　a crown radiated above.　1797.　Conder, 212 ; 21.

　　　This is in white metal.

✓ 52. *O*: Laureate bust to right.　GEORGE . III . REX . .

　　　R: TO COMMEMORATE HIS MAJESTY VIEWING THE DUTCH PRIZES
　　　　　AT THE NORE . OCTR. 30, 1797.　In eight lines.

　　　E: Milled.　　　　　　　　　　　　　Conder, 212 ; 22.

✓ 53. *O*: Two busts to right.　GEORG . III . ET . CHARLOT . REX . ET
　　　　　. REG .

　　　R: Rose, shamrock, and thistle.　QUIS NON SEPARABIT.

　.　*E*: Milled.　　　　　　　　　　　　　Conder, 212 ; 23.

　　　This is struck in copper and brass.

　 54. *O*: Two busts to left.　LONG MAY THEY REIGN OVER A
　　　　　GRATEFULL PEOPLE.

　　　R: A man-of-war sailing.　THE GUARD & GLORY OF BRITAIN.

　　　E: PAYABLE AT ANGLESEY LONDON OR LIVERPOOL.

✓ 54a.　　As last, but *E* : Milled.

　　　　　　　　Conder, 212 ; 24.—Pye, 52 ; 3.—Virt : 98.

　 54b.　　　　　　,,　　,,　　*E* : Plain (not in collar.)

　 55. *O*: The same as last.

　　　R: A man-of-war sailing.　THE WOODEN WALLS OF OLD
　　　　　ENGLAND.

　　　E: PAYABLE AT ANGLESEY LONDON OR LIVERPOOL.

　.55a.　　As last, but *E* : Milled.

✓ 56. *O*: Bust to left. CHARLOTTA DEI GRATIA.
  R: In a shield HER PEOPLE'S FRIEND. A crown above. BRITAIN'S HONOR.
  E: Milled. Conder, 214; 31.

∨ 57. *O*: Laureate bust to right. GULIELMUS . III . DEI . GRATIA . . 1688 . .
  R: NOVR. 4TH. 1788 within a wreath. GLORIOUS . REVOLUTION . JUBILEE.
  E: Scalloped. Conder, 235; 210.
  This is struck in brass.

Briton.

∨ 58. *O*: A man handcuffed and ironed, a padlock on his mouth. A . FREE . BORN . BRITON . OF . 1796.
  R: A knife, fork, and plate, chained down to a table. USELESS. Conder, 217; 61.

∨ 59. *O*: The same as last.
  R: A man holding a cutlass in one hand, and broken fetters in the other, leaning upon an anchor. A . FRENCH . REPUBLICAN. Conder, 217; 62.

Collectors' Tokens.

∨ 60. *O*: A connoisseur smoking a pipe, at a table spread with medals, an old man behind him putting on his head a fool's cap. TOKEN COLLECTORS HALFPENNY . PAYABLE ON DEMAND . 1796.
  R: An ass and a mule saluting. BE ASSURED FRIEND MULE YOU NEVER SHALL WANT MY PROTECTION.
  E: ANY SUM GIVEN FOR SCARCE ORIGINAL IMPRESSIONS. Conder, 219; 76.

∨ 61. *O*: The same as last.
  R: Two boys riding a race upon asses. ASSES RUNNING FOR HALFPENCE.
  E: The same as last. Conder, 219; 77.

Cooper.

∨ 62. *O*: Bust to left. W. COOPER AGED . 20 . YEARS.
  R: An open book. HOLY BIBLE EX I CHAP. I. Radiation above, branches below. RELIGION. Conder, 219; 78.

Corn.

∨ 63. *O*: Laureate bust to right. * HE FEELS HIS PEOPLES WANTS & RELIEVES THEM *
  R: A ship sailing. CORN IMPORTED BY GOVERNMENT * * * Conder, 212; 18.

This obv. appears with the following reverses :—

✓ 64. *R*: A plough and harrow. SUCCESS TO THE CULTIVATION OF WASTE LANDS *　　　Conder, 284; 197.

✓ 65. *R*: A wheatsheaf. * RELIEF * AGAINST * MONOPOLY * *
　　　Conder, 283; 195.

✓ 66. *R*: A pair of scales. THE SALE OF CORN BY WEIGHT PROPOSED 1796.　　　Conder, 284; 201.

✓ 67. *R*: A pair of scales " $3\frac{1}{2}$ lb." 1s. WORTH OF BREAD 1795 . 96 * GOOD LORD DELIVER US *　　　Conder, 284; 198.

✓ 68. *R*: A pair of scales " $6\frac{1}{2}$ lb." BREAD FOR 1s. APRIL 1796 * GOD BE PRAISED *　　　Conder, 284; 199.

O: A ship. As No. 63.
This obverse has the following reverses :—

✓ 69. *R*: A plough and harrow. As No. 64.　Conder, 295 ; 315.

✓ 70. *R*: A wheatsheaf. As No. 65.　　　Conder, 295 ; 316.

✓ 71. *R*: A pair of scales. As No. 66.　　Conder, 295 ; 317.

✓ 72. *R*: Scales, $3\frac{1}{2}$ lb. As No. 67.　　Conder, 295 ; 313.

✓ 73. *R*: Scales, $6\frac{1}{2}$ lb. As No. 68.　　Conder, 295 ; 314.

O: A plough and harrow. As No. 64.
This obverse has the following reverses :—

✓ 74. *R*: A wheatsheaf. As No. 65.　　Conder, 219; 82.

✓ 75. *R*: A pair of scales. As No. 66.　　Conder, 219; 81.

✓ 76. *R*: Scales, $3\frac{1}{4}$ lb. As No. 67.　　Conder, 293 ; 297.

✓ 77. *R*: Scales, $6\frac{1}{2}$ lb. As No. 68.　　Conder, 294; 302.

O: A wheatsheaf. As No. 65.
This obverse has the following reverses :—

✓ 78. *R*: A pair of scales. As No. 66.　　Conder, 302 ; 398.

✓ 79. *R*: Scales, $3\frac{1}{2}$ lb. As No. 67.　　Conder, 302 ; 396.

✓ 80. *R*: Scales, $6\frac{1}{2}$ lb. As No. 68.　　Conder, 302 ; 397.

O: A pair of scales. As No. 66.
This obverse has the following reverses :—

✓ 81. *R*: Scales, $3\frac{1}{2}$ lb. As No. 67.　　Conder, 293 ; 300.

✓ 82. *R*: Scales, $6\frac{1}{2}$ lb. As No. 68.　　Conder, 294; 305.

✓ 83. *O*: A pair of scales, $3\frac{1}{2}$ lb. As No. 67.
R: A pair of scales, $6\frac{1}{2}$ lb. As No. 68.　Conder, 215 ; 37.

Dimsdale.

84. *O*: A deformed man. SR. HARRY DIMSDALE MUFFIN MERCHT.
R: ELECTED MAYOR OF GARRAT 1796. Encircled with sprigs of roses.　　　Conder, 220; 83.

Erskine and Erskine & Gibbs.

✓ 85. *O*: Bust to left. HON. T. ERSKINE.
R: A FRIEND | TO FREEDOM | & RIGHTS | OF MAN.
　　　Conder, 221; 93.

86. *O*: Two barristers standing, holding a label, inscribed
    " RIGHTS OF MAN." Another label above them has
    " MAGNA CHARTA " inscribed upon it. ERSKINE AND
    GIBBS AND TRIAL BY JURY.
    R: T. HARDY | I. H. TOOKE. | T. HOLCROFT. | I. A. BONNEY. | J.
    JOYCE, S. KID. | J. THELWALL. | I. RICHTER. | I. BAXTER.
    | 1794.
    E: Engrailed.   Conder, 221 ; 94.
    Also struck in silver.
✔ 86a.   As last, but *E* : Milled.
✔ 87. *O*: The same as last.
    R: A WAY | TO PREVENT | KNAVES | GETTING | A TRICK.
                                          Conder, 221 ; 95.

Fox.

✔ 88. *O*: Bust to right. RT. HONOURABLE C. J. FOX.   1797.
    R: A cypher *P S Co.* in a circle. DEDICATED TO COLLECTORS
    OF MEDALS & COINS. See Middlesex, No. 413.
                                          Conder, 222 ; 98.
89. *O*: The same as last.
    R: Minerva. TRUTH FOR MY HELM & JUSTICE FOR MY SHIELD.
    See Middlesex, No. 394.   Conder, 222 ; 99.

France (King and Queen of).

90. *O*: Two busts. LOUIS . XVI ET M. ANTOINETTE . ROI ET REINE
    DE FRANCE.
    R: MURD. BY | THE FACTIOUS. | LOUIS XVI. JAN. 21 | M. ANTOIN-
    ETTE | OCT. 16. | 1793.
    E: Milled.
✔ 90a.   As last, but *E*: Plain (not in collar).
    This obv. occurs with the following reverses :—
✔ 91. *R*: Bust of DAVID GARRICK ESQ. See Middlesex, No. 156.
    E: Milled.
91a.   As last, but *E*: Plain (not in collar).
92. *R*: A cypher *P S Co.* &c. See Middlesex, No. 413.
    E: Milled.
✔ 93. *R*: An anchor and cable, &c. See No. 117.
    E: Milled.   Conder, 278 ; 141.
94. *O*: Similar to No. 90; but with the date 17—95 at the
    sides.
    R: Bust of DAVID GARRICK ESQ. As No. 91.
    E: SKIDMORE HOLBORN LONDON.   Conder, 278 ; 143.
94a.   As last, but *E*: Milled.
95. *O*: As last.
    R: Anchor and cable, &c. As No. 117.
    E: As No. 94.
95a.   As last, but *E*: Milled.

France (Dauphin).

V 96. *O*: Bust to right, a crown above. THE ✳ DOPHIN ✳ OF ✳ FRANCE ✳

R: MAY . THE . DOPHIN | BE . RESTORED . TO . THE | CROWN . OF . FRANCE . | *I. W.* A crown above.

France (Louis Rex).

97. *O*: Bust to right, JAMES under it. LOUIS REX. See Middlesex, No. 329.

R: Three fleurs-de-lis, 1790. See Middlesex, No. 396.

France (Map of).

98. *O*: A square of daggers, " FIRE " at each corner; " HONOR " under foot; FRA—NCE (divided); " *throne* " upside down; " GLORY " defaced; RE | LI | GI | ON (broken). A MAP OF FRANCE 1794.

R: MAY | GREAT BRITAIN | EVER REMAIN | THE | REVERSE. Radiated within a wreath of oak. The first and last letters of second line of legend touch the wreath.

E: CURRENT EVERY WHERE.

98a. As last, but *E*: PAYABLE AT THE WAREHOUSE OF THOMAS CLARKE.

V 98b. As last, but *E*: Engrailed. Conder, 213; 26.
V 98c. „ „ *E*: Milled.
98d. „ „ *E*: Plain (not in collar).
99. *O*: and *E*: The same as No. 98.

R: The same legend but in smaller letters, which do not touch the wreath.

99a. As last, but *E*: PAYABLE AT CLOUGHER OR IN DUBLIN.
99b. „ „ *E*: PAYABLE AT I. IORDANS DRAPER GOSPORT.
99c. „ „ *E*: PAYABLE IN LONDON BRISTOL & LANCASTER.
v 99d. „ „ *E*: Engrailed.
v 99e. „ „ *E*: Plain (not in collar).

Garbett.

100. *O*: Bust to right. SAMUEL GARBETT.
R: Blank.
E: Engrailed. Conder, 222 ; 101.
v 100a. As last, but *E* : Plain.
Very rare.

General Convenience.

101. *O*: A helmed bust to right. FOR GENE—RAL CONVENIENCE.
R: Shield of arms. HALFPENNY-TOKEN 1795.
E : PAYABLE IN LONDON. The remainder engrailed.

24

✓ 101*a*.   As last, but *E*: Milled. Conder, 223; 110.—Virt: 70.

✓ 102. *O*: and *E*: The same as No. 101.

     R: A figure of Britannia seated. ✱ ✱ RULE BRITANNIA ✱ ✱
     Ex: 1797. See Middlesex, No. 751.

                                    Conder, 223; 111.

✓ 103. *O*: and *E*: The same as last.

     R: A plough. INDUSTRY ✱ SUPPLIETH WANT. *Ex*: 1796.
     See Middlesex, No. 749.

Handel.

✓ 104. *O*: Bust to left. G. F. HANDEL. I KNOW THAT MY REDEEMER
                 LIVETH.

     R: BENEVOLENT CHORAL FUND INSTITUTED 1791—FOR ITS
     DECAY'D WIDOWS AND ORPHANS.   Conder, 224; 116.

✓ 105. *O*: The same as last.

     R: BENEVOLENT CHORAL FUND INSTITUTED 1791 FOR ITS
     DECAY'D MEMBERS WIDOWS AND ORPHANS.

                                    Conder, 224; 117.

✓ 106. *O*: Similar to preceding, but the name is in a straight
       line.

     R: The same legend as last, but smaller letters and with
     four dots at the end, thus ∴   Conder, 224; 118.

Hardy.

✓ 107. *O*: Bust to left. TRIED FOR HIGH TREASON. *Ex*: T. HARDY
       1794.

     R: ACQUITTED | BY HIS | JURY | COUNSEL | HON. T. ERSKINE |
     V. GIBBS ESQR. In six lines.   Conder, 224; 120.

✓ 108. *O*: The same as last.

     R: ACQUITTED | BY HIS JURY | COUNSEL | HON. T. ERSKINE |
     V. GIBBS ESQR. In five lines.   Conder, 224; 121.

Howard.

109. *O*: Bust to left. IOHN HOWARD F. R. S. HALFPENNY.

     R: A female seated, instructing a boy with a key to
     unlock the prison doors, GO FORTH radiated above,
     the whole within a beaded circle. REMEMBER THE
     DEBTORS IN GOAL.

     E: PAYABLE IN ANGLESEY LONDON OR LIVERPOOL.

109*a*.   As last, but *E*: PAYABLE IN DUBLIN OR LONDON . + .+ .

✓ 109*b*.   „   „   *E*: PAYABLE BY HENRY OLIVERS +

109*c*.   „   „   *E*: PAYABLE IN LANCASTER OR BRISTOL.

109*d*.   „   „   *E*: PAYABLE AT LONDON OR DUBLIN.

109*e*.   „   „   *E*: MASONIC HALFPENNY TOKEN MDCCXCIV.

109*f*.   „   „   *E*: CURRENT EVERY WHERE.

                                    Conder, 225; 125.

109*g*.   „   „   *E*: Milled.

109*h*.   „   „   *E*: Plain (not in collar).

v 110. *O* : The same as last.
 R : A figure of Britannia seated. RULE BRITANNIA. See
 Middlesex, No. 243. Conder, 224; 124.

111. *O* : The same as last.
 R : A female seated, holding mining tools. HALFPENNY.
 Ex : 1790. See Cheshire, No. 19. Conder, 225; 127.

Howe.

112. *O* : Bust to left in cocked hat. EARL HOWE & THE FIRST OF
 JUNE . 1794 . HALFPENNY . 1795.

 R : A man-of-war sailing to right. THE GUARD & GLORY OF
 GREAT BRITAIN.

 E : PAYABLE AT BANBURY OXFORD OR READING.

112*a*. As last, but *E* : PAYABLE AT DUBLIN OR AT BALLYMURTAGH.
112*b*. ,, ,, *E* : PAYABLE IN DUBLIN OR LONDON + . + .
v 112*c*. ,, ,, *E* : PAYABLE IN SUFFOLK BATH OR MANCHESTER.
112*d*. ,, ,, *E* : Engrailed.
112*e*. ,, ,, *E* : Plain. On a very small flan.
  Conder, 226 ; 137.

v 113. *O* : The same as last.
 R : A smaller ship sailing to left. THE WOODEN WALLS OF
 OLD ENGLAND +

 E : PAYABLE IN LANCASTER LONDON OR BRISTOL.

v 113*a*. As last, but *E* : PAYABLE AT LONDON. +.+.+.+.
113*b*. ,, ,, *E* : PAYABLE AT LONDON OR DUBLIN.
113*c*. ,, ,, *E* : CURRENT EVERY WHERE.
  Conder, 226 ; 138.
This obverse occurs with the following reverses :—
114. *R* : Britannia seated. RULE BRITANNIA. As No. 110.
 E : Engrailed.

v 115. *R* : Female seated holding mining tools. HALFPENNY. *Ex* :
 1790. As No. 111. Conder, 226 ; 139.
116. *R* : MUR'D BY THE FACTIOUS, &c. See No. 90.
 E : Milled.

v 117. *O* : A rather different bust. MAY THE FRENCH EVER KNOW
 HOWE TO RULE THE MAIN. +
 R : An anchor and cable. IN COMMEMORATION OF THE
 GLORIOUS FIRST OF JUNE+17—94.
 E : Milled. Conder, 226 ; 140.—Virt: 91.
117*a*. As last, but *E* : Plain (not in collar).
This obv. occurs with the following reverses :—
118. *R* : Bust of DAVID GARRICK, ESQ. As No. 91.
 E : SKIDMORE HOLBORN LONDON. Conder, 282 ; 182.
119. *R* : A cat, &c. See Middlesex, No. 514.
  24 *

120. *O*: A much smaller bust than before, with sprigs under it. INSCRIBED TO THE TARS OF OLD ENGLAND.
R: An anchor and cable. IN COMMEMORATION OF THE GLORIOUS FIRST OF JUNE 1794. Conder, 227 ; 142.
This is struck in white metal.

Industry.

120*bis.O*: A beehive and bees, within a wreath of flowers. INDUSTRY THE SOURCE OF CONTENT. *T. P.*
R: A shield, inscribed FOR CHANGE IN TRADE, between sprigs of oak. TO CONVENIENCE THE PUBLIC 1801.
This piece is strictly speaking of the 19th century.

Jervis.

121. *O*: Bust to left dividing the date 17—97. THE GALLANT JERVIS DEFEATED THE SPANIARDS 14 FEB.
R: A man-of-war sailing to right. BRITISH VALOR TRIUMPHANT.
E: Milled. Conder, 227 ; 147.

122. *O*: The Union Jack, within a circle. MAY IT BE DISPLAYD AT ALL POINTS OF YE COMPASS ❖
R: A fleet of ships sailing. *Ex*: CAPE ST. VINCENT Feby. 14. 1797.
E: A VALENTINE PRESENTED TO SPAIN BY ADML. JERVIS.
Conder, 214 ; 30.

Loyal Briton's Lodge.

123. *O*: An anchor and cable, and cap of liberty radiated. LIBERTY+PEACE+COMMERCE.
R: A crown in a radiated circle, sprigs of leaves below. + LOYAL ✿ BRITONS ✿ LODGE + Conder, 230 ; 169.

124. *O*: Similar to last, but the radiation is shorter, and the crosses larger.
R: Similar, but with stars of six rays between the words, three dots at beginning, and four at end of legend.
Conder, 230 ; 170.

125. *O*: As before.
R: The arms of Orchard, &c. See Middlesex, No. 285.
Conder, 285 ; 213.

Masonic. (See London.)
Newton.

126. *O*: Bust to left. SR ISAAC NEWTON.
R: A caduceus, olive branch, and cornucopia. HALFPENNY . 1793. The right hand wing of caduceus nearly touches the second limb of the first N of "HALFPENNY."
E: Engrailed.

✓ 127. *O*: Similar to last, but without the dot under the small R
of SR.
R: and *E*: The same as last.
A flaw in the die may possibly account for the absence
of the dot.
127*a*.   As last, but *E*: Plain (not in collar).
128. *O*: Similar, but the small R is smaller, and the legend
approaches nearer to the bust.
R: The right hand wing of caduceus points between the
two N's of "HALFPENNY."
E: PAYABLE IN HULL AND IN LONDON . × . × .
✓ 128*a*.   As last, but *E*: PAYABLE IN LONDON BRISTOL & LANCAS-
TER. × .
128*b*.   As last, but *E*: PAYABLE AT THE WAREHOUSE LIVERPOOL.
128*c*.   „   „   *E*: Engrailed.
Conder, 231 ; 177.—Pye, 51 ; 9.—Virt: 59.

Noted Advocates.

✓ 129. *O*: Three men hanging on a gibbet.   NOTED ADVOCATES FOR
THE RIGHTS OF MEN 1796.
R: A WAY | TO PREVENT | KNAVES | GETTING | A TRICK.
Conder, 231 ; 178.
Also struck in silver.
✓ 130. *O*: The same as last.
R: An open book, inscribed THE WRONGS OF MAN JANY.
21: 1793.   Conder, 231 ; 179.

Odd Fellows. (See London.)
End of Pain.

131. *O*: A man hanging on a gallows.   END OF PAIN.   Within a
border of dots and hands pointing.
R: MAY THE | KNAVE | OF JACOBIN CLUBS | NEVER GET A |
TRICK.   In five lines within a similar border.
E: PAYABLE AT SHREWSBURY.
✓ 131*a*.   As last, but *E*: Plain.   Conder, 232 ; 188.
132. *O*: Similar to last, but with a milled border, and the work
coarser.
R: The same as last, but with a milled border.
E: Plain (in collar).   Conder, 232 ; 189.
✓ 132*a*.   As last, but not struck in collar.
133. *O*: Similar to preceding, but the gallows is smooth, and
the man's legs hang straight down.   The vane on
top of church points to the second limb of the A.
R: An open book, &c.   As No. 130.
E: Milled.   Conder, 232 ; 190.
✓ 133*a*.   As last, but *E*: Plain (not in collar).   *This may be
from having been struck on smaller flans.*

✓ 134. *O*: Similar to last, but the vane on spire points to the
first limb of the **A**.
   R: Similar, but from different dies.   Conder, 233 ; 191.
✓ 135. *O*: The same as last.
   R: A number of combustibles intermixed with labels,
issuing from a globe inscribed " FRATERNITY." The
labels are inscribed " REGICIDE," " ROBBERY,"
" FALSITY," " REQUISITON." FRENCH REFORMS 1797.
                                          Conder, 233 ; 192.
✓ 136. *O*: Similar to preceding, but with a demon seated on the
gallows smoking a pipe.
   R: A man and a monkey, each standing on one leg. WE
DANCE, PAIN SWINGS.
For other End of Pain tokens see Middlesex, Nos.
651-2.

Priestley.

✓ 137. *O*: Bust to right. J. PRIESTLEY CITIZEN OF THE WORLD.
   R: The flame of liberty proceeding from the tomb of
" HAMPDEN & SIDNEY." SACRED TO LIBERTY.
   E: Milled.   Conder, 234 ; 203.
See also No. 147.

Romaine.

✓ 138. *O*: Bust front face, JACOBS F. under. REVD. W. ROMAINE,
M.A. 1795.
   R: Arms in a double circle. I LIVE BY THE FAITH OF THE
SON OF GOD.   Conder, 235 ; 212.

Shakespeare.

139. *O*: A bust to left. SHAKESPEARE.
   R: A female seated holding mining tools. HALFPENNY.
Ex: 1790.
   E: PAYABLE AT BANBURY OXFORD OR READING. +.
139*a*.   As last, but *E* : PAYABLE IN DUBLIN OR LONDON +.+
139*b*.   ,,   ,,   *E* : PAYABLE IN LANCASTER LONDON OR LIVER-
POOL.
139*c*.   As last, but *E* : PAYABLE IN SUFFOLK—BATH OR MANCHES-
TER +.×.
139*d*.   As last, but *E* : Milled.
✓ 139*e*.   ,,   ,,   *E* : Plain (not in collar).
                                          Conder, 236 ; 217.
This obv. occurs with the following reverses :—
140. *R*: Similar to last, but dated 1794.   Conder, 236 ; 218.
141. *R*: A man-of-war sailing. THE WOODEN WALLS OF OLD
ENGLAND.
   E: PAYABLE IN LANCASTER LONDON OR LIVERPOOL.
141*a*.   As last, but *E* : Plain (not in collar).
                                          Conder, 236 ; 219.

142. *R* : A harp. ✶ NORTH ✶ ✶ WALES ✶
    E : PAYABLE AT MACCLESFIELD LIVERPOOL OR CONGLETON . ✕ .
✓ 142*a*.   As last, but *E* : Plain (not in collar).
Conder, 157 ; 26.

✓ 143. *O* : A very similar bust. SHAKESPEAR.
    R : Figure of Britannia seated. RULE BRITANNIA.
Conder, 236 ; 222.

Slave.

✓ 144. *O* : A chained negro kneeling, in supplication. AM I NOT A
    MAN AND A BROTHER.
    R : Two hands joined. MAY SLAVERY & OPRESSION CEASE
    THROUGHOUT THE WORLD +
    E : PAYABLE IN DUBLIN OR LONDON + . +
144*a*.   As last, but *E* : THIS IS NOT A COIN BUT A MEDAL.
144*b*.   ,, ,, *E* : Milled.   Conder, 237 ; 229.
145. *O* : The same as last. The negro's head is under the
    space between MAN and AND.
    R : Similar to last, but OPPRESSION is spelt correctly.
    E : PAYABLE IN DUBLIN OR AT BALLYMURTAGH.
145*a*.   As last, but *E* : PAYABLE IN DUBLIN OR LONDON.
✓ 145*b*.   ,, ,, *E* : PAYABLE IN LANCASTER LONDON OR LIVER-
    POOL.
145*c*.   As last, but *E* : YORK BUILT A.M. 1223 CATHEDRAL RE-
    BUILT A.D. 1075.
145*d*.   As last, but *E* : Engrailed.
145*e*.   ,, ,, *E* : Milled.
✓ 145*f*.   ,, ,, *E* : Plain (not in collar).
Conder, 237 ; 230.

146. *O* : Similar to last, but the negro's head is under the AND
    and the letters of legend are smaller.
    R : The letters of legend are smaller, and terminate with
    a rosette instead of a cross.
    E : BIRMINGHAM REDRUTH & SWANSEA.
146*a*.   As last, but *E* : PAYABLE AT DUBLIN CORK OR BELFAST.
✓ 146*b*.   ,, ,, *E* : PAYABLE AT LONDON LIVERPOOL OR
    BRISTOL.
146*c*.   As last, but *E* : Milled.
146*d*.   ,, ,, *E* : Plain (not in collar).
Conder, 237 ; 231.

    See also No. 172.

Stanhope.

✓ 147. *O* : Bust to left. STANHOPE NOBLE WITHOUT NOBILITY.
    R : The tomb of Hampden, &c. As No. 137.
    E : Milled.

Tom Tackle.

∨ 148. *O* : A sailor brandishing a cutlass. TOM TACKLE IS RICH. FOR KING AND COUNTRY.

R : A sailor with a wooden leg and crutches. TOM TACKLE IS POOR * MY COUNTRY SERVED * Conder, 238 ; 236.

Tooke.

149. *O* : A full face bust. IOHN HORNE TOOKE ESQR.

R : The names of the jury in a square ; ERSKINE above, GIBBS below. BRITISH JUSTICE DISPLAY'D NOVR. 22 1794.

E : PAYABLE AT BIRMINGHAM   BRIGHTON OR LIVERPOOL ✕

149a.   As last, but *E* : PAYABLE AT LONDON LIVERPOOL OR BRISTOL . — .

∨ 149b.   As last, but *E* : Plain (not in collar).
Conder, 238 ; 237.

∨ 150. *O* : Bust to right, J. H. TOOKE ESQR. 1794 under. TRIED FOR HIGH TREASON.

R : ACQUITTED | BY HIS JURY | COUNSEL | HON. T. ERSKINE | V. GIBBS ESQR.   Conder, 238 ; 238.

∨ 151. *O* : The same as last.

R : NOT GUILTY | SAY THE JURY | EQUAL JUDGES OF | LAW AND FACT | COUNSEL | HON. T. ERSKINE | V. GIBBS ESQR.
Conder, 238 ; 239.

152. *O* : Differs from the preceding in several particulars, but may best be identified by noticing that the name below the bust is more spread so as to come under the beginning and end of upper legend.

R : The same as last.   Conder, 238 ; 240.

Wales (Prince of).

∨ 153. *O* : Bust to left. PRINCE REGENT OF GREAT BRITAIN FRANCE & IRELAND &c.

R : The Prince's crest and motto. BORN . AUGT. 12 . 1762 ✛ APPOINTED . FEB. 1789 ✛   Conder, 239 ; 243.

∨ 154. *O* : Bust to left. PRINCE REGENT. There is a flaw at the letter C in " PRINCE."

R : A crown. HE HOLDS IT FOR THE KING. *Ex* : 1789.

E : Milled.   Conder, 239 ; 244.

∨ 155. *O* : Very similar to preceding, but without the flaw, the tie of periwig comes close to the foot of the T in "REGENT."

R : and *E* : The same as last.

156.   Similar to preceding, but with the date on *obv.* and not on *rev.*   Conder, 239 ; 245.
This is struck in brass.

157. *O* : A full face bust. GEO. PRINCE OF WALES. HALFPENNY.

R : The Freemasons' Arms, &c. PRINCE OF WALES ELECTED G.M. 24 NOV. 1790.

E : PAYABLE IN LANCASTER LONDON OR BRISTOL .

✓ 157a.   As last, but *E* : PAYABLE AT LONDON OR DUBLIN ✕.✕.
Conder, 239 ; 246.—Virt : 77.
✓ 158. *O* : The same as last.
R : The Prince's crest and motto. INDUSTRY IS THE PARENT OF SUCCESS. HALFPENNY 1795. See Norfolk, No. 6.
E : The same as No. 157.   Conder, 239 ; 247.
✓ 159. *O* : Bust to right. GEORGE PRINCE OF WALES
R : and *E* : The same as No. 157.   Conder, 240 ; 250.
✓ 160. *O* : The same as last.
R : and *E* : The same as No. 158.
160a.   As last, but *E* : PAYABLE IN LONDON .+.+.+.+.+.
Conder, 240 ; 251.
161. *O* : The same as last.
R : The Prince's crest and motto. HALFPENNY 1795.
E : PAYABLE AT LONDON LIVERPOOL OR BRISTOL.
161a.   As last, but *E* : Milled.
161b.   „   „ *E* : Plain (not in collar).
162. *O* : The same as last.
R : Similar, but with a period after "HALFPENNY."
E : PAYABLE AT DUBLIN CORK OR BELFAST. ✕ ✕.
✓ 162a.   As last, but *E* : The same as No. 161.
163. *O* : Similar to last, but with a period at end of legend.
R : The same as last.
E : PAYABLE AT W. PARKER'S OLD BIRMINGHAM WAREHOUSE. ✕.
✓ 164. *O* : The same as last.
R : Without the period after " HALFPENNY " as No. 161.
E : PAYABLE IN LANCASTER LONDON OR BRISTOL.
✓ 165. *O* : Similar to preceding, but the line of forehead comes to the E OF " PRINCE."
R : Similar to No. 161, but dated 1794.
E : PAYABLE AT W. GYE'S PRINTER BATH ✕.✕
165a.   As last, but *E* : PAYABLE AT IOHN SAWYER'S ROMNEY .✕.
165b.   „   „ *E* : The same as No. 164.

Wales (Prince and Princess of).

166. *O* : Two busts to left. GEO. & CAROLINE PRINCE & PRINCESS OF WALES ❖
R : The Prince's crest, between sprigs of laurel. MAY THE UNION BE CROWNED WITH HAPPINESS . APRIL 8 1795.
E : Milled.
✓ 166a.   As last, but *E* : Plain (not in collar).
Conder, 240 ; 256.

Wales (Princess of).

✓ 167. *O* : Three-quarter bust to left. PRINCESS OF WALES.
R : The Prince of Wales' crest above a portcullis. HALF PENNY 1795.
E : Milled.   Conder, 240 ; 257.—Pye, 51 ; 6.—Virt : 79.

✓ 168. *O* : Similar to last, but showing an eardrop.
   R : Similar, but the crest and chains are smaller.
   E : The same as last.

✓ 169. *O* : Similar to last, but not from the same die.
   R : A portcullis and crest as before. RENDER TO CÆSAR THE
    THINGS THAT ARE CÆSAR'S.
   E : The same as last.
        Conder, 241 ; 258.—Pye, 51 ; 5.—Virt : 79.

✓ 170. *O* : Similar to No. 167.
   R : The Prince's crest, within a radiation, 1795 under. MAY
    THE UNION BE CROWNED WITH HAPPINESS +
   E : BIRMINGHAM REDRUTH & SWANSEA.
 170*a*. As last, but *E* : PAYABLE AT DUBLIN CORK OR BELFAST. × ×.
 170*b*.   „ „ *E* : PAYABLE AT LONDON CORK OR BELFAST. × ×.
 170*c*.   „ „ *E* : PAYABLE AT LONDON LIVERPOOL OR BRISTOL.
 170*d*.   „ „ *E* : Milled.   Conder, 241 ; 259.
 170*e*.   „ „ *E* : Plain (not in collar).
 171. *O* : Similar to preceding.
   R : The same as No. 161.
   E : NOTED FOR PURE AIR AND SEA BATHING.
 171*a*. As last, but *E* : Plain.   Conder, 241 ; 260.

✓ 172. *O* : The same as last.
   R : Two hands joined. MAY SLAVERY, &c. See No. 144.
            Conder, 241 ; 261.

Washington.

✓ 173. *O* : Bust to left. WASHINGTON PRESIDENT 1791.
   R : An eagle holding in his beak a label inscribed " UNIM E
    PLURIBUS " ONE CENT.
   E : UNITED STATES OF AMERICA . ×.

✓ 174. *O* : A similar bust to last. WASHINGTON PRESIDENT.
   R : A smaller eagle with eight stars and a cloud above it.
    ONE CENT 1791.
   E : The same as last.
 174*a*. As last, but *E* : PAYABLE AT THE WAREHOUSE OF THOS.
    WORSWICK & SONS . ×.

✓ 175. *O* : The same as last.
   R : A ship. HALFPENNY 1793.
   R : PAYABLE IN ANGLESEY LONDON OR LIVERPOOL . ×.
      Conder, 6 ; 41.—Pye, 51 ; 10.—Virt : 118.

✓ 176. *O* : Bust to right. GEORGE WASHINGTON.
   R : Shield and crest of the United States. LIBERTY AND
    SECURITY 1795.
   E : BIRMINGHAM REDRUTH & SWANSEA.
 176*a*. As last, but *E* : PAYABLE AT LONDON LIVERPOOL OR BRISTOL.
 176*b*.   „ „ *E* : AN ASYLUM FOR THE OPPRESS'D OF ALL
    NATIONS.

176c.　As last, but *E*: Plain (not in collar).
　　　　　　Conder, 241; 262.—Virt: 119.
This is of similar design to the penny, No. 43, but from different dies. They are all rare.

Duke of York.

✓ 177. *O*: Bust to left. DUKE OF YORK.
　　R: A female standing, leaning upon a pillar. GOD SEND PEACE.　　Conder, 243; 278.—Virt: 81.
✓ 178. *O*: Bust to right. FREDK. DUKE OF YORK HALFPENNY 1795. The top of the 1 in date is sloping.
　　R: A man-of-war sailing to the left. THE WOODEN WALLS OF OLD ENGLAND ⁙
　　E: PAYABLE AT LANCASTER LONDON OR BRISTOL.
✓ 178a.　As last, but *E*: PAYABLE AT LONDON OR DUBLIN. ×.×.
178b.　　„　　„　*E*: PAYABLE AT LONDON .+.+.+.+.+.
　　　　　　Conder, 243; 279.—Pye, 51; 2.—Virt: 80.
✓ 179. *O*: The same as last.
　　R: A large man-of-war sailing to right. The same legend as before.
　　E: PAYABLE IN DUBLIN OR LONDON .+.+.
　　　　　　Conder, 243; 280.—Pye, 51; 3.—Virt: 80.
180. *O*: Similar to preceding, but there is a period at end of legend, which is more spread out and the top of the 1 in date is flat.
　　R: Man-of-war sailing to right. THE GUARD & GLORY OF BRITAIN.
　　E: PAYABLE IN DUBLIN OR LONDON .+.+.
180a.　As last, but *E*: PAYABLE IN SUFFOLK—BATH OR MANCHESTER .×.
✓ 180b.　As last, but *E*: Milled. Conder, 243; 281.—Virt: 80.
180c.　　„　　„　*E*: Plain (on smaller flans).
　　The obv. of No. 178 occurs with the following reverses:—
✓ 181. *R*: The Freemasons' Arms, &c. As No. 157.
　　E: PAYABLE IN DUBLIN OR LONDON .+.+.
181a.　As last, but *E*: Milled.　　Conder, 243; 282.
✓ 182. *R*: The Prince of Wales' crest, &c. As No. 161.
　　　　　　Conder, 243; 283.
✓ 183. *R*: Female seated holding mining tools. HALFPENNY 1794.
　　　　　　Conder, 244; 286.
✓ 184. *R*: Figure of Britannia seated. RULE BRITANNIA. 1797.
　　The obv. of No. 180 occurs with the following reverses:—
✓ 185. *R*: Female seated holding mining tools. HALFPENNY 1790.
　　　　　　Conder, 243; 284.
✓ 186. *R*: The same as No. 183.
　　E: PAYABLE IN LANCASTER LONDON OR LIVERPOOL.
　　　　　　Conder, 243; 285.

✔ 187. *O* : Bust different from any preceding and in high relief.
     * DUKE * OF * YORK *
     R : A cypher *D Y* within a circle.   A MEMBER OF THE
     BRITH. SENATE.   1797.   Conder, 244 ; 289.

FARTHINGS.

British.

✔ 188. *O* : Laureate bust to left.   GOD SAVE THE KING.
     R : MAY A | FLOWING | TRADE FOLLOW | A SPEEDY AND |
     HONOURABLE | PEACE | 1796.   Conder, 246 ; 11.
✔ 189. *O* : The same as last.
     R : A stork standing upon a cornucopia of flowers.
     FARTHING.   Conder, 246 ; 12.
190. *O* : The same as last.
     R : An anchor and cable.   PROMISSORY NAVAL FARTHING ❖
     E : Milled.   Conder, 246 ; 13.
✔ 191. *O* : Laureate bust to right, c.ı under it.   GEORGIVS III DEI
     GRATIA.
     R : RESTORED | TO | HEALTH | MARCH : II : | 1789.   A crown
     between sprigs of laurel and palm above.
         Conder, 245 ; 5.
192. *O* : Similar, but with ı.ıı & co under the bust.
     R : RESTORED | TO HIS | SUBJECT'S | MARCH : | 1789.
193. *O* : The same as No. 191.
     R : A harp crowned.
✔ 194. *O* : Two busts to right, K . F under.   GEORGIUS III ET
     CHARLOTTE REX ET REG.
     R: A palm branch across a lyre.   PEACE AND HARMONY.
         Conder, 246 ; 14.
195. *O* : Similar to last, but with W . F under bust.
     R : PATRONS OF VIRTUE within a laurel wreath, ı . D under.
     A PRESENT FOR THE NEW YEAR.   Conder, 246 ; 15.
✔ 196. *O* : Similar to preceding, but without the initials under bust.
     R : The same as last.
     E : Milled.
197. *O* : The same as No. 195.
     R : A crown above two hearts.   PATRONS OF VIRTUE.
     E : Milled.   Conder, 246 ; 16.
     Also struck in silver.
✔ 198. *O* : The same as 196.
     R : The same as last.
✔ 199. *O* : Two busts, similar.   GEO. III ET CHAR. REX ET REG.
     R : The same as last.
✔ 200. *O* : Laureate bust to right.   GULIELMUS . III . DEI . GRATIA .
     1688.
     R : NOVR. 4th. 1788 within a wreath.   REVOLUTION . JUBILEE.
     Davies.
     E : Scalloped.   Conder, 252 ; 75.
✔ 201.   As last, but ı . D on rev. instead of " *Davies.*"

Maximus.

✓ 202. *O* : A rude bust to left. MAXIMUS *
     R : A plain shield. NON . PLUS . ULTRA *

Naval.

✓ 203. *O* : Bust to left in naval uniform. ADML. LORD BRIDPORT.
     R : A naval crown, between sprigs of oak. PROMISSORY
          NAVAL FARTHING ❖   Conder, 245 ; 3.—Virt : 146.
✓ 204. *O* : The same as last.
     R : An anchor and cable. PROMISSORY NAVAL FARTHING ❖
                                 Conder, 245 ; 4.—Virt : 146.
✓ 205. *O* : Bust to right, in naval uniform. ADML. LORD HOOD.
     R : The same as No. 203.   Conder, 248 ; 36.—Virt : 147.
✓ 206. *O* : The same as last.
     R : The same as No. 204.   Conder, 248 ; 37.—Virt : 147.
✓ 207. *O* : Bust to right, in naval uniform. ADML. EARL HOWE.
     R : A man-of-war sailing to left, FARTHING under it in
          curved line. GLORIOUS FIRST OF JUNE 1794.
                                 Conder, 249 ; 38.
✓ 208. *O* : Similar to last, but both bust and legend smaller.
     R : A smaller ship sailing to right, FARTHING in a straight
          line under it, and a straight line under FARTHING.
          Legend as last, but with a small annulet before
          date.
     E : Milled.   Conder, 249 ; 39.—Virt : 148.
✓ 208a.   As last, but *E* : Plain.
✓ 209. *O* : The same as last.
     R : No annulet before date, and no line under FARTHING.
✓ 210. *O* : A slightly different bust. ADML. EARL HOWE.
     R : The same as No. 203.   Conder, 249 ; 40.
✓ 211. *O* : A still different bust, with a period before as well as
          after legend.
     R : The same as last.
     E : Milled.   Conder, 249 ; 41.
✓ 212. *O* : and *E* : The same as last.
     R : The same as No. 204. Conder, 249 ; 42.—Virt : 171.
✓ 213. *O* : and *E* : The same as last.
     R : The same as No. 188.   Conder, 249 ; 43.
✓ 214. *O* : Bust to right, in naval uniform. ADML. SR. JNO. JERVIS.
     R : The same as No. 203.
     E : Milled.   Conder, 249 ; 45.—Virt : 169.
✓ 215. *O* : and *E* : The same as last.
     R : The same as No. 204. Conder, 249 ; 46.—Virt : 169.
  216. *O* : and *E* : The same as last.
     R : The same as No. 188.   Conder, 249 ; 47.
✓ 217. *O* : Bust to left, in naval uniform. ADML. MACBRIDE.
     R : The same as No. 203.
     E : Milled.   Conder, 250 ; 51.—Virt : 170.

218. *O* : and *E* : The same as last.
    R : The same as No. 204.   Conder, 250; 52.—Virt: 170.
219. *O* : and *E* : The same as last.
    R : The same as No. 188.   Conder, 250; 53.

Newton.

220. *O* : Bust to left.   SR. ISAAC NEWTON.
    R : A cornucopia and olive branch.   FARTHING.   1793.
    E : Milled.   Conder, 250; 55.
220a.   As last, but *E* : Plain.
221.   A very poor copy of the above, evidently a counterfeit.
222. *O* : The same as No. 220.
    R : A shield bearing the Prince of Wales' plume, between
        sprigs.   PRO BONO PUBLICO 1795.
223. *O* : Bust to left.   ISAAC NEWTON.
    R : Female seated holding spear and palm branch.
        FARTHING.   *Ex* : 1771.
    E : Milled.   Conder, 251; 56.
224. *O* : The same as last.
    R : Similar to last, but dated 1793.   The 3 has a flat top.
                                           Conder, 251; 61.
225. *O* : A poor imitation of last.
    R : Similar to last, but the top of the 3 is round.
226. *O* : The same as last.
    R : The same as No. 222.
227. *O* : The same as last.
    R : A naval crown above a harp.   COMMERCE PROTECTED.
        See No. 239.   Conder, 251; 64.
228. *O* : Bust similar to No. 220, IC. NEWTON.
    R : A cypher, *T. H.*   FARTHING 1793.   Conder, 251; 57.
229. *O* : The same as last.
    R : The same as No. 224.   Conder, 251; 58.
230. *O* : Similar to last, but with the legend closer, and a period
        after it.
    R : The same as No. 225.   Conder, 251; 59.
231.   A poor copy of No. 229.   Conder, 251; 60.
232. *O* : Similar to No. 229.
    R : A female as before.   FARTHING.   1794.

End of Pain.

233. *O* : A man hanging on a gibbet, and a distant view of a
        church.   END OF PAIN.
    R : MAY THE KNAVE OF JACOBIN CLUBS NEVER GET A TRICK.   An
        ornament above and below.   Conder, 252; 67.
234. *O* : The same as last.
    R : An open book inscribed—"JANY. 21 1793." THE .
        WRONGS . OF . MAN .   Conder, 252; 68.

235. *O* :. The same as last.

    R : An open book inscribed—"THE WRONGS OF MAN JANY. 21 1793." Conder, 252 ; 69.

236. *O* : The same as last.

    R : A cap of liberty radiated upon a pole, which is crossed by a sword and palm branch. Conder, 252 ; 70.

236a .

End of P. ☾ T.

237. *O* : A man hanging from a gallows, against which a ladder is resting. END . OF . P ☾ T.

    R : SUCH IS THE REWARD OF TYRANTS 1796.

    E : Milled.

237a. As last, but *E* : Plain. Conder, 252 ; 74.

238. *O* : The same as last.

    R : A man hanging, &c., as on obv. of No. 233.

    E : Milled. Conder, 306 ; 436.

Peace.

239. *O* : Laureate bust to right. MAY PEACE BE ESTABLISHED.

    R : A coronet above a harp. COMMERCE PROTECTED.

        Conder, 252 ; 72.

240. *O* : Very similar to last, but from a different die.

    R : A naval crown above a harp. Legend as last.

        Conder, 252 ; 73.

    See also No. 227.

Pro Bono Publico.

241. *O* : Bust of Brutus to left, between sprigs.

    R : A shield bearing the Prince of Wales' plume. PRO BONO PUBLICO 1796.

242. *O* : A Druid's bust to left.

    R : A shield as last, between sprigs. PRO BONO PUBLICO.

243. *O* : A cypher, *W P* FARTHING ⁘

    R : A canister inscribed "TEA." PRO . BONO . PUBLICO . 1757.

244. Similar to last, but instead of the canister being defined in outline it stands up solid from the field of the token.

245. *O* : A cypher, *H B* FARTHING 1803.

    R : A cask with TOBACCO above it. PRO . BONO . PUBLICO.

Prince of Wales.

246. *O* : Bust to left. PRINCE OF WALES.

    R : The Prince of Wales' crest. ✳ ICH ✳ ✳ DIEN ✳

    E : Milled. Conder, 252 ; 79.

246a. As last, but *E* : Plain.

247. *O* : Similar to preceding, but coarser work, and with a
     star over bust.

   R : Similar, but with several small ornaments above and
     below crest.
   This is struck in brass.

Prince‾ and Princess of Wales.

248. *O* : Two busts to left.   GEO & CAROLINE PRINCE & PRINCESS
     OF WALES.

   R : The Prince's crest, between sprigs.   MAY THE UNION BE
     CROWNED WITH HAPPINESS APRIL 8 1795.

                                        Conder, 253 ; 82.

   This is struck in brass.

Imitation of the Regal Coinage.

UNDER this head are gathered together several so-called half-penny tokens of Conder as follows:—Surrey, Nos. 5-9; North Wales, 1, 2, 11-41; South Wales, 42-44; Warwickshire, No. 113; and the following from Not Local, Nos. 7, 8, 39-60, 79, 114, 143-146, 164, 200, 201, 214-216, 221-228, 233, 254, 255, 287, 288, together with a few farthings, Nos. 6-10, 27, 32, 44, 63, and 83; also Not Local.

To these are added all of a similar kind which have come to hand, making in all a list of some 500 pieces, which it is hoped may be of interest to collectors; many of the varieties are exceedingly rare, and with the exception of some few they are all scarce.

The initials *R* or *L* on obv: denotes bust looking to right, or left, as the case may be, and those of *f* or *h*, on rev: will denote a figure seated, more or less resembling Britannia; or the harp for Ireland.

HALFPENNIES.

	OBVERSE.		REVERSE.		
1.	*R.* ✻ ADMIRAL JERVIS ✻	‾*f.*	RULE BRI TANNIA.	*Ex:*	1797
✓ 2.	„ AL FRED	„	BRI TON'S	„	GLORY
3.	„ ALFRED THE GREAT	*h.*	✻ MUSIC . CHARMS		
4.	„ „ „	„	✻ SOUTH WALES ✻		
5.	„ „ „	*f.*	UNITY AND PEACE		
6.	*L.* ALFRED . THE . GREAT	*h.*	SHEBERNIA ❖		17-96
7.	„ ✻ AUCTORI ✻✻ PLEBIS ✻	*f.*	✻ INDEP: ET. LIBER ✻	*Ex:*	1787
8.	*R.* „ „	*h.*	HISPANIOLA		17-36
9.	*L.* BRUTUS SEXTUS	*f.*	BEL ONA	*Ex:*	1777
10.	„ „ „	„	BRITAN . NIA	„	1771
11.	„ „ „	„	BRITANNIA RULES	„	„
12.	„ „ „	„	BRITONS RULE	„	1772
13.	„ „ „	„	DELECTAT . RUS .	„	1775
14.	„ „ „.		NOBIEGTA	„	1696
15.	„ „ „	*h.*	NORTH WALES		1769
16.	„ „ „	„	„ „		1799
17.	„ „ ribbons longer	„	MUSIC ✻ CHARMS .		1775
18.	„ „ „	*f.*	NORTH WALES	*Ex:*	1792
19.	„ „ „	„	PAX . PLA . CID	„	1777
20.	„ „ „	„	DELECTAT . RUS .	„	1775·
21.	„ „ „	*h.*	MUSIC ✻ CHARMS		17-75
✓ 22.	„ T F under „	„	DELECTAT RUS ✻		
23.	„ „ „	*f.*	PAX . PLA . CID	*Ex:*	1775
24.	*R.* BRUTUS SEXTUS	„	BRITAN NIA	„	1771

25.	*R.* BRUTUS SEXTUS	*f.*	BRITAN NIA	*Ex:* 1774
26.	„ „ „	„	BRITONS RULE	„ 1772
27.	„ „ „	„	DELECTAT RUS	„ 1775
28.	„ „ „	„	MAY BRITONS RULE	„ 1779
29.	*L.* CELESTIN II POPE .	*h.*	NORTH WALES TOKEN	
30.	„ „ „	„	NORTH WALES	17-69
31.	„ CHARLES FOX . M.P	*f.*	BRITAN NIA . RULES THE MAIN .	
32.	„ „ „	*h.*	NORTH . WALES	1761
33.	*R.* CLAUDIUS ROMANUS	*f.*	BRITAN NIA	*Ex:* TOKEN
34.	*L.* CLAUDIUS . . ROMANUS	„	BRITAN NIAS.	„ ISLES
35.	„ „ „	„	BRITAIN§ ISLES	„ 1771
36.	„ „ „	„	DELECTAN DUS	„ 1771
37.	„ „ „	„	DELECTAT RUS . * C	„ 1774
38.	„ CLAUDUIS ROMANUS	„	BRITAIN RULES	„ 1771
39.	„ „ „	„	BRITANNIA§ ISLE .	„ 1774
40.	„ „ „	„	DELECTAT RUS . * C	„ 1774
41.	„ CLAUDUIS . . ROMANUS .	„	DELECTAT . RUS .	„ 1771
42.	„ „ „	„	PAX . PLA CID	„ 1773
43.	„ CLAUDUIS . ROMANUS .	*h.*	HEBRIDES	17-81
44.	„ „ „	„	HIBERNIA	17-71
45.	„ „ „	„	NORTH . WALES	„
46.	*R.* CLAUDUIS ROMANUS	„	DELECTAT . RUS *	
47.	„ „ „	*f.*	PAX . PLA . CID	*Ex:* 1775
48.	„ „ „	„	BRITANNIA§ ISLE .	„ 1774
49.	„ „ „	„	„ „ „	„ 1777
Ɣ50.	„ CLAUDUIS ROMANUS .	„	DELECTAT . RUS .	„ 1775
51.	„ „ „	„	MAY BRITONS RULE	„ 1779
52.	„ CLAUDUIS . ROMANUS .	„	DELECTAT RUS .	„ 1774
53.	„ „ „	„	PAX PLA CID.	„(1772 ?)
54.	„ CLAUDUIS : ROMANUS .	„	DELECTAT . RUS .	„ 1771
55.	„ „ „	„	DELECTAT RUS . * C	„ 1774
56.	„ „ „	„	PAX . PLA . CID .	„ 1773
57.	„ „ „	„	BRITAN NIA	„ 1771
58.	„ „ „	*h.*	MUSIC CHARMS	
59.	*L.* CLEMENT PONT MAX		HINC.NOSTRÆ.CREVERE.ROSÆ.	
60.	„ COLONEL KIRK	*f.*	BRITONS HAPPY ISLE	
61.	„ „ „	*h.*	NORTH WALES .	
62.	„ „ „	„	* NORTH WALES *	
63.	„ „ „	„	NORTH WALES	17-95
64.	„ „ „	„	„ „	17-96
65.	*L.* COLONEL PERCIE KIRK	*f.*	BRITONS OWN HAPPY ISLE	1686
66.	„ „ „	„	BRITAN NIA . RULES THE MAIN	
67.	„ CORNWAL LIS IND	„	BRITAN. NIA	*Ex:* 1771
68.	„ „ „	„	„ „ „	„ 1774
69.	„ „ „	„	BRITAIN RULES .	„ 1771
70.	„ „ „	„	BRITISH TARS	„ 1797
71.	„ „ „	„	DELECTAN DVS .	„ 1690
↙72.	„ CORNWAL LIS . IND	„	BATER SEA	„ 1779
73.	„ „ „	„	BRITAN NIA . RULES THE MAIN	
74.	„ „ „	„	BRITAIN RULES	„ 1771

75.	*L.*	CORNWAL LIS . IND	*f.*	BRITAN . NIA	*Ex:* 1771
76.	,,	,, ,,	,,	BRITAN RULE	,, 1771
77.	,,	CORNWAL LIS . IND .	,,	BONNY GIRL .	,, 1779
78.	,,	,, ,,	,,	BRITAN NIA . RULES THE MAIN	
79.	,,	,, ,,	,,	BRITISH GIRL [s]	*Ex:* 1788
80.	*R.*	CORNWAL LIS . IND .	*h.*	HEBRITES	17-69
81.	,,	,, ,,	,,	HIBERNIA	17-76
82.	,,	, ,,	,,	HIRARMIA	17-69
83.	,,	CORNWAL LIS IND	*f.*	BRITAINS ISLES	*Ex:* 1771
84.	,,	, ,,	,,	BRITONS RULE	,, ,,
85.	,,	,, ,,	,,	BRITISH TARS	,, 1797
86.	,,	,, ,,	,,	DELECTAN DOS	,, 1690
87.	,,	,, ,,	*h.*	HIBERIA	17-76
88.	,,	,, ,,	,,	HIBERNIA	,,
89.	*L.*	CORNWAL LIS . IR[D]	*f.*	BONNI FACE	*Ex:* 1771
90.	,,	,, ,,	,,	BRITAN NIA .	,, ,,
✓ 91.	,,	,, ,,	,,	BRITAN RULE	,, ,,
92.	*R.*	DUKE OF BEDFORD	,,	BRITISH TARS	,, 1797
93.	,,	,, ,,	*h.*	* MUSIC CHARMS *	
94.	,,	DUKE OF YORK	,,	BRITANNIA [s] HERO	
95.	,,	DUKE OF . YORKE	*f.*	BRITAN NIA	*Ex:* 1775
96.	,,	,, ,,	*h.*	HALFPENNY	17-81
97.	,,	,, ,,	,,	HIBERNIA	17-69
✓ 98.	,,	GANGES . III . RATE .	*f.*	BRITANNIA . RULES	
99.	,,	,, ,,	*h.*	STRATFOR DENSIS .	17-81
100.	,,	GBOIUISE INI RAX	,,	HIBERNTA	1766
101.	,,	GDOR OVIS . PEL . LEW	*f.*	BRITISH TARS	
102.	,,	GDOROVIS . TII RDX .	,,	BERTAN NUA .	*Ex:* 1775
103.	,,	,, ,,	,,	BERTEN NOE .	,, 1771
104.	,,	,, ,,	,,	BRITAN NIA .	,, TOKEN
105.	,,	GDOROVIS TII RDX	,,	BRITAIN RULES	,, 1731
106.	,,	GDORIOUS TII RDX :	,,	BRITAIT RULES	
107.	,,	,, ,,	,,	BRITAN NIAS ISLES	
108.	*L.*	GEORGUIS TI ROX .	,,	BERTAN NUA	*Ex:* 1775
109.	,,	,, ,,	,,	BRITAN NIA	,, TOKEN
110.	,,	,, ,,	,,	BRITAT RULES	,, 1771
111.	,,	,, ,,	,,	PAX PLA CET	,, 177?
112.	*R.*	GEORCIVS III BEX	,,	BRITAN NIA	
113.	*R.*	GEORCIVS III KEX	*h.*	NORTH WALES	
114.	*L.*	GEORGE FOR EVER	*f.*	BRITONS FOR EVER	,, TOKEN
✓ 115.	,,	GEORGE GORDON	,,	BATER SEA	,, 1779
116.	,,	,, ,,	,,	BRITAN . NIA .	,, 1771
117.	,,	,, ,,	,,	BRITONS RULE	,, 1791
118.	,,	,, ,,	*h.*	SOUTH WALES	17-96
119.	*R.*	,, ,,	*f.*	BRITAN NIA	*Ex:* 1771
120.	,,	,, ,,	,,	BRITONS RULE .	,, 1772
121.	,,	,, ,,	,,	,, ,,	,, 1776
122.	,,	,, ,,	,,	DELECTAT . RUS	,, 1775
123.	,,	,, ,,	,,	BONNY GIRL	,, 1779
124.	,,	,, ,,	,,	BRITANNIA RULES THE MAIN .	

25 *

125.	*R.* GEORGE GORDON	*f.* BRITISH TARS		1797
126.	„ „ „	*h.* NORTH WALES		1769
127.	*L.* GEORGE II. MAG	*f.* BRITISH TARS	*Ex* :	1797
128.	„ „ „	*h.* NORTH WALES	TOKEN	
129.	„ GEORGE II REX	*f.* BRITAN NIA	*Ex* :	1752
130.	*R.* „ III „	„ „ „	„	1771
131.	„ „ „ RULES	„ „ „	„	1775
132.	*L.* GEORGEIVS WASHINGTON	*h.* * NORTH WALES *		
133.	„ „ „	„ * * NORTH WALES * *		
134.	*R.* GEORGE KING OF B	*f.* HALF PENNY	*Ex* :	1777
135.	„ „ REN	*h.* YELARIES		17-71
136.	„ GEORGEON II PES	„ HIBERNIA		16-96
137.	„ GEORGE P.R WALES	„ BRITANNIA'S HERO		
138.	*L.* „ REIGN'D .	*f.* PITT FOR EVER	*Ex* :	1730
139.	„ „ REIGNS	„ BATER SEA	„	1776
140.	„ „ „	„ „ „	„	1779
141.	„ „ „	„ BRITONS RULE	„	1791
142.	„ „ „	„ DELECTAN DUS	„	1771
143.	„ „ „	*h.* SOUTH WALES		17-96
144.	*R.* „ „	*f.* BATER SEA	*Ex* :	TOKEN
145.	„ „ „	„ „ „	„	1776
146.	*L.* „ RULE	*h.* DELECT TATRUS		17-71
147.	„ „ RULED	*f.* BRITAIN'S ISLES	*Ex* :	1721
148.	„ „ „	„ „ „	„	1731
149.	„ „ „	„ „ „	„	1756
150.	„ „ „	„ „ „	„	1771
151.	„ GEORGE . RULED .	*h.* „ „		17-56
152.	„ GEORGE RULES .	*f.* BATER SEA .	*Ex* :	1776
153.	„ „ „	„ BOENNY GIRL	„	1777
154.	„ GEORGE . RULES	„ BRITAIN RULES	„	1771
155.	„ „ „ (No dot)	„ BRITAIN'S ISLES	„	1721
156.	„ „ „ „	„ „ „	„	1730
157.	„ „ „ „	„ „ „	„	1731
158.	„ „ „ „	„ BRITANNIA GUARDS	„	1771
159.	„ GEORGE . . RULES .	„ BRITAN NIA .	„	ISLES
160.	„ „ „	„ BRITANNIA.S ISLES	„	1773
161.	„ „ „	„ „ „	„	1777
162.	„ (No dot before Rules)	„ BRITISH TARS +	„	1771
163.	„ „ „	„ DELECTAN DUS .	„	„
164.	„ „ „	„ DELECTAT RUS . C	„	1774 .
165.	„ „ „	*h.* NORTH WALES		17-69
166.	„ GEORGE . . RULES .	*f.* BRITANNIA.S EARD .	*Ex* :	1771
167.	„ „ „ (No dots)	*h.* DELECT TATRUS		17-71
168.	„ „ „ „	„ NORTH WALES		17-81
169.	„ GEORGE . RULES . I.G.	*f.* DELECTAT RUS. * C	*Ex* :	1774
170.	„ „ „	*h.* HEBRIDES		17-81
171.	„ (No dots or initials)	„ HILAR IES		17-71
172.	„ „ „	„ HISPAN IOLA .		17-36
173.	„ „ „	„ NORTH WALES		17-60
174.	„ „ „	„ „ „		17-69

175.	*L.*	(No dots or initials)	*h.*	NORTH WALES			17-71
176.	,,	,, ,,	,,	,, ,,			J7-7J
177.	,,	,, ,,	,,	,, ,,			17-75
178.	,,	GEORGE . RULES I.G.	*h.*	,, ,,			J7-8J
179.	,,	,, ,, (T under)	,,	,, ,,			,,
180.	,,	,, (No initial)	,,	,, ,,			17-82
181.	*R.*	GEORGE . RULES .	*f.*	BRITAN NIA		*Ex :*	1771
182.	,,	,, ,, (No dots)	*h.*	BRITAIN'S . ISLES			1756
183.	,,	,, (With dots)	*f.*	BRITAIN NIAS . ISLE .	*Ex :*		1791
184.	,,	,, (Rude work)	,,	BRITONS RULE		,,	,,
185.	,,	,, ,,	*h.*	NORTH WALES			17-56
186.	,,	(Same as No. 184)	,,	,, ,,			17-61
187.	,,	,, ,,	,,	,, ,,			17-69
188.	,,	,, ,,	,,	,, ,,			17-75
189.	,,	,, ,,	,,	,, ,,			17-82
190.	,,	,, ,,	,,	NORTH WALES			,,
191.	,,	,, ,,	,,	NORTH WALES			,,
192.	,,	,, ,,	*f.*	BRITANNIA'S BARD			1771
193.	,,	,, ,,	*h.*	HEREKNIA			1769
194.	,,	,, ,,	,,	HIBEKNIA T D			1760
195.	,,	,, ,,	*f.*	HILARITAS			1771
196.	,,	,, ,,		HISPAN NIOLA			1791
197.	,,	,, ,,		MUSIC CHARMS			1775
198.	,,	,, ,,		PAX PLACID			1772
199.	,,	GEORGERY . TOL . REN		BONNEY GEL			
200.	*L.*	GEORGES . RULES .	*h.*	HEBR IDES			1771
201.	*R.*	GEORGE SUSSEX .	*f.*	BATER SEA		*Ex :*	TOKEN
202.	,,	,, ,, (No dot)	,,	,, ,,		,,	1772
203.	,,	,, ,, ,,	,,	,, ,,		,,	1779
204.	,,	,, ,, ,,	,,	BRITONS RULE		,,	1791
205.	,,	,, ,, ,,	,,	DELECTAN DUS		,,	1771
206.	,,	,, ,, ,,	*h.*	NORTH WALES			17-61
207.	,,	GEORGE . SUS-SEX .	*f.*	BRITAIN RULES		*Ex :*	1771
208.	,,	,, ,,	,,	BRITAN . . NIA .		,,	,,
209.	,,	,, ,,	,,	BRITAN RULE		,,	,,
210.	,,	GEORGE . TEL . REN .	*h.*	YELAREBIH			17-77
211.	*L.*	GEORGIAS II REX	*f.*	BRITAN NIA		*Ex :*	1731
212.	*R.*	GEORGIAS III REX	*f.*	BRITAN NIA		,,	1771
213.	*L.*	GEORGIVS II REN	,,	BUNNY GIRL			
214.	*R.*	GEORGIUS III REX	*h.*	NORTH WALES			1782
215.	*L.*	GEORGIVS II REX	*f.*	BRITAN NIA		*Ex :*	1737 .
216.	,,	GEORGIVS . II REX .	,,	,, ,,		,,	1751
217.	,,	,, ,,	,,	,, ,,		,,	1771
218.	,,	,, ,,	,,	,, ,,		,,	1775
219.	,,	,, ,,	,,	,, ,,		,,	1792
220.	,,	,, ,,	,,	BRITAN RULES		,,	1771
221.	,,	,, ,,	,,	BRITANNIA		,,	1775
222.	,,	,, ,,	*h.*	HIBERNIA			17 51
223.	*R.*	,, ,,	,,	,,			17 81
224.	,,	,, ,,	*f.*	BRITAN NIA		*Ex :*	1771

No.		Obverse		Reverse	Date
225.	*R.*	GEORGIVS III REX	*f.*	BRITAN NIA	*Ex*: 1775
226.	,,	,, ,, ,,	,,	,, ,,	,, 1778
227.	,,	,, ,, ,,	,,	,, ,,	,, 1787
228.	,,	,, ,, ,,	*h.*	HIBERNIA	1769
229.	,,	,, ,, ,,	,,	,,	1781
230.	*L.*	XƎR . III SVI ƧOЯOƎ	*f.*	AIN NATIRꓭ	*Ex*: 1771
231.	*R.*	GEORGIVS TIL REN	*h.*	HIDERALA	17-69
232.	,,	GEORGIVS TRIUMPHO .	*f.*	*(in box)*. VOCE POPOLI	*Ex*: 1783
233.	*L.*	GEORGLVS II RER	,,	BRITAIN RULES	1771
234.	,,	GEORGUIS II REX	,,	BRITAN NET	,,
235.	,,	,, ,, ,,	*h.*	HIBERNIA	17-76
236.	,,	GEORGUIS III RUS	*f.*	BRITAN NIA	1771
237.	,,	GEORGUIS III RUX	,,	BRILLA NGE	,,
238.	,,	,, ,, ,,	,,	BRITAN NET	,,
239.	*R.*	,, ,,	,,	BRITAN NIA	,,
240.	,,	GEORG VIS II RFX	,,	BRIT AIN	1770
241.	,,	GEOR IOUS III VIS	*h.*	NORTH WALES	17-61
242.	*L.*	GEOR IVS II . REN	*f.*	BONNY GIRL .	*Ex*: 1771
243.	,,	,, ,, ,,	,,	,, LAS .	,, (1774 ?)
244.	*R.*	,, . PIL . SEX .	,,	BRITAN NIA	,, 1775
245.	,,	,, ,, ,,	,,	BRITISH TARS	,, 1767
246.	,,	GEORIVVS III VES	,,	BRITT	
247.	,,	,, ,, ,,	,,	BRITAN NIA	*Ex*: 1771
248.	,,	GEORUGIS III . RUX	,,	BRITAN RULES	,, ,,
249.	,,	,, ,, ,,	*h.*	HIBERNIA	17-76
250.	,,	GEORUMS III	*f.*	BRITAN NIA	*Ex*: 1771
251.	,,	GEOTUISR INI RAX	*h.*	HIBERNTA	17-66
252.	*R.*	GIVE US PEACE	*f.*	PITT FOR EVER	*Ex*: 1770
253.	*L.*	GLACIOVS DEI . PAX	,,	BONNEY GERL	,, 1779
254.	,,	,, ,, ,,	,,	BRITAN RULES	,, 1771
255.	,,	GLACIOUS DEI . PAX	,,	BRITAN NIA	,, ,,
256.	,,	,, ,, ,,	,,	,, ,,	,, 1774
257.	,,	,, ,, ,,	,,	BRITAN RULE	,, 1771
258.	,,	,, ,, ,,	,,	,, RULES	,, ,,
259.	*R.*	,, ,,	,,	,, ,,	,, ,,
260.	,,	,, ,, ,,	*h.*	HEBRIDES	17 ( )
261.	*L.*	GLAUCOVS . DEI . PAX .	*f.*	BONNEY GERL .	*Ex*: 1777
262.	,,	,, ,, ,,	,,	BONNY GIRL	,, 1771
263.	,,	GLORIOVS II REN	,,	BRITAN NIA	,, 1775
264.	,,	,, ,, ,, ,,	,,	,, ,, ,,	,, 1797
265.	,,	,, ,, ,, REX	,,	,, ,, ,,	,, 1777
266.	*R.*	GLORIOVS III VES	*h.*	HEBRIDES	17-81
267.	,,	,, ,, ,, ,,	,,	HIBEKNIA	
268.	,,	,, III . VIS .	*f.*	BONNY GIRL	*Ex*: 1779
269.	,,	,, ,,	,,	BRITAN NIA	,, 1775
270.	,,	,, ,,	,,	BRITAN RULES	,, 1771
271.	,,	,, ,,	,,	BRITISH TARS	,, (1771?)
272.	,,	,, ,,	,,	BRITON S RULE	,, 1788
273.	,,	,, ,,	,,	BITIT	
274.	,,	,, IER VES	,,	BRITAN NIA	*Ex*: 1771

275.	*R.*	GLORIOVS . IER . VES .	*h.*	HEBRIDES	17-91
276.	*L.*	GLORIOVS . IER VIS .	,,	HIRAROSA .	17-69
277.	*R.*	,, ,,	*f.*	BRITAN NIA . RULES THE MAIN	
278.	,,	,, ,,	,,	BRITISH TARS .	*Ex:* 1771
279.	,,	,, IER . VIS	,,	BRITAN NIA . RULES THE MAIN	
280.	,,	,, ,,	,,	BRITAN RULE	*Ex:* 1771
281.	,,	,, ,,	,,	BRITA IN RULES	,, ,,
282.	,,	,, ,,	,,	BRITONS RULE .	,, ,,
283.	,,	,, ,,	,,	BRITISH TARS .	,, 1797
284.	,,	,, ,,	*h.*	NORTH WALES	17-61
✦285.	,,	,, ,,	*ship.*	VAL . T BRIT TISH TARS	-
286.	*L.*	,, JAR . VIS	*f.*	BRITAN NIA	*Ex:* 1774
287.	,,	,, ,,	,,	BRITAN RULES	,, 1771
288.	,,	,, NE . SON	,,	BRITISH TARS	,, 1767
289.	,,	,, PELLEW .	*f.*	HALFPENNY .	,, 1796
290.	,,	,, ,,	,,	INCORPORATED BY ACT OF PARLIAMENT	,, 1792
291.	,,	,, ,,	*h.*	* MUSIC CHARMS	
292.	,,	,, PE . LEW	*f.*	BRITAN NIA . RULES THE MAIN	
293.	,,	,, ,,	,,	BRITISH TARS	*Ex:* 1771
294.	,,	,, ,,	,,	,, ,,	,, 1797
295.	,,	,, ,,	,,	BRITONS RULE	,, 1771
✦296.	,,	,, ,,	*ship.*	VAL . T BRIT TISH TARS	
297.	*R.*	GLORIOUS PEL-LEW .	*f.*	BRITISH TARS .	*Ex:* 1797
298.	,,	GLORIOUS . TIL . ROX .	*h.*	HOS SANNA .	17-61
299.	,,	GLORIVS IER . VES	,,	HEBRIDES	17-81
300.	,,	,, PIT . SEX	*f.*	BONNY GIRL .	*Ex:* 1779
301.	,,	,, ,,	,,	BRITISH TARS	,, 1767
302.	,,	,, ,,	,,	BRITONS RULE	,, ,,
303.	,,	GLORIUS IES . VES	*h.*	HEBRIDES	17-97
304.	,,	GLORIUVS . III . VIS	*f.*	BRITAT	
305.	*L.*	GOD SAVE THE KING .	,,	BRITAN NIA .	*Ex:* 1771
306.	,,	,, ,,	,,	BRITAN NIAS .	,, ISLES
307.	,,	,, ,,	,,	BRITAN RULES .	,, 1771
308.	,,	GOD SAVE THE KING	*h.*	NO BE BGTA	16 96
309.	,,	,, ,,	*f.*	OF ENG LAND	*Ex:* 1772
310.	*R.*	,, ,,	,,	BRITAN NIA .	,, ISLES
311.	,,	,, ,,	,,	,, ,,	,, 1771
312.	,,	.GOD.SAVE.THE.KING.	,,	BRITANNIA RULES	,, ,,
313.	,,	,, ,,	*h.*	MUSIC * CHARMS	17-75
314.	,,	GOD SAVE THE KING		BE AS YOU SEEM TO BE	*Ex:* 1796
315.	,,	,, ,,	*f.*	BRITAN NIA	,, 1774
316.	,,	,, ,,	*h.*	* NORTH * * WALES *	
317.	,,	,, ,,	*f.*	NORTH WALES	*Ex:* 1792
318.	,,	GOD SAVE THE REALM	*f.*	DELEÇTAT . RUS	,, 1775
319.	,,	,, ,,	*h.*	MUSIC * CHARMS	17-75
320.	,,	,, ,,	*f.*	PAX PLA . CID	*Ex:* 1775
321.	*L.*	GOD SAVE US ALL .	,,	BEL * ONA	,, 1777
322.	,,	,, ,,	,,	BRITAN NIA	,, 1774
323.	,,	,, ,,	*h.*	HIBERNIA	16-96

324.	*L.*	GOD SAVE US ALL .	*h.*	MUSIC ✳ CHARMS		17-75
325.	,,	,, ,, ,,	,,	NOBEBGTA		16-96
326.	,,	,, ,, ,,	,,	✳ NORTH ✳ ✳ WALES ✳		
327.	,,	GOERGAIS TII RAX	*f.*	BIRMIN RAI		1777
328.	,,	,, ,, ,,	,,	BRITAIN RULES		1777
329.	*R.*	GOERGIUV . III . PAX	,,	BRITAN NIA	*Ex:*	1774
330.	,,	,, ,, ,,	*h.*	HIBEKNIA		17-69
331.	*L.*	GORDIUS REYS	*f.*	BRITAIN RULES	*Ex:*	1777
332.	,,	,, ,, ,,	,,	BRITAN NIA	,,	1771
333.	,,	,, ,, ,,	*h.*	DELECTATRUS		17-81
334.	*R.*	,, ,, ,,	*f.*	BRITAN NIA	*Ex:*	1771
335.	,,	,, ,, ,,	,,	DELECTAN DUS	,,	1777
336.	,,	,, ,, ,,	,,	DRLECTAN RUS	,,	1777
337.	,,	,, ,, ,,	*h.*	DELECTATRUS		17-81
338.	,,	,, ,, ,,	*h.*	HEBRIDES		,,
339.	,,	GORGIVS III . REX .	,,	HIBERNIA		,,
340.	,,	GRAGRORY . III . RUS .	*f.*	PAX PLA CID .	*Ex:*	1770
341.	,,	GREGORIVS . III . PON .	,,	BRITAN RULES	,,	1771
342.	,,	,, ,, ,,	,,	BRITISH GIRLS	,,	1788
343.	,,	,, ,, ,,	*h.*	HEBRIDES		17-81
344.	,,	,, ,, ,, PONT .	*f.*	BRITAN RULES	*Ex:*	1771
345.	,,	GREGORS III PON	,,	BRITAN NIA . RULES THE MAIN		
346.	,,	,, ,, ,,	,,	BRITA IN RULES	*Ex:*	1771
347.	,,	GREGORVS III PAX	*h.*	HEBRIDES		17-81
348.	,,	,, ,, ,,	,,	,,		17-97
349.	,,	,, ,, ,, PON	*f.*	BRITAN NIA	*Ex:*	1771
✓ 350.	*L.*	GREGORY . II .	,,	BELLONA	,,	1756
351.	,,	GREGORY . II . BAN		BON GEL		
352.	,,	GREGORY . TI . ROW .	*h.*	HIBERNIA (?)		17-71
353.	,,	,, ,, ,,	,,	NORTH WALES		17-71
354.	,,	GREGORY . III PAX	*f.*	BONNI FACE	*Ex:*	( )
355.	*R.*	GREGO^{RY} . III . PON	,,	BEL ✳ ONA	,,	1777
356.	,,	GREGOR^{Y} III . PONT .	,,	,, ,,	,,	,,
357.	,,	,, ,,	,,	BRITAN NIA	,,	1771
358.	,,	GREGORY . III . PON .	,,	BOENY GIRL	,,	,,
359.	,,	,, ,, ,,	,,	BONNY GIRL	,,	,,
360.	,,	,, ,, ,,	,,	BRITAIN RULES	,,	1731
361.	,,	,, ,, ,,	,,	,, ,, ,,	,,	1771
362.	,,	,, ,, ,,	,,	,, ,, ,,	,,	1777
363.	,,	,, ,, ,,	,,	BRITAIN S ISLES	,,	1721
364.	,,	,, ,, ,,	,,	,, ,, ,,	,,	1730
365.	,,	,, ,, ,,	,,	,, ,, ,,	,,	1771
366.	,,	,, ,, •,	,,	BRITAIN^s ISLES	,,	,,
367.	,,	,, ,, ,,	,,	BRITAN NIA	,,	,,
368.	,,	,, ,, ,,	,,	PAX PLA CID .	,,	1773
369.	*R.*	GREGORY . III . PON .	*f.*	BONNY GIRL .	,,	1779
370.	,,	,, ,, ,,	,,	BRITONS RULE .	,,	1771
371.	,,	,, ,, ,,	,,	PAX PLA CID .	,,	1779
372.	,,	GRUMRUIS . ITI NEX	*h.*	HIBERNIA		17-76
373.	,,	,, ,, ,, ,,	,,	IIIRARMIA .		,,

374. *R.* GSOIUISE . INI . BAX	*h.* NTBRRNIA		17-66
375. ,, GVLIELMVS SHACKSPIRE	*f.* BRITANNIA: ISLES		
376. *L.* GULIELMUS.SHAKESPEAR.	,, BRITANNIA . RULES .		
377. ,, ,, ,,	,, BRITANNIA: BARD	*Ex:*	1771
378. ,, ,, ,,	,, BRI TON'S	,,	GLORY
↲ 379. ,, ,, ,,	,, ENG LANDS	,,	,,
380. *R.* GULIELMUS SHAKESPEAR	,, BRITAN NIA	,,	1771
381. ,, ,, ,,	,, ,, ,,	,,	1774
382. ,, ,, ,,	,, BRITAN NIA . RULES THE MAIN		
383. ,, ,, ,,	,, BRITAN RULE	*Ex:*	1771
384. ,, ,, ,,	,, BRITON S RULE .	,,	1771
385. ,, ,, ,,	,, ,, ,,	,,	1772
386. ,, ,, ,,	,, ,, ,,	,,	1791
387. ,, ,, ,,	*h.* MUSIC * CHARMS		17-75
✓ 388. ,, ,, ,,	,, STRATFOR DIENSIS .		17-81
389. *L.* GULIELMUS SHAKSPEAR	,, HISPAN NIOLA		17-91
390. *R.* GULIEMUS SHAKESPEAR	*f.* BRITAN NIA	*Ex:*	1771
391. ,, ,, ,,	,, ,, ,,	,,	1774
392. ,, ,, ,,	*h.* * NORTH * * WALES *		
393. ,, ,, ,,	*f.* NORTH WALES	*Ex:*	1792
394. *R.* GUSTAVAS ADOLPHUS .	,, BEL * ONA	,,	1777
395. ,, ,, VASA	,, BRITANNI CUS	,,	1771
396. *L.* GUSTAVUS ADOLPHUS .	*f.* BRITAIN RULES .	,,	,,
397. ,, ,, ,,	,, BRITAN NIA	,,	1774
↲ 398. ,, -H -L	*Arms.* NON . PROCUL . DIES . 1696		
399. *R.* IOHN HOW ARD F.R.S.	*f.* UNITY AND PEACE		
✓ 400. ,, IOHN KEMP .	*h.* NORTH WALES		17-96
401. ,, ,, ,,	*f.* UNITY AND PEACE		
402. ,, IOHN SON PUGALIST	*h.* * MUSIC CHARMS		
403. ,, ,, ,,	,, * NORTH * * WALES *		
404. ,, ,, - ,,	,, * * NORTH WALES * *		
405. ,, LONG LIVE THE KING .	*f.* BATER SEA	*Ex:*	1776
406. ,, ,, ,,	,, BRITAN NIA	,,	1772
407. ,, ,, ,,	,, BRITAN NIA RULES THE MAIN		
408. ,, ,, ,,	*h.* NORTH . WALES		17-61
✓ 409. ,, LOUIS THE SIXTEENTH	*f.* BRITONS HAPPY ISLE		
410. ,, ,, ,,	*h.* * MUSIC CHARMS		
411. ,, LUD . XX . DEI . GRA .	*f.* BRITANNIA: BARD .	*Ex:*	1771
412. ,, ,, ,,	*h.* . FRAN . E T . NAVR .		17-71
413. *L.* MAY . PEACE . BE . ESTABLISHED	,, HILA RIAS		,,
414. *R.* OLIVER CROMWELL	,, * SOUTH WALES *		
415. ,, ,, ,,	*f.* BRITANNIAS ISLE	*Ex:*	1791
↲ 416. ,, PAYABLE * AT . I . WILLIAMS .	*h.* MUSIC * CHARMS		17-75
417. ,, ,, ,,	*f.* NORTH WALES	*Ex:*	1792
418. *L.* PAYABLE . AT . W . WILLIAMS .	,, BRITANNIAS . ISLE	,,	1791
♥ 419. ,, ,, ,,	*h.* NORTH WALES		17-82
420. ,, ,, ,,	*f.* BRITANNIA: BARD	*Ex:*	1771

421.	L.	PAYABLE . AT . W . WILLIAMS .	f.	NORTH WALES	Ex: 1792
422.	„	„ „	h.	NORTH * WALES	
423.	„	„ „	f.	NORTH WALES	Ex: 1792
424.	„	„ „	„	BRITANNIA RULE	„ 1771
425.	„	PAYABLE . AT . WM .	h.	DELECTAT RUS *	
426.	R.	PRINCEPS WALLIÆ .	h.	DELECTAT * RUS *	
427.	„	„ „	f.	PAX . PLA . CID	Ex: 1775
428.	„	QUINTUS SEXTUS .	h.	MUSIC * CHARMS .	„
✔429.	L.	ROMULUS		VIRTVS NUNQ DEFICIT ICXXX	
430.	„	SFORGIVS LLUDOVICUS XVI		. IE . NE | VIS . QVA | REGRET | 17 . 93	
431.	„	SHAKESPEAR	f.	HALFPENNY	Ex: 179
432.		„	,,	INCORPORATED BY ACT OF PAR-LIAMENT	
433.	„	SHAKES PEARE	„	RULE BRIT AN NIA .	Ex: 1771
434.	„	„ „	„	RULE BRI TA NNIA .	„ „
435.	R.	Sᴿ BEVOIS SOUTHAMTON	h.	* NORTH * * WALES *	
436.	„	(Hair tied with 2 bows)	„	„	„
437.	„	(One bow and an end)	„	„	„
438.	„	(Helmed)	„	„	„
439.	L.	THOMAS SEYMOUR .	f.	BRITONS HAPPY ISLE	
✔440.	„	„ „	h.	* MUSIC CHARMS	
441.	„	(Larger and older bust)	„	„ „	
442.	„	„ „	„	* SOUTH WALES *	
443.	R.	THOMAS SEYMOUR .	„	* * NORTH WALES * *	
✔444.	L.	TVRCVPELLERIVS	f.	HISPANNIOLA	
445.	R.	WILLIAM . PIT . P . M .	„	RULE BRI TANNIA	Ex: 1797
446.	L.	WILLIAM WILLIAMS	h.	HIBERNIA	17-66
447.	„	WILLIAM S WILLIAMS	f.	BRITAN NIA	Ex: 1774
448.	„	„ „	h.	* NORTH * * WALES *	
449.	„	Bust only.		Harp only.	
450.	„	Different bust.		Female seated (?)	

FARTHINGS.

451.	L.	DUKE OF YORK	f.	FARTHING	Ex: 1756
452.	R.	ENONA ATKNE	Arms.	KETEC GATVC	1791
453.	„	GEOGIS III BEX	h.	BRITANNIA	1777
454.	„	GEORGEV GORDON	Arms.	PEACE AND PLENTY	
455.	L.	GEORGE II REN	f.	BRITANNIA	
456.	„	„ „ RULES	„	BRITAN RULES	Ex: 1779
457.	„	„ REIGNS .	„	BRITAN NIA	„ 1777
458.	„	„ „	,,	BRITON S RULE	„ 1776
459.	„	„ RULE	„	FARTHING	„ 1798
460.	„	GEORGE .. RULES	„	BRITAIN RULES	„ 1771
461.	„	GEORGE . RULES .	„	BRITAN NIAᴱ	„ ISLES
462.	„	GEORGE .. RULES .	„	BRITAN .. NIA .	„ „
463.	„	„ „	„	BRITA NIAᴱ	„ „

464. L. GEORGE .. RULES (Different bust)   f. BRITAN NIA.   *Ex*: ISLS
465. ,, ,, ,,   ,, FARTHING   ,, 1793
466. ,, ,, ,,   ,, MNITH INO
467. R. GEORGE RULES .   ,, BRITAN NIA.   *Ex*: ISLES
468. ,, ,, ,,   ,, BRITAN RULES   ,, 1771
469. ,, ,, ,,   ,, FARTHING   ,, 1793
470. ,, ,, ,,   ,, OLD   *Ex*: ENGLAND STILL
471. ,, GEORGE SUSSEX   ,, FARTHING   *Ex*: 1771 .
472. ,, GEORGIVS . HI REX   ,, BRITAN NIA   ,, 1774
473. L. GEOR . GIS III KEX   ,, BRITANNIA   ,, 1778 .
474. ,, GEORGIES II REN   ,, ,,   ,, 1771
475. ,, ,, ,, ,,   ,, ,,   ,, 1777
476. ,, ,, ,, ,,   ,, BRITONS RULE   ,, 1776
477. ,, ,, ,, REX   ,, FARTHING   ,, 1778
478. ,, GEVRCV ATOETE   *Stork, &c.*, ETA ENA NOA
479. ,, GLORIOUS DUNCAN   f. BRITAN NIA .   *Ex*: ISLES
480. ,, ,, ,,   ,, BRITAN RULES   ,, 1771
481. ,, ,, ,,   ,, OLD ENGLAND STILL
482. ,, GLORIOUS H OWE   ,, BRITAN NIA   *Ex*: 1794
483. R. GLORIOUS PEL : LEW   ,, ,, ,,   ,, 1771
484. ,, ,, ,,   ,, BRITONS RULE   ,, 1776
485. L. GORGUS . RUN .   ,, BRIANIA   ,, 1771
486. ,, GRAGORY II . PON .   ,, BRITANNIA RULES   ,, 1777
487. ,, ,, ,,   ,, BRITAIN RULES   ,, 1771
488. ,, GREGOIVS III PAX   ,, ,, ,,   ,, ,,
489. ,, GREGORY II PAX   ,, BRITANNIA   ,, 1777
490. ,, ISAAC NEWTON   ,, BRITAN RULES   ,, 1797
491. R. LORD CAMDEN   ,, PEACE AND TRADE

Silver Proofs.

The following pieces occur struck in Silver :—

Buckinghamshire, Nos. 3, 20, 22, 23, 24, and 26.
Cambridgeshire, Nos. 4, 7.
Cornwall, No. 4.
Devonshire, No. 2.
Durham, No. 5.
Essex, No. 4.
Gloucestershire, Nos. 40, and 42, and the Gloucester buildings.
Hampshire, Nos. 40, 41, and 58.
Herefordshire, No. 1.
Kent, No. 22.
Lancashire, Nos. 86, and 89.
Leicestershire, No. 2.
Lincolnshire, No. 6a.
Middlesex, Nos. 13, 23, 31, 95, 103, 105, 106, 110, 152, 196, 211,
     217, 236, 237, 265, 266, 279, 348, 350, 353, 361, 725, and 748.
Norfolk, Nos. 4, 7, 14, 20, 25, 35, 47, and 54.
Shropshire, No. 13.
Somersetshire, No. 74.
Staffordshire, Nos. 6, 17, and 19.
Suffolk, Nos. 8, 9, 17, 25, 29, 31a, and 33.
Sussex, No. 14.
Warwickshire, Nos. 1, 21, 22, 30, 42a, 43, 44, 45a, 54, 233, 236,
     251, 276, and the Birmingham and Coventry buildings.

Anglesea, Nos. 2a, 4, 6, 80, 100, 175.

Angusshire, Nos. 1, 2, 3, 7, 8, 12, 14, 15, 16, and 17.
Ayrshire, Nos. 1, and 3.
Lanarkshire, No. 2.
Lothian, No. 5.
Perthshire, Nos. 1, and 4.

Not Local, Nos. 2, 3, 4, 12, 16, 35, 40, 44, 86, 129, and 197.

Index of Edges.

In the following index will be found all the different edges, arranged in alphabetical order. Where more than one number is affixed, the first will refer to the proper edge, the others being references to false or incorrect edges, which either by accident, or design, were used for the various pieces. The numbers refer to the page on which they are found.

PAYABLE IN HULL AND IN LONDON, 252, 26, 27, 36, 56, 61, 62, 65, 69, 103, 174, 190, 211, 259, 313, 355, 356.

„ „ LANCASTER LIVERPOOL & MANCHESTER, 58.

„ „ „ LONDON OR BRISTOL, 56, 12, 13, 14, 25, 49, 50, 53, 59, 61, 63, 64, 93, 95, 99, 100, 101, 102, 111, 140, 152, 158, 171, 172, 173, 187, 188, 189, 198, 201, 209, 212, 221, 222, 232, 233, 234, 237, 238, 241, 255, 276, 278, 285, 286, 305, 314, 342, 355, 357, 370, 371, 376, 377.

„ „ LANCASTER LONDON OR LIVERPOOL, 58, 12, 171, 209, 256, 285, 306, 355, 374, 375, 379.

„ „ LEITH EDINBURGH & GLASGOW, 315.

„ „ LIVERPOOL OR BRISTOL, 255.

„ „ LONDON, 141, 7, 15, 24, 26, 36, 37, 38, 39, 51, 58, 63, 65, 84, 85, 109, 126, 131, 135, 156, 171, 176, 183, 198, 206, 246, 260, 282, 284, 285, 296, 305, 306, 358, 369, 377.

„ „ LONDON BRISTOL & CARMARTHEN, 288.

„ „ LONDON BRISTOL & LANCASTER, 27, 36, 56, 68, 69, 153, 189, 206, 209, 232, 252, 259, 305, 313, 314, 356, 357, 358, 369, 373.

„ „ LONDON EVERY WHERE, 13, 37.

„ „ „ LIVERPOOL OR ANGLESEY, 250.

„ „ „ LIVERPOOL OR BRISTOL, 13, 61, 197, 223, 234, 238, 255, 282, 284, 354.

„ „ „ OR ANGLESEY, 211, 237.

„ „ „ „ BRIGHTON, 62.

„ „ „ „ LIVERPOOL, 236.

„ „ SUFFOLK BATH OR MANCHESTER, 61, 209, 285, 371, 374,

„ „ „ LONDON OR LIVERPOOL, 209. [379.

„ „ „ -STREET HAY-MARKET, 111, 57, 188.

PAYABLE * IN * LONDON * OR * ANGLESEY * 273, 281, 282.

„ ON DEMAND, 38, 208, 290.

„ „ „ BY JOHN FERRIER, 324.

„ „ „ „ THOS. WEBSTER JUNR. 294.

PAY THE BEARER ONE HALFPENNY IN DUBLIN, 342.

PAYNE & TURNER SILVER SMITHS BATH, 174.

PENNY TOKEN PAYABLE AT THE HOUSE OF IOBN HARDING CALICO PRINTER TAMWORTH, 181.

„ „ „ BY E . W . PERCY COVENTRY, 205.

„ „ „ „ RICHARD WRIGHT LICHFIELD, 181.

„ „ „ ON DEMAND, 205.

PORTSMOUTH HALFPENNY PAYABLE AT THO'S SHARPS, 40, 36.

PROMISSORY PENNY TOKEN PAYABLE ON DEMAND, 79.

PUBLISHED BY JOS. DANL. & JNO. BOULTER, 156, 297.

„ „ R . LODER 1796, 186.

RICHARD BACON COCKEY LANE, 151, 26, 27, 97.

„ DINMORE & SON NORWICH, 152.

S . & . T . ASHLEY, 150.

26 *

General Index.

The abbreviations are as follows : *p.* = penny ; *h.* = halfpenny ;
f. = farthing.

Addenda.

[*The figures on left-hand side of page, thus 58/25 denotes page 58, No. 25.*]

Since going to press the following additional Tokens have been noted.

49/50 *bis.* *O*: The same as No. 50.

R: The same as No. 46.

58/25 *bis.* *O*: The same as No. 25.

R: The same as No. 24.

E : PAYABLE IN LANCASTER LONDON OR LIVERPOOL.

60/49 *bis.* *O*: A rather poor imitation of No. 47, but the bowsprit nearly touches the last limb of the Y.

R: The bulrush heads are above the shield, and the top of the 1 is pointed.

E : PAYABLE IN DUBLIN OR LONDON . ×.

„ „ *a* As last, but *E*: PAYABLE IN LANCASTER. The remainder illegible.

70/6 *bis.* *O*: The same as No. 6.

R: A globe inscribed BRITAIN between a rose and thistle . BRITISH . PENNY . 1797.

E: I PROMISE TO PAY ON DEMAND THE BEARER ONE PENNY +

73/31 *bis.* Different rev: die, which may be distinguished by noting the T of THO.S which touches the U of JURY in this, and in No. 31, touches the Y.

80/111 *bis.* Slightly different to No.111 on both *O*: and *R*: which may be distinguished by the handles of the plough coming, the one to the foot of the L, and the other between the T and H.

132/638 *bis.* *O*: Cain and Abel. As No. 521.

R: Bust of Thelwall. As No. 535.

159/2 *bis.* *O*: The same as No. 2.

R: MATHER FURNISHING IRONMONGER HARDWAREMAN PATENT STOVE GRATE MANUFACTURER N⁰ 14 DEAN STREET NEWCASTLE UPON TYNE in eight lines. This is struck in tin.

165/3 *bis.* *O*: The same as No. 3.

R: Two boys riding a race upon asses. ASSES RUNNING FOR HALFPENCE.

E : Milled.

169/1 *bis.* *O*: and *E*: The same as No. 1.

R: The arms of West Cowes. See Hampshire, No. 63.

192/5 *bis.* O: A large building and trees . WEST . CLANDON . PLACE . SURRY *Ex* : JACOBS. See Middlesex, No. 94.

R: and E: The same as No 1.

216/103 *bis.* O: The same as No. 103.

R: SUB MONITOR in the centre . BLUE COAT CHARITY SCHOOL ERECTED 1724 BIRMINGHAM.

216/115 *bis.* O: The same as No. 115.

R: The same as obv. of No. 146. (*This is struck in tin.*)

219/166 *bis.* O: The same as No. 166.

R: Two men in a foundry &c. See Middlesex, No. 361.

E: Milled.

Slight variations of die have been noted as follows:—

41/48	Variations of rev. die.
41/50	,, ,,
56/9	,, ,,
59/37	,, · ,,
59/39	,, ,,
59/40	,, ,,
60/48	Variation of both obv. and rev.
222/186	,, ,, rev. die.
254/41	,, ,, obv. die.
263/4 *et seq.*	There are many variations of both obv. and rev. dies in the Anglesey series, other than those specified, which are too slight for description.

There are also the following additional edges :—

1/2*b.* E: PAYABLE AT W. GOLDSMITHS BRAINTREE ESSEX.

3/4*a.* E: PAYABLE AT F. WHEELER AYLESBURY BUCKS.

15/52*a.* E: PAYABLE AT SHARPS PORTSMOUTH AND CHALDECOTTS CHICHESTER.

22/6*b.* E: PAYABLE AT BANBURY OXFORD OR READING.

25/9*a.* E: LONDON LIVERPOOL OR MONTROSE.

,, ,, *b.* E: PAYABLE AT S. SALMONS I COURTNEY & E FROST PORTSEA ✕

26/3*a.* E: PAYABLE IN LONDON BRISTOL & LANCASTER.

26/4*b.* E: WE PROMISE TO PAY THE BEARER ONE CENT.

36/11*c.* E: PAYABLE AT W. GOLDSMITHS BRAINTREE ESSEX.

37/22*b.* E: PAYABLE IN LONDON BRISTOL & LANCASTER.

39/31*a.* E: PAYABLE IN LONDON. The remainder engrailed.

,, ,, *b.* E: Plain (not in collar).

40/38*a.* E: PAYABLE AT ADAM SIMPSONS ROMNEY.

40/39*a.* E: COVENTRY TOKEN.

40/41*a.* E: Plain (not in collar).

40/42*a.* E: Plain (not in collar).

42/54*a.* E: PAYABLE AT MACCLESFIELD LIVERPOOL OR CONGLETON . ✕ . (An Artists proof.)

43/58a.   E : PAYABLE IN ANGLESEY OR LONDON. (An Artists proof.)

„ „ b.   E : Plain (not in collar).

49/7a.   E : Plain (not in collar).

49/11c.   E : AT RICHARD SHIPDENS.

52/28a.   E : PAYABLE AT W. PARKERS OLD BIRMINGHAM WAREHOUSE.

52/29b.   E : MASONIC TOKEN I. SCETCHLEY FECIT . 1794 . +

54/40b.   E : Plain (not in collar).

57/18f.   E : HALFPENNY PAYABLE AT THE BLACK HORSE TOWER HILL

57/19a.   E : MASONIC HALFPENNY TOKEN MDCCXCIV . × . × .

58/26a.   E : PAYABLE IN LONDON. The remainder engrailed.

61/55d.   E : The same as No. 51.

61/56b.   E : PAYABLE AT THE WAREHOUSE OF THOS. & ALEXR. HUTCHISON.

74/36a.   E : The same as No. 33.

92/208a.   E : Plain (not in collar).

99/249c.   E : PAYABLE AT BECCLES SUFFOLK.

„ „ d.   E : Milled.

103/275a.   E : Plain (not in collar).

„ „ b.   E : PAYABLE AT I. IORDANS DRAPER GOSPORT.

109/341a.   E : PAYABLE IN DUBLIN OR LONDON.

„ „ b.   E : Milled.

109/343c.   E : PAYABLE AT THE WAREHOUSE OF IONATHAN GARTON & Cº . × .

109/344b.   E : PAYABLE AT THE WAREHOUSE OF SAMUEL KINGDON.

„ „ c.   E : WILLEY SNEDSHILL BERSHAM BRADLEY.

115/414a.   E : SKIDMORE HOLBORN LONDON.

„ „ b.   E : Plain (not in collar).

118/457   E : Milled over SKIDMORE HOLBORN LONDON.

152/22d.   E : Milled.

169/6a.   E : Plain (not in collar).

175/61a.   E : PORTSMOUTH HALFPENNY PAYABLE AT THOS . SHARPS . × .

176/74f.   E : PAYABLE AT DALLYS CHICHESTER.

190/30b.   E : Plain (not in collar).

193/10a.   E : Engrailed.

197/14d.   E : RICHARD BACON COCKEY LANE.

206/30i.   E : PAYABLE AT LEEK STAFFORDSHIRE.

207/33a.   E : PAYABLE AT THE HOUSE OF IOHN CLARKE BULL STREET +

214/91a.   E : Milled.

215/95a.   E : COVENTRY TOKEN. And a wavy line.

217/123a.   E :   „   „

252/27d.   E : PAYABLE IN LANCASTER LONDON OR BRISTOL.

www.ingramcontent.com/pod-product-compliance
Lightning Source LLC
Chambersburg PA
CBHW032308280326
41932CB00009B/745